SOCIETY AND CULTURE IN AMERICA

The
New American Nation Series

EDITED BY

HENRY STEELE COMMAGER

AND

RICHARD B. MORRIS

SOCIETY AND CULTURE
IN AMERICA
1830 ★ 1860

By RUSSEL BLAINE NYE

ILLUSTRATED

HARPER TORCHBOOKS
Harper & Row, Publishers
New York, Evanston, San Francisco, London

A hardcover edition of this book is available from Harper & Row, Publishers, Inc.

Contents

Illustrations

Editors' Introduction

IN his previous volume in this series, *The Cultural Life of the New Nation*, Professor Russel B. Nye delineated the features of American character and culture in the early years of the Republic and traced, with a masterly hand, the interplay of Enlightenment ideas, nationalism, and the impact of environment on the making of a new society. This volume, which covers the years from Jackson to the eve of the Civil War, discovers an almost revolutionary transformation of those forces, but one that took place within the framework of the original institutions and even—surprisingly enough—of the original philosophy. The influence of environment persisted, but it was a new environment, one profoundly modified by technology—often by the technology which it had itself called forth. In philosophy, religion, literature, art, education, and even in some areas of political thought and style, romanticism supplanted enlightenment—a special American form of romanticism which (outside the South) was prospective rather than retrospective, and optimistic rather than forlorn and which, for all its emphasis on individualism, inspired far-reaching social reforms. Nationalism persisted and flourished, but in the shadow of a deepening sectionalism which, by the 1850s, had already posed the question whether the Union would or could endure.

The one constant was growth—a growth so prodigious and so various that it took on qualitative dimensions. Within a thirty-year period the national territory effectively doubled and the population more than doubled. Growth in agricultural and industrial production almost required a new arithmetic and, as a kind of special tribute to the success of the new Republic, more immigrants landed on American shores in these thirty years than the total population of the United States at the time Washington took office. Of primary interest to the cultural historian was the impact of material growth on social institutions such as the church, schools, and colleges, as well as in journalism and literature, and on the practices and principles of equality and the principles and practices of reform; the demands such growth made on science and technology, and the extent to which these in turn conditioned that growth; and what it contributed to the American's sense of his own identity and to the cultural and moral relationships with the Old World.

This search for an American identity was a paradoxical affair. Intellectually almost everything in American culture was derivative: transcendentalism flowed out of German idealism; the passion for nature from English and German Romanticism; architecture was neo-Greek or Italian or Gothic; sculpture was nurtured in Florence or Rome; the new educational ideas came at one level from Rousseau and Pestalozzi and at another from Göttingen; and revolutionary scientific ideas bore the stamp of Humboldt or Liebig or of Lyell and Darwin. It was almost symbolic that the Smithsonian Institution was made possible by the generosity of an Englishman. But Americans did, nevertheless, put their mark upon these importations and, to a degree, Americanize them. New England transcendentalism differed deeply from Kantian idealism; Emerson's romanticism was not at all like that of Carlyle, and Ticknor was unable to make a Göttingen out of Harvard or Alcott to create a Hofwyl at the Temple School. Nor did the new nation fail to make its own contributions. If these were not as distinguished in the realms of politics and law as during the earlier history of the Republic, they were far more distinguished in the areas of literature, philosophy, education, and even science. All of these Professor Nye has explored, and mapped, with a sure hand.

However different the Enlightenment and Romanticism in character and in philosophy, the American approach to them had one common denominator. As it might be said that the Old World invented the Enlightenment and America realized it, so it could be said with almost equal justification that Romanticism had its roots in Old World soil, but flowered in New World expression. Nowhere is this contrast more dramatic than in that development which so fascinated Tocqueville: the achievement of an equalitarian (white) society, and the ferment of the principle of equalitarianism in a complex of social, economic, political, cultural, and moral forms.

Society and Culture in America is a volume in the New American Nation Series, a comprehensive and cooperative survey of the history of the area now embraced in the United States from the days of discovery to our own time. Each volume of the series is part of a carefully designed whole, fitted as well as possible to other volumes in the series; each is designed to be complete in itself. For the most part the series follows a chronological organization, but separate volumes, or groups of volumes are devoted to such subjects as constitutional history, foreign affairs, and westward expansion. This book by Professor Nye is the third of a group of volumes interpreting the cultural life of America from the founding of Jamestown to our own day.

HENRY STEELE COMMAGER
RICHARD BRANDON MORRIS

Preface

THE purpose of this book is to present, as comprehensively and concisely as one can in a single volume, a study of the cultural life of the United States from about 1830 to the Civil War. There is no magic, of course, about the year 1830, but it does mark, more or less accurately, the assumption of leadership of that generation born after the Revolution. Their fathers won independence; this generation had to confirm it. The year 1861 lies like a sword slash across nineteenth-century America. Things were never the same after it, and consideration of the alterations of American cultural and social life which followed belongs in a subsequent volume. While this period covers only a brief span of three decades, they were—culturally—crucial ones and deserve a volume of their own.

I have interpreted cultural history to mean chiefly the development of key American ideas and institutions, that is, of those ways of thinking and acting (as Tocqueville once said) held in common by members of a society. This is a study, then, of those assumptions which, joined together, influenced the style of life and motivated the behavior of Americans through these years. There is naturally a great deal left undone; the complex, fugitive thing called American culture cannot be captured and explained in one book. Deciding what to include in such a survey is necessarily subjective, and I am well aware that much remains to be said. For example, I have not been able to treat the development of American business or law or family life, among other aspects of the period. Some of these have been treated better elsewhere, and others may be soon.

My indebtedness to the dozens of scholars whose books, monographs, and articles I have used is enormous. A study of this kind must necessarily build on the work of many others, and I have tried to acknowledge this debt fully in the footnotes and Bibliography. I wish also to express my thanks to the Library staff at Michigan State University, and most of all to Henry Steele Commager, whose editorial guidance had much to do with giving this book whatever usefulness it may have.

East Lansing, Michigan

RUSSEL B. NYE

SOCIETY AND CULTURE IN AMERICA

CHAPTER 1

The Frame of American Belief

The Idea of Nationalism

IT is impossible to choose a particular year in American history and say, "Here American nationalism began." The development of an American identity was a long and subtle process that began with the first settlers. That they were Englishmen who intended not to return to England must have made them feel, perhaps, a sense of difference which could have been the beginnings of some faint national feeling. Some colonists, of course, from the cutpurse fleeing justice to the Puritan seeking a new Jerusalem, came to escape Europe, expecting America to be different and better. Yet to use the word "nationalism" to describe the seventeenth-century American state of mind would be misleading. Those who lived in British North America considered themselves Englishmen even though they did not live in England.

The growth of a feeling of commonality among the colonies was slow but inevitable. As the century wore on, they developed a dim yet perceptible sense of relationship among themselves and the term "American" took on a meaning different from "British" or "West Indian." By the early eighteenth century the word seems to have been used to describe a particular kind of British colonist—Eliza Pinckney of South Carolina in 1750 made sure she was presented at court as an "American," and colonial newspapers used the term with the connotation of separate identity. John Adams, for his part, called himself "John Yankee" to distinguish himself from a "John Bull."[1]

There were also dividing factors at work, of course, which tended to reduce the tendency toward nationality. Each colony had its own past, distances were great, communications unreliable, rivalries strong. As late as midcentury Jonathan Boucher was unable to see how thirteen disparate colonies could ever discover a common cause, or how Virginians could "form a cordial union with the saints of New England."

Yet there were other elements which tended to unite the colonies and to give them a sense of solidarity. Living for over a century in a new environment across a sea was bound to produce Englishmen whose habits diverged more and more from those who remained at home. By the eighteenth century, the majority of colonists had been born on American soil, had never seen England, and never would. They were still *British* colonists, of course, but as English and European travelers rarely failed to observe, they had developed a style of their own that could only be called "American." The colonies were tied together by trade; newspapers circulated freely among all of them; travelers moved through them with increased ease; interchanges of ideas were as common as of goods.

The relationship of the colonies to England in the first half of the eighteenth century was curiously ambivalent. The colonists were loyally British. Francis Hopkinson, ten years before he signed the Declaration of Independence, wrote that "We in America are in all respects Englishmen, notwithstanding that the Atlantic rolls her waves between us and the throne to which we owe our allegiance." But the colonist also thought of himself as a special kind of Briton, entitled to special consideration and to recognition of his identity. Franklin did not call himself a British subject, but "an American subject of the King." When the time came to choose, American colonists had to decide between their imperial loyalties and their sense of Americanism. Franklin, a loyal American subject in 1765,

1. Hans Kohn, *American Nationalism* (New York, 1957), is a useful general treatment of the subject; see also Yehoshua Arieli, *Individualism and Nationalism in American Ideology* (Cambridge, 1964), and Paul C. Nagel's study, *This Sacred Trust: American Nationality 1798–1898* (New York, 1971). A briefer general survey is that of Russel B. Nye, in *This Almost Chosen People* (East Lansing, 1966), on which portions of this discussion are based.

was a rebel leader eleven years later. The Reverend Jonathan Boucher, on the other hand, stayed with his king, trying to explain that he was American, yet British too. America, he said, he might "love as I do my own soul," but he could not leave his sovereign for it.

The Declaration of Independence, if it did not create a nation, made it clear that although there were *thirteen* colonies, they were *united*. "Our great title is Americans," wrote Thomas Paine, nor could the problems of independence and war be confronted and solved except in nationalistic terms. All the materials needed for a powerful nationalistic tradition came directly from the wartime experience, and afterwards American leaders agreed that a strong sense of national identity was vital to the new country's survival. Therefore, said Noah Webster, "Every engine should be employed to render the people of this country *national* . . . , and to inspire them with the pride of national character."

The War of 1812, near-disaster that it was, nonetheless did help to hasten the completion of national feeling. It might have been averted by better statesmanship and might have been fought with France, yet from the American viewpoint it gave notice to the world that the United States had arrived as a power. "The war has given strength and splendor to the chain of union," wrote a South Carolinian. "Every link exhibits the lustre of the diamond. Local feelings are absorbed in the proud feelings of being an American." "The people . . . are more American," said Albert Gallatin afterwards. "They feel and act more as a nation."

The eagle never screamed more loudly and proudly than in Jacksonian America. Thomas Low Nichols, writing of those years, remembered that

We were taught every day and in every way that ours was the freest, the happiest, and soon to be the greatest and most powerful country in the world. . . . We read it in our books and newspapers, heard it in sermons, speeches, and orations, thanked God for it, in our prayers, and devoutly believed it always.

American holidays were given over to skyrocketing oratory, parades, pageants, and other evidences of patriotic enthusiasm, especially on the Fourth of July. Monuments and statues dedicated to national events and heroes appeared in profusion (exceeded only by the post–Civil War decades) while biographies of American heroes sold by hundreds of thousands.[2]

The nineteenth century was also much concerned with developing symbols to express this nationalistic pride and confidence. The United States began its existence with none of the symbolic equipment—heroes, songs, legends, flags, monuments, and so on—needed to express and demonstrate national feeling. Since it had rejected England, the nation turned to Greece and Rome (particularly to Rome, the most powerful republic in history) for symbols it might adapt to its own uses. Thus the eagle, both a Roman and an American bird, furnished an equivalent for the British lion, while the Great Seal of the United States, adopted in 1776, with its slogan of "E Pluribus Unum" and related devices, was directly derived from similar Roman apparatus. Roman architecture furnished patterns for American public buildings; the upper house of the Congress became a Senate; even Horatio Greenough's statue of Washington, done in 1841, clothed him in a Roman toga. Without a nationalistic tradition of its own, the United States drew heavily on classicism for the forms and symbols it needed to affirm its sense of nationality.

For heroes Americans turned naturally enough to the recent war, to Marion the Swamp Fox, Ethan Allen's sturdy mountaineers, the defenders of Bunker Hill, the martyred Nathan Hale, the ragged veterans of Valley Forge, and most of all to Washington, who even before the war ended had attained almost the status of a national deity. Parson Weems's biography (c. 1800) and John Marshall's *Life* (1805–1807) fixed the Father-of-His-Country image in the American nationalist tradition. His place was subsequently more firmly secured by his likeness on coins, Gilbert Stuart's portrait in thousands of homes, his name on hundreds of towns and streets, Emanuel Leutze's "Crossing the Delaware" in uncounted reproductions, and of course the Washington Monument. Washington served as the major symbol of American unity.

For national holidays, Americans chose Washington's birthday and the Fourth of July—the day on which Congress finally adopted the amended Declaration. The Fourth of July celebration soon

2. For a contemporary analysis of nationalistic feeling, see "Patriotism," *The New England Magazine* VI (April, 1834), 318–24. A useful collection of documents is Selim H. Peabody, ed., *American Patriotism* (New York, 1886).

became the most important American national ceremonial; anniversaries of the adoption of the Constitution never aroused as much interest. No token of nationalism became more important than the American flag, which at first played a relatively small part in the development of nationalist psychology. Created in 1777 by substituting thirteen stars for the crosses of Saint Andrew and Saint George in the "Great Union" flag flown by Washington's army, the familiar stars and stripes remained chiefly a naval flag until 1834, when the army adopted it. Although Francis Scott Key's "Star-Spangled Banner" emerged from the War of 1812, neither the song nor the flag attained great importance as national symbols until the Civil War. "My Country 'Tis of Thee," rather lamely put to the tune of "God Save the King" in 1832, never really provided a satisfactory national anthem, nor did the much later "America the Beautiful." "Brother Jonathan" and "Yankee Doodle," at first conceived simply as comic Down East rustics, had been transformed into national prototypes in the late eighteenth century, but "Uncle Sam," a creation of the War of 1812, soon displaced them.[3]

Certainly, by 1840, the United States possessed a clear understanding of its identity. Francis Grund, the Austrian intellectual who came to the United States in 1826, commented in *The Americans* (1837) on the differences between American patriotism and the European brand. American nationalism was based, he believed, on three things. First, on equality of expectation—each American could legitimately hope for personal and material security. Second, on religious sentiment, for Grund found the churches to be perhaps the most powerfully cohesive factors in American civilization. Third, on the American conviction that the nation had a moral commitment to lead the world to a better future. These beliefs, Grund felt, largely motivated the vigorous, distinctive nationalism he observed in America.

During the forties, however, because of the nature of the American political system, the term *nationalism* began to take on a narrower and more specialized meaning, prescribed both by the

3. Merle Curti, *The Roots of American Loyalty* (New York, 1946), chapter V, *passim*. An excellent discussion of the nationalistic drive is chapter I of Henry Steele Commager, *The Search for a Usable Past* (New York, 1967). Contrary to legend, Betsy Ross neither designed nor made the flag; see Milo Quaife, *The History of the United States Flag* (New York, 1961), chapters XVI and XVII on "Fictions and Myths."

unique nation-state relationship inherent in the federal political structure and by the double set of allegiances which the Constitution recognized and perpetuated. *Nationalism,* in contrast to *states' rights,* meant that national authority should take precedence over that of the states when the two sets of interests did not coincide. After 1820 debates over the issue of *political* nationalism appeared more frequently as the conflict between federal and state loyalties sharpened. What was needed was a workable balance between the forces of nationalism and sectionalism, those "two opposite tendencies" in American life, as Tocqueville called them in 1835, "like two distinct currents flowing in contrary directions in the same channel."

The problem grew partly from national expansion and national diversity. In the seventy years between 1790 and 1860 the national population rose from four million to thirty-one million, while the country quadrupled in size to include new areas of highly diverse climates, topography, resources and population. Europe, crammed into a much smaller area, was divided into ten nations; it was freely prophesied in England and Europe (with some logic) that the United States might well go the same way. When California and Oregon joined the Union, for example, the best way to reach them was by a 20,000-mile journey around Cape Horn.

There were a number of reasons why the United States did not dissolve as Europeans frequently predicted it would. Internal migration settled new states from old, while the old states renewed themselves by immigration from abroad. Half the people in Illinois, Missouri, and Texas, according to the census of 1850, came from established communities in the East and South, and so did almost two-thirds of those in Michigan, Wisconsin, and California. Despite their distance from Washington, the new states were children of the federal government, which distributed their land, protected them from Indians, governed them as territories, and supervised their admission to the Union. Their orientation was always national. And providentially for the United States, the revolution in transportation and communication joined the country together with turnpikes and canals, steamboats and railroads. During the years between Jefferson and Lincoln, the nation developed a highly integrated economic system and a complex network of internal communications which unified it more closely than ever before.

But while nationalism grew, so did sectionalism, at an equally swift rate. Whatever the commitments of the American public to the national purpose, there were regions within the nation which were so geographically and socially unified as to possess their own sense of identity. Throughout the first half of the nineteenth century there was a constant exploration of the issue of national versus sectional interests; the controversy over states' rights was part of an attempt to establish what a reasonable and acceptable definition of nationalism, in this peculiarly American situation, really was. The issue was most clearly brought into focus by the constant argument over state and national sovereignty that ran through the politics of the period between the close of the War of 1812 and Lincoln's election in 1860.

On one side, sentiment in the Northeast and Northwest polarized about the concept of nationalized union; on the other, sentiment in the South, strongly influenced by the economic and social conditions of slavery, crystallized about a more diffused, particularized concept of states' rights. It was not a question of patriotism—the Southern point of view was as thoroughly American as the Northern—but one of fixing the boundaries of national authority. The North called for the recognition of a centralized, nationalized power that represented the majority will and was responsive to it; the South demanded a redefinition of nationalism that recognized sectional and minority rights.

These differing concepts of the nature of the Union were most dramatically presented in 1830 during the Senate debate over tariffs. When Senator Robert Hayne of South Carolina advanced the prevailing Southern theory of state sovereignty, he was answered by Massachusetts's Daniel Webster, whose strongly nationalist interpretation of the Constitution represented the consensus of Northern opinion. His "Reply to Hayne," as it became known, soon attained the status of an oratorical classic, and his motto, "Liberty and Union, now and forever, one and inseparable!," became his generation's slogan in the North. To the South, whatever Webster's eloquence, the Union—if it meant, as Jefferson Davis believed it did, "the despotism of a majority"—represented the instrument of a "hostile government" which might rob the Southerner of "the equality, the liberty, and the sovereignty" to which he was born. The Constitution, in the Southern view, was more important than the Union, and if war were inevitable over it, as Reverdy Johnson thought, the Union ought to be dissolved.[4]

The development of nationalistic feelings, centered on the nature of the Union, could clearly be traced from Washington's day. To the generation that ratified the Constitution, the concept of a strong federal union seemed an essential device for preserving national unity, security, and liberty, but not as an end in itself. So long as this opinion held true, the majority of Americans, North and South, believed the exact nature of this union not to be irrevocably fixed, but rather subject to change and modification according to need. Within the next generation, however, the feeling grew that the idea of the Union was in itself so exalted, so crucial to the pursuit of American ideals, that it represented something much more than a mere political arrangement. William Ellery Channing, speaking in 1835, expressed the change precisely. "Most men value the Union as a means," he wrote, "to me it is an end." "The Union," said Emerson succinctly, "is part of the religion of this people."[5]

This belief in the United States as the ideal union, gathering greater emotional charge as the years passed, came into direct conflict with the concept of state sovereignty emerging in the South. From the Northern point of view the Union was (as Edward Everett called it) "a metaphysical and theoretical thing." William Seward, Charles Sumner, and many others expanded the theme, creating in the North a deification of Union that went far beyond argument or analysis. Nations, wrote Congressman Owen Lovejoy of Illinois, required "some central idea which they could enshrine." For the United States, it was union, that "holy instrument around which all American hearts cluster and to which they cling with the tenacity of a semi-religious attainment."

Unionism and *Nationalism* were virtually synonymous by Lincoln's time, an identification illustrated most clearly, perhaps, by his attitude toward the issue of war. The concept of a nationalized democracy—represented by the principle of union—was the guid-

4. For an interesting contemporary analysis, see "The Infancy of the Union," *The New-York Review* VII (October, 1840). The most comprehensive treatment of nationalism and unionism is Paul C. Nagel, *One Nation Indivisible: The Union in American Thought, 1776–1861* (New York, 1964).

5. For numerous examples of such unionist sentiment, see the anthology compiled by the Reverend Samuel Fallows, *Liberty and Union* (Chicago, 1882), of "patriotic oratory, poetry, and music."

ing doctrine of Lincoln's life, one that he erected into an almost mystical principle. "The world's best hope depended on the continued Union," he believed, and the war in which he reluctantly engaged was to him a war for the Union, nothing else. Its aim was to preserve the United States as a nation and not a federation; his "paramount object," he told Horace Greeley, always was "to save the union." While there were those in the North, as in the South, who did not like the idea of a union maintained by the force of arms, there were many more who agreed with Lincoln that without force there would be no union, and without union no nation. Why thousands of Northern boys who had never seen a slave went to war to maintain that union was expressed directly and simply by a popular song of the Union Army camps:[6]

> The Union forever, hurrah! boys, hurrah!
> Down with the traitor, up with the star,
> While we rally round the flag, boys, rally once again,
> Shouting the battle cry of Freedom!

The Civil War marked the climax of the American nationalizing process. Terrible as the war was, it preserved the Union and made an end to the constitutional issue of nationalism. But more important than any military settlement was the emotional validity of the victory for the Union, reflected in thousands of commemorative orations and celebrations over the next half century. The war, Charles Sumner explained in an oration titled "Are We a Nation?," gave a conclusive answer to that question, for it made the country "One and Indivisible, with a new consciousness of national life." James Russell Lowell, writing in 1865, concluded that the United States had gained from that bitter experience a "conscious feeling of nationality," and he went on, with admirable lucidity, to explain what was meant by this new consciousness of nationality:[7]

Loyalty has hitherto been a sentiment rather than a virtue; it has been more often a superstition or a prejudice than a conviction of the conscience or the understanding. Now for the first time it is identical with patriotism,

6. See, for example, the sentiments expressed in the speech by Daniel Stevens Dickinson at the Union Mass Meeting, New York, April, 1861, in Peabody, *op. cit.*, 515–20; and the speeches at the Union Meeting of February 26, Indianapolis, Indiana, Frank Freidel, ed., *Union Pamphlets of the Civil War* (Cambridge, 1967), II:591 ff.

7. Lowell's essay "E Pluribus Unum," in *Works* (Boston, 1904), V:55–91.

and has its seat in the brain, not the blood. . . . Every man feels himself a part, sensitive and sympathetic, of this vast organism, a partner in its life or death.

The Sense of Mission

The search by Americans for a national identity included a parallel search for a national purpose, a *raison d'être* for existence. Almost from the beginnings of settlement, the colonists conceived of themselves as a special people, providentially chosen for a particular mission in history.[8]

One component of this concept of mission arrived with the New England settlers, who believed themselves destined to found a new Jerusalem in America's green and pleasant land. Edward Johnson, who came to Massachusetts in 1630, saw the new country as a "place where the Lord will create a new Heaven, and a new Earth, new Churches, and a new Common-wealth together." Johnson and his fellow settlers were convinced that God had brought them to New England as He had once directed Moses and the children of Israel. Jonathan Edwards, a century later, agreed that God had chosen America to be His agent as "glorious renovator of the world," just as He had chosen certain human ministers to renovate souls. Seventeenth-century Americans saw their mission as theological—and evangelical—in that they were to serve as agents for Christianizing the continent.

In the eighteenth century, however, the nature of the American mission began to show an increasingly secular tinge. First of all, to develop a conviction of purpose was, for that emergent society, a historical necessity. American colonists had to ask questions about themselves and their society to which their transplanted traditions provided no ready answers. They needed to establish (even as *British* colonists) some meaning for their lives, institutions, and destinations. The eighteenth-century American (before any thought of independence) needed to have a set of long-range principles with

8. For a comprehensive study, see Edward McNall Burns, *The American Idea of Mission* (New Brunswick, 1957). Specialized studies are Ernest C. Tuveson, *Redeemer Nation: The Idea of America's Millennial Role* (Chicago, 1968), and Frederick Merk, *Manifest Destiny and Mission in American History* (New York, 1963).

which to handle the problems and issues arising out of the novelty of his peculiarly American situation.

Second, the growing diversity and power of the colonies demanded some sort of definition of this new society, and the identification of a national purpose was one way of giving a bundle of separate colonies a sense of coherence. American society was a mixture of attitudes, traditions, and ideas, all imported at different times; it became imperative for Americans who had no single identifiable tradition to attempt to evolve one out of what was borrowed, old, and new. To establish a sense of national purpose was one method of providing colonial society with the unity and security it needed.

Lastly, the development of an American sense of mission helped to compensate for the American lack of a past. Even in comparison to the more recent countries of Europe, America was embarrassingly new. American colonists were conscious of this and properly respectful of their cultural elders; as members of a new country (after 1776) they were equally aware of their infancy, and often aggressively sensitive about it. But if their nation had been chosen to do something no other nation could do, it obviously possessed a distinction granted to no other. Jedidiah Morse, the scientist and historian, explained this in the preface to his *American Geography,*

Here the sciences and the arts of civilized life are to receive their highest improvement. Here civil and religious liberty are to flourish, unchecked by the cruel hand of civil or ecclesiastical tyranny. Here Genius, aided by all the improvements of former ages, is to be exerted in humanizing mankind —in expanding and enriching their minds with religious and philosophical knowledge, and in planning and executing a form of government . . . , which shall be calculated to protect and unite, in a manner consistent with the natural rights of mankind, the largest empire that ever existed.

Americans could say with Morse, in effect, our country is new and young, but we have a unique and special destiny; we have a brief and perhaps negligible past, but we have a significant future.

The Declaration of Independence, of course, was the final statement of national purpose, and the Revolution a necessary first step toward accomplishing it—as John Adams phrased it, the war was part of "a grand scheme and design of Providence." The Revolutionary generation was acutely conscious of the responsibility which rested upon the new nation to provide a model for the world. The Declaration carried with it the feeling that its framers believed that they were doing something of great significance to the future of mankind—certainly it must have been issues of far greater importance than taxes or parliamentary authority which led them to ask the judgment of "The Supreme Judge of the World" and "the protection of Divine Providence." The poet Philip Freneau had a vision of America as "a new Jerusalem sent down from Heaven" to serve "a pattern for the world beside," while the Continental Congress expressed the same idea concisely in 1789:

If justice, good faith, honor, gratitude, and all the other qualities which ennoble a nation and fulfill the ends of government, shall be the fruits of our establishment, then the cause of liberty will acquire a dignity and lustre it has never yet enjoyed, and an example will be set which cannot but have the most favorable influence on mankind.

So too Jefferson, in his belief that his generation "acted not for ourselves alone, but for the whole human race," implied that those ideals which motivated their revolution were ultimately exportable. The Founding Fathers thus agreed that the goal of the United States was to furnish to the world a model of democracy, and to convince others of its worth and workability by the force of the American example.

By the time the nation was ready to celebrate the twenty-fifth anniversary of the Declaration, Americans generally believed that they held a divinely bestowed responsibility—as part of God's plan for human progress—to do three things:

—to lead others toward a future world-state of freedom and liberty, and to serve as surrogate or agent for the rest of mankind in achieving it.
—to serve as an example to the rest of the world of God's intentions for mankind, and as proof that man can govern himself in peace and justice.
—to serve as a haven for the oppressed, and as a place of opportunity for the deserving, ambitious, and godly.

The Jacksonian generation inherited this multileveled concept of mission and built upon it. The thirties and forties rang with the self-confidence of a nation that knew where it was going, and exactly why. William McGuffey's *Eclectic Reader* taught students that "the United States holds out an example . . . to nine-tenths of the human race who are born without hereditary rank or fortune . . . , that it is practicable to elevate the mass of mankind . . . , to raise them to self-respect." Samuel F. Smith, whose song "America" (1832) nearly became a national anthem, expressed it well in his concluding stanza:

> Beneath Heaven's gracious will
> The stars of progress still
> Our course do sway;
> In unity sublime,
> To broader heights we climb,
> Triumphant over time,
> God speed our way!

In the opinion of John L. O'Sullivan, the Jacksonian editor, the United States was

destined to manifest to mankind the excellence of divine principles; to establish on earth the noblest temple ever dedicated to the worship of the Most High—the Sacred, and the True . . . , governed by God's natural and moral law of equality, the law of brotherhood,

—rhetoric matched by hundreds of other editors, orators, statesmen, and plain citizens through the forties and fifties. Certain that Providence had chosen the United States to serve as leader of the world, the editors of *Harper's* in 1858 reviewed the history of the missionary concept and concluded that "everything connected with our position, history, progress, points out the United States of America as the land of the future."[9]

Conscious of their responsibilities to the rest of the world, Americans were quick to welcome revolutions elsewhere which seemed to reflect the purpose of their own. The American experience of 1776, said John Quincy Adams in 1821, stood as a model for all others, as "a beacon . . . on the summit of the mountains, to which all the inhabitants of the earth may turn their eyes." It would be but a short time, a Massachusetts orator told his Fourth of July audience in 1827, until "the spark kindled in America, shall spread and spread, until all the earth shall be illuminated with its light." The reaction in the United States to the upheavals in Europe early in the nineteenth century was one of expectant approval; it was commonly hoped, historian George Bancroft wrote, that within twenty years not a crowned head would be left in Europe. The

9. "Providence in American History," *Harper's*, XVII (1858) , 697–8.

Greek uprising against Turkey enlisted the passionate support of hundreds of prominent Americans; mass meetings were held in major cities to raise funds for arms, and men of the stature of Webster, Clay, Monroe, and Calhoun spoke out for Greek independence.

The overthrow of Louis Philippe's government in France in 1848 produced a sensation throughout the United States, eliciting dozens of speeches, celebrations, and orations in Congress. This second French Revolution, it was assumed, was lit from the sparks of 1776; the American Revolution was the "leaven to the millions of the world," according to the New York *Sun,* "a light and a fire, illumining their souls and warming their hearts until they have dared to shout in the ears of tyrants, 'we too are men—we will be free!' " More revolutions could be expected, and in anticipation Senator William Allen introduced a resolution into Congress congratulating the French on their "efforts to consolidate liberty by imbodying its principles in a republican form of government."

The Hungarian revolutionist leader Louis Kossuth, called by the American press "the General Washington of Hungary," came to the United States in 1851 on a ship officially furnished by the American government, and his subsequent tour provided him with a hundred thousand dollars in contributions and left streets named in his honor all over the nation. Italy, Germany, Switzerland, Prussia, and Belgium were soon to follow in America's path, the New York *Sun* predicted; England's monarchy might be the last to go, but go it must. The mission of the United States at this point in history, the *Sun* continued, was "by our sympathy and counsel, to nerve and help guide the sinews of the liberty-seeking masses," to serve as "the watchword, the polestar of their struggle"—even, perhaps, "if freedom were in danger . . . , to fly to her rescue." "Already the age," wrote Joseph Story, "has caught the spirit of our institutions."[10]

It has ascended the Andes, and suffused the breezes of both oceans. It has infused itself into the lifeblood of Europe . . . , touched the philosophy of Germany and the North . . . , warmed the sunny plains of France and the lowlands of Holland.

The concept of America's mission contained a significant portion of ethnic and theological content. It was taken for granted that the

10. J. P. McCaskey, ed., *Butler's Literary Selections* (Philadelphia, 1882), 164; similar quotations abound in the collection.

nation's Anglo-Saxon, Protestant elements were among its major qualifications as a missionary nation. The idea of "God's Englishman," as Milton had explained it, was as current in the colonies as in England. In its nineteenth-century form it could be clearly identified in John Lothrop Motley's history of the Dutch Republic, or Parkman's studies of New France, or Bancroft's spread-eagle American histories. Motley's *Rise of the Dutch Republic* (1856), which showed how a Germanic Protestant people successfully resisted the tyranny of Catholic, Latinate Spain, was accepted by the public as an excellent example of what the *Presbyterian Quarterly Review* called the Anglo-Saxon's "intense love of freedom, indomitable valor, steadiness, sobriety, industry, receptivity to culture, and sagacious intellectuality." Implicit in the drive of the forties and fifties toward continental domination was the belief that it was the duty of "Teutonic" peoples (of whom the United States was an acknowledged leader) to redeem "lesser" nations from darkness. Senator Thomas Hart Benton thought the Mexican War "illustrated the Anglo-Saxon character" by showing that "liberty, justice, valor—moral, physical, and intellectual power—discriminate that race wherever it goes."[11]

The missionary concept found concrete expression in the "manifest destiny" expansionism of the midcentury years. Although the phrase itself did not appear until 1845, the idea was not new.[12] Derived in part from the natural rights theories of the eighteenth century, it was based on the belief that nations had a "natural right" to do certain things by reason of their geography, history, theology, or conviction. It was America's right to occupy the continent, since, as one Congressman explained in 1819, "The great Emperor of the Universe has fixed the natural limits of our country, and . . . to that boundary we shall go." Various limits were suggested, but most Americans agreed with John Quincy Adams who in 1824 said it was "a law of nature" that "our proper dominion be the continent of North America."[13] Since the conformation of the continent indicated that the United States was destined to control

11. See Tuveson, *op. cit.*, chapter V, "Chosen Race, Chosen People."

12. The earliest known use of the phrase was in an unsigned editorial in the July–August issue of the *United States Magazine and Democratic Review*, attributed to John L. O'Sullivan.

13. Albert K. Weinberg, *Manifest Destiny* (Gloucester, Mass., 1958), chapter I. See also Merk, *op. cit.*, chapters I–III.

it, reference to laws of "natural growth" added further support to expansionism. Like any organism, a nation grew and matured—this is "as organic and vital in the youth of states as in individual men," thought Edward Everett.

Mere possession of territory, however, was not enough; it was America's mission to use it for those purposes decreed by Nature and God. One such purpose, as the Bible stated, was to subdue the earth and make it bloom. As John Winthrop had pointed out to the first colonists, it was clearly not God's intent to "suffer a whole continent, as fruitful and convenient for the use of man to be waste without any improvement," and it was equally clear that if Americans did not possess the land, they could not achieve their mission. It was the nation's destiny to own the continent, from sea to sea and perhaps even pole to pole, since, said the *Democratic Review* in 1858, "no race but our own can either cultivate or rule the Western hemisphere."

There were other, more abstract elements of the continental mission, not the least of which was the belief that in extending its control over America the United States was also extending freedom and enlightenment to people who needed it. In the Revolution and the War of 1812 Americans included "oppressed" French and English Canadians in their plans for a liberated continent, and in the forties added the Caribbean and Mexico. "This continent was intended by Providence," said one Congressman, "as a vast theater in which to work out the great experiment of Republican government, under the auspices of the Anglo-Saxon race," while O'Sullivan believed it was "the right of our manifest destiny to overspread and possess the whole of the continent which Providence has given us for the development of the great experiment of liberty and federated self-government entrusted to us."

In the process of expansion, therefore, the United States must assume the responsibility of raising inferior peoples to a higher level of civilization. American soldiers, said the Reverend McVickar, were in a sense "chosen carriers to introduce into less favored lands a higher and purer civilization"; the New York *Herald* in 1847 was confident that the United States could

regenerate and disenthrall the people of Mexico in a few years; and we believe it is part of our destiny to civilize that beautiful country and enable its inhabitants to appreciate some of the many advantages and blessings they enjoy.

The Mexican War, to some expansionists, represented only the first phase in the process. Senator Daniel Dickinson of New York, in 1848, felt strongly that the country had not yet[14]

fulfilled the destiny allotted to us. New territory is spread out for us to subdue and fertilize; new races are presented for us to civilize, educate, and absorb; new triumphs for us to achieve for the cause of freedom.

The ultimate statement was perhaps that of William Gilpin, soldier, explorer, and governor of Colorado Territory, who believed it to be America's "yet untransacted destiny,"[15]

to subdue the continent—to rush over this vast field to the Pacific Ocean—to animate the many hundred millions of its people, and to cheer them upward—to set the principle of self-government at work—to agitate these herculean masses—to establish a new order in human affairs—to set free the enslaved—to regenerate superannuated nations—to change darkness into light—to stir up the sleep of a hundred centuries—to teach old nations new civilization—to confirm the destiny of the human race—to carry the career of mankind to its culminating point—to cause stagnant people to be reborn—to perfect science—to emblazen history with the conquest of peace—to shed a new and resplendent glory upon mankind—to unite the world in one social family—to dissolve the spell of tyranny and exalt charity—to absolve the curse that weights down humanity and to shed blessings around the world.

Nonetheless, the missionary confidence of the era was tempered with misgivings. There were those who feared "a gradual and unperceived decline of moral sentiment and moral purpose" in the land, and who advocated less self-praise and more self-examination.[16] Even the normally ebullient *Democratic Review* wondered if the country were not "at a critical stage of our national progress," while Ralph Waldo Emerson, in *Lectures on the Times* (1842–1843) expressed uneasiness about the nation's goals—"Will it not

---

14. Quoted from Weinberg, *op. cit.*, 72–79, ff. For a representative contemporary statement of the missionary aspects of manifest destiny, see "California," *The American Review*, III (n.s., April, 1849), 3–18.

15. Clark Spencer, ed., *The American West* (New York, 1966), 108.

16. For an excellent discussion of the doubts and doubters, see Nagel, *This Sacred Trust*, chapters II and III, from which these quotations are taken.

be dreadful," he asked, "to discover that this experiment made by America, to ascertain if men can govern themselves, does not succeed?"

The country had more than its share of shocks and turbulences in the forties and fifties—boom-and-bust times, the Texas question and the Mexican War, mob violence and ugly nativism, the increasingly acrimonious debates over slavery, the undeclared civil war in Kansas and Nebraska, fugitive slaves, Dred Scott, eventually Harper's Ferry.

The more thoughtful journals of the fifties were filled with essays titled "On the Times" or "The Nation Today," which attempted to identify some of the dangers facing the nation. For one thing, the country suffered from what Alexander Everett called "a too urgent love of worldly gain," a materialism that had blunted the nation's idealism. It suffered too from a diminution of religious energy, a loss of its historic Christian purpose. Americans, said Henry Ward Beecher, had to learn to live once again "by divine truths," to become once more "an evangelized and Christian people." Third, the people at large needed to rededicate themselves to their ideals; the lack of interest in "the democratic principle" which seemed to pervade the times was, the *Democratic Review* warned, "portentous of incalculable evil" and the nation needed new, enlightened leadership, above "intrigues of party and the allurements of ambition"—new Washingtons to whom the nation was more important than personal power.[17]

But confidence prevailed. William Cullen Bryant, returning from Europe in 1846, found the contrast heartening. In his poem "O Mother of a Mighty Race!" he considered the United States—despite divisions over war and slavery—at the peak of its strength:

> Thine eye, with every coming hour,
> Shall brighten, and thy form shall tower;
> And when thy sisters, elder born,
> Would brand thy name with words of scorn,
> Before thine eye,
> Upon their lips the taunt shall die.

Walt Whitman defined America itself as "essentially the greatest poem" and took from it his poetic theme. Philip Schaff's *America*

17. See Nagel, *This Sacred Trust*, "Search," 47–129.

(1855) concluded that the nation's "soundness and vitality" would carry it through its testing time, while Carl Schurz, in his 1859 address, "True Americanism," was certain that a country based on the eternal verities of liberty and self-government was bound to endure—even as the storm of war gathered.

The High Tide of Romanticism

The rise of Romanticism introduced another important factor of thought. In the latter years of the eighteenth century, European and British philosophers and critics revived interest in a body of ideas which had been relatively neglected in the seventeenth and earlier eighteenth centuries. These ideas were developed, extended, ramified, and diffused throughout Europe, Britain, and America. In the process men on both sides of the Atlantic questioned and revised many of their concepts and altered the framework of their thinking. These Romantic ideas were not "new" in the narrow sense of the word; but they were new in the sense that they represented a sharp break with the dominant ideas of the preceding century. Romanticism was never wholly assimilated into a unified system. Sometimes Romantic concepts existed side by side with much older ideas, and sometimes they contradicted themselves. Nonetheless, the body of ideas termed Romanticism was one of the elements which served to separate the mind of the first half of the nineteenth century from that of the later eighteenth, and from the latter decades of the nineteenth.

Romantic thought rested on three general concepts. First, on the idea of organism. Things were conceived as wholes, or units, with their own internal laws of governance and development. This held true for men as individuals, or for the state as an aggregation of persons, or for nature as an organism, or for a work of art as a unit. Second, on the idea of dynamism, that is, of motion and growth. Beliefs and institutions were assumed to be fluid, changing, capable of adaptation. The age had, as the philosopher A. O. Lovejoy has pointed out, "a dislike of finality." Third, on the idea of diversity, the value of differences of opinions, cultures, tastes, societies, characters—as opposed to the uniformitarian norm of the Enlightenment. To the earlier eighteenth century, rationality meant uniformity; diversity meant irrationality, and therefore error. To the late eighteenth century the *consensus gentium* seemed less important than private, individual judgment, and diversity seemed both "natural" and right.[18]

The United States was formed during an era of great cultural change—from Classicism to Romanticism—and it attained its cultural maturity at Romanticism's high point. Rousseau and Franklin were contemporaries; so were Irving, Byron, and Scott. Young Emerson visited Coleridge, and young Bancroft talked with Byron and Goethe, who completed *Faust* the year Andrew Jackson began his second term.[19] Romanticism, by then, was peculiarly an American article of faith.

The term "Romanticism" is virtually impossible to define precisely and difficult to circumscribe generally. However, there were common factors which together created the Romantic point of view and the Romantic personality. The Romantic, whatever his moments of melancholy, tended to be optimistic—if not wholly convinced of the inevitability of human progress, at least hopeful of it. He lived in an optative mood. Second, the Romantic was aware of life's complexities, its infinite detail, its variety and richness of difference. The Enlightenment's reaction to experience was to explain it and reduce it to rules; the Romantic's was to explore it, and to wonder at it. The Romantic recognized (and accepted) irrationality in the world; he knew that life was not always explicable, and much more complicated than the Enlightenment supposed. Third, the Romantics caught the first suggestions, from the scientists, of evolutionary development—in nations, ideas, plants, animals, men, governments, and all things. Whereas the Age of Reason postulated a world of fixed laws—in astronomy, chemistry, physics—the Romantic age searched for the *origins* of things and the laws of their development. Every branch of thought in the nineteenth century was influenced by this methodology.[20]

18. A. O. Lovejoy, "The Meaning of Romanticism for the Historian of Ideas," *Journal of the History of Ideas,* II (1941), 257–78.

19. Keats, Vigny, and Bryant were all born in the same decade; so were Longfellow and Hugo.

20. For consideration of American literary Romanticism, see G. H. Orians, "The Rise of Romanticism," in H. H. Clark, ed., *Transitions in American Literary History* (Durham, 1954). For general discussions of Romanticism see Robert F. Gleckner and Gerald Ensue, eds., *Romanticism: Points of View* (Englewood Cliffs, 1970). A provocative discussion of the movement and its characteristics is W. T. Jones, *The Romantic Syndrome* (The Hague, 1961), 15–20, 117–35.

The two central, related doctrines of Romanticism, from which the others sprang, were the importance it placed on the emotions and the importance it placed on the individual. The Romantics unseated Reason, declared that the oracle of truth was intuition (under various names) and affirmed that what one felt within was true. Believing that the impulses of the "heart" were of greater interest and cogency than those of the "head," the Romantics placed their trust in that "moment of intense feeling" as opposed to the calculations of logic.

What a man must do to find the truth, Emerson wrote in *The American Scholar*, was "to learn to detect and watch that gleam of light which flashes across his mind from within." Philosopher Caleb Sprague Henry explained that "the instantaneous but real fact of spontaneous apperception of truth" took place in "the intimacy of individual consciousness." Theodore Parker believed that truth could be perceived best in those "great primal Intuitions of Human Nature, which depend on no logical process of demonstration." Thus the Romantic age stressed the emotional aspects of man's nature until they became a higher source of truth than reason— —until emotion, passion, and intuition blended into a power called (among other names) the Imagination, an indefinable, intuitive power which, wrote a critic in 1844,[21]

is always above and around us, as gentle and familiar as the airs of home. As electricity to nature, so imagination to man's reasoning or material part. It is not always apparent to his drowsy consciousness; yet it always is, subtle and silent. . . . The Chieftain, the Architect, the Sculptor, the Painter, the Poet, are her slaves—and at her bidding, the world is showered with splendors.

Placing importance on the emotions enhances the importance of he who feels and follows them; if the test of truth lies within, in the flash of inward intuition, then the individual takes on primary significance. The individual becomes paramount; the most dynamic ideal of Romanticism was its vision of greater freedom for the individual. Emerson said it many times in many ways. "I have taught one doctrine," he wrote, "namely, the infinitude of the private man," which he summarized in *Self-Reliance*, with its stirring

21. C. W. Eimi, "Instinct—Reason—Imagination," *The Democratic Review*, XV (October, 1844), 418.

message, "Trust thyself. Every heart vibrates to that iron string." Or again, speaking politically, "The root and seed of democracy is the doctrine, judge for yourself. Reverence thyself." Henry David Thoreau, of course, lived out at Walden Pond the experiment that tested Emerson's concept of individualism.

Trusting the individual, believing in his unlimited potential, releasing him from restraints and freeing him from the past, made the Romantic era one of dynamic, explosive vitality. Combining optimism and energy with an endless curiosity about everything imaginable, Romanticism energized every area of interest and endeavor. It experimented with religion and philosophy (transcendentalism, idealism, evangelism, unitarianism), with social systems (Oneida, New Harmony, Brook Farm), and with social change (abolition, prohibition, criminology, women's rights). Its extraordinary list of inventions, from the locomotive to the tin can; its jigsaw-carpentered houses, parlors crammed with drapes, rugs, souvenirs, pictures, furniture, chairs, and the like; the teeming streets, parks, beaches, stores, and homes; its sculptors who mass-produced busts, poets who published a thousand poems, novelists who produced fifty volumes, the prints and engravings by hundreds of thousands that pictured the age—everywhere one looked one found testimony to the bursting energy of the times. The individual could, the Romantics felt, do almost anything God would allow him to do. Each man was unique and important—"you for you," wrote Emerson, "as mine for me." There was nothing greater than one's own identity, that "precious idiosyncrasy and special nativity and intuition that he is, the man's self."

The Enlightenment studied nature and man in order to establish their relationships as parts of an intricate machine in which they were locked in mutual interdependency. It studied the external world to find evidences of God, laws of morality and development, and even hints about man's own nature. It studied man, as Alexander Pope said, to find what kind of being he was and where he fitted into the great, universal, mechanistic scheme. Looking at man and the world, the Enlightenment concluded that mind and nature were very much the same, that the internal structure of man replicated the external structure of nature—that is, both were based on laws of order and reason. When man and his environment (or nature and mind) were in balance, all would be perfection—but man was imperfect, partly through ignorance and partly through will, so that often he and his society were out of harmony with nature. The ideal of the Enlightenment was, quite simply, to bring man and his society into line with nature in one unitary, harmonious system.

Romanticism stressed the study of man. The Romantics questioned the very basis of the Enlightenment by suggesting that the mind of man and the nature of the world were not at all the same, but quite different. Nature to the nineteenth century became less important for itself and more so for the impact it had on man—important chiefly insofar as men perceived and used it with their inner senses. The Romantics, depending for their comprehension of things on intuitive insight and emotional revelation, neither tried to understand nor succeeded in understanding man and nature as a whole. The earlier age associated man and nature with reason; the later, with "feeling," "sensibility," or Imagination. This shift of viewpoint separated man from nature and made him an object for study in his own right. It also introduced a new question—if the mind was not like nature, orderly, rational, harmoniously related to the world, then what was it like? The implications of this question occupied the best minds of the nineteenth century.

Much of American Romanticism, of course, derived from Britain and Europe and held much in common with them; certainly its basic ideology was similar, and its manifestations often the same. Yet there were differences. Americans did not accept all of European and British Romanticism, for they did not need all of it, and some of it was hardly applicable to American conditions. In America Romanticism turned out to be a much more constructive, individualistic, and democratically based movement than in Britain or Europe, a trend reinforced by the frontier tradition.

In Europe, Romantic individualism frequently took the form of an attack on established institutions, mores, social and political and economic codes; the Romantic rebelled, sometimes spectacularly, against the status quo. In America, where feudalism, traditionalism, and political privilege had been under attack successfully for at least two generations before the Romantic movement was well under way, the Romantic needed to be much less the rebel or iconoclast than his European counterpart. The American Romantic tended to be more constructive than destructive; he had much less to destroy, and much more opportunity to create. American Romanticism thus produced not Byron but Longfellow, not Marx but Thoreau; instead of attacking the status quo with Byron's *Manfred,* it did it with Emerson's *Self-Reliance.* Despite their admiration for the European and British Romantics, the young Americans were of a different temper and temperament. They simply could not accept the rebelliousness of Schiller, the anti-institutionalism of Byron, the outlaw morality of the young Goethe, the moody, sentimental return to original sin that marked much of contemporary European poetry and philosophy. They had too much faith in and respect for the individual, too much left of their hereditary intensity of moral feeling. They put their own distinctive stamp on the Romantic movement as they absorbed it.[22]

Not everyone, of course, saw things through the bright Romantic prism. Alcott argued with Emerson and Channing over what he called their "excessive individuality." Orestes Brownson joined the Catholic Church and concluded that individual freedom was to be obtained only within the realm of the imaginative. Where Emerson could say that "God himself culminates in the present moment" and concentrate on that personal intuitive instant, Hawthorne instead spoke of "that visionary and impalpable *now,* which if you look at it closely, is nothing." Herman Melville said "No, in thunder," and where Thoreau found certainty in the Individual Self, Melville's theme was the failure of Self. *Moby Dick, Pierre, Young Goodman Brown,* and *The Marble Faun* were shadowed books that did not belong with the optimism of American Romanticism. And after 1860 it was harder to be a Romantic than before; that generation faced not only war, but Darwin.

The Certainty of Progress

The belief in progress—that man moves always toward a better world—is perhaps as old as man and certainly, in the Western world, as old as the Greeks. It received its modern articulation in the seventeenth and eighteenth centuries, growing out of the Enlightenment's belief in rationalism and its faith in man's perfect-

22. Useful essays on the differences are Robert E. Spiller, "Critical Standards in the American Romantic Movement," *College English,* VIII (1947), 344–52; and Tony Tanner, "Notes for a Comparison between American and European Romanticism," *Journal of American Studies,* II (April, 1968), 83–103.

ibility. It reinforced, with powerful authority, the age of revolutions, political and social, for if—as Locke said—evil and error came from institutions, man could change his institutions by his own reason and effort. It also attained a kind of quasi-theological status, representing God's plan for mankind and evidence of his guidance, and beneficence. The continental philosophers, especially, seized on this idea with enthusiasm. Condorcet, whose *History of the Progress of the Human Spirit* (1793) was much read in America, believed that it could be demonstrated

that there is no limit set to the perfecting of the powers of man; that human perfectibility is in reality indefinite; that the progress of this perfectibility, henceforth independent of any power that might wish to stop it, has no other limit than the duration of the globe upon which nature has placed us.

This concept of progress, as it took shape in the eighteenth century, found ardent supporters in America; the Revolution and the Constitution, in American opinion, marked a new phase in the inexorable march of events toward a better world. Americans believed what Condorcet suggested: that mankind had passed through nine epochs of civilization, each better than the last, and that the tenth, soon to come, would be by far the best of all. The United States, they felt, might well be the harbinger of that fortunate tenth.[23]

The agent of this advance, the Enlightenment believed, was human reason, the power which provided both the instrument and the substance of improvement. If there was unanimity among American commentators on human nature, it was on the concept of man's perfectibility through reason. In this they resembled the French rather than the British philosophers, who tended to view the presumed upward march of humanity in more conservative terms. The confident optimism of such Frenchmen as Condorcet, Turgot, and Helvétius—and of a few more self-assured Englishmen such as William Godwin—appealed to Americans who believed their

23. There are a number of general treatments of the idea of progress, the earliest of which is J. B. Bury's classic *The Idea of Progress* (London, 1928). An excellent treatment of the doctrine in America occurs in Stow Persons, *American Minds* (New York, 1958); and in Ralph H. Gabriel, *The Course of American Democratic Thought* (New York, 1940). Rush Welter, "The Idea of Progress in America," *Journal of the History of Ideas*, XIV (1955), 401–15, is a useful essay.

nation might well lead the march into the future. Jefferson felt that "no definite limits can be assigned to the improveability of the human race"; Joel Barlow believed that "all things in the physical world, as well as in the moral and intellectual world, are progressive in nature." Even John Adams, not given to enthusiasms, agreed that there was "hope for splendid improvement in human society and vast amelioration in the condition of mankind." The American experience itself helped to reinforce this conviction. Americans who had wrested a civilization out of the wilderness and were building a nation where none had existed most certainly had evidence to believe in progress, and there seemed to be nothing in the United States to hold it back. William Ellery Channing, who belonged to the next post-Revolutionary generation, echoed it in 1824 in words that might easily have been written in 1774: "If there be one striking feature in human nature, it is the susceptibleness of improvement."[24]

The eighteenth-century American's belief in progress presupposed a world improved by reason, moving forward toward an inevitable, divinely-ordained perfection, approached a step at a time as divinity willed it. Men could hasten it by revising their ideas and institutions, but not by much. Yet the "melioration" of man's problems, to use a favorite contemporary term, *would* come; progress was part of a huge cyclic change, a wave in the tide of human affairs that could be neither hurried nor diverted.

After the turn of the nineteenth century, the American idea of progress became much more kinetic and positive. The nineteenth century believed that men could so manipulate their society that progress could be materially hastened. They concluded that social change was not simply a series of events, arranged by chronology, that shifted the direction of some institutions, but that they could change the character and quality of those institutions to make them new and different in kind and result. It was a rule of nature, wrote Emerson, that it "slept no moment of an old past, but every hour repaired itself and improvement was its law." Man was also equally improvable, for he was endowed with reason, will, and conscience, inwardly impelled by God's decree to seek betterment. "We learn

24. Arthur Ekirch, *The Idea of Progress in America, 1815–1860* (New York, 1944), a thorough study of the period, has furnished much material for this discussion.

that the highest is present in the soul of man," Emerson noted. "Who can set bounds to the possibilities of man?"

There were good reasons, American thinkers of the opening decades of the nineteenth century assumed, for believing that the rate of man's advancement could be spectacularly accelerated. They saw evidence, as they looked around them, that this was exactly what was happening. Conditions of life had improved visibly over the preceding century; economic standards were higher, scientific discoveries more numerous, technological advances easily noticeable. Advances in machinery had transformed the physical aspects of living and had reduced much of its drudgery and danger. Education and social improvements were on the way to reducing poverty, ignorance, and crime—or so it seemed. The peace that followed the War of 1812 and the obvious success of the great American political experiments of 1776 and 1787 lent further proof to progress far beyond what the eighteenth century had dreamed of. The philosophers were certain that men had discovered new ways of perceiving truth, by way of the inward intuition—that faculty identified by Emerson and the transcendentalists as the great primal power that made God's truth available *immediately* to man.

During the first half of the nineteenth century the doctrine of progress took on an emotional validity for American thinkers that it had not had before. "No word in the English language," said a writer in *The Southern Quarterly Review* in 1854, "is so much used as the disyllable progress. In America we use it so much, that we have made a verb of it." Man sometimes stumbled or lost his way, but he always moved ahead. The impediments he encountered were surmountable; he contained within himself the elements of his ultimate success. He was by no means a helpless sinner in the hands of a Calvinist God, but a self-reliant, free-standing individual, capable of making choices to his own benefit. John O'Sullivan summarized it superbly in an editorial for *The United States Magazine and Democratic Review* in 1840:[25]

In all history . . . , the reflecting mind can observe the operation of one mighty principle. On all is written the great Law of Progress. This is indeed

25. "The Progress of Society," *United States Magazine and Democratic Review*, VIII (July, 1840), 67–88. See also Mark Hopkins's oration, "The Law of Progress of the Human Race," *Ibid.*, XX (August, 1844), 195–200. For an earlier essay, see "Indefinite Improvement," *The United States Literary Gazette*, I (November, 1834), 218–20.

the distinguishing mark of our species, obviously dividing it from the beasts that perish. One after another the generations may pass from the stage of action . . . , empires may sink in ruin, and whole nations be swept from the face of the earth but the course of the whole race is onward. Every age takes some one step in advance of its predecessors.

Emerson, quite typically, wrote in his essay *Fate* that the "indwelling necessity" and "central intention" of all creation was nothing less than "universal harmony and joy"; his friend William Ellery Channing felt that a man need only "to trust, dare, and be." Their fellow minister Theodore Parker believed that progress was inherent in God's plan for mankind, since "from the infinite perfection of God there follows unavoidably the relative perfection of all that He creates." The whole force of history, these men believed, pointed toward the United States as the climax of a divinely-ordained march toward human betterment.

The thinkers of the early nineteenth century made the principle of progress into a rule of life; theirs was no tentative acceptance, but a fervent, clear belief. There were a number of reasons for this. Some of the responsibility for improving the world had shifted from God to man, who was held much more accountable for determining his future than before, and much more capable of it. Progress was conceived not simply to be part of a remote, ageless cycle, but something accessible, responsive to manipulation. As Albert Brisbane wrote, men could find ways of "*hastening* this progress, and of anticipating results, which if left to the gradual movement of society would require centuries to effect." By using government as one of the instruments of change, many Americans believed that in the United States, at least, one might obtain "progress by legislation," a kind of self-willed bootstrap-lifting by statute.

Nowhere was the impact of this newly-affirmed belief in progress more visible than in the growth of American reform, which swelled over the early nineteenth century like a wave. "Perhaps there has been no age," the *North American Review* editorialized in January of 1827,

since the world was established as the abode of man, so generally confident of progress, and so full of anticipation of further advancement, as our own. It looks back at the ages that are past, and asserts it is wiser and better than they. It looks forward on the ages to come, and acknowledges they will far surpass it.

Convinced of both the possibility and the availability of progress, the men of Emerson's and Jackson's time looked ahead toward an improved society, a perfected democracy, an inspiring future. "No reform is now deemed impossible," said the Reverend Orville Dewey of Massachusetts in 1844, "no enterprise for human betterment impracticable. Everything may be made better."

In science and technology, especially, Americans believed they had powerful allies in the drive toward betterment. Through science, which liberated man from bondage to matter and enlarged his control over the world, he could channel his energies toward improving his condition—and in America, a democracy, its benefits were open to all. Thus Edward Marshall of California wrote that "this unseen influence"

cheapened literature, and drove a myriad-headed free press into existence. It strewed the land with railways . . . , netted the Republic over with streams of thought, subdued the earth and the elements, and made all things equal to all men.

"Wrought by that 'active principle,' the history of the United States therefore 'is a history of progress; physical and geographical progress; intellectual, moral, civil, social, and political progress.' "[26] The steam engine, the reaper, the printing press, the telegraph, and other inventions were hailed as powerful tools of progress. Jacob Bigelow, writing in *The Elements of Technology* (1829), predicted that though "the strides of the past" seemed rapid indeed, "we have scarcely crossed the threshold of the temple of human knowledge" in the application of machinery to "the tasks of life." The potentialities of the telegraph *DeBow's Review* found almost unimaginable: "Scarcely anything now will appear to be impossible. We limit not what man may achieve, nor determine what is beyond his reach." Walt Whitman, for his part, wrote that "a passing glance at the fat volumes of the Patent Office Reports" in 1857 made him "bless his fate for being born."[27]

Americans of the early nineteenth century, then, believed deeply in a kind of progress which could be hastened by science, govern-

26. "The Progress of Democracy," *Democratic Review*, XXX (April, 1852), 300, 304.

27. An impassioned summary of the nation's future is Gamaliel Bailey's "Lecture before the Young Men's Mercantile Association of Cincinnati," *The Herald of Truth*, I (1847), 253–66.

ment, education, technology, and by the efforts of individuals and groups in combination. This progress was a real thing, visible in the life of their own times. To the contemporary European intellectual, the idea of progress was a philosophical abstraction to be defined and explored, an intellectual principle by which one's interpretation of history could be manipulated. In the United States, however, the idea had much more dynamic reality. The achievements of the American people, illustrated by their successful revolution, their establishment of a new kind of government that seemed to work, their conquest of a great, untapped continent, all helped substantially to make the concept of progress a real and demonstrable fact in America, rather than simply a philosophical theory. The American could look around him and see its results. "The former wild prairie, now a cultivated farm," wrote N. H. Parker of the frontier lands in 1857,

the floating palaces upon the bosom of the river which but a little while ago rolled on undisturbed in its lonely beauty; the churches and school-houses where stood a few summers ago the Indian's wigwam

were positive evidences of the Americans' progress in settling and peopling this new empire.

Since it was assumed that all men, not merely a chosen class, profited from this upward trend, the idea of progress was built into America's social and intellectual framework. The consideration of almost every issue of general importance to the early nineteenth century was formulated and in some way influenced by the era's assumption of unlimited, available progress, and almost every leader of contemporary thought affirmed his faith in it. "The law of man's nature," wrote Salmon P. Chase, "impressed on him by God, is onward progress." Whitman believed the near future promised "such unparalleled happiness and national freedom, such unnumbered myriads," that "the heart of a true man leaps with a mighty joy to think of it." George Bancroft, the era's reigning historian, in an 1854 oration titled "The Necessity, the Reality, and the Promise of the Progress of the Human Race," gave the idea of progress its most eloquent contemporary exposition. "The course of civilization," he concluded,[28]

28. George Bancroft, *Literary and Historical Miscellanies* (New York, 1855).

flows on like a mighty river through a boundless valley, calling to the streams from every side to swell its current, which is always growing wider, and deeper, and clearer, as it rolls along. Let us trust ourselves upon its bosom without fear; nay, rather with confidence and joy. Since the progress of the race appears to be the great purpose of Providence, it becomes us all to venerate the future. . . . Everything is in movement, and for the better, except only the fixed eternal law by which the necessity of change is established.

Longfellow, more succinctly, heard the same message in the sound of the Bells of San Blas:

> Out of the shadows of night
> The world rolls into light;
> It is daybreak everywhere.

Through the first half of the nineteenth century, then, Americans expected a continual unfolding of benefits, to be attained by taking best advantage of all the available scientific, technological, and intellectual advances. Even James Fenimore Cooper, a man not overly sanguine about society's ability to improve itself, felt that in America things might be different; in the United States, he admitted grudgingly, "all that reason allows may be hoped in behalf of man."

This fervent, deep-rooted belief in what George Bancroft called "the necessity, the reality, and the promise of progress" was the result of a re-evaluation—in terms of the American experience—of the Enlightenment and of four subsequent decades of territorial expansion, nationalistic confidence, and growing wealth. The nation was proud of its development from thirteen weak and divided colonies to a powerful, united nation. What had happened in America since Yorktown seemed to furnish convincing proof that there was such a thing as progress, as the Enlightenment promised, and that it was especially swift and decisive in its American manifestations. If any portion of the world had the right to assume the reality of progress, Americans believed, they did.[29]

29. Even on the verge of the Civil War, "Glimpses of the American Future," *Harper's Monthly*, XVIII (December–May, 1859) , 119–24, seemed bright. In a five-page paean of hope, the editor believed America "destined to be the continent of the future," and the American mind to be the "pioneer mind of the world in coming stages of progress."

CHAPTER 2

The Thrust of Reform

THE American of the early nineteenth century faced the future with magnificent self-assurance. "There is at hand," remarked William Ellery Channing in 1830, "a tendency and a power to exalt the people," founded on "devotion to the progress of the whole human race." Emerson, commenting on the state of the nation, noted a spirit of "restless, prying, conscientious criticism" abroad, and summarizing it in a single question, asked, "What is man born for, but to be a Reformer, a Remaker of what man has made?" To the men of the era, the problem of attaining perfection seemed clear, if not simple. One could reasonably assume that man was intended by God to live in peace, plenty, and morality; if he did not, whatever interfered with God's plan ought to be eliminated—poverty, injustice, ignorance, sin, sickness.

Reform in nineteenth-century America, though part of a larger world movement sweeping England and Europe, had its own characteristics. The majority of reforms it proposed were pragmatic, practical ways of improving a practical society. The American habit of paying more attention to practice than theory, however, sometimes led to hurried failures; studies of the sources of crime, disease, poverty, and allied ills were neglected in the rush to cure them. American reform was comprehensive rather than selective; reformers, with supreme confidence, attacked on all fronts. Nothing was too large or too small—one could work for the abolition of slavery or of Sunday mails, or for sensible dress for women and

Christianizing Asia at the same time and with equal fervor. Bronson Alcott once even suggested forming a "Club for the Study and Diffusion of Ideas and Tendencies Proper to the Nineteenth Century" that included the study of nearly everything wrong with the world.[1]

In addition, American reform was infused with the characteristically American tradition of "good works" and benevolence, compounded of Calvinism, Quakerism, Enlightenment deism, frontier democracy, and evangelical missionary zeal. Tocqueville, in 1831, was impressed by the pervasive humanitarianism of American society, particularly in the attitude of the wealthy toward the poor. This tradition of philanthropy and mutual aid had deep native roots, and the principle of "giving" was strongly established by the nineteenth century, whether it meant money or spiritual aid.[2] American reform was essentially conservative, nonviolent, primarily peaceful in method and intent. It was curative, intended to forestall disruption and dissent; unlike Europe, there were no barricades in American streets nor cavalry riding down mobs. Despite the violent rhetoric and the powerful emotions unleashed by reform, there were only a few American martyrs, excepting Elijah Lovejoy and perhaps (as the era considered him to be) John Brown. Nobody dragged Theodore Parker from his pulpit; Greeley's *Tribune* presses were never destroyed; eggs and vegetables were usually the most dangerous things thrown at Garrison.

American reform was also primarily regional, its dynamics Northern and later Western, leaving the South relatively untouched. One "ism" could lead to another, and the South could afford to take no risks with any of them, lest they lead to abolitionism. A writer in *DeBow's Review* in 1856 warned that any book in "the whole range of moral science, if not written by Southern authors, written within

1. An excellent summary of nineteenth-century reform is Henry Steele Commager's introduction to *The Era of Reform* (Princeton, 1960), 1–18. The enthusiasm generated by reform may be judged by the fact that in one two-week period in May in New York in the forties, there were meetings of the American Antislavery Society, the New York Antislavery Society, the American Temperance Union, the American Women's Educational Association, the American Bible Society, the American Tract Society, the American Female Guardian Society, and the American Seaman's Friend Society, not counting meetings of church missionary societies and other charity-related groups.

2. Robert Bremner, *American Philanthropy* (Chicago, 1960), chapters II and III trace the roots of American humanitarianism.

the last twenty or thirty years," was likely to "inculcate abolitionism either directly or indirectly." Until the fifties American
reform was for the most part nonpolitical, doing its work outside
the usual partisan political framework. There was no single national reform party or leader; reformers usually worked through the
machinery of the state—as Horace Mann did with public schools or
Neal Dow with prohibition of liquors or Dorothea Dix with prisons
—and not through political parties. The Workingman's Party was
an exception, and not a particularly successful one, but no con-
certed effort was ever made until late in the fifties to co-opt either
major party for reform. Even the antislavery movement divided
sharply over the question.

If the roots of reform lay deep in the soil of the eighteenth
century, the plant drew vitality from the climate of the nineteenth.
First, from the past the reformers inherited the Enlightenment's
faith in progress, the conviction that the world could be made
better if only men would try. Americans had science, technology,
democracy, and divine guidance to help them; they believed that
the process of improvement could be so directed and accelerated
that perfection on this earth *could* be attained and not simply
dreamed of. Nineteenth-century reformers were absolutely certain
of this.

Second, American reformers inherited the Enlightenment's faith
in the individual's ability to control himself and his society and to
direct both toward higher ends. This was reinforced by Romanticism's faith in the individual and its belief that all men possessed
an intuitive faculty that directed them toward right thinking and
acting. Together the two strains of thought produced in the nineteenth century an aggressive, almost mystical conviction that each
man, by using those powers within him, could achieve in his life
and institutions something approaching perfection. "There is an
infinite worthiness in man," Emerson wrote, "which will appear at
the call of worth," and which would enable him to surmount all
obstacles.[3]

3. For discussions of the ideological backgrounds of American reform, see Commager, *op. cit.*, 7–18, and his *Theodore Parker* (Boston, 1937) ; Arthur M. Schlesinger, *The American as Reformer* (Cambridge, 1951) ; Merle Curti, *The Growth
of American Thought* (New York, 1943) , chapter 15; and Ralph Gabriel, *The
Course of American Democratic Thought* (New York, 1940) , chapters I–III. The

Third, nineteenth-century reformers were heir to the Enlightenment tradition of benevolence, reinforced by the evangelical ethic of social responsibility. As Franklin had considered the "most acceptable service to God the doing good to man," so the nineteenth-century reformer accepted the responsibility of being his brother's keeper. "It is part of Christian duty," wrote the directors of the American Bible Society, to rescue one's fellowman from "thoughtlessness, ignorance, and peril; it becomes Christians to imitate their Master, and to seek the good of those who are careless of their own good."[4]

Fourth, nineteenth-century reform was an integral element of the belief that it was America's national mission to serve the world as an example of what it could and ought to be. The United States represented the hope of the future; its "high purpose," said William H. Seward, was to show "that throughout the rise, progress, and decline of nations, one divine purpose runs, the increasing felicity and dignity of Human Nature." All the reforms of pre–Civil War America, however disparate their aims, merged into the single great mission of making the United States the model for the world's future.

Reform was in the air on both sides of the Atlantic, and the winds of change blew equally strong in London, Paris, Frankfurt, and Boston. American reformers' strongest connections, of course, were with England. English and American churches exchanged ministers and reprinted each other's publications; English reformers visited the United States while Americans served as delegates to conventions of peace, antislavery, and temperance societies in England and Scotland. Fourier and Robert Owen, Harriet Martineau and Frances Wright and Father Matthew were known in the United States as well as they were in England and Europe.[5] From Eng-

---

relationship between Romanticism and reform is brilliantly treated in John L. Thomas, "Romantic Reform in America, 1815–1865," *American Quarterly*, XVII (Winter, 1965) , 656–81.

4. Clifford S. Griffin, *Their Brother's Keepers: Moral Stewardship in the United States 1800–1865* (New Brunswick, 1960) , 46 ff.

5. See Frank Thistlethwaite, *The Anglo-American Connection in the Early Nineteenth Century* (Philadelphia, 1959) , 76–100. American temperance societies were models for similar British and Scottish groups; London peace societies were patterns for American ones. British and American antislavery societies in particular were closely linked.

land, too, Americans drew inspiration from philosopher Jeremy
Bentham's "utilitarianism," expressed in *Principles of Morals and
Legislation* (1789) and subsequent books. His criterion of judgment, "the greatest good to the greatest number," and his belief
that *utility* constituted the final test of ideas and institutions struck
Jacksonian America as exactly right. If prisons did not deter crime,
change them so they did; if war settled nothing, outlaw it. Nothing
could have provided a more practical basis for reform.[6]

Reform in the United States received its most powerful support
from the religious evangelism that swept the country in the twenties
and thirties. From evangelical revivalism sprang two beliefs: one,
"perfectionism," the conviction that American life could be reformed and rearranged to meet the moral requirements God had set
down for the perfect society; the other, that the "saved" or "perfected" Christian must, to make his salvation complete, apply his
religion to life and make his piety practical. Salvation was not the
end, but the beginning of a useful life; each Christian should, said
the Reverend Charles Grandison Finney, "have the determination
at being *useful* in the highest degree possible." As a Methodist
hymn put it,

> To save the present age,
> My calling to fulfill;
> O may it all my powers engage,
> To do my Master's will.

Evangelical religion made social reform a moral imperative. If
social evil were the result of individual sin and selfishness, then
progress came from reforming individuals by religious conversion.
The duty of the reformer, then, was to convert the nation, rather
than to try to argue it into virtue or legislate it into benevolence.
John Humphrey Noyes, founder of Oneida Community, explained
that real social change was simply religious perfection translated
into action:

The Revivalists had for their one great idea the regeneration of the soul.
The great idea of the Socialists was the regeneration of society, which is the

6. Curti, *op. cit.*, 362–4. John Quincy Adams bought twenty-five copies of each
of Bentham's books for American libraries; novelist and critic John Neal lived
at Bentham's house and edited his works for American use; reformer Gilbert Vale
of New York in 1840 founded a journal, *The Diamond,* devoted to utilitarian
ideas.

soul's environment. These ideas belong together and are the complements of each other.

Leadership of the major reform groups was thus closely tied to the churches, and for good reason.[7] Later, as reform by moral suasion seemed to be losing momentum, some societies turned to political action, but until then most of the reform leaders hoped to change society by conversion rather than legislation.

The instrument chosen to accomplish reform was the voluntary society, an organized group of like-minded individuals who together could exert more effort, more effectively, than an individual alone. There were societies everywhere in 1845, wrote one minister:

Missionary societies, tract societies, education societies, moral societies, and other societies of various names for the purpose of feeding the hungry, clothing the naked, instructing the ignorant, saving the lost, and promoting peace on earth and mutual amity among mankind.

In the principle of "association" the reformers believed they had found a powerful tool. As William Ellery Channing wrote,

Men, it is justly said, can do jointly, what they cannot do singly. . . . Union not only brings to a point forces which before existed, and which were ineffectual through separation, but, by the feeling and interest which it rouses, it becomes a creative principle, calls forth new forces, and gives the mind a consciousness of powers, which would otherwise have been unknown.

These societies of clergy and laymen—local, regional, and national in scope—published journals, organized speakers' bureaus, sent out lecturers, held conventions, and later proved to be powerful lobbies in state capitals and in Congress. Their directorates often interlocked; some men belonged to half a dozen, and some held influential posts in several, establishing a kind of empire that eventually

7. Thomas, *op. cit.,* 670–81. A useful discussion is Roy F. Nichols, "The Religion of American Democracy," in *Religion and American Democracy* (Baton Rouge, 1959), 50–102; see also Louis Filler, "The Dynamics of Reform," *Antioch Review,* XXVII (Fall, 1967), 362–78. A thorough treatment of religion and reform during the period is Charles C. Cole, *The Social Ideas of the Northern Evangelists 1826–1860* (New York, 1954); and Timothy Smith, *Revivalism and Social Reform in Mid-Nineteenth Century America* (Nashville, 1957).

held the whole movement under loosely centralized control.* As Channing remarked,[8]

So extensive have coalitions become, through the facilities now described, and so various and rapid are the means of communication, that when a few leaders have agreed on an object, an impulse may be given in a month to the whole country.

On the other hand, there were those who preferred not to place too much trust in associations, and who felt that possibly one should reform one's self before reforming society. Organizations, Channing also warned, had "a tendency to fetter men, to repress energy"; neither Thoreau nor Emerson would join reform societies with the zeal of a Parker. Even Greeley, a champion joiner, wrote in his *Recollections of a Busy Life* (1869) that "the true reformer turns his eyes first inward, scrutinizing himself. . . ."[9]

Despite its reliance on organization and its belief in the effectiveness of collective action, the American reform movement was highly individualistic. Both the intellectualized transcendentalist and the emotional evangelist (like their Calvinist forebears) placed great emphasis on the right of private judgment. As a result, many of the reform societies were plagued by schisms and divisions. The history of the antislavery movement, a prime example, was one of constant internal quarrels. In effect, American reformers could never really decide which counted most, the society or the member, and kept up an uneasy compromise between them.

Some reform societies were broadly religious, others had general social goals, and still others were directly aimed at changing specific practices.[10] Women figured prominently in many of them; their

8. "The Principle of Association," *The Christian Examiner,* VII (September, 1829) , 105–40; Filler, *op. cit.,* 366. Arthur Tappan, for example, at one time was on the governing boards of six societies; the Reverend Anson Phelps on four, Jasper Comins on three. Garrison was involved with six different reform societies, Theodore Parker with seven, Horace Greeley with eleven.

9. Contemporary discussions of the philosophy of reform are too numerous to list. However, representative essays are J. H. Moore, "Social Reform," *The Herald of Truth,* II (1848) , 129–34 and "Hints to Reformers," *Ibid.,* 398–406; "Social Reforms," *The New Englander,* VIII (1850) , 452–70, and "Reforms and Reformers," *Ibid.,* 507–15; "On Doing Good," *Christian Examiner,* XXII (January, 1837) , 320–24.

10. Typical of the first variety were the American Home Missionary Society, the American Tract Society, and the American Bible Society; the second was represented by the American Sunday School Union, the American Peace Society, and

participation in the reform movement, in fact, became a powerful force in the feminist struggle for equal rights. An upper-class urban woman often had time on her hands, and a socially-acceptable outlet for her talents was Christian good works. "While the husbands are in business," James Buckingham wrote, their wives could "direct their energies into useful channels" by joining a charitable or reform society. Visiting the poor, teaching children, gathering old clothes, and caring for the sick were, of course, traditionally female activities.

In the search for perfection, few aspects or institutions of American society escaped scrutiny; minor flaws in the conduct of life received the same attention as major social problems. A good digestion, a ten-hour working day, whole wheat bread, better jails, and the abolition of slavery were each considered to be steps that might advance humanity a few paces toward the ideal society. Dueling, for example, though rapidly disappearing, was still a way gentlemen settled disputes in certain parts of the country. Laws against it were lax, and the Anti-Duelling Society (founded in 1809) worked for years for stricter enforcement. Public opinion finally ended the custom by the thirties.[11] The Sabbath Union (1828) lobbied for laws to preserve Sunday as a holy day, in opposition to the tendency to use it for work, play, and business. One of the most sensational campaigns was that to abolish flogging in the navy. The use of the lash was common punishment for a variety of crimes, ranging from laziness to mutiny, and twenty lashes could permanently injure the recipient. After long agitation, in which Richard Henry Dana played a prominent part, the practice was outlawed in 1850 over the strenuous objections of many old navy men.[12]

---

the American Education Society; of the third class, typical organizations were the Anti-Duelling Society, the Sabbath Union, the Boston Prison Discipline Society, and the American Bethel Society for seamen and canal workers.

11. New Jersey and New York, after the Burr-Hamilton affair in 1804, enforced their laws strictly. Congressmen and military officers fought duels in Maryland, where the law was winked at; here Commodore James Barron killed Commodore Stephen Decatur in 1820. The last duel between prominent politicians was Henry Clay versus John Randolph, in 1826, in which neither was injured. New Orleans bloods, however, met at the "Duelling Oaks" for some years.

12. Some captains were notorious sadists. Captain Mackenzie of the *Somers* prescribed 2,313 lashes to ninety sailors in one four-month cruise; the captain of the *Independence* gave out 40,000 lashes in one Pacific tour of duty. Allan Nevins, *Ordeal of the Union* (New York, 1947), I:120–1.

American Quakers were long-time pacifists, while many of the liberalized men of the Enlightenment—among them Paine, Rush, and Franklin—supported antiwar societies. The long Napoleonic Wars, which involved the United States itself in the War of 1812, further encouraged the growth of the peace movement. David Low Dodge, a wealthy New York manufacturer, wrote a brief tract, *War Inconsistent with the Religion of Jesus Christ* (1815), which found a sympathetic public.[13] That year Dodge and others formed a Peace Society in New York and Noah Worcester another in Boston; Worcester's journal, *The Friend of Peace,* was probably the first publication of its kind in the world. The movement spread swiftly —there were at least seventeen peace societies scattered over the United States by 1820—supported by clergy, judges, educators, and other civic leaders. The spark that turned the reform into a crusade was struck by William Ladd, a wealthy Maine merchant, who believed that only if it were nationally organized could the movement prosper. In 1828, with the help of Dodge and others, he founded the American Peace Society and began a national campaign against war.

The peace movement, however, was sharply divided between those who believed all wars were wrong and those who believed only offensive wars should be condemned. The American Peace Society's convention in 1837 split over the issue and a substantial number seceded. The movement at the same time was divided by the "non-resistants," who carried pacifism to its logical extreme— since all governments were based on force, they refused to support any government in any way, "offering no physical resistance to any of its mandates, however unjust and tyrannical." Non-resistants declared themselves against all war, militia, appropriations for war, or any war-related activities; they also refused to vote, hold office, or recognize the courts, or participate in any governmental affairs.[14]

13. For studies of the peace movement, see Arthur C. F. Beales, *The History of Peace* (New York, 1931) ; W. Freeman Galpin, *Pioneering for Peace: A Study of American Peace Efforts to 1846* (Syracuse, 1933) ; Peter Brock, *Pacifism in the United States* (Princeton, 1968) ; and Chapter 15 of Alice Felt Tyler's *Freedom's Ferment: Phases of American Social History to 1860* (Minneapolis, 1944) .

14. At the 1838 meeting of peace society delegates William Lloyd Garrison and his followers swung the group to their point of view and created the New England Non-Resistance Society, whose paper, *The Non-Resistant,* gained a good deal of notoriety for its blazing attacks on government.

The real crisis came with the declaration of war against Mexico in 1846, which was opposed by a number of prominent men—among them Charles Sumner, Theodore Parker, Emerson, Henry Thoreau (whose refusal to pay his poll tax put him in jail overnight), and James Russell Lowell, whose indictment of the war in *The Biglow Papers* (1848)

> Ez fer war, I call it murder—
> There you hev it, plain an' flat;
> I don't want to go no furder
> Than my Testyment for that,

reflected the views of the peace advocates.

One of the most effective leaders of the American Peace Society, a self-educated blacksmith named Elihu Burritt, believed that peace could be gained only by international effort. With Joseph Sturge and other English pacifists he formed the League of Human Brotherhood, whose members signed a pledge,

never to enlist or enter into any army or navy, or to yield my voluntary support or sanction to the preparation for or prosecution of any war, by whomsoever or for whatsoever proposed, declared, or waged,

which brought up once more the issue of offensive versus defensive war. Ironically, the fifties saw the Crimean War, bloody revolts in Italy and Poland, and rising tensions in the United States over the slavery issue, where some felt that force might be the only way to abolish the system and others the only way to preserve it. What can you do, asked Horace Greeley, with people *"who won't have* Peace, nor let others have it, what then?"* Was peace with slavery worth having? Garrison, after much soul-searching, defended John Brown; so did Emerson. What was in Garrison's mind, as he watched his son, Lieutenant George Garrison, march through Boston's streets with the Fifty-fourth Massachusetts (a black regiment) on his way to war, one cannot know.

Since poverty and vice were urgent and highly visible urban problems, the cities were focal points of a great deal of reform effort. Churches were particularly sensitive to these problems, recognizing, as the Congregational *Independent* said, that "the immense class of working poor" needed immediate practical as well as spiritual aid. Church groups set up mission homes, slum churches, and refuges for special groups like old sailors, recent immigrants, juveniles, alcoholics, and reformed prostitutes. The Reverend John McDowell, a Presbyterian minister, established a home for the rehabilitation of prostitutes in New York City in 1830, organized the Magdalen Society, and in 1832 brought out the famous "Magdalen Report," a study of prostitution. Other societies appeared—the American Society for the Prevention of Licentiousness and Vice, the Seventh Commandment Society, and the most successful, the American Female Reform Society (1834), which published a journal called *The Advocate of Moral Reform* and had 20,000 members in 1838.[15] The savage old laws of imprisonment for debt worked especial hardship on the poor man, the apprentice, workman, small shopowner, and street vendor, and it was argued with some justification that the laws made ill-fortune a crime. Clearly, it made no sense to put a man in jail, where he could not earn money, for not having it. In 1817 New York set twenty-five dollars as the minimum debt for imprisonment; in 1821 Kentucky abolished the law itself and other states did so before 1860.[16]

The urban poor presented an especially difficult and puzzling problem. The public, to some extent, still clung to the old idea that poverty was somehow a moral as well as an economic condition, and that in a country where labor was scarce and land plentiful, a man was poor by his own fault.[17] Yet despite the efforts of missionary societies, tracts, pamphlets, and sermons, and despite all the earnest good works done by the churches, the poor continued to increase and the slums to grow. Cities opened almshouses and improved sanitation; charitable societies and missions did the best they could; and editors and legislators advocated closing saloons, restricting immigration, or opening savings banks in the slums. No one really knew why some people were poor, nor did anyone know how to find out. For that matter, no one knew how many poor there were, nor

15. See Cole, *op. cit.*, 160 ff., 172 ff., and chapter VII on the church and reform.
16. Tyler, *op. cit.*, 283–5. From January, 1820, to April, 1822, Boston had 3,000 people in jail for debt, of whom 2,000 owed less than twenty dollars, or less than it cost the state to keep them.
17. Reports of the New York Society for the Prevention of Pauperism for 1818–1824, for example, listed as the causes of poverty ignorance, idleness, intemperance, gambling, imprudent marriage, lack of economical habits, and prostitution.

was there any standard for defining who was poor and who was not.[18]

In fact, poverty in its nineteenth-century setting was a new thing to American society, neither fully understood nor defined. It was assumed that in any society most people would be poor—as the Bible said—but in the new, urbanized, industrialized society of the nineteenth century, the whole problem needed redefinition. In rural America poor relief was informal; churches gave clothes and food to the poor, neighbors cared for the sick, orphans were put into county homes, labor "sold" for its keep. But what did *poor* mean in either rural or city terms? At what level was one no longer *poor*, so that the condition could be identified and measured?[19]

The attitude toward poverty in the forties and fifties was ambivalent. Some people were poor, it was assumed, because they were morally incapable of living a better life; they were, said one investigator, "content to live in filth and disorder with a bare subsistence." Some, on the other hand, were poor because environment forced them to be; Horace Greeley, among others, believed many people were poor simply because they had no other choice. For the most part, poverty was considered a personal rather than a social responsibility, to be cured by reforming the person himself and rewarding him for ridding himself of those habits that made him poor.

Poor relief and charity work, therefore (at least until the sixties), consisted chiefly of providing moral instruction for the poor, with some direct assistance to alleviate present suffering. "Moral and Religious culture," said William Ellery Channing in *The Ministry for the Poor* (1835), "is the great blessing to be bestowed on the poor." Work among the poor in the cities was thus predominantly under the direction of religious and quasi-religious groups. The New York Mission and Tract Society, for example, which had over forty missionaries at work in the city in 1860, did good work in

18. For a discussion, see Nevins, *op. cit.*, I:129–32. A Philadelphia report of 1854 showed 700 professional beggars in the city and 1,800 vagrant children. Official New York State reports in 1855 revealed that there was one pauper, living on state charity, to every seventeen persons. Massachusetts in 1853 had 26,000 persons on relief rolls, 2,600 of them under fourteen.

19. The best study of the era's thinking about poverty and wealth is Robert Bremner, *From the Depths: The Discovery of Poverty in the United States* (New York, 1964), especially chapters I and II.

housing, employment, and direct relief, but its primary purpose was to distribute tracts in jails and almshouses and to operate its mission churches. There were dozens of similar societies, sponsored by every major Protestant sect. The Catholic Church, with long experience in dealing with Europe's poor, began its work early. The Sisters of Charity of St. Vincent de Paul arrived in 1809, and other orders, like the Little Sisters of the Poor (1840), were active in the cities throughout the century. Their emphasis, like that of the Protestant groups, was on the moral causes of poverty.[20]

Some, however, who studied the problem of poverty groped toward the semblance of a methodology. The Reverend Joseph Tuckerman of Boston, for example, organized all the city's major charitable societies into a cooperative agency for greater effectiveness. Robert Hartley, a New York merchant, organized the New York Association for Improving the Condition of the Poor in 1843 on the principle that health, housing, employment, education, and not morality, were the keys to social betterment, and under Hartley's direction the thirty-odd philanthropic societies in the city began to coordinate their efforts. Charles Loring Brace, who addressed himself to the problem of New York's ten thousand vagrant children and adolescents, founded the Children's Aid Society in 1853 to provide housing, education, and supervision for them. These and other such efforts marked a significant shift in the attitude of reformers toward the poor. The idea that poverty was a social as well as an individual or moral problem laid the foundation for modern social work.[21]

Reformers also re-examined the plight of the insane and the handicapped, the blind, deaf, and orphaned. Traditionally, such handicaps had been considered acts of God—inscrutable perhaps, but obviously to some purpose, else God would not have allowed

20. For a general study, see Frank D. Watson, *The Charity Organization Movement in the United States* (New York, 1922) and John O'Grady, *Catholic Charities in the United States* (Washington, 1930).

21. A good study is Daniel McColgan, *Joseph Tuckerman, Pioneer in American Social Work* (Washington, 1940). Charles Loring Brace's *Dangerous Classes of New York and Twenty Years' Work Among Them* (New York, 1872) is still a fascinating study. Several of Theodore Parker's sermons are excellent summaries of the enlightened social thought of the period; see especially "The Dangerous Classes of Society," *Speeches, Addresses, and Occasional Sermons* (Boston, 1871), I:279–333.

them. Christian sympathy led some, who had no particular qualifications for the work save love of humanity, to make careers out of helping the unfortunate. The Reverend Thomas Gallaudet, Congregational minister, was drawn into curative work by caring for the deaf child of a friend. He studied in France and England and returned to open a school for the deaf in 1817, the first of its kind in the country. Before 1850 thirteen states had established similar schools, all based on Gallaudet's model. Samuel Gridley Howe, a Harvard medical graduate, began teaching the blind in his home in Boston. He was so successful that a wealthy Bostonian, Colonel Perkins, gave him his home as a school in 1832 and helped Howe solicit funds for what became Perkins Institute, the best school for the blind of the time. His greatest achievement was teaching Laura Bridgman, a blind deaf-mute child who entered the school in 1837, to communicate with the world. The orphan received renewed attention. Orphanages, whether publicly-supported or run by private charitable societies, were few in number and disgracefully casual and cruel. "Houses of Refuge" for waifs appeared in the cities in the twenties, but the first recognition that the orphaned or wayward child was a ward of the state and a public responsibility came with Massachusetts's "reform" school for boys (1845) and girls (1847), a pattern followed by other states.[22]

Treatment of the insane presented a somewhat more complicated problem. The old idea that the mentally ill were afflicted by God died hard. The work of the French, particularly of Philippe Pinel, had great influence in the United States, as did that of William Tuke in England. During the early decades of the nineteenth century "asylums" for the insane appeared, separating the mentally ill from the paupers and criminals with whom they had previously been confined—Philadelphia's Quaker Retreat (1817), McLean Asylum in Massachusetts (1818), New York's Bloomingdale (1821), the Kentucky State Asylum (1824). Some state mental hospitals opened in the thirties, but most asylums were privately run and public expenditures were woefully inadequate. But if attitudes toward the insane were changing, their treatment was not. Doro-

22. For a summary, see Tyler, *op. cit.*, 283–96. Robert S. Pickett, *House of Refuge: Origins of Juvenile Reform in New York State 1815–1847* (Syracuse, 1969) is a useful study. Harold Schwartz, *Samuel Gridley Howe* (Cambridge, 1956) is a good biography.

thea Dix, a Boston school mistress, taught a Sunday school class at the East Cambridge House of Correction and what she saw there started her on a lifelong career.

In 1841, with the help of Samuel Gridley Howe and Charles Sumner, Miss Dix began a two-year survey of jails, asylums, and reform schools that touched off a comprehensive program of reform. She next made surveys in Rhode Island, New Jersey, and Pennsylvania, leaving behind a shocked public and better prisons and asylums wherever she went. By 1854 she had reported on the institutions of every state east of Indiana; by 1860 she covered the rest. She also investigated jails and asylums in Canada, England, Hungary, Turkey, and even Japan. Her "sad, patient, deliberate" investigations stung the world's conscience. Few persons have ever had such far-reaching effect on public policy toward reform.[23]

The concept of incarceration as therapy and punishment was essentially a nineteenth-century development; colonial jails were intended chiefly to hold lawbreakers until courts had imposed sentence, of whatever nature that might be. Later, however, the idea emerged that all those members of society who did not or could not follow society's rules should be placed in institutions where they could be rehabilitated and returned to normal life. If the deviant did not respond properly, his continued confinement served both as punishment and as incentive to reform. In the contemporary view, crime, delinquency, poverty, debt, and even mental instability stemmed from lack of self-discipline, character weakness, and bad habits such as laziness, intemperance, profligacy, and the like. These could be cured, possibly, by forced labor, learning obedience, and social isolation.[24]

Prison reform in the United States was part of a world movement; Americans were familiar with the ideas of British and French penologists, and particularly with the work of an Italian, Cesare

23. Albert Deutsch, *The Mentally Ill in America* (New York, 1937); Samuel Hamilton, "The History of American Mental Hospitals," in Gregory Zilboorg, ed., *One Hundred Years of American Psychiatry* (New York, 1944), 73–167; Gerald N. Grob, *The State and the Mentally Ill: A History of Worcester State Hospital in Massachusetts 1830–1920* (Chapel Hill, 1966). The best biography is Helen Marshall, *Dorothea Dix: Forgotten Samaritan* (Chapel Hill, 1937).

24. This thesis, and its relation to the developing industrial-urban society of the period, is studied in David J. Rothman, *The Discovery of the Asylum: Social Order and Disorder in the New Republic* (Boston, 1971).

Beccaria. Several states revised their penal codes in the 1790s; new prisons like Philadelphia's Walnut Street and New York's Newgate represented attempts to treat criminals as individuals who might be reclaimed for society. Central to the new attitude toward the criminal, of course, was the assumption that he was, at least in part, a product of his environment, and that society perhaps shared some responsibility for him. As the Philadelphia Society for Alleviating the Miseries of Public Prisons (founded in 1787) phrased it, a Christian's "obligations of benevolence" extended to all whose "follies and crimes" had put them in prison.

In 1816 New York commissioned a new prison at Auburn, the first experiment with the cell system, instituted later in the state's second new prison at Ossining. Prisoners had separate cells and met together in dining and work halls; they were forbidden to talk and discipline was harsh, but there was less confinement than before and somewhat less brutality.[25] Pennsylvania's Eastern State Penitentiary, begun in 1829, kept prisoners in separate cells—in what amounted to constant solitary confinement—on the theory that isolation afforded the criminal time for reflection and protected him from the influences of evil companions. Isolation solved a number of supervisory problems, but it also caused an exceptionally high rate of suicide and insanity; perhaps more important, it produced a lower rate of work productivity than the Auburn system. Both systems were copied by those states (at least eleven) which built new prisons in the forties and fifties, with New York's favored by most.

Prison discipline changed slowly. Tattooing of prisoners gradually disappeared, flogging decreased, sightseeing tours of curious visitors were discouraged; more enlightened jailers hired chaplains and prison doctors and some instituted schools for the illiterate. Nonetheless, in 1853 the warden at Auburn, one of the more advanced institutions, reported that over two hundred prisoners that year had been given the "bath" (which took a man to the drowning point) and a hundred the "buck," an extremely painful torture. Ossining, another showplace, still used the ball-and-chain; in other prisons the lash was common day-to-day punishment.[26]

25. W. David Lewis, *From Newgate to Dannemora: The Rise of the Penitentiary in New York 1790–1845* (New York, 1965) is a full study.

26. Cole, *op. cit.*, 141 ff. Blake McKelvey, *American Prisons: A Study in American Social History* (Chicago, 1936) is one of the best general sources.

The eighteenth was a hard-drinking century. Alcoholic over-indulgence was more or less socially accepted, innkeepers held rather high social status, and there were well-known alcoholics in positions of public trust. Cider, beer, wine, and whisky were cheap; whisky, in fact, was one of a farmer's cash crops and rum an international trade item. The breaking up of the older social order, the rise of cities, the growth of a poor working class, the diminished influence of the clergy—these and other factors helped to create after 1800 what was clearly a drinking problem of national proportions.[27] Captain Basil Hall, traveling in the United States in 1828, observed that Americans had "the practice of sipping a little at a time [every] half-hour to a couple of hours, during the whole day." Drinking was customary on holidays, at marriages, dances, quiltings, funerals, meetings, or anywhere else people gathered. Belief in liquor's medicinal values made it a common household remedy for any number of ills.[28]

The movement for temperance in the use of alcohol—not necessarily abstinence—derived from a number of sources. One was evangelistic religion; the saved, obviously, ought to lead lives of moral rectitude and usefulness. Reformers were well aware of the relation between drinking, poverty, and vice; the laborer who spent money on whisky could not spend it on his other needs. "Drink," said a pamphlet distributed by the Sons of Temperance, "is the prolific source (directly or indirectly) of nearly all of the ills that afflict the human family." Nor could the man who drank vote intelligently. When the laboring classes "are perverted by intemperance," asked Lyman Beecher, how can they be responsible citizens?

27. John A. Krout, *The Origins of Prohibition* (New York, 1925) is still a major study. Gerald Carson, "The Dark Age of American Drinking," *Virginia Quarterly Review*, XXXIX (Winter, 1963), 94–104 is a good brief account of drinking habits. J. C. Furnas, *The Life and Times of the Late Demon Rum* (New York, 1965) is a useful popular history of the temperance and prohibition movements.

28. Production of alcoholic beverages during the early nineteenth century is difficult to estimate, since manufacturing reports include production of industrial alcohol. However, whisky in the fifties cost 7 to 15¢ a quart, and as low as 25¢ a gallon—in the West, however, transportation costs and demand might run the price to as high as $3 a gallon. A respectable bar in the East charged 10¢ a glass, including free lunch, in 1859. Whisky began to replace rum as a popular drink in the fifties. Edgar Martin, *The Standard of Living in 1860* (Chicago, 1942), 78–82.

Drink, he believed, could "dig the grave of our liberties, and entomb our glory."[29]

Much of the motive power behind the temperance movement came from the churches. Whatever its social and economic wastefulness, most of the evangelical sects considered drinking a sin; the moral crusade against drink, said Neal Dow of Maine, was "Christ's work . . . , a holy war, and every true soldier of the Cross will fight in it." The General Association of Presbyterian Churches in 1811 declared drinking an evil, and in 1813 the Congregational and Presbyterian churches of Massachusetts joined to create the Society for the Suppression of Intemperance. Local and state church-sponsored societies began to appear across the nation, while in 1826 the American Society for the Promotion of Temperance, patterned on the missionary societies, began work on a national scale. By the early thirties there were five thousand or more temperance societies, enrolling a half-million members, which sponsored revivalistic camp meetings, sent out speakers and organizers, published pamphlets, and gave essay prizes. They founded "temperance hotels" which served no liquor, organized children's groups, administered "temperance pledges," and adopted all the apparatus of evangelism.[30]

Powerful and popular as it was, the temperance movement nevertheless developed internal tensions. Were all liquors, or only hard liquors, under attack? Should the movement's goals be accomplished by conversion or legislation? Should the objective be temperance or abstinence? The so-called "New Pledge," adopted by the American Temperance Union in 1836, for example, called for absolute abstinence from *any* alcoholic beverage. And as the church societies argued among themselves, a new element appeared; the Washington Temperance Society, formed in 1840 by a group of "reformed drunkards" (actually not all were), infused new energy into the crusade. Led by laymen and not ministers, the Washingtonians used new and spectacular techniques—"cold water" parades, bands, pledges, badges, rituals, banners, and the like. "Reformed drunkards" like John Hawkins (who was reported to have given 2,500 lectures in two years) and John B. Gough were major attractions on the lecture circuit, while pamphlets and

29. Beecher gave six sermons on intemperance in 1825 which were published under that title in 1826; see *Autobiography* (New York, 1864) , I:383.
30. Cole, *op. cit.*, chapter IV.

novels, like Timothy Shay Arthur's *Ten Nights in a Barroom and What I Saw There* (1854), sold in the thousands.[31]

The leaders of the temperance movement could not agree whether the answer lay in education, exhortation, moral regeneration, or legislation. Some felt that as a moral crusade temperance had been only partially successful; as Horace Greeley pointed out in the *Tribune*, New York still had six thousand licensed saloons and one thousand unlicensed ones, operating at full capacity daily and Sundays. Some societies preferred the political approach. Massachusetts in 1838 passed an act regulating liquor sales and repealed it in 1840; several states experimented with local-option laws, but enforcement was indifferent. An intensive campaign in Maine led to the passage of a state prohibition law, strengthened in 1846 and again in 1851. Other states followed. Prohibition forces were strongest in New England and the West; by 1855 New Hampshire, the last of the New England states to succumb, passed a version of the Maine law, and every state from Ohio to Iowa was dry. Pennsylvania's law, however, was defeated in a popular vote; New York finally passed one which was immediately tied up in litigation. New Jersey and Maryland held out, and it was never an issue in the South. In practice these laws were less successful than their sponsors had hoped, and by 1868 all had disappeared except Maine's. The solution, if there were to be one, was left to another time, yet the impact of thirty years of debate was lasting. The American conscience was never again easy with liquor; drinking habits changed, control was established over the trade, social acceptance of the drinker was never so certain again.

The status of the American woman, married or single, remained to a large degree much as it had been in the eighteenth century. Legally, women were minors, unmarried women the wards of relatives, married women husbands' chattels. A wife's rights to property were closely limited; she could not make a will, sign a contract, or witness a deed without her husband's permission. Although obviously women were not ill-treated in American society, the legal

31. Arthur's novel ranked just below *Uncle Tom's Cabin* in sales, and in dramatized form was a tent-show favorite for another thirty years. Father Theobald Matthew, an Irish Capuchin, spent two years, 1849–51, in the United States, lectured in twenty-five states, and signed a half-million people to the total pledge.

system denied them protection in situations where it was vitally necessary. Sexual double standards were almost universally accepted; divorce was so difficult as to be next to impossible; almost all professions were closed to women; women could neither vote nor hold office.[32]

British and European writers on women's rights were well known in the United States. Mary Wollstonecraft's *Rights of Women* (1792) was widely read; Englishwomen like Harriet Martineau and Frances Wright lectured in America,[33] and American feminists were closely in touch with their British counterparts. They were also developing their own leaders. The various reform societies enrolled many women, to whom such societies provided an opportunity for the middle-class female to define her place in society (and to express her frustrations) in ways to which masculine society could not object. Women held important offices in the reform societies, demanded from them and got the right to speak in public, and learned from experience about parliamentary procedures, organizing techniques, and public relations.[34] At the same time young women were attending colleges and academies, claiming the right to equal education and equal access to professions like the law, medicine, and the ministry. They were not supposed to do these things. As the Congregational Association of Massachusetts told the Grimké sisters, who were abolitionist speakers,[35]

The power of Woman is in her dependence, flowing from the consciousness of that weakness which God has given her for her protection, and which keeps her in those departments of life that form the characters of individuals and of the nation.

32. Elizabeth Cady Stanton, *et al.*, *A History of Woman Suffrage* (Rochester, 1889) is still a classic source. More recent and useful is Eleanor Flexner, *Century of Struggle: The Woman's Rights Movement in the United States* (Cambridge, 1959).

33. Miss Wright, a resolute Scotswoman, came to the United States at twenty-three, joined Robert Owen's New Harmony Colony, founded a colony of her own in Tennessee, and became one of the best-known American feminist leaders. Presumed to be an advocate of free love and an atheist, she shocked as many women as she convinced. Ernestine Rose, a Polish Jewess who spoke on numerous reform topics, similarly scandalized audiences by her aggressiveness.

34. See Carroll Smith Rosenberg, "The Militant Woman in Jacksonian America," *American Quarterly*, XXIII (October, 1971), 562–84.

35. A useful article is Barbara Welter, "Anti-Intellectualism and the American Woman 1800–1860," *Mid-America*, XLVIII (October, 1966), 258–71.

Despite nervous and occasionally bitter opposition—from anti-feminist women as well as from men—women leaders kept up a constant pressure on society. In the reform societies, which could not have existed without them, they learned political techniques quickly. Lucy Stone, Ann Phillips, Antoinette Brown, Lydia Child, Susan Anthony, Elizabeth Cady Stanton, and others like them put what they learned there to good use. Margaret Fuller, whose *Woman in the Nineteenth Century* (1845) was possibly the key statement of the feminist movement, wrote it down thus:

What woman needs is not as a woman to act or rule, but as a nature to grow, as an intellect to discern, as a soul to live freely and unimpeded, to unfold such powers as were given her when we left our common home.

Feminist leaders contended that women, if given proper education and the opportunity to use their talents, could compete equally in a number of professions. They captured the teaching profession first, for the swift expansion of schools created a teacher shortage which only they could fill. Was it not silly, Susan Anthony remarked, to concede that a woman had the brains to be a teacher, but not a lawyer, minister, or doctor? Harriet Hunt, twice rejected by Harvard Medical School, made it, graduated, and entered practice in 1835. Elizabeth Blackwell forced her way in Geneva Medical School and graduated first in her class in 1849.[36] The great market for children's books, women's magazines, Sunday School publications, household books, cookbooks, and the like opened new opportunities for women. Lydia Child published a children's magazine and was one of the editors of *The Antislavery Standard;* Sarah Josepha Hale was an editor of *Godey's.* Women novelists dominated the popular market—Susan Warner, Mrs. E.D.E.N. Southworth, Mary Jane Holmes, "Grace Greenwood," "Fanny Fern," and of course there was Harriet Beecher Stowe. Women could also point to the achievements of Maria Mitchell, an astronomer; Harriet Hosmer, a sculptor; Jane Swisshelm, an editor; as well as many other

36. Of the five Blackwell sisters, Elizabeth and Emily received M.D. degrees and the other three were prominent in the arts and reform. One Blackwell brother married Lucy Stone and another Antoinette Brown, who was one of the first women to be ordained a minister. Emily became Dean of the Women's Medical College of New York, Elizabeth joined the staff of the London School of Medicine for Women.

women in successful careers as lawyers, merchants, lecturers, and educators.

When Lucretia Mott visited Elizabeth Cady Stanton at her house at Seneca Falls, New York, in 1848, the two decided to call a convention to discuss "the social, civil, and religious condition and rights of women." The hastily called meeting attracted a number of enthusiastic supporters, who passed a series of resolutions framed in a clever parody of the Declaration of Independence based on the "self-evident truth" that "all men and women were created equal." A second convention, held later that year, attracted wider notice and a great deal of ponderous journalistic humor. Nonetheless, the leaders of the movement pushed on, organizing conventions, petition drives, and lecture tours. Susan B. Anthony, already a person of influence in temperance and antislavery societies, joined the women's rights movement in the fifties, and, as one observer put it, Mrs. Stanton "forged the thunderbolts and Miss Anthony hurled them."

Constant pressure brought results. Prominent men, like Emerson, Channing, Parker, Higginson, and Garrison, lent their support and so did editor Horace Greeley, although James Gordon Bennett fulminated against all "Lucy Stoners," claiming that the rights of women "like her duties, are bounded by her household." Women did not win the ballot, but they won a number of other things, particularly the right to be heard and the right to be educated. New York in 1848 passed a Married Woman's Property Act which gave a wife some control of her own property, and by the sixties eleven other states had passed similar laws. Other rights followed—to sue and be sued, to joint guardianship of children, to make wills and leave bequests. It would be more than a half century before women obtained anything resembling equality, but in 1860 to attain it no longer seemed impossible.[37]

America's search for Utopia in the nineteenth century was only a continuation, of course, of the search that began centuries earlier with Christians seeking a heaven on earth. The first half of the century, however, was a golden age of utopian experiment. More than a hundred communities, numbering over a hundred thousand people, appeared in the course of the century, the majority of them

37. See Tyler, *op. cit.*, 424–30; Nevins, *op. cit.*, 130–36.

during its third to sixth decades. Conditions for social experimentation in the United States were favorable; land was cheap, society
open, government controls few, religious toleration the rule, the
economic system flexible. Refugees from a Europe in turmoil found
in the United States a chance for a fresh start with new ideas.
Everyone was hopeful. "We are all a little mad here," Emerson
wrote Thomas Carlyle in 1840, "with numberless projects of social
reform. Not a reading man but has the draft of a new community in
his pocket."[38]

Religious groups, seeking a place to try out their ideas in safety
and quiet, arrived in the seventeenth century—the Labadists, followers of Jean de Labadie; Johann Kelpius's "Woman in the
Wilderness" colony; and others like Johann Beisell's Ephrata group
and Mother Ann Lee's Shakers in the eighteenth. George Rapp's
German Harmonists established a colony in Pennsylvania in 1805
and others later in Ohio and Indiana; Joseph Bimmeler formed his
Zoar colony in Indiana in 1817.[39] The great wave, however, came
after 1820. There were sixteen communities founded between 1820
and 1830, forty-two between 1830 and 1850, ten between 1850 and
1870.[40] They tended to fall into three general groups: those based
on a particular economic theory or plan of organization; those
whose origins and theories were religious; and those who owed their
existence to a particular leader or circle of leaders whose ideas,
economic or otherwise, provided the motives.

The earliest of the economically-based experiments was Robert
Dale Owen's. Owen, a wealthy Scottish manufacturer, gained a
worldwide reputation after 1800 for progressive experiments in

38. An excellent summary of the historical and ideological backgrounds of
American utopianism is Mark Holloway, *Heavens on Earth: Utopian Communities in America 1680–1880* (New York, 1951), 17–32.

39. For these and other early colonies, see Arthur Bestor, *Backwoods Utopias*
(Philadelphia, 1949); and V. F. Calverton, *Where Angels Dared to Tread* (New
York, 1941).

40. F. A. Brashee, "Communistic Societies of the United States," *Political Science Quarterly*, XX (1905), 625–64. Between 1800 and 1900 there were 113 such
colonies founded; over one-third appeared between 1830 and 1850. About one-
third lasted less than one year, one-third for two or three years, one-third from
four to twenty years. The most common cause of failure was internal dissension;
other causes were the death of the leader, poor location, bad management, legal
problems, and epidemic illness.

housing and education for his factory workers. In his plan for a model community (he thought units of about 2,500 people were best) each able-bodied member would work at a compatible job assigned by the community's administration; all labor was accounted equal, paid for by credit at the community's stores. Its economy would combine factory work (beginning with textiles) and farming, with the workshops placed on the periphery, removed from the residential and cultural center. All members shared in the community's profits. Laws governing the community were to be made by vote of an assembly of all adults; executive power was granted to a council and to the superintendents of activities— manufacturing, agriculture, science, literature, education, domestic economy, general economy, and commerce. This, Owen said in 1825, would introduce "an entire new system of society . . . , change it from an ignorant, selfish system to an enlightened social system which shall gradually unite all interests into one, and remove all causes for contest between individuals." The truly enlightened society, he believed, substituted cooperation for competition, benevolence for selfishness.

François Marie Charles Fourier, in France, had much more detailed and disciplined plans. He conceived of his communities as "phalanxes," with about 1,500 to 2,000 residents living within a district of three square miles at the center of 4,000 to 6,000 acres of land, occupying a "phalanstery" or set of buildings for common living. From here workmen and farmers would travel to outlying farms or workshops, or they might work within the phalanstery at some craft. About three million phalanxes, he believed, would take care of the entire population of the world.[41] Life within the phalanx was to be strictly regimented, with each individual assigned tasks commensurate with his disposition and talents. Government was by a Council of seven Arbiters, five of them women. Fourier's point was to replace competitive capitalism with cooperative enterprise, promote individual happiness, and distribute the profits from

41. Fourier planned, although perhaps not seriously, a completely phalansterized world, with one language, one government, and a society based on a polyandry-concubinage system. Constantinople would be its capital, where the ruler, or Omniarch, lived with a court of subsidiary rulers including three Augusts, twelve Caesarinas, forty-eight Empresses, 114 Kalifs, and 576 Sultans.

labor equitably.[42] Albert Brisbane, who studied with Fourier in France, adapted his ideas to the American situation in *The Social Destiny of Man: Or Association and Reorganization of Industry* (1840), a book of great influence on American utopian thinking.

The majority of other economically-based communities were cooperative common-property arrangements, sometimes with religious overtones. A large number of communities were founded on the religious convictions of a charismatic leader, or a theological principle, or a particular interpretation of a Biblical injunction. Among religious colonists, George Rapp's Harmonists believed that by work and worship men and women might become as they were before the expulsion from Eden. A mystic to whom Gabriel sometimes spoke, Rapp ran his colonies (in Pennsylvania, Indiana, and Ohio) with an iron hand and unusual success. The arrival of a shrewd adventurer who called himself "Count Maximilian de Leon" created a problem for Rapp until the Count was finally banished. Bethel Colony in Missouri, established in 1844 by Dr. Keil, a mesmerist and faith healer, was, like Rapp's, tightly disciplined; Keil moved it to Oregon in 1855 and renamed it Aurora. Grown to over a thousand members, it dissolved after his death in 1877.

Amana Colony, established by Christian Metz near Buffalo between 1842 and 1844, was founded by German pietists who called themselves "Inspirationists." A wealthy and efficiently organized group, they moved to Iowa in 1855, introduced cooperative industrial work as well as farming, and maintained their existence for another century. Eric Jansen, who believed himself the returned Christ, founded Bishop Hill in Illinois in 1846 on a kind of Christian communism. Jansen was shot by an angry member and his successor could not hold the colony together. At Hopedale, a much more loosely governed colony organized by a Universalist minister, Adin Ballou, members hoped to put New Testament ethics into social and economic practice. They called their system "Fraternal Communism," by which they would "inaugurate the kingdom of heaven *on earth*." Hopedale grew to a 500-acre farm with 200 mem-

42. The phalanx's working population was divided into four major groups—Industry, Agriculture, Science, and Finance—each group into "series" charged with specific tasks, and each series into "compatibles" assigned to particular jobs. An agricultural worker, therefore, might be assigned to the planting series and fruit tree compatible.

bers, three machine shops, and twenty houses, but after Ballou resigned in ill-health in 1853, some shrewd local farmers in Milford, Massachusetts, bought the place out.

A number of other colonies combined socialism, individualism, and occasionally plain eccentricity in varying proportions. Étienne Cabet's Icarian communities were patterned after his utopian novel, *Voyage en Icarie* (1840). In 1847 a group of Cabetians bought a million acres of Texas land (actually they got about 100,000) but the advance party, riddled by illness and bad luck, gave up. The second party stayed in New Orleans and finally three hundred moved to Nauvoo, Illinois, which the Mormons had left in 1849. Squabbles, depression, and Cabet's death had ruined it by 1859. Brook Farm, established in 1841 in Massachusetts by George Ripley, a Unitarian minister, received wide publicity because it was supported by Emerson and other Boston intellectuals. Ripley conceived it as a kind of vaguely socialistic intellectual oasis in a materialistic world, but a joint community school, which accepted tuition students from outside, was the chief money-maker.

Though Brook Farm never had more than eighty or ninety members, the presence there of people like Hawthorne and Margaret Fuller gave it greater publicity than the rest. The farm work was never very efficiently done, but the picnics, charades, boating parties, debates, and lectures made it, perhaps more than any other, a place of real intellectual stimulation. After Horace Greeley and Albert Brisbane persuaded Ripley to turn it toward Fourierism in 1844 the experiment lost much of its savor and its buildings were destroyed by fire in 1846. Bronson Alcott's Fruitlands, so called because its main diet was to be fruit, was based on high thinking and very plain living. It lasted but seven months, and Alcott had few disciples.[43]

Although the primary Owenite community was at New Harmony, Indiana, satellite communities sprang up elsewhere in Indiana, and a few in Ohio, Tennessee, New York, and Pennsylvania. The

43. Hawthorne used portions of his Brook Farm experience for his novel *The Blithedale Romance* (1852). Alcott's suggested diet included nothing which caused suffering to any living creature or robbed it of its sustenance—no meat, milk, or any food of animal substance. Nature was not to be forced by fertilizers, nor would fuel be wasted by heating water or burning lamps. There would be no clothes of wool, since they exploited sheep. A useful article is Aurele Durocher, "The Story of Fruitlands," *Michigan Academician*, I (Spring, 1969), 37–45.

Preliminary Society of New Harmony was formed on May 1, 1825, ran through seven constitutions in two years, and split into six different groups which lived in the town in utter confusion. Owen admitted defeat in 1827, but many colonists stayed on at New Harmony anyway, where some of their descendants still live. The other Owenite communities quickly expired; the longest-lived, Frances Wright's Nashoba in Tennessee, lasted nearly four years, but none were left in 1830. Despite its short span, life at New Harmony was nonetheless exciting. It attracted men like geologist William Maclure, Thomas Say, the zoologist, scientists like Constantin Refinesque and Gerhard Troost; it had excellent schools, libraries, and art collections, a good newspaper, a superb lecture series, and several social societies. Its farming, hat and boot shops, soap, candle, and glue works were fairly successful; its cotton, dye, and pottery works did poorly. It simply did not have the organization needed to hold together such a diverse and individualistic group of members, nor was the idealistic but impractical Owen the man to lead it.[44]

American Fourierism had persuasive exponents in Albert Brisbane and Horace Greeley of the New York *Tribune*, both of whom tirelessly promoted "associationism." Phalanxes dotted the country in the forties and fifties, twenty-five or more in all, one group in upper New York State, a cluster near Cincinnati, others scattered across the midwest to Iowa. The North American Phalanx at Red Bank, New Jersey, which lasted twelve years, was one of the strongest. The Wisconsin Phalanx, also successful, lasted six years. Almost all, however, were gone by the sixties.

Three experiments in communal living, all religious in nature, deserve special notice because of their unique qualities. The Shakers, founded by Ann Lee Stanley, or "Mother Ann" Lee, came to Watervliet, New York, after a revelation had told her to leave England and found a new faith in the new land. She died in 1784, but her teachings became the canon of a new sect, called Shakers because of their trembling religious ecstasy, but more accurately named The United Society of True Believers in Christ's Second Appearing. Mother Ann taught that God was of dual sex, Jesus the male principle and she the female. Members lived in celibacy,

44. By far the best account is William Wilson, *The Angel and the Serpent* (Bloomington, 1964).

minimum literacy, absolute equality, and with as little contact as possible with the outside world. Communities were divided into "families" of thirty to one hundred members, governed by a ministry of elders of men and women in equal numbers. Each member had a job, given by the elders; men and women were separated at worship, women wore black with a distinctive starched cap, men black and unadorned clothes. Shakers worshipped God in many ways—in song, dance, prayer, meditation, drawings, sermons, labor, and most of all by the example of quiet Christian brotherhood.

Since they were celibate, they propagated their communities by recruitment and by adopting orphans. Their economy was self-sufficient and agricultural, though they did produce a few things for sale to the outside market—seeds, herbs, hats, brooms, jellies, furniture, farm tools, and leather or woodcraft specialties. There were about ten Shaker communities by 1820, and during the wave of evangelical religion that followed more communities appeared in Pennsylvania, Ohio, Kentucky, Indiana, and Iowa. The minimum community was usually about fifty members and a thousand acres of land; large communities, like the Ohio group near Cleveland, might have two hundred members and considerable holdings. The Shaker way of life, however, was ill-equipped to survive in the industrialized, urbanized society of the postwar years, and most of their communities gradually disappeared. Two communities, totaling nine members, still existed in the 1960s.[45]

John Humphrey Noyes's Oneida Community was an interesting blend of religious idealism, cooperative economics, and capably-managed business. Noyes, a Yale-graduated minister, read Fourier and Brisbane and visited several other communities before he formed his own in Vermont in 1840, combining socialist economics and evangelical religion. Knowing that many communities suffered from internal bickerings, Noyes instituted what he called "Mutual Criticism," a weekly meeting at which any member could state a grievance, have it discussed, and receive advice. There were clashes and disagreements, of course, but Noyes's community escaped much of the spite and anger that blew many others apart. He also instituted "complex marriage," a system whereby men and women

45. See Holloway, op. cit., 53–64; Margaret F. Fellows, The Shaker Adventure (Boston, 1941); and Edward Andrews, The People Called Shakers (New York, 1953).

might live together without legal sanction while still maintaining association with the community—by no means "free love," but a domestic arrangement rather rigidly supervised by the group. The community practiced birth control and later embarked on a eugenics experiment involving fifty-three young women and thirty-eight men that produced fifty-eight children of "perfect" eugenic lineage.

In 1847 Noyes moved some of his community to Oneida, New York, where by 1851 he had two hundred members and substantial capital. Oneida branched out into manufacturing, at first making steel animal traps; later the community sold canned fruits, textiles, dyes, silverware, and a dozen other products. Oneida sent its young men and women out into the world to study and return as doctors, lawyers, teachers, engineers, technicians, and agronomists. By the late sixties the community had assets of over a half-million dollars, profits of $50,000 a year, 500 acres of land, a string of workshops, and employed 250 workmen from outside. But as the founding generation aged, the next grew restive—some had been to war, others to universities, cities, factories, and knew the outside world. Oneida simply began to run down, and finally in 1881 it re-formed as a joint stock company called Oneida Community Limited. Noyes, that odd combination of dreamer and organizer, died in 1886 and with him the "holy experiment" ended. Oneida was the most successful, ideologically and financially, of all the American utopian communities, certainly the least dreary, the best regulated, and in the long run apparently the happiest. None of Oneida's survivors remembered it with anything but pleasure.[46]

Except for those groups held together by religious agreements, nearly all of the experimental communities were gone by the opening of the Civil War, terminated partly, at least, by the controversies that brought it on. Only seven new communities were launched between 1850 and 1861, eight in the seventies, and eight more in the eighties and nineties, few of them durable. The thrust toward utopia was strongest among the dissatisfied or frustrated, or among those who had aims that could be pursued nowhere else; in

---

46. A good account is Karen Lockwood Carden, *Oneida: Utopian Community to Modern Corporation* (Baltimore, 1969). Pierrepont Noyes, *My Father's House* (New York, 1937) is a first-hand account; Robert A. Parker, *A Yankee Saint* (Boston, 1935) is a good biography of Noyes.

the open, optimistic, opportunistic society of the nineteenth century, there were never large numbers of these. The competitive, challenging excitement of contemporary America stirred the eager and ambitious, to whom the placid, planned life of even the better utopias seemed unadventurous. Public opinion, furthermore, never took kindly to the eccentric fringe that showed always at the edges of the movement, nor did many of the experiments, if closely examined, really live up to their claims.

The antislavery movement began as a minor part of the whole great stirring of nineteenth-century humanitarianism. It was a reform motivated by the same drives that produced Jacksonian democracy, utopian communities, and other humanitarian and social experiments. Until the mid-forties antislavery was simply one of many such reform enthusiasms, one frowned on, in fact, by the more stable and conservative-minded reformers. Gradually it rose to eclipse the others, because its appeal was wider, its leadership more skillful, its relation to politics more direct, its relevance to the future of American democracy more unmistakable.[47]

The slavery question became eventually a question of whether the nation would continue to exist, as Lincoln observed, and if so, of whether it would exist as a democratic nation. Slavery existed near enough to touch the orbit of every individual's future, yet geographically far enough removed from some to allow it to be judged and evaluated more or less impersonally. It was also confined to a portion of the nation whose political and economic interests differed sharply from those of the nonslaveholding portions. In addition, the slavery system was politically accessible, subject to state and federal law.

Neither slavery nor its abolition became an important issue in America until 1830. Opposition to slavery was common in colonial days, but it was not until after the formation of the Republic and the enunciation of eighteenth-century doctrines of liberty and equality that a serious examination of the institution began. There was a strong tradition of antislavery thought derived from eigh-

47. The most comprehensive secondary study is Louis Filler, *The Crusade Against Slavery, 1830–1860* (New York, 1960). An excellent essay is Dwight L. Dumond, "The Controversy Over Slavery," in A. M. Schlesinger, Jr., and Morton White, eds., *Paths of American Thought* (Boston, 1963), 86–105.

teenth-century humanitarianism—Franklin, Paine, and Benjamin Rush among others spoke against it—and from Christian commitments to brotherhood, for John Wesley himself denounced it and Quakers like John Woolman had long opposed it. In a wave of legislation after the Revolution the New England and Middle Colony states all outlawed the system, while slavery was barred from the new Northwest territories by the Ordinance of 1787.

Federal prohibition of the slave trade in 1808 aroused little real opposition; there was, in fact, after it a surge of antislavery sentiment in the South. State societies, beginning with Pennsylvania's in 1777, were working in nearly all the states outside the South before 1830. But with the increasing importance of cotton as the basic Southern crop, Southerners began to consider slavery essential to their economic and social welfare. The cotton boom made slaves an indispensable labor force and sent their value soaring; sensitive to abolitionist talk, Southern states asserted that the prosperity of the region depended on retaining and even expanding the system. Discussion of the question soon stopped south of Mason's and Dixon's line.

At the same time the temper of Northern antislavery sentiment changed. What had once been mild approval of some sort of emancipation, or at best mild disapproval of slavery in principle, became an aggressive, forthright, sometimes intemperate demand for the instant abolition of the entire institution.[48] William Lloyd Garrison, the New England firebrand, struck the keynote of the new crusade in the first number of his abolitionist paper, *The Liberator*. "I am in earnest," he wrote. "I will not equivocate—I will not excuse—I will not retreat a single inch—AND I WILL BE HEARD." Under the leadership of Garrison and others, newly organized societies carried abolitionist doctrines through the North and Northwest. British organizational techniques, publications, and arguments were widely copied in the United States; leaders like Zachary Macaulay, Thomas Clarkson, and William Wilberforce

48. For contrasting views of the abolitionists, see Hazel Wolf, *On Freedom's Altar: The Martyr Complex in the Abolition Movement* (Madison, 1952) and Martin Duberman, *The Antislavery Vanguard* (Princeton, 1968). Lorman Ratner, *Powder Keg: Northern Opposition to the Antislavery Movement 1831–1840* (New York, 1968) is an indispensable study. See also Ratner's "Northern Concern for Social Order as a Cause for Rejecting Antislavery 1831–65," *Historian*, XVIII (November, 1965), 1–19.

were well known to Americans and British speakers constantly toured the country.[49]

Garrison and a few friends founded the New England Anti-Slavery Society in Boston in 1832. Within the next year similar groups appeared in New York City, Providence, Philadelphia, and Ohio. In 1833 representatives of these societies met in Philadelphia to organize a national body, the American Anti-Slavery Society, whose purpose was to persuade the nation that "slave-holding is a heinous crime in the sight of God, and that the duty, safety, and best interests of all concerned, require its *immediate abandonment* without expatriation." In 1840, however, a large number of moderates withdrew to form the American and Foreign Anti-Slavery Society. Both societies sent out speakers and organizers, published newspapers and tons of pamphlets and books, founded state and local branches, and publicized the abolitionist cause with unflagging zeal. By then the entire complexion of the argument had changed; compromise or understanding among antislavery, abolitionist, and pro-slavery adherents seemed no longer possible.

The arguments on both sides of the slavery question were extremely complex, nor were pro- and antislavery groups always able to agree among themselves. The antislavery societies intended to appeal to the nation by fact and argument, to change public opinion, and thus to build a great body of Northern and Southern antislavery sentiment that would eventually (by legal and political means) abolish slavery. Their attack on slavery rested on several principles, any one of which might be stressed to the exclusion of others.[50]

First, said some, slavery was wrong on moral grounds. The system was cruel, barbaric, and inhuman; Theodore Weld's study, *American Slavery As It Is* (1839), Mrs. Stowe's *Uncle Tom's Cabin*

49. Frank Klingberg, *The Anti-Slavery Movement in England* (New Haven, 1926) ; Reginald Coupland, *The British Anti-Slavery Movement* (London, 1964) ; Christine Bolt, *The Antislavery Movement and Reconstruction: A Study in Anglo-American Cooperation 1833–1870* (London, 1969) ; and Betty Fladeland, *Men and Brothers* (Urbana, 1972).

50. In addition to Filler, *supra cit.*, an excellent brief explanation of the antislavery position with illustrative documents are John L. Thomas, ed., *Slavery Attacked: The Abolitionist Crusade* (New York, 1965) and William and Jane Pease, eds., *The Antislavery Argument* (Indianapolis, 1965). A useful article is Donald Mathews, "The Abolitionists on Slavery," *Journal of Southern History*, XXXIII (May, 1967), 163–83.

(1852), and countless other studies and novels appeared to document the accusation with stories of whippings, tortures, confinements, bloodhounds, slave marts, and separated families. Slavery, said others, was unchristian and irreligious, a clear violation of both the Christian ethic of brotherhood and the law of Christian charity. It was impossible, in the Garrisonian view, for a man to be a slavery sympathizer and a Christian; it was equally impossible for an American church to remain Christian while condoning or supporting slavery.[51]

In addition to being unchristian, slavery was also believed to be undemocratic, irreconcilable with other American institutions and with the American tradition. It produced a small, powerful, minority class of aristocratic landholders who, it was claimed, had entered into a secret "slave-power conspiracy" to extend slavery everywhere and to impose their rule on the nation at large. After the Compromise of 1850, the progress of this "malignant and potent agency," as Henry Wilson of Massachusetts called it, was carefully charted by the abolitionists; as some pointed out after the Dred Scott decision of 1857, one more favorable Supreme Court decision would make slavery a national rather than only a Southern institution. "You young men," wrote Walt Whitman in 1856, "American mechanics, farmers, boatmen, manufacturers, and all work-people of the South, the same as North! you are either to abolish slavery, or it will abolish you!"

Slavery, it was also argued, was economically unsound, wasteful, and inefficient. The poor white man in the South could not compete with unpaid slave labor; neither could he break the political and economic domination of the slaveholding aristocracy over the South. Last of all, some antislavery men claimed that slavery was simply illegal. The Declaration of Independence, they said, banned slavery by its enunciation of man's natural rights. If the Constitution were neutral on the subject, as some claimed it was, the abolitionists reasoned that since the Declaration had abolished slavery prior to 1787, the framers of the Constitution had not considered it

51. For the role of the church and of evangelical religion in the antislavery movement, see Gilbert H. Barnes, *The Antislavery Impulse 1830–44* (New York, 1933); Timothy Smith, *Revivalism and Social Reform in Mid-Nineteenth Century America* (Nashville, 1957) chapters XII, XIII; and Anne C. Loveland, "Evangelicalism and Immediate Emancipation in American Antislavery Thought," *Journal of Southern History*, XXXII (May, 1966), 172–89.

necessary to label as illegal an institution already outlawed. If the Constitution did actually sanction slavery, as certain commentators believed it might under the guaranteed property clause, the Christian must then obey "a higher law" of morality and reject the authority of the Constitution. Thus William Lloyd Garrison publicly ground a copy of the Constitution under his heel, exclaiming, "It is an agreement with Death and a covenant with Hell!"

Antislavery sympathizers, whatever their reasons, agreed generally that slavery was wrong and that it must be abolished, but they found great difficulty in agreeing on how and when to abolish it. The question of "when" caused especial trouble. One faction favored instant emancipation and "immediate enfranchisement of our slave population," the policy generally approved by the New England societies. The "gradualist" school of thought favored a type of emancipation extended over several generations, with gradual absorption of the Negro into the social and political structure—a policy attacked by Garrison as "gradualism in theory and perpetualism in practice." The so-called New York doctrine, adopted by the New York Society, compromised on "immediate emancipation, gradually accomplished," a theory difficult to understand and equally hard to publicize. In the West the Lane Seminary group evolved a theory of "gradual emancipation, immediately begun." The Garrisonian and Lane groups found most supporters but never reached agreement.

The "how" of abolition proved no less troublesome. One group, basing its opposition to slavery on moral and religious grounds, believed that a national campaign for moral regeneration—an evangelical religious crusade—would abolish slavery by unanimous consent, North and South. Appeals to the national conscience, thought Theodore Weld, would by "moral suasion" convince slaveholder and nonslaveholder alike that the system was against God and Christianity. Another school of thought believed that slavery could best be abolished by legal action within the existing political framework, either through existing parties, which could legislate slavery out of existence, or through a third party which might gain control of the federal government to accomplish the same end. For this reason abolitionists founded the Liberty Party and nominated James G. Birney for President in 1840 and 1844. Not long after that the abolitionists found political leaders—Henry Wilson, Salmon

Chase, William Seward—to carry their battle into Congress. The political phase of the abolition movement, culminating in the Liberty, Free-Soil, and Republican parties, rested primarily on the Lane doctrine, though it held Democratic-flavored ideas on the tariff, bank, and internal improvements issues. A small but vocal third group, believing that the Constitution legalized slavery and that there were no proper legal means of abolishing it, advocated either abandoning the Constitution for a new one or seceding from any government based on it. If the Constitution sanctioned a system which violated "higher laws" of morality and natural right, a man must follow his conscience and refuse to remain in the Union. Garrison's *Liberator* carried on its masthead for years the slogan "No union with slave-holders!" Disunionism, however, was an extreme position, never acceptable to even a sizable minority in the movement.

The "colonizationists" proposed to extirpate slavery by sending Negro slaves elsewhere, either to Africa or to some unsettled portion of the West. The American Colonization Society, founded in 1817 and counting among its members such men as Bushrod Washington, James Madison, Charles Carroll, and Henry Clay, established the colony of Liberia in West Africa for this purpose in 1822. After 1830 the abolitionists attacked the colonizationists both for their lack of success and for their refusal to face the problem directly; understandably, the colonizationists never found much support in the West. In forty years of activity the Society shipped about eleven thousand Negroes to Africa at a cost of more than a million dollars—a number replaced within a few months by the birth rate. Various other methods received some notice. Quaker groups argued that a boycott of slave-state products would force the South into emancipation. Some recommended paying wages to slaves so that they might buy their own freedom, and others proposed an appropriation of state and federal funds to purchase slaves for expatriation.

Free-Soilism, a doctrine developed in the forties in the Northwest, was less a scheme for the abolition of slavery than for its containment within existing Southern boundaries. The Northwest farmer, who could not afford slaves and who found slavery unadaptable to his type of agriculture, did not want the fertile land of the plains states given over to slavery nor did he want the Negro as an economic competitor. Gradually the Free-Soil position moved closer to the legalistic, humanitarian, natural-rights theories of the abolitionists. By the mid-fifties the Free-Soil and Liberty parties, both opposed to slavery but on different grounds, joined with the new Republican party. "Immediate" abolitionism eventually killed off or engulfed its opponents, until by 1860 the single great issue became—not if, how, and when slavery must be abolished—but one of freedom versus oppression, right versus wrong.

The pro-slavery forces from the outset presented a much more united front than the antislavery group.[52] There were, however, some disaffected areas in the South (western Virginia, western North Carolina, parts of upland Georgia, eastern Tennessee and Kentucky) which refused to cooperate. Antislavery thought in the South was generally very well controlled, either by legal intimidation or by social pressure, and the pro-slavery cause was so efficiently propagated that by 1850 the slaveholding states formed a solid bloc of opinion on the issue. In order to obtain solidarity Southern leaders were forced to make clear infringements on freedom of the press, speech, thought, and education, to condone and encourage mob action, and to appeal to distinctly antidemocratic political, social, and racist theories.[53]

The pro-slavery argument was both defensive and offensive in nature. In rationalizing the existence of slavery in a democratic nation, its proponents encountered stumbling blocks in the old Virginia liberal tradition and in the Declaration of Independence it had produced. The only alternative was to discredit both the tradition and the document, which Southern writers proceeded to do. The Declaration of Independence, said Calhoun, represented an admirable theory but no guide for practical life. "The universal law of nature is force," Thomas Cooper wrote. "By this law the lower animals are subdued to man, and the same law governs the relations

52. A useful brief summary of the pro-slavery argument with illustrative documents is Eric McKittrick, ed., *Slavery Defended: The Views of the Old South* (New York, 1963). Standard sources are William S. Jenkins, *Pro-Slavery Thought in the Old South* (Chapel Hill, 1935), and Arthur Y. Lloyd, *The Slavery Controversy* (Durham, 1939). A brilliant re-examination is David Donald's "The Proslavery Argument Reconsidered," *Journal of Southern History*, XXXVII (February, 1971), 3–18.

53. For further consideration, see R. B. Nye, *Fettered Freedom: Civil Liberties and the Antislavery Controversy* (East Lansing, 1963).

between men." Slavery, from a Southern point of view, had deep roots in natural law, the Declaration notwithstanding.

Replying to Northern critics, the exponents of slavery retorted that no matter what Jefferson said men were born neither free nor equal. *Natural* rights to liberty do not exist; men possess only such rights as society grants to them; that which society gives it can also take away. As Calhoun summarized the argument, men are born into a political and social state, subject to its laws and institutions. A Negro, being socially, mentally, and anthropologically inferior to white men, had no natural rights and could not make responsible use of them if he had them. "The Negro," wrote J. B. D. DeBow, "cannot be schooled, nor argued, nor driven into a love of freedom." Southern preachers scrutinized the Bible for arguments justifying slavery as carefully as Northern divines examined scripture for arguments against it. Both Jesus and the apostles exhorted slaves to obedience and fidelity to their masters; the sons of Ham were cursed to eternal servitude by divine decree.[54]

Having once established slavery on religious and political grounds, its supporters proceeded to prove that its continued existence was both necessary and desirable. Slavery was best for the Negro, since he needed the care and guidance that only some system of servitude could provide. "Providence has placed him in our hands for his good," wrote Governor Hammond of North Carolina, "and has paid us from his labor for our guardianship." Economically, the pro-slavery writers continued, slavery was absolutely necessary to the South and to the world. The slave represented a huge investment in property, whose loss would mean financial ruin for one-third of a nation and probably for the nation itself. David Christy, in *Cotton Is King* (1855), reasoned that since cotton depended on slavery, and the world economy depended on cotton, therefore the world economy depended on slavery.

Slavery was, said the South, an absolute social necessity. Only by declassing and subduing the Negro could the white race keep itself racially pure; if the black man gained social status, miscegenation inevitably followed. Freeing the Negro might mean reprisals on white masters, murder, pillage, and destruction. Nat Turner's slave

54. The anthropological argument was extremely important; see chapters IV–VII of Thomas Gossett, *Race: The History of an Idea in America* (Dallas, 1963), and William Stanton, *The Leopard's Spots* (Chicago, 1960).

revolt in 1831, which cost the lives of sixty-one white men, women, and children, served to emphasize the point. The argument for plain personal safety was a powerful one, and the specter of the "Black Terror" hung always over and behind pro-slavery talk.[55]

As time passed the South produced a flood of pro-slavery literature proclaiming slavery not only necessary and justifiable, but the best possible system—a "positive good"—that should be extended to the North and West, perhaps to white men. "Free society," editorialized the Richmond *Enquirer*, "is in the long run an impracticable form of society." John C. Calhoun pointed out that a real democracy, like the Athenian, could exist only in a clearly stratified society; slavery therefore was "the most safe and stable basis for free institutions in the world." Furthermore, the conservatism of the established master class guaranteed social stability, since the classes that could make revolutions had no power to do so. The "demoralized, insurrectionary" free society of the North contrasted ill with the "harmony, union, and stability" of the slave-holding states; Senator Downs of Louisiana challenged anyone "to prove that the white laborers of the North are as happy, as contented, or as comfortable as the slaves of the South." George Fitzhugh of Virginia, in *Sociology for the South* (1854) and *Cannibals All!* (1857) carried the "positive good" argument to its ultimate conclusion. Slavery, he said, was "a form, and the very best form, of socialism." One sentence penned by Fitzhugh—"Slavery is the natural and normal condition of the laboring man, whether black or white"—probably did more damage to the pro-slavery cause in the North than all that Garrison ever did or wrote. When war came Fitzhugh's words were used as concrete evidence of what a Southern victory might mean— white slaves in the North, as well as black ones in the South.

The argument achieved its purpose. One antislavery editor printed two quotations side by side in 1855. The first, from the Richmond *Enquirer* in 1832, called slavery "a dark and growing evil." The second, from the same paper in 1855, called it "a natural and necessary and hitherto universal, hub, element, or institution of society." The contrast, representing more than twenty years of agitation, illustrated the effective work of the Southern pro-slavery

55. See Robert Abzuz, "The Influence of Garrisonian Abolitionists' Fears of Slave Violence on the Antislavery Argument 1829-40," *Journal of Negro History*, LV (January, 1970), 15-29.

forces. William Ellery Channing, at the beginning of the controversy, realizing the inevitability of what was to come, had written sadly and prophetically, "It has stirred up bitter passions, and a fierce fanaticism, which have shut every ear, and every heart."

The bright promise of the age of reform never quite came true. Women had to wait another half century to increase their rights, the prohibition crusade dwindled out, the utopian communities vanished, the peace movement disappeared in war, the antislavery crusade was engulfed in four years of bloody conflict. Yet none of these causes died, nor did the hope that animated them disappear. Prisons and hospitals *were* better, the poor and unfortunate and handicapped *did* become people, society *did* recognize and assume responsibilities that it never would have considered a century earlier. All the reforms left marks; the spirit beneath them was an inspiring force and a powerful instrument in shaping the future. America was by no means perfect by midcentury, nor would it ever be, but it still seemed to Americans the brightest hope of mankind.

CHAPTER 3

History and Literature in a Romantic Age

TWO major factors influenced the development of American literature in the period 1830 to 1870: nationalism and Romanticism. The first generation of post-Revolutionary writers and critics—Dennie, Freneau, Webster, Brown, Neal, and others—who argued long and convincingly for the creation of a native, nationalized literature did their work well.[1] To the next generation, those writers born between 1800 and 1820, this issue was already resolved. William Ellery Channing's "Remarks on a National Literature" (1830) and Emerson's clarion call in "The American Scholar" (1837) summarized the belief of their generation that American literature had finally come of age, and, in Channing's words, "springing up in this new soil would bear new fruits, and in some respect, more precious fruits, than are elsewhere produced."

Romanticism and nationalism in American literature, then, developed together—unlike Europe, where England, France, Germany, and Spain already possessed strongly identifiable national characteristics before Romanticism came. In the United States, which had no native literary tradition, the Romantic movement supplied both means and vehicle for creating one. True, American Romanticism drew its central ideas from British and European sources—from Wordsworth, Coleridge, and Carlyle in England;

1. See Benjamin T. Spencer, *The Quest for Nationality* (Syracuse, 1957), 47–51, *passim,* for the trends of this period. George Boas, ed., *Romanticism in America* (New York, 1961) is a useful collection of essays on Romanticism.

from Herder, Schelling, and the Schlegels in Germany; from Taine and others in France. Traces of nearly every major Romantic critic or philosopher could be found in the essays and reviews published in American periodicals after 1820. But American critics and authors put these ideas to their own uses. The American variety of Romanticism was not simply a mélange of British and European principles and practices transported across the Atlantic, for though Americans may have imported them, they utilized them within an American environment, and within the context of a different past.

The traditional moral earnestness that pervaded American literature since colonial times led American critics to warn artists against what they and the public considered some of the excesses of the European and British brand. In America, the restraints of Calvinistic culture, the respect for tradition and aversion to extremes characteristic of colonial society, and Yankee common sense exerted a tempering discipline to some of the excesses and chaos of Romanticism elsewhere. There was also a cultural time lag. Keats and Shelley, for example, were not well known to American literary circles until the 1850s; neither Wordsworth's criticism nor his poetry were so influential as Coleridge's until the late thirties; while Byron's poetry fascinated many readers, his morals were suspect; George Sand, Eugene Sue, and other French writers were welcomed only with reservations; even some of the much-admired Germans were suspected of "contradictory moral qualities." George Bancroft, who in his "Studies in German Literature" made one of the more perceptive explorations of Romanticism of the period, counseled American writers to avoid the imbalances, disproportions, and over-enthusiasms of the Europeans in favor of "moral charm," "moral propriety," and "earnestness and moral beauty" in art.[2]

American Romanticism, then, is to be construed within its own context. The concept of Romanticism as a revolt against neoclassicism, for example, does not apply to the American situation in 1820. Eighteenth- and early-nineteenth-century American writing

2. See Hyder Rollins, *Keats' Reputation in America to 1848* (Cambridge, 1946); Julia Power, *Shelley in America in the Nineteenth Century* (Lincoln, 1940); Arnold Newton, *Wordsworth in American Criticism* (Chicago, 1928). Bancroft's essays on German literature were collected in *Literary and Historical Miscellanies* (New York, 1855). For expressions of the moral point of view, see the contrast of Longfellow's "Psalm of Life" with Byron's work, in *Christian Examiner*, XXVIII (1840), 244–5, and the criticisms of Byron's morality, *ibid.*, X (1842), 226.

was, to be sure, neoclassic, but never so strongly so that Romanticism could be called a revolt against it. Romanticism in America was less a reaction against something than the beginning of something new. The British Romantic's medievalism, for example, came from a desire to escape from stereotyped materials into a remoter, more exotic past; the United States, with no such past to escape to, chose instead its own frontier as a substitute. The European's "return to nature" was in part a reaction against a set of conventional responses to the natural world, developed and codified over the years by neoclassic poets; American Romantics did not need to "return" to nature since they had never been away from it. The British Romantic's experiments in literary forms were attempts to break out of traditional models conventionalized over the previous two centuries; since American literature was just beginning, it had nothing to break away from. Whereas British and European Romanticism, then, was in large part a set of reactions against previously-established traditions, American writers used Romanticism as a new way of articulating their feelings about their land, their culture, their experiences, and themselves. Nationalism provided the center and framework for their Romantic movement.[3]

The heart of American Romanticism lay in three major precepts: that literature was expression; that it was organic; that it was imaginative.

The neoclassical critic, as Dr. Johnson did, conceived of literature as an "imitation" of life. Rejecting this, the Romantics viewed literature as "expression"—primarily an expression of self and a projection of the writer's interpretations of experience. Thus Emerson exclaimed of a piece of writing that it was "bloodwarm," while Whitman, to whom literature was the culmination of self, wrote of *Song of Myself*

> Comrade, this is no book,
> Who touches this touches a man.

Romanticism in America (as in England and Europe) became autobiographical and confessional; what the writer felt became of

3. Robert E. Spiller, "Cultural Standards in the American Romantic Movement," *College English*, VIII (1947), 344–52; Walter F. Taylor, *A History of American Letters* (Chicago, 1936), "The Romantic Impulse," 69–86; and Tony Tanner, "Notes for a Comparison Between American and European Romanticism," *Journal of American Studies*, II (April, 1968), 83–102.

paramount importance. Romantic writing emphasized the integrity
of self, the validity of individual experience. "Judge for yourself,"
wrote Emerson, "Reverence thyself," and again, "Trust thyself.
Every heart vibrates to that iron string."

Second, if (as the Romantic assumed) literature derived from
experience and expressed it, it grew—like other forms of life—in
organic form.[4] As opposed to the neoclassic writer, who conceived of
literature as essentially static, fixed, controlled, the Romantic saw it
as responsive, fluid, changing, shaped from within by its own laws,
each artifact possessed of its own form and unity. The parts of a
work of art were related to each other not as parts of a watch, but as
the branches and roots and trunk of a tree—as Emerson made clear
in his poem "Each and All." A work of art had to have some
principle of life "pervading, uniting the whole," wrote Lowell:[5]

> Roots, wood, bark, and leaves together singly perfect may be,
> But clapt hodge-podge together, they don't make a tree.

Third, art was to the Romantics a product of the "imagination,"
that intuitive quality of the mind (whatever name it might be
given) which saw nature and experience not literally, but colored
and enhanced by beauty, truth, and morality. It was, in Emerson's
phrase, "a higher power of the soul." The poet's "direct lessons of
wisdom," Bryant wrote in the first of his *Lectures on Poetry* (1826),
were delivered to him intuitively; they were "truths" which the
mind instinctively acknowledges. The vital meanings of experience were not to be discovered through the operations of reason or
logic, but rather by those flashes of intuition granted to the artist.

Romanticism thus set up a particularly intimate relationship
between viewer and viewed, between artist and material, for it was
the artist's imagination that gave life to the object by relating it to

4. Coleridge, in his notes for a lecture on Shakespeare, distinguished between
mechanic form, "when on any given material we impose a predetermined form,
not necessarily arising out of the properties of the material," and *organic* form,
which is ". . . innate, it shapes as it develops itself from within." See Richard H.
Fogle's discussion, "Organic Form in American Criticism, 1840–70," in Floyd
Stovall, ed., *The Development of American Literary Criticism* (Chapel Hill,
1955) .
5. Cf. Emerson in "The Poet" (1844) : "For it is not metre, but metre-making
argument that makes a poem—a thought so passionate and alive that like the
spirit of a plant or animal it has an architecture of its own, and adorns nature
with a new thing." See E. G. Sutliffe, *Emerson's Theories of Literary Expression*
(Urbana, 1922) .

the life of the beholder. "The inner world," wrote Hegel, "is the content of Romantic art," and the artist penetrated into it not by the head, but by the heart; not by a conscious intellectual process but an inward burst of perception which was, in Emerson's words, "a very high sort of seeing."

From these premises, Romanticism in America developed certain distinguishing literary characteristics, which may be grouped as follows:

An emphasis on the emotional and imaginative aspects of life and literature, with a corresponding emphasis on the "intimations," the "fancy," or the imagination, over the reason as a source of aesthetic and moral truth.

A recognition of the importance of individual and subjective values as equal to social values.

A belief (especially emphasized in American Romantic thought) in the dignity and worth of the common man, his freedom from restraints, and his capacity for improvement.

A new kind of interest in external nature, directly experienced, both in its spiritual and sensuous aspects; "I enter some glade in the woods," wrote Thoreau, "and it is as if I had come to an open window."

A renewed interest in the literary uses of the past, particularly the unique, colorful, primitive, exotic, and distant, as in Irving's use of Dutch legends, Cooper's frontier, or Freneau's Indians.

An interest in the symbolic as a method of expressing indefinite, complex meanings, making the emotional and abstract tangible—as in Shelley, or Poe, or Melville, or Hawthorne.

A tendency to use (with restraint) "the real language of man in a state of vivid sensation," in Wordsworth's phrase, or to restore to art what Whitman called "the indescribable freshness and unconsciousness" of natural man's expression.

Conditions were more favorable to the American writer during the middle decades of the nineteenth century than ever before. Not only was the population growing by millions annually, but it was an increasingly sophisticated and literate audience. The proliferation of colleges and public schools, the growth of lyceums, reading rooms, and libraries all contributed to the creation of a larger reading public. An expanding network of roads and railroads and canals meant swifter, cheaper, and wider distribution of news-papers, magazines, and books; improved oil lamps meant more reading hours per day. Ten thousand miles of new railroad, laid before 1860, carried books and authors and lecturers into places where few had been before.

At the same time, improvements in printing and bookmaking changed the technology of publishing. The Napier steam press, introduced in 1825, could produce two thousand copies an hour; the Hoe rotary press in 1847 could produce ten times that. Stereo-typed book plates were in use by the thirties, electrotyping by the forties, while improved machines for binding and embossing and cheaper processes for making paper and ink made it possible to turn out books like any other mass-produced article.

These new methods of production and distribution were immedi-ately reflected in the book market. Publisher Samuel Goodrich estimated the gross sales of books in the United States in 1820 at $2,500,000, in 1850 at $12,500,000, and in 1860 at nearly $20,000,-000. During the same period, through decreased production costs, the actual number of titles published increased as much as twenty times. Goodrich also estimated that whereas in 1820 British authors sold twice as many books in the United States as American authors did, by 1850 the ratio was exactly reversed. Meanwhile the organi-zation of publishing houses changed. Whereas authors previously often paid publishers to manufacture their books, which booksellers then sold on commission, publishers began to sell them to book-sellers who in turn sold them for profit, with the publisher paying royalties to the author. A sounder method of business, it made possible the rise of the great publishing houses—Harper, Putnam, Carey, Thomas, Fields, Cummins and Hilliard—which dominated the trade in the forties and fifties.[6]

The great burst of magazine and newspaper publishing over these years gave American writers an even better market. In 1860 there were more than six times the number of magazines published in 1825—by count 575 magazines, 372 daily newspapers, and 271 weeklies, many of which published stories, essays, and verse. Among

6. Robert E. Spiller, ed., *The Literary History of the United States* (New York, 1948), I:235–40. See also H. Lehmann-Haupt, C. C. Wroth, and Rollo Silver, *The Book in America* (New York, 1952), and John C. Oswald, *Printing in the Americas* (New York, 1937).

the best outlets were those aimed at a mass market: *The Casket* (1826–40), *The Knickerbocker* (1833–65), *The United States Magazine and Democratic Review* (1837–59), *The Southern Literary Messenger* (1834–64), *Graham's* (1840–58), *The Union Magazine* (1847–52), *Godey's Lady's Book* (1830–98). In the fifties *Harper's*, *The Atlantic Monthly*, and the *New York Ledger* appeared. In addition, there were annuals, gift books, and anthologies by the score—during their most popular years, gift books and annuals alone appeared at the rate of sixty a year.[7]

Although a writer could do well in the market, competition was heavy and payment not high. *Graham's*, *Godey's*, and the mass-circulation magazines paid best. Poe received $4 to $5 a page from *Graham's*, but Nathaniel P. Willis, probably the most successful writer of the fifties, received $10. Longfellow received the highest fees for poetry—only $15 for "The Village Blacksmith" in 1841, but $1,000 later for "Morituri Salutamus" and $3,000 for "The Hanging of the Crane." The popular female novelists of the fifties and sixties did best; Susan Warner for example in 1855 published three novels, all of which sold over 75,000 copies, netting her in excess of $25,000. However, this happy state of affairs applied to only a few. Copyright laws, both domestic and international, were so loosely drawn and easily evaded that best-sellers were consistently pirated. Not until the passage of satisfactory copyright legislation in 1891 did the situation change.

American critics and American authors were deeply concerned about developing a distinctively American literature, equal to or surpassing Britain's and Europe's best. While no author had any intention of abandoning his great English literary inheritance, yet he hoped to find his own way of expressing himself and his culture outside the confines of the Old World's critical rules and aesthetic

7. Frank Luther Mott, *A History of American Magazines 1741–1850* (New York, 1930); William L. Charvat, *Literary Publishing in America 1790–1850* (New York, 1959); Ralph Thompson, *Annuals and Gift Books 1825–65* (New York, 1930). Annuals and gift books were richly bound ornamental volumes designed as gifts or prestige possessions; Poe, Bryant, Hawthorne, Willis, Simms, and others wrote for them. Rufus Griswold, the best known of the anthologists, compiled *Poets and Poetry of America* (1842), *Prose Writers of America* (1847), and *Female Poets of America* (1848), all of which sold in the thousands. Meanwhile Evert and George Duyckinck's *Cyclopaedia of American Literature* (two volumes, 1855) familiarized the public with American writers.

judgments. This was not easy to do. Critics, over the first third of the century, tended to follow the safe, Addisonian standards of the British eighteenth century, evaluating literature for the familiar qualities of taste, genius, and originality. Taste meant the ability to discriminate between beauty and deformity; genius was a blend of inspiration and diligence; originality meant to be creative but controlled, stopping short of the eccentric or bizarre.[8]

American criticism, like British, was primarily judicial, concerned with clearly enunciated standards and conservative in their application. The deities of American criticism were Lord Kames's *Elements of Criticism* (1762), Hugh Blair's *Lectures on Rhetoric and Belles Lettres* (1783), and Archibald Alison's *Essays on the Nature and Principles of Taste* (1790). American periodicals like the Baltimore *Portfolio* and the Boston *Monthly Anthology* judged all literature by their rules. It was to be evaluated by reference to certain invariable "constants," founded on the permanent elements of human nature, nature, ethics, and reason. Literary criticism, wrote Andrews Norton of Harvard, must always be written in the light of "unalterable principles of taste, founded in the nature of man, and the eternal truths of morality and religion."[9]

After 1840, however, American literary criticism began to change. Reflecting the influence of the new Romantic criticism from Europe (especially from Coleridge and Germany), critics showed an increasing tendency to judge a work on its own terms, to consider it less as an exemplification of rules than as the expression of the individual artist. Emerson spoke of "creative reading" in which critic and writer joined in the creative act; a book, he wrote, is "to be interpreted by the same spirit which gave it forth." George Allen used the phrase "reproductive criticism" to describe the new approach. The critic, he explained (following Goethe), by bringing his mind "into contact with the mind of the artist," tried to reproduce "step by step, the creative process." Instead of judging literature, as Norton said, by the "unalterable rules" of the past,

8. See William Charvat, *The Origins of American Critical Thought 1810–1835* (Philadelphia, 1936), chapter I. An excellent survey of the period is that of John Pritchard, *Criticism in America* (Norman, 1956), 19–25.

9. See H. H. Clark, "Changing Attitudes in Early American Literary Criticism, 1800–1840," in Floyd Stovall, ed., *The Development of American Literary Criticism* (Chapel Hill, 1955).

critics suggested that a work of art ought to be interpreted in relation to its time, place, society, and also in terms of the author's own
life and personality.[10]

Behind the evolution of a new American literary criticism after
1835 was the argument between the so-called Young Americans who
wrote chiefly for *The Democratic Review* and those conservative
critics who wrote for *The Whig Review, The New York Review,
The New England Magazine,* and *The Knickerbocker.*[11] The
Young Americans rejected the "bilious," "dogmatic" rules of Blair
and Kames and refused to submit to the old "dictatorship of letters" which, they claimed, ruled American criticism. American
literature ought to be, they argued, strongly American, fitted to
"the New Man in the New Age," filled with "the animating spirit
of democracy," near to "the thinking heart of humanity," expressive
of "the Spirit of the Age." To the Whig critics, literature (as John
Quincy Adams said) "in its nature must be, aristocratic"; there
could be no such thing as "a democracy of numbers and literature."
Whereas the Young Americans thought of literature as a vehicle for
ideas, the Whig critics thought of it in terms of its aesthetics—the
"spurious democracy" of the *Democratic Review* group, said H. N.
Hudson, simply "perverted" literature into polemics. Although the
Young America group began to break up in the fifties, it was influential in encouraging the development of a democratically and
ideologically oriented American literature and instrumental in
encouraging writers such as Emerson, Hawthorne, and Melville.
Most of all, the Young Americans prepared the way for Whitman.
To Whitman, the true poet merged himself with the spirit of his
times and immersed himself in his country's culture, incarnating its

10. H. H. Clark, *op. cit.,* 51.
11. See Clarence A. Brown, *The Achievement of American Criticism* (New
York, 1954), 149–56. The best study is John Stafford, *The Literary Criticism of
"Young America"* (Berkeley, 1952); but see also John P. Pritchard, *Literary Wise
Men of Gotham* (Baton Rouge, 1963). *The Democratic Review* was founded in
1837 by John O'Sullivan and Samuel Langtree to counteract the political-literary
establishment represented by the New York and Boston journals. The "Young
American" group included Evert Duyckinck, William A. Jones, Parke Godwin,
and Cornelius Matthews, while the ranking "Whig" critics were E. P. Whipple,
H. N. Hudson, Rufus Griswold, and Lewis Gaylord Clark. Thoreau, Hawthorne,
Whittier, Bryant, and Emerson all contributed to *The Democratic Review.*

"geography and national life and rivers and lakes," encompassing all its people in his inclusive "I."[12]

Artists and critics considered the poet as the representative artist who sought beauty—the aesthetic counterpart of the philosopher (who sought truth) and of the moralist, who sought virtue. The poet, unlike other men, possessed a greater command of that inner perceptive faculty or "creative power" with which all men were endowed and greater skill in its use. In the prevailing terminology this power could be called "reason," "imagination," or other names, but whatever its label it was from this principle of the mind that the poet gained those "deeper insights" which made him the "interpreter of Heaven."

The poet lived, as George Bancroft (who wrote literary criticism as well as history) explained, in a kind of permanent excitement of "sacred enthusiasm" which lent color and fire to his view of things. Great poets received their creative impulses from inward inspirations; they possessed the power of expressing those insights in original and exact terms, drawn from "the high heaven of inventiveness." They did not imitate, but assimilated experience; they did not copy, but created. Bancroft made this view of poetry clear in explaining in a *North American Review* article in 1825 why Herder was not a great poet. His mind

was of a poetic character, yet not inventive, and his sensibility to the beautiful and his lively and busy fancy never conducted him to highly original efforts in verse. . . . The character of his mind was poetic, yet nature had denied him the highest qualification of the poet, and he was conscious of his own inability to tread firmly in the heaven of invention.

The poet, then, transforms as well as interprets the truth he perceives; he seizes "a beautiful idea . . . and giving it a form suited to his own taste, presents it to the world anew." His enthusiasm, intuition, and originality, however inspired, must yet be

12. For a good example of Young America criticism, see William A. Jones, "Critics and Criticism of the Nineteenth Century," *The Democratic Review*, XV (August, 1844), 158–63; and "Criticism in America," *Ibid.* (September, 1844), 241–49. John Stafford, "William A. Jones, Democratic Literary Critic," *Huntington Library Quarterly*, XII (1949), 289–302, is an excellent study of his work. See also James E. Mulqueen, "The Literary Standards of the American Whigs, 1845–1852," *American Literature*, XXXXI (November, 1969), 355–72.

disciplined by taste and judgment, for the creative power must harmonize with morality.[13]

Second, the artist possessed "genius," a term seldom clearly defined but one which seemed to mean (as Coleridge suggested) the power of feeling life and of understanding it. It was a matter of "the heart," said the Young America critics, of an "honest enthusiasm" for experience. A writer for the *Knickerbocker* agreed that *genius* was "a peculiar and felicitous combination of mental faculties, moral qualities, and physical organization. . ." which provided the artist "the ability to conceive, comprehend, and reproduce truth, beauty, and harmony."[14] Third, the artist must be "true to nature," a requirement which elicited a good deal of discussion. How true *must* he be? Should he depict wrong, evil, and disharmony, under what circumstances, and to what purpose? The rise of the novel, in particular, gave critics—to whom poetry had always been the literary touchstone—new aesthetic problems. Somewhat tentatively critics suggested that Dickens, Thackeray, George Eliot, and the emergent realists might be "true to nature" in a fashion not applicable to Longfellow, Scott, or Mrs. Hemans. Even the conservative *Whig Review* in 1852 conceded that the novelist, at least, could deal with real people, giving the reader a sense of "the strong pulse of nature throbbing beneath the turf he treads upon."

Artistic creation was conceived of in highly subjective, individually intuitive terms. E. P. Whipple's Coleridgean definition of the imagination as the power which "evolves from material objects the latent spiritual meaning" was typical. The majority of critics agreed with Bancroft's explanation of the poetic process. The poet's original inspiration, he wrote, may arise from within or without himself. It may come "communing with his own soul, or with nature, or with God." From the external world of nature he may

---

13. For a clear, concise treatment of this contemporary, somewhat avant-garde aesthetic theory, see Bancroft's review of Mrs. Hemans, *North American Review,* XXIV (April, 1827), 443–63, and his essays on German literature in *The American Quarterly Review,* II (September, 1827), 171–86; III (March, 1828), 150–73; IV (September, 1828), 157–90; VII (June, 1830), 436–49; and X (September, 1831), 194–200.

14. Pritchard, *The Literary Wise Men of Gotham,* 11–36. Talent was a lesser power, defined as "the ability to explore, gather up, and reproduce truth, beauty, and harmony."

draw materials with which "to enrich the world with images, excite and diversify his inventive powers, and impart a poetic impulse to all his faculties." But those who derive their inspiration solely from the outward world of nature and experience—those "nature poets" and "nature philosophers" who "look for God among the rivers and forests"—are incomplete artists. The promptings of the inner world provide higher exaltations, more elevated ideas. Since "it is mind only which can exhibit the highest beauty," the great artists search for inspiration not only in nature, but "in the hearts of men." The origins of art are thus neither wholly external nor internal, neither all sense nor all soul, but derive from interaction of the two.[15]

Most of the principles of American literary criticism established during the years 1830 to 1870 were derived from British and German sources, from Wordsworth, Coleridge, Carlyle, and the Schlegels. Critics assumed that there was a hierarchy of ideal forms beyond the material world, which were both source and standard of beauty. By means of the "imagination" or creative power the artist could penetrate beyond matter into the realm of the ideal, finding there and expressing in finite terms its infinite perfection.[16] The greatest artists "strive to present, under sensible forms," an "ideal" beauty "more perfect, purer, loftier, brighter than anything human eyes have seen . . . of a more perfect loveliness and excellence than the actual world shows." To represent and symbolize that ideal, the artist used the beauty of nature and of human action.[17]

American literature of the nineteenth century, critics and authors agreed, while striving to reproduce the ideal, must also embody the specific characteristics of its time and place. That the importance placed upon morality in literature by the seventeenth and eighteenth centuries had not disappeared was clear from the fact that

15. "Studies in German Literature," *Literary and Historical Miscellanies* (New York, 1855), 103–206.

16. Brown, *op. cit.*, 149–53. See Emerson: "For poetry was all written before time was, and whenever we are so finely organized that we can penetrate into that region where the air is music, we hear those primal warblings and attempt to write them down. . . ." ("The Poet").

17. Thomas L. Haines, *The Royal Path of Life* (Chicago, 1876), 486–93, explains the artist's role clearly. The artist's imagination "fashions the ideal conception" of beauty, while to illustrate it his intellect chooses materials from lesser levels—the beauty of nature, visible in "every leaf, stem . . . rock and diamond, sun, plant, and star"; the beauty of the human form, "animated by the intelligence within"; and the beauty of "soul, mind, heart, and life."

except for Poe (who attacked "the heresy of the didactic") no major literary critic suggested that literature should be judged solely on aesthetic grounds. While the artist might strive to find and express the ideal-beautiful, it was assumed that there could be no such beauty without morality. Beauty, said Bancroft, cannot exist "independent of moral effect." For this reason American critics found it difficult to accept enthusiastically all of Byron, Goethe, George Sand, and Balzac. It seemed doubtful that an "impure life" (as Bancroft and Longfellow thought Byron's was) could produce art of "moral charm" or "moral propriety." Great art, wrote the *North American Review*'s critic in 1829, "deals with man's higher and better nature."[18]

> Uniting these two qualities which we would deem most essential, we should esteem that the highest poetry, which unfolded moral excellence in its greatest amplitude and expansion, and in a way that should communicate the expansion of being, in the highest degree possible, to the reader's nature.

In addition to being beautiful and moral, art must also be true—"true" in a double way, that is, "natural" or consistent with the reality of the object perceived; and "true" in the sense that it is presented in a way that "coincides with virtue and moral law." Art is untrue if it falsifies the facts of nature; it is doubly so if it falsifies the facts of moral law by "investing vice with beauty." Art is also false if it deals only with the inconsequential or impermanent instead of with the highest and most enduring "truths," for great art should express "the most exalted thoughts and kindling aspirations of which human nature is capable."[19]

Great *American* art, of course, had also to reflect and embody American culture and American ideals. An American author, said *The Knickerbocker* in 1842, must express in his work "national sentiments and domestic habits" and "as from a faithful mirror, reflect the physical, moral, and intellectual aspects of the age." Since the age was characterized by democracy, literature therefore

---

18. "American Poems," *North American Review*, XXIX (July, 1829), 220. An excellent discussion of beauty and morality in art is Bancroft's review of Mrs. Hemans, *Ibid.*, XXIV (April, 1827), 443–63.

19. Bancroft, "American Poems," 221. Thus Milton's art is true, in contrast to Dryden's, which "lacks virtue, the soul of song," and Voltaire's, which "trifles with topics of highest moment."

must reflect democracy's respect for and belief in individual man. America needed "poetry for the people," said *The Democratic Review*, ". . . filled with the animating spirit of democracy." From the thirties on, critics and writers emphasized the necessity of encompassing in American literature the feeling and meaning of America, itself leading to Whitman's preface to *Leaves of Grass*, in which he visualized the United States itself as "essentially the greatest poem of all."[20]

Though the essay remained a popular literary form in the United States, it lost ground to fiction and poetry during the middle third of the century. Since the spirit of Irving still dominated the familiar essay, his adaptations of the Addisonian style and temper remained the model by which essayists were judged.[21] The proliferation of magazines and newspapers still provided a good market, and "Loungers" and "Scribblers" and "Bachelors" filled their columns. Americans read the newer British essayists, especially Lamb and Hazlitt, and imitated them enthusiastically, as in Richard Henry Dana's *Idle Man* (1822), Theodore Fay's *Dreams and Reveries of a Quiet Man* (1832), and Henry Tuckerman's *Rambles and Reveries* (1841). Nathaniel Parker Willis, who wrote well in several styles, was especially admired for his light, witty collections like *Dashes at Life* (1845) and *Hurry-Graphs* (1851). The increased cosmopolitanism of American society was reflected in the popularity of the travel essay, filled with gossip, sketches, and impressions of Europe, the Mediterranean, and the Holy Lands. Longfellow's *Outre-Mer* (1834) was one of the most thoughtful collections; Willis's *Pencillings by the Way* (1836) and his expanded version of it (1844) were best-sellers. There were many others: DeKay's *Greece;* Tuckerman's *Italian Sketch Book;* Stephen's *Incidents of Travel in Egypt, Arabia, Petrea, and the Holy Land;* Slidell's *Spain.* (Mark Twain, of course, was later to burlesque the type.)

Meanwhile the example of the British and Scots critical journals —*Blackwood's, The Edinburgh Review, The London Magazine*—

20. See also Channing's "Remarks on a National Literature" (1830). See the quotations and discussions in Pritchard, *Literary Wise Men of Gotham*, chapter I; *Criticism in America*, 98–100; and Brown, *op. cit.*, 149–50.

21. For a survey, see Adaline M. Conway, *The Essay in American Literature* (New York, 1914).

and of critics like Francis Jeffrey, Hazlitt, J. G. Lockhart, and Leigh Hunt encouraged Americans to imitate them. The formal critical essay became standard in such American journals as *The North American Review*, *The Southern Literary Messenger*, and *The American Quarterly Review*, which published critics like Poe, Lowell, Channing, Whipple, Bryant, and Dana. At the same time these men and others used the essay as formal discourse, for philosophical discussion (as in the case of William Ellery Channing), or for social criticism, as Cooper did. In this form, the essay was clearly allied to the sermon and the lecture, retaining much of their organizational density and dialogue quality, as well as using many of the rhetorical devices of platform and pulpit style. For Emerson and Thoreau the essay became their primary vehicle of expression, the chief medium for developing their ideas.

Since many of Emerson's essays were first presented as lyceum lectures, they displayed something of the oracular style which made him effective on the platform; and something too of the terse, laconic quality that he learned from Thomas Carlyle. Emerson sprinkled his prose with epigrams—"Beauty is the mark God sets on virtue"; "Life only avails, not the having lived"; "Man is a stream whose source is hidden"—which prompted Carlyle to liken Emerson's essays to buckshot in a canvas bag. Emerson used few transitions, letting the reader absorb his ideas a thought at a time, and (except in a few essays) he paid little attention to tight organization. His method of composition had much to do with his style. He might jot down in his journal, in a few sentences, the essence of a day's thought; later he might put these crammed, cryptic statements in an essay without much change. Thus an Emersonian page might represent the distillation of hours or days of reflection; some of his sentences were in effect topic sentences of paragraphs that were never written. Except for his journals and lectures, the great body of Emerson's work lay in the essay, which he shaped and molded into his own distinctive kind of literary self-expression.[22]

22. His work appeared in *Essays, First Series* (1841); *Essays, Second Series* (1844); *Nature, Addresses, and Lectures* (1849); *Representative Men* (1850); *English Traits* (1856); *The Conduct of Life* (1860); and *Society and Solitude* (1870). The best biography is Ralph L. Rusk, *The Life of Ralph Waldo Emerson* (New York, 1949); for discussion of his ideas, see Stephen Whicher, *Freedom and Fate* (Philadelphia, 1953); and Sherman Paul, *Emerson's Angle of Vision* (Berkeley, 1952).

Henry David Thoreau, like Emerson, chose the essay as his medium—amended by his own unique adaptation of the journal, itself an old New England form—and learned much in his early years from both Emerson and Carlyle. He once said, not wholly in jest, that keeping his journal was his main business, and it served him through his life as storehouse and factory of his thought. Two congruent themes pervaded his writings—how to live truly and simply; how to enjoy and understand nature—whether they were lectures or reviews or essays. He was not as popular a lecturer as Emerson, nor did he publish as many essays as Lowell, but he wrote so well that even without *Walden* (1854) he would have been counted among the major practitioners of the genre in his time.[23] "Ktaadn," "Chesuncook," "Walking," and "Wild Apples," with collections like *A Week on the Concord and Merrimack Rivers* (1849) and *A Yankee in Canada* (1853), were sufficient to establish him as one of the finest stylists of the era. *Walden,* the series of essays derived from his famous residence in Walden Woods, 1845–47, and integrated into a book, remains one of the great accomplishments in American literary prose. Though cast as an autobiographical journal, *Walden* is really an extended familiar essay, whose message finds appreciative listeners in every generation. Live directly and simply; get straight with Nature; master yourself and the world you live in; determine for yourself what in life need not be done. In Thoreau the Yankee epigrammatic quality was as strong as in Emerson—"The mass of men lead lives of quiet desperation"; "Money is not required to buy one necessary of the soul"; "Sell your clothes and keep your thoughts; God will see that you do not want society"; "The cost of a thing is the amount of what I call life which is required to be exchanged for it." Thoreau worked at a deliberately rhythmic, artfully cultivated style, often with a humorous twist and an ironic aftertaste. The rolling prose of *Walden* is Thoreau the stylist at his best.

James Russell Lowell followed Longfellow as Smith Professor of Belles Lettres at Harvard, became the first editor of *The Atlantic Monthly*, and served also as joint editor of *The North American Review*. Though better known as a poet by literary historians, he

23. For a study of Thoreau and *Walden,* see Sherman Paul, *The Shores of America* (Urbana, 1961). Walter Harding, *A Thoreau Handbook* (New York, 1959) is the best introduction.

wrote more prose than poetry, much of it concerned with the political and social issues of his time. Far from being an ivory-tower
scholar, Lowell (who wrote for three newspapers and served as
Minister to Spain and England) was deeply involved with contemporary life. He wrote excellent historical essays—"Cambridge
Thirty Years Ago" (1854), and "New England Two Centuries
Ago" (1865)—while his contributions to the antislavery press
totaled two volumes, collected as *Antislavery Papers* (1902). The
onset of the Civil War led him to explore, more thoughtfully than
most men, the nature of the Union, in essays such as "E Pluribus
Unum" (1861), the war itself in essays like "The Rebellion"
(1864), and postwar policy in "Reconstruction" (1865). His observations of Europe, combined with those commenting on American
society, produced a series of penetrating studies, among them
"Democracy" (1884) and "The Independent in Politics" (1888).
Lowell's most distinguished prose appeared in his critical essays; he
belonged in the first rank of American literary critics and was so
recognized by his contemporaries.[24] He wrote a clear, viable prose,
marked by lively erudition and reasonable argument. If his essays
had little of Emerson's gnomic wisdom or Thoreau's pungency, they
had nonetheless an air of authority and clarity of Lowell's own
making.

The essays of Dr. Oliver Wendell Holmes, Boston's court wit,
would have found an appreciative audience in the eighteenth-
century London coffeehouses. Holmes in 1831 published two essays,
titled "The Autocrat at the Breakfast Table," in *The New England
Magazine,* and when Lowell in 1857 asked him to continue the
series for *The Atlantic Monthly,* Holmes gladly agreed. As it happened, the essay form fitted Holmes's talents perfectly; a sparkling
conversationalist, he simply transferred his own table talk to the
Atlantic's pages, assuming the character of the Autocrat, who ruled
the morning conversation at a Boston boardinghouse. Like his
eighteenth-century predecessors, Holmes assumed the identity of a
wise and witty commentator, surrounded with a cast of charac-

24. Lowell's critical essays are collected in *Among My Books* (1870, 1876), *My
Study Windows* (1871), *Literary Essays and Addresses* (1891), and *The Old En-
glish Dramatists* (1892). See H. H. Clark and Norman Foerster, *Lowell* (New
York, 1947), "Lowell as Critic" for a thorough discussion. The best biography is
Martin Duberman, *James Russell Lowell* (Boston, 1966).

ters—a poet, a landlady, a minister, a servant, a sweet young thing—drawn from different social strata, so that, like Addison and Irving, he could comment on the "fads, follies, and fashions" of the day. The effectiveness of his essays lay in his use of surprise and his flashing prose style, for Holmes had a real gift for the quick twist of an idea. He could find humor in the solemn and solemnity in the humorous, and he had the knack of surprising his reader with a sudden shift of direction. A man who found everything interesting, Holmes wrote with authority and wit about horse racing and trees and universities and tobacco or anything else that caught his eye. He also sprinkled his pages with pithy Yankee apothegms that stuck in the mind—"Put not your trust in money, but your money in trust"; "Sin has many tools, but a lie is the handle that fits them all." It was typical of Holmes that he began his new series of *Autocrat* essays, after a twenty-six-year lapse, with the words, "As I was just going to say when I was interrupted. . . ."[25]

Another variety of essay, however, developed swiftly during the prewar years, descended not from the familiar or formal essay favored by the New England circle, but rather from the anecdote, almanac, travel book, and tale. The American essay of humor had a sturdy ancestor in Poor Richard; it emerged as a thriving form in 1830 with Seba Smith's "Major Jack Downing" series, centered on the character of an earthy, shrewd Down East Yankee who commented on the American scene for the next thirty years. Some of the Major's descendants surpassed the original in expertise and effectiveness. T. C. Haliburton's cunning Yankee, Sam Slick; B. P. Shillaber's Mrs. Partington; Frances Whitcher's Widow Bedott; and Lowell's Hosea Biglow were major creations. Writers in the South and Southwest developed a tougher, rougher brand of frontier humor, first in Augustus Longstreet's *Georgia Scenes* (1835) and later in characters like Johnson J. Hooper's Simon Suggs, William Thompson's Major Jones, and George Harris's Sut Lovingood. By the fifties the humorous essay, built about a central character who served as comedian and critic, was a journalistic standard, and in the sixties some of its practitioners moved to the lecture circuit as

25. The best introduction to Holmes is S. I. Hayakawa and H. M. Jones, *Oliver Wendell Holmes* (New York, 1939). A good biography is Eleanor Tilton, *Amiable Autocrat* (New York, 1947).

well. Most assumed comic names, talked and wrote in dialect, and used "phunny" spellings like *wuz, kum,* and *sed.* Among the better known were Charles Farrar Browne, who wrote and lectured as "Artemus Ward"; David Ross Locke, who called himself "Petroleum V. Nasby"; and Henry Wheeler Shaw, or "Josh Billings." Samuel L. Clemens, who broke into print with his "Jumping Frog" story in 1865, derived directly from them.[26]

The most striking development in American literature after 1820 was the rise of fiction. Whereas at the turn of the century there was a considerable belief among critics that novels tended to diminish the reader's morals and give him a false impression of life, twenty years later *The Western Literary Journal* characterized the country as "a nation of newspaper readers and novel readers," while another journal admitted that "there are few who do not read novels openly or by stealth." For one thing, the great popularity of Sir Walter Scott did much to remove lingering prejudice against the form; for another, novelists' constant claims that they instilled morality and virtue in their readers helped to remove objections. In larger numbers, year by year, talented and sophisticated men and women took up fiction as serious art.

The ground had been prepared, of course, by the floods of sentimental, Gothic, Richardsonian-style novels that had gone before. At the same time, Americans had both as model and competitor the burgeoning English novel as practiced by Jane Austen, Maria Edgeworth, the Brontës, Dickens, George Eliot, Thackeray, Trollope, and an army of others. American fiction had nothing to match them, and American novelists did not try to imitate them very closely. Though Scott died in 1832, veneration of him in the United States did not. Americans were aware of Dickens as a humorist in the mid-thirties; by the forties his novels were selling well; and by the time of the Civil War he was undoubtedly the most popular British novelist in the United States. The Brontës were well known (E. P. Whipple in 1847 said that "Jane Eyre fever was a national epidemic"), and so were G. P. R. James (a Scott imitator) and Edward Bulwer-Lytton. French writers like Paul de Kock and

26. Walter Blair, *Native American Humor* (New York, 1937).

George Sand, though widely read, were considered somewhat shock-
ing, their novels interesting though morally doubtful.[27]

American authors still maintained the eighteenth-century distinction between a "romance" and a "novel," which Hawthorne so
carefully explained in his preface to *The House of the Seven Gables*
(1857).[28] Whether the romance or the novel was the higher form of
fiction was a subject for argument. Some agreed with Hawthorne
and Melville that fiction's function was "idealizing," that it was less
concerned with a picture of life than with life's meanings. The
world required, Hawthorne wrote, "a deeper moral and closer and
severer truth" than either Scott or Dickens furnished; to him an
important function of art was "spiritualizing the grossness of actual
life."[29] The major American novelists tended to agree. None
worked in the contemporary British realistic tradition; the "romance" and "tale" dominated American fiction. Instead of dealing
with contemporary society and its factual surfaces, American novelists worked an older vein, concerned with ideas, symbols, allegories,
and history.

At the same time, critics were reluctant to relieve fiction of its
moral function, emphasizing (as in poetry) the relationship between art and morality. The general consensus was that the novel
should instruct, but not obviously; the didactic element should be
integrated into the work and not superimposed upon it. As critical
and public interest in the romance faded, a vague but definable

27. Edward Wagenknecht, *Cavalcade of the American Novel* (New York, 1952).
Other general histories of the novel are Alexander Cowie, *The Rise of the American Novel* (New York, 1951); Richard Chase, *The American Novel and Its Tradition* (New York, 1957); and Arthur H. Quinn, *American Fiction* (New York,
1930).

28. The distinction developed in the later eighteenth century, when, as Clara
Reeve put it, the novel presented "a picture of real life and manners, and of the
times in which it is written," while the Romance dealt with "what never happened or is likely to happen." The novel, then, became a documented narrative
(as in Jane Austen) and the romance an imaginative narrative (as in Scott and
Cooper). Hawthorne made the difference clear in his preface by saying that the
novel is "presumed to aim at minute fidelity, not merely to the possible but to
the probable and ordinary course of man's experience," whereas the writer of
romance could present "the truth of the human heart . . . under circumstances,
to a great extent, of the writer's own choosing and creation."

29. Emerson, for example, criticized Jane Austen's "pinched and narrow" realism, and did not like Dickens because "his eye always rests on surfaces." Melville
did not believe that the reader should expect "severe fidelity to real life" in fiction, but that it "should present another world. . . ."

realism began to emerge in fiction. *Putnam's* reviewer in 1854, pitting Hawthorne against Dickens, argued that since the novel was produced by the Imagination and the romance by the Fancy, the novel was the higher form. By the fifties, critics had accepted the novel as a legitimate form of artistic endeavor, comparable in status to other genres, subject to the same considerations by serious artistic standards. Dickens, George Eliot, and Thackeray were carefully reviewed by major American periodicals, and the issue of realism versus romance thoroughly explored. Parke Godwin's review of Thackeray in 1855 praised the "reasonable realism" which gave his novels "the aspect of an actual transcript of the life of society," while the *Atlantic* in 1858 complimented George Eliot for basing her fiction "securely upon a broad groundwork of truth." From this point it was not a long distance to William Dean Howells.[30]

The greatest factor in the rise of the American novel, however, was its use as a vehicle for nationalism. When writers discovered how to exploit the American past and the American landscape, the novel became a powerful instrument for defining and developing the national personality. Reviewer John Gorham Palfrey pointed out in the *North American Review* in 1821 "the unequalled fitness of our early history for purposes of a work of fiction" at almost the same time that Cooper was writing *The Spy*. Novelists responded by the score—the Indian, the forest, the sea, American history and legend opened fields ripe for literary harvest. The anniversary of the Pilgrims' landing in 1820, the semicentennial celebrations of 1826, the beginning of the Bunker Hill monument, Lafayette's visit to the United States, and many other such events stirred up what Edward Everett called a mood of "comprehensive patriotism." Novels like John Neal's *Rachel Dyer*, Catharine Sedgwick's *New-England Tale*, Lydia Child's *The Rebels*, and Cooper's *Lionel Lincoln* dotted the decade; the year 1825 alone produced seven novels about the Revolution. Another favorite topic was the Indian. Indian removals and treaties (ninety-four between 1829 and 1837) and books by authorities such as Schoolcraft and Catlin focused attention on the red man's plight as a "dying race," eliciting a series

30. Brown, *op. cit.*, 153–67. See also Mrs. M. J. Sweat, "A Chapter on Novels," *North American Review*, LXXXIII (1856), 337–51; and E. P. Whipple's essay on Fielding, *Ibid.*, LXVIII (1849), 41–82. The appearance of photography quickly influenced the critical view of the novel; the analogy of the camera and the novel appears more frequently after 1856.

of novels like *Tadeuskund, or the Last King of the Lenape,* and *Tokeah, or the Last of the Cochi,* as well as Cooper's *Last of the Mohicans.*

The appearance of writers of the caliber of Irving and Cooper marked the beginnings of a distinctively American, distinctively mature American fiction. Irving, though he represented a well-established British and Continental tradition, yet inspired by his example the whole next generation of young Americans. But Cooper, more than Irving, represented a thoroughly native point of view. The fact that he was called (inaccurately) "the American Scott" obscured for the moment his real place in American fiction—at the beginning of a maturing nationalistic, romantic strain, with *The Spy* (1821), *The Pioneers* (1823), and *The Last of the Mohicans* (1826).

Between Charles Brockden Brown and beyond Cooper, however, a number of novelists continued to work in the older British-based popular traditions. Isaac Mitchell's *Alonzo and Melissa* (1804) and George Watterson's *Glencairn* (1810) were anachronistic Gothic; John Neal's *Logan* (1822) and *Rachel Dyer* (1828), plus a dozen more, were Gothic-flavored romances, despite their American historical content. James Kirke Paulding, part of Irving's Knickerbocker circle, wrote old-fashioned historical novels like *Konigsmarke* (1823), *The Dutchman's Fireside* (1831), and *The Old Continental* (1846).[31]

Of the lesser novelists, three Southerners, Robert Montgomery Bird, John Pendleton Kennedy, and William Gilmore Simms, were among the best. Bird, who made his reputation first as a playwright, had more talent as a novelist; his *Nick of the Woods* (1837) was the first of the blood-and-thunder, Indian-killing novels that later provided a pattern for the whole tradition of dime-novel violence. *Calavar* (1834) and *The Infidel* (1835) dealt with the Spanish conquest of Mexico, *The Hawks of Hawk-Hollow* (1835) with the

31. Others were Daniel Thompson, who wrote several historical romances, of which *The Green Mountain Boys* (1839) was the most successful. William Carruthers's *Cavaliers of Virginia* (1835) used Bacon's Rebellion as its central plot; Theodore Fay's *Norman Leslie* (1835) combined elements of the sentimental, Gothic, and the novel of manners. Timothy Flint's *Frances Berrian: or The Mexican Patriot* (1826), James Hall's *Legends of the West* (1832), and Caroline Kirkland's *A New Home, Who'll Follow?* (1839) were among early novels of pioneer life.

Revolutionary War. Kennedy's *Swallow Barn* (1832), a series of vignettes rather than a novel, was the first significant treatment of Southern plantation life; *Horseshoe Robinson* (1835), laid in the Revolutionary South, seemed to some critics to equal Cooper; *Rob of the Bowl* (1838), a novel of colonial Maryland, ranked with the better historical romances of the times. Simms, a man of considerable talent, wrote in several fields. *Guy Rivers* (1834), the story of a frontier desperado, was the first of his "border" series; *The Yemassee* (1835) was the most widely read of his Indian novels; *The Partisan* (1835) was the first of a Revolutionary War series. A man of tremendous energy and the South's most distinguished man of letters, Simms also wrote history, biography, essays, and plays, edited ten magazines at different times, and filled eighty volumes with his total output.[32]

James Fenimore Cooper, of course, dominated American fiction through the twenties and thirties. Raised in upstate New York, at Cooperstown, where his father, Judge William Cooper, held thousands of acres of virgin forest land, young Cooper studied at Yale, shipped out as a merchant seaman, and later joined the navy. He left the sea, married well, and returned to New York State as a wealthy country squire. He tried his hand at a novel of manners, *Precaution* (1820), and in 1821 published *The Spy*, a superb novel of the American Revolution. He laid his next novel, *The Pioneers* (1823), at Cooperstown, introducing into it one of the most famous characters in all fiction, the frontiersman Natty Bumppo, known later as "Leatherstocking," "Pathfinder," and "Deerslayer." Natty appeared as a younger man in *The Last of the Mohicans* (1826), with the Indians Uncas and Chingachgook. *The Prairie* (1827), *The Pathfinder* (1840), and *The Deerslayer* (1841) completed the series, but Cooper had already, in *The Pilot* (1824), written the first of eleven sea novels. Thus within three years Cooper established three great themes of American fiction—the national past, the wilderness, and the sea—which occupied the talents of his successors for another century.

32. Curtis Dahl, *Robert Montgomery Bird* (New York, 1963); Charles H. Bohner, *John Pendleton Kennedy: Gentleman from Baltimore* (Baltimore, 1961); and Joseph V. Ridgeley, *William Gilmore Simms* (New York, 1962). John Esten Cooke, in the fifties, continued what Simms had begun in *Leather Stocking and Silk* (1854), *The Virginia Comedians* (1854), and *Henry St. John, Gentleman* (1859).

Cooper continued to write novels (thirty-two in all) and after publishing a dozen books of social criticism, travel narrative, and satire returned to historical fiction in the "Littlepage" series, dealing with the conflict of aristocrat and commoner in upper New York State, in *Satanstoe* (1845), *The Chainbearer* (1845), and *The Redskins* (1846).[33] His fictional techniques, unfortunately, were already out of date when he began his major work, so that his novels fell into an awkward interval between the discursive, artificial, sentimental style of the eighteenth century and the more sophisticated, symbolic, and realistic practices of the nineteenth.

Nonetheless, his readers were willing to accept his old-fashioned format in recompense for his powerful sense of narrative, his action, and his magnificent articulation of the red-white, frontier-civilization conflict that lay at the center of American history. Deerslayer, Uncas, Long Tom Coffin the sailor, the spy Harvey Birch, and the crude squatter Ishmael Bush are major character creations, all part of American literary mythology, and the novels that contain them stand at the headwaters of the stream of American fiction. There was implicit in Cooper much that later novelists drew upon and developed—the lonely forest hero, the "natural" man, the "white hunter," the poor white, the doomed Indian, as well as the good Indian and the bad one, the literature of the hunt and the chase, and most of all the theme of innocence destroyed by experience, of the American Adam expelled from his wilderness Eden.

Though Edgar Allan Poe began his literary career as a poet, he found that if he were to make a living by his pen, he could do it only by writing the kind of short fiction bought by the magazines. The tendency of the times, he wrote, "was magazineward" and the market demanded "the curt, the well timed, the terse." One of his early tales, *Ms. Found in a Bottle,* won a prize in 1833, and through the help of one of the judges, John P. Kennedy, he obtained a succession of editorial jobs and concentrated his efforts on fiction.

33. Robert E. Spiller, *Fenimore Cooper, Critic of His Times* (New York, 1931), is the best study of his social criticism. Donald Ringe, *James Fenimore Cooper* (New York, 1962), and James Grossman, *James Fenimore Cooper* (New York, 1949), are excellent critical studies. Cooper wrote several European historical romances including *The Bravo* (1831), *The Heidenmauer* (1832), and *The Headsman* (1833). *Homeward Bound* (1838), and *Home as Found* (1838) are representative social criticism; *The Monikins* (1835), and *The Crater* (1848) are satire and allegory.

His projected collection of stories, *Tales of the Folio Club,* which was to appear in 1833, never did, but most of the tales appeared in magazines over the next few years. Poe at the same time was writing criticism, developing his ideas on fiction as he wrote his own stories and reviewed those of others. By the time his collection, *Tales of the Grotesque and Arabesque,* was published in 1840, he had evolved a clear, well-constructed theory of fiction. To him the tale, as he called it, was a complete, finalized moment of emotional tension; he strove, he said, for "a single effect," with the story so unified and self-contained that not a word or phrase could be eliminated without destroying the completeness and symmetry of the whole.[34]

Poe published forty-three tales, not including articles and sketches, during the forties, all so carefully designed that after him no man dared write short fiction without acknowledging his debt. Though he reviewed numerous novels and praised good ones, he felt that their length—and especially serial publication—destroyed the unity and brevity that marked the best artistic fiction. His own attempt at a novel, *The Narrative of Arthur Gordon Pym of Nantucket,* published in 1837, he simply left unfinished.

Nathaniel Hawthorne gained recognition first for his tales and sketches, collected in *Twice-Told Tales* (1837, 1842) and *Mosses from an Old Manse* (1846). After the success of *The Scarlet Letter,* his "romance" that appeared in 1850, he turned to longer works, *The House of the Seven Gables* (1851), *The Blithedale Romance* (1852), and another set of tales, *Tanglewood Tales* (1854). *The Marble Faun,* his last major effort and his most enigmatic, did not appear until 1859. He completed nothing else before his death in 1864.[35]

34. General critical studies of Poe are Edward Davidson, *Poe* (Cambridge, 1959), and Vincent Buranelli, *Edgar Allan Poe* (New York, 1961); a good biography is Edward Wagenknecht, *Edgar Allan Poe: The Man Behind the Legend* (New York, 1963). Poe's remarks on fiction appear in his reviews of *Undine* (1839), *Night and Morning* (1841), *Barnaby Rudge* (1841), and Hawthorne's *Twice-Told Tales* (1842). An excellent summary of his critical principles is chapter III of the introduction to Margaret Alterton and Hardin Craig, eds., *Poe* (New York, 1935).

35. A good biography is Edward Wagenknecht, *Nathaniel Hawthorne: Man and Writer* (New York, 1961). Critical studies include Richard Fogle, *Hawthorne's Fiction: The Light and the Dark* (Oklahoma, 1952); Hyatt H. Waggoner, *Nathaniel Hawthorne* (Cambridge, 1963); and Terence Martin's brief but brilliant *Nathaniel Hawthorne* (New York, 1965).

Hawthorne brought intensity, depth, and craftsmanship to American fiction, but, unlike Poe, his concern was not solely with emotional effect; Hawthorne's fiction probed inside man's mind, to the center of his soul. The descendant of two centuries of New England Calvinism, he could never accept Emerson's ebullient optimism or place so much trust in self-reliant man. Unlike Thoreau, Hawthorne did not celebrate Nature, nor did he, like Poe, explore the effects of fear or irrationality on the psyche. Seeing the world emblematically, as his Puritan ancestors did, Hawthorne's method was to probe action for its significance, "to construct an incident into a thought." Whether it was a short tale like "The Minister's Veil" or a complex novel like *The Marble Faun* (1860), Hawthorne's art moved inward, from fact to symbol, from web of experience to cluster of symbols. Through all his work, whether tale, allegory, or romance (for Hawthorne did not consider himself a novelist), he was concerned with a single question—what lies in the heart of man? What he found there was a complicated mixture of good and evil, of free will and compulsion, of fear and hope. Hawthorne gave no answers, only implications. It was this symbolic, unfinished quality in his fiction that led Poe to suggest that he get "a bottle of visible ink" and Melville to remark that all of Hawthorne's conclusions were inconclusive.

Herman Melville tried clerking in a bank and teaching school before he ran off to sea at eighteen. In 1841, when he was twenty-one, he spent eighteen months on the whaler *Acushnet,* jumped ship in the South Seas, and lived for four months with friendly cannibals in the Marquesas Islands. The *Acushnet* was to him, he said later, "my Yale College and my Harvard," and from the memories of that voyage, refined in recollection, came the main thrust of his literary work. Melville returned to Boston and wrote accounts of his adventures in *Typee* (1846) and *Omoo* (1847). *Redburn* (1849) and *White Jacket* (1850) were based on his experiences aboard a United States naval frigate. These books, while popular, were also controversial. *Typee* and *Omoo* suggested that the missionary's influence on pagan life was not entirely beneficial; *Redburn* and *White Jacket* did not portray the navy in flattering terms. *Mardi* (1849) was a curious mixture of satire, allegory, and philosophizing, keyed to the contemporary scene; it had, as his naval books did, disturbing, darker elements which puzzled a public which expected something different from him. That he could write stories of sea life and naval adventure Melville knew by the fifties; instead of writing more of these, he told a friend, he wanted to be "a thought-diver."

From the summer of 1850 to the fall of 1851 Melville and Hawthorne were neighbors. Melville was writing *Moby Dick,* ostensibly a whaling story, and, as Hawthorne wrote later, they talked often "about time and eternity, things of this world and the next, and books and publishers, and all possible and impossible matters." Meanwhile, what Melville may have begun as the story of the pursuit of the huge malevolent white whale by Captain Ahab turned into something much more. Dedicated to Hawthorne, the book appeared in 1851. It received mixed reviews, since most of Melville's readers expected another kind of sea tale, which they found, of course, but beneath it another story that reverberated with meanings.[36]

Moby Dick, Melville told Hawthorne, was a book "broiled in hellfire." He felt that he had poured all his talent into it, and although he was only thirty-three his art fell into decline and his reputation into semiobscurity. "I feel I am now come to the inmost leaf of the bulb," he wrote Hawthorne, "and shortly the flower must fall to the mold." *Pierre, or the Ambiguities* (1852), an almost despairing study of good and evil, *Israel Potter* (1855), a sea tale, and *The Confidence Man* (1857), an odd allegory, were interesting books but did not appeal to the public. He wrote some superb short fiction in *Piazza Tales* (1856) and left *Billy Budd* for posthumous publication. Yet whatever its falling-off, Melville's late work was by no means a failure. "Benito Cereno" and "Bartleby the Scrivener," in *Piazza Tales,* remain two of the finest short tales in the language. *Pierre,* for all its unevenness, is an exploration of fate and failure unequaled for its time except by Hawthorne, while the tale of the handsome sailor, *Billy Budd,* is a provocative study of good, evil, and justice.

The most prolific type of fiction of the period, however, was the

36. Among the numerous studies of Melville, the more useful are Leon Howard's biography, *Herman Melville* (Berkeley, 1951) and Jay Leyda's documentary collection, *The Melville Log* (New York, 1951); Milton Stern, *The Fine Hammered Steel of Herman Melville* (Urbana, 1957); Howard Vincent, *The Trying-Out of Moby Dick* (Boston, 1949); William Ellery Sedgwick, *Herman Melville: The Tragedy of Mind* (Cambridge, 1944).

sentimental-domestic novel, produced by what Hawthorne once angrily called "a damned mob of scribbling women." The swift growth of a huge market of educated, literate women promised great rewards for writers who could satisfy it. The parallel growth of gift books, annuals, and women's magazines like *Godey's, The National Magazine, The Casket, The Token,* and others furnished lucrative outlets. *Godey's,* for example, at one time had eighteen regular female contributors; Mary Agnes Fleming, one of the more popular women novelists, had a $15,000 annual retainer from *The New York Weekly.* What the market demanded was fiction that spoke directly to women and dealt with women's problems. It was no accident that many of the female novelists also conducted household-hints columns or advice-and-counsel departments in the magazines, while others edited cookbooks, etiquette books, and guides to child care.

Legitimate descendants of the Richardsonian novels of sentiment that flooded England and America in the eighteenth century, these tales dealt with children, husbands, love and marriage, illness and death, and all the sorrows and joys of domestic life. Their plots were chains of episodes which, taken together, served to show the reader that bliss could come from suffering; that conventional morals were best; that church, home, and family were anchors against unhappiness and evil. Soft and lachrymose as most of these stories were, they had nonetheless a real social function, in that they defined the moral boundaries of life, delineated some of its problems, and gave advice on how to cope with them. The English novelist Mrs. Gaskell characterized them exactly. "They unanimously reveal," she wrote, "all the little household secrets. . . .We hear the little family discourses, we enter into their home struggle, and we rejoice when they gain the victory." The early domestic novels struck a balance, usually, among religious, sentimental, moral, and romantic elements; as time passed the emphasis shifted until by the latter years of the century some were almost wholly love novels, occasionally with surprisingly erotic undertones.[37]

37. Cowie, *op. cit.,* chapter X, is an excellent brief treatment. Herbert R. Brown, *The Sentimental Novel in America 1790–1860* (Durham, 1940) is a substantial treatment. Individual novels and novelists are treated by James Hart, *The Popular Book* (Berkeley, 1957) , and Frank L. Mott, *Golden Multitudes* (New York, 1947) .

Catharine Maria Sedgwick, a New England lady who was called "the American Maria Edgeworth," was the first of the successful female novelists and the best-known of her sex before Harriet Beecher Stowe. *The North American Review* called *A New England Tale* (1822) "a beautiful little picture of native scenery and manners"; *Redwood* (1824), a historical romance, was compared to Scott and Cooper. Her novels were moralistic as well as sentimental—The New York *Mirror* said they aimed "at higher ends than the mere imparting of interest"—and she produced many of them over the years, including *The Linwoods* (1835), *Home* (1835), *The Poor Rich Man* (1836), and *Live and Let Live* (1837).

In the forties and fifties the sentimental-domestic novel inundated the market. Caroline Lee Hentz, whose first novel appeared in 1846, lived in the South and produced a series of novels about Southern life—*Linda, or the Young Pilot of the 'Belle Creole'*, *The Planter's Northern Bride*, and *Ernest Linwood*, among others. Ann S. Stephens wrote *The Old Homestead;* "Fanny Fern" (Sarah Payson Willis Parton) wrote *Ruth Hall;* Mrs. Marion Harland's first novel, *Alone* (1854), sold 100,000 copies a year for five years, and her last novel came in 1919. Mary Jane Holmes averaged a book a year from 1854 to 1907; both *Tempest and Sunshine* (1854) and *Lena Rivers* (1856) remained in print for thirty years. Susan Warner's *Wide, Wide World* (1850) and *Queechy* (1852) were second only to *Uncle Tom's Cabin* in sales. Her novels, said one reviewer, did more good than any writing outside the Bible.

Maria Susanna Cummins' *The Lamplighter* (1854), the story of an orphan girl, was not far behind in sales. Augusta Jane Evans Wilson's *Beulah* came out in 1859, her last novel, *The Speckled Bird*, in 1902. Her story of how Edna Earl reformed and married the handsome, dangerously attractive St. Elmo, *St. Elmo* (1866), ranks among the thirty most popular novels ever published in the United States. Sylvanus T. Cobb, a New Englander who wrote women's novels as well as they could, began the full-time manufacture of fiction in 1850, eventually publishing 122 novels, 937 shorter pieces, and 2,143 essays and sketches; his novel *The Gunmaker of Moscow* (1888) remained popular for years. The queen of the domestic novel was no doubt Mrs. E. D. E. N. Southworth, who after her husband deserted her wrote *Retribution* (200,000 copies) followed by sixty-one more. Her combination sentimental-domestic-mystery novel *The Hidden Hand* (1859) appeared in forty drama-tized versions and remained in print continuously for fifty years.[38]

The instant fame of Mrs. Harriet Beecher Stowe's *Uncle Tom's Cabin* obscured the fact that she had been writing for eighteen years before the novel appeared serially in *The National Era* in 1851–52.[39] Her concern over the slavery question led her to write, she said, a book which would "give the lights and shadows of the 'paternal institution,'" showing *"the best side* of the thing and something *faintly approaching the worst."* Nobody was prepared for what happened. The first edition of five thousand copies sold out in forty-eight hours, and for the next two years the presses never caught up with the demand. Total sales in the United States reached a million within the next seven years, and nearly that many (chiefly in pirated editions) in Britain. There were thirty different British editions of the book before 1860, later twelve German, five French, and translations into twenty-three other languages, includ-ing Armenian, Bengali, Siamese, and Welsh.

Critical opinions of the novel tended to polarize about extremes. By late 1853 the book had been suppressed in most of the slave states, and abusive letters poured into the Stowe mailbox in Maine. About thirty replies, or "anti-Tom" books, appeared in the next few years, nearly all condemning Mrs. Stowe's picture of slavery as sensational, exaggerated, or unjust. She was surprised and hurt by the violence of some of the attacks on her book and her intentions. She never meant, she repeated many times, that her novel should serve as a symbol of anger and discord. But whatever her intentions, it was soon plain that she had written a book destined to become one of the most powerful instruments of moral force and social change ever published. Lincoln's remark to Mrs. Stowe at a White House reception during the Civil War, "So this is the little lady

38. Russel B. Nye, *The Unembarrassed Muse: The Popular Arts in America* (New York, 1970), chapter II.

39. Mrs. Stowe's novel was not the first antislavery novel. Richard Hildreth's *Archy Moore* (1836), written as if it were a slave autobiography, preceded it. After the success of Mrs. Stowe's book, Hildreth brought out an expanded edition of his own, titled *The White Slave* (1853), which portrayed the militant Negro as contrasted to Uncle Tom.

who wrote the book that made this great war" was only half in jest.[40]

During the first half of the nineteenth century Americans expended a great deal of energy in the writing of history. The nation was, of course, bent on establishing an identity while the surge of nationalism that swept across the United States after the War of 1812 made the study of American history a matter of vital interest. Every citizen, it was assumed, needed to know where his country came from and how it came to be. Certainly, Americans believed, one of the keys to an understanding of the country's future lay in the study of its past.[41]

The Americans who wrote history during the nineteenth century were heirs of a long tradition of Puritan historical writing, stretching back to the chronicles of Massachusetts Bay. To the seventeenth-century Calvinist, history was theology exemplified, a record of God's "ordering and governing time and chance according to his own good pleasure," in the words of the Reverend Urian Oakes. The nineteenth-century American was also heir to an older concept of history—as the Enlightenment saw it—and to a newer one the Romantic. In the eighteenth century, the greatest influence on the historian was the critical, naturalistic attitude of Locke, Bacon, and Descartes that challenged the old ideas of history, ultimately defeated them, and created a new "rationalist" view of the past. The old concept of history as a record of retrogression, of mankind's movement away from a golden age, was replaced by the belief that the past showed a progressive march up from the lower stages of civilization—a theory developed by Fontenelle, Vico, Hume, Gibbon, Turgot, Kant, Condorcet, and others. The basis for history in the nineteenth century thus broadened, turned scientific (in the

40. Forrest Wilson, *Crusader in Crinoline* (New York, 1943) is a good biography. John R. Adams, *Harriet Beecher Stowe* (New York, 1963) , and Charles H. Foster, *The Rungless Ladder: Harriet Beecher Stowe and New England Puritanism* (Durham, 1956) are excellent critical studies.

41. "Materials for American History," *North American Review*, XXIII (October, 1826) , 276. For the backgrounds of American historical writing, see the preface and chapter I of George Calcott, *History in the United States 1800–1860: Its Practice and Purpose* (Baltimore, 1970) . See also Fred Somkin, *Unquiet Eagle: Memory and Desire in the Idea of American Freedom 1815–1860* (Ithaca, 1967) , on historical writing.

contemporary sense of the term) and, most of all, rationalistic. The field of history widened to embrace the study of societies and cultures as well as of church and state; historians rejected folklore, supersitition, legend, or anything that could not be called to the bar of reason's judgment.

Eighteenth-century rationalist historians tended to see the past as cause and effect—God the cause, history the effect. Beneath historical phenomena, they believed, lay general natural laws which governed the course of events. By studying the record of the past, historians might trace in it the operation of these laws and discover how a particular society came to be. This view of history made all facts relevant to a larger plan or scheme behind them; history, in Bolingbroke's famous phrase, became "philosophy teaching by example." Such historical writing was, since it hoped to deduce general laws from specific evidence, "scientific." In a narrow sense of the term it was, for the historians who wrote it tried to cut away accretions from historical evidence and to find reasonable explanations for events. In the later sense of the term, it was not. The historians knew what they expected to find, and the conclusions they searched for were fixed before they began. God's great design was there beneath the palimpsest of the past, and all they asked was that the facts fall into place so that they might reveal that design.

The rationalist school of historical interpretation in Britain and Europe was shortly challenged by a group of Romantic historians who were as intuitional as their opponents were rational. They believed that every nation possessed a unique "national spirit"—a combination of traditions, customs, laws, language, and culture—which produced (as the German historian Ranke named it) a *Zeitgeist* peculiar to its people. History became, then, the task of tracing out of the past the development of this "national genius" and of identifying its elements. Since such a "spirit" existed in every age and every society, all ages and societies responded equally to historical examination. No eras were "better" or "worse" than others, as earlier historians had assumed; history assumed the *total* study of a nation's past, not meaningless segments.[42]

42. Russel B. Nye, *George Bancroft* (New York, 1964), 135–40. See also David Levin, *History as Romantic Art* (Stanford, 1959), and Bert J. Loewenberg, *American History in American Thought* (New York, 1972), chapters XI–XVI, for studies of American historians and historical theory of the period.

In addition, German historians (of whom at least a dozen were writing between 1790 and 1860) were exploring an idea that Americans needed to believe, that is, that the study of a nation's past was the best way to understand its present and predict its future. French historians, who emphasized the color, drama, and conflict of history, also found enthusiastic American readers. Both French and German historians stressed the "organic" nature of history; they assumed that a nation had growth, life, and could be studied as one studied a living thing.[43] This Romantic approach to history, with its emphasis upon nationalism and progress, led historians to study single nations or peoples, to explain the emergence of their "national genius," and to show how it manifested itself in their national culture. Historians, eager to discover the reasons for the rise and fall of nations and to trace the course of their development, searched national records, collected and published documents, and claimed the right to use them in their own way.

Early-nineteenth-century American historical theory, then, drawing from both rationalist and Romantic sources, was marked by these traits: an attitude of objectivity toward the facts of the past, asking for impartiality and freedom from preconception; a belief in progress, buttressed by transcendental idealism and reinforced by the rationalist faith in an upward social tendency; the recognition of a master plan or controlling scheme behind the shifting facts of history; an interest in the evolution of national institutions, leading to an emphasis upon "national genius" as the creative force underlying historical development.

Historians in the United States faced a difficult problem in the fact that neither of the two traditionally accepted theories of historical writing seemed to fit American needs. The seventeenth-century view of history as a chain of events, though old-fashioned, still had its adherents. The eighteenth century liked the chain analogy—George Thomson in 1791 spoke of history as "a chain consisting of many links, and to strike off one would be to discompose the whole." Others preferred the recent cyclical theory, which conceived of history as a series of cyclical movements, based on the

43. Calcott, op. cit., 8–15. Schiller was translated in 1799, Herder in 1800, Karl von Schlegel in 1835, Fichte in 1838; over a hundred articles on German historians appeared in American magazines before 1846. Among French historians, American periodicals excerpted or reviewed Thierry, Thiers, Guizot, and Michelet.

assumption that societies and nations rose and fell in endless sequences according to their observance or disregard of natural law—as in Gibbon's *Decline and Fall of the Roman Empire,* the first volume of which appeared in 1776. John Adams, for example, remarked that "there is never a rising meridian without a setting sun," and Noah Webster noted that all nations "progress from their origins to maturity and decay."

Both "chain" and "cycle" theories, however, contained implications Americans found difficult to accept. Neither theory placed much value on individual action; both were essentially pessimistic and deterministic. If all history was linked together by a chain of preordination, no individual could change it; if nations rose only to fall, there seemed to be no reason to hope for a better future. Neither view fitted the American's feeling for his own past and future. He had, so he believed, already changed the course of history to found a new kind of nation; there must be some way to break the chain or stop the cycle, to exempt the United States from the inexorable fate of other nations in the past. The answer came in a new view of history, best summarized in Condorcet's *Tableau historique du progrès de l'esprit humain* which appeared in France in 1793. Condorcet saw history as a series of stages, each an improvement over the last, moving ever upward by the law of progress. The theory of historical progress (not new, but redefined and reinvigorated by the Enlightenment philosophers) took man off the cyclical treadmill of history and freed him from the chain of historical causation.

This was precisely the view of the past that Americans needed to write their own history, for it showed that past and present ages were preludes to better ones, and suggested that the creation of the United States was a step forward toward that better world. America was not, therefore, the crest of a movement bound to decline; it was instead a new stage in an ever-upward succession of stages. The concept of history as the record of human progress, and of American history as the most recent and convincing chapter of that record, provided the basic theory for American historical writing for the next generation. Thus George Bancroft, dean of the Romantic school of historians, beginning his monumental *History of the United States* in 1834, could see the whole sweep of history coming into focus at Lexington as the embattled farmers faced the redcoats—for this, he wrote, "was the slowly ripened fruit of Providence and time . . . and the light that led them was combined of rays of the whole history of the race."[44]

Both historian and public believed that history was to do certain things; most important, it was supposed to express "the spirit of the age" or "the genius of the people." The people of each nation, said a writer in 1852, were distinguished "by the manifestations of some predominant thought" that "gives vitality . . . , stimulates their energies, and makes them great." Because of this "spirit," the Romans, or the Spanish, or the English Puritans, or the American colonists acted as they did; understanding the "genius" of a nation was one of history's major functions. Second, history was a way of locating right and wrong in human behavior; it taught "lessons," provided moral guideposts for present and future actions. "The province of history is to establish a tribunal," wrote a reviewer in 1831, "where princes and private men alike may be tried and judged"; it should "furnish instruction . . . in political, moral, and even private affairs (and) information for some department of life."

Third, history showed the law beneath the fact, the meaning behind the event, for it was assumed that historical phenomena exemplified general laws governing "not merely the history of government and politics" (wrote the directors of the American Antiquarian Society), "but the history of man in all his nature and interests." History "developed those great principles," said the *New England Magazine* in 1834, "which, by divine appointment, diffuse their influence through every human being." These were God's laws of moral order made manifest in action; it was the function of the historian to locate and explain them. Each page of history, wrote George Bancroft, "may begin with Great is God and marvellous are his plans among men."[45]

44. Russel B. Nye, *American Literary History 1607–1830* (New York, 1970), 205–8. An excellent study is Stow Persons, "Progress and the Organic Cycle in Eighteenth Century America," *American Quarterly*, VI (Summer, 1954), 147–63. For examples of contemporary discussions of the cyclical theory, see "Growth and Decay of Nations," *DeBow's Review*, XXX (January, 1861), 19–30; and "Living and Dying Nations," *Popular Science Monthly*, LIII (September, 1898), 705–8.

45. Calcott, *op. cit.*, 154–56, 178–80; Nye, *Bancroft*, 140 ff.; "History and Biography," *The New England Magazine*, VI (March, 1834), 197; "The Philosophy of History," *The American Magazine of Entertaining and Useful Knowledge*, III (1837), 13–20.

Surveying the past, American historians believed they could discern clearly the shape of God's plan. First, *progress*, the "all-embracing, basic law" of history. The past was a battlefield on which the forces of right and wrong eternally contested, the one for humanity's advancement, the other against it. Men and nations might go astray, but what historian John Lothrop Motley called "the inexorable laws of Freedom and Progress" always led upward to the same victorious resolution.[46] Second, *order* and *unity*. The historian searched for proofs of the relationship that existed among the infinite number of segments of God's design. As Bancroft phrased it, beneath "the movements of nations" there existed "a marshalling intelligence which is above them all, and which gives order and unity to the universe." To discover this divine unity in the past's variety, to find connections among men and facts and acts and eternal principles—this too was the historian's calling. Third, history seemed to show that there was inherent in natural law an inexorable trend to *freedom*, and that the American people were apparently destined to lead the world toward it. Few doubted, after the Revolution, that the Americans were a chosen people; the nation needed historians who could find out why, and for what purpose. Jeremy Belknap was convinced that man had been created by God "to make various experiments for happiness," and that "one of the grandest of these experiments has been made in our own part of this continent." Bancroft, with greater sophistication, made the concept of the United States as God's instrument for liberty a controlling theme of his *History*.[47]

To the citizens of the new republic history had a particularly important function. Since an intelligent awareness of one's national past served as a sort of patriotic cement to bind the nation together, Benjamin Trumbull wrote, Americans should know their history, in order "to awaken their mutual sympathies and promote their general union and general welfare." Noah Webster, who thought

46. His fellow historian George Bancroft likened the law of progress to the Mississippi in which, though "there are little eddies and sidecurrents . . . the onward course of the mighty mass of waters is as certain as the laws of gravitation." See Levin, *op. cit.*, 239 and the discussion of progress, *passim*.

47. See Ralph Miller, "American Nationalism as a Theory of Nature," *William and Mary Quarterly*, XI (January, 1955), 74–95; "Providence in American History," *Harper's Monthly*, XVII (June–December, 1858), 694–700; "California," *The American Review*, III (April, 1849), 331–38; Nye, *Bancroft*, 143, 158–9.

that an American history book "should be the principal school book
in the United States," felt that an American child, "as soon as he
opens his lips, should rehearse the history of his own country."
Naturally, therefore, Americans urged (and some states required)
the study of American history in the schools, not only as a mark of
the educated man, but as an effective way of instilling pride in
every citizen.[48]

Texts and readers came in a flood. Readers and grammars contained historical materials, American and otherwise, and so did
texts like Jedidiah Morse's geographies. The first real history text
was John McCulloch's, which appeared in 1787, with another edition in 1795. Histories aimed at the general public also sold well,
and writers who knew the market, like John Barker, Jacob Abbott,
and Benson J. Lossing, wrote and sold thousands of copies of flam-
boyantly patriotic histories.[49] During the fifties history emerged as
a separate academic discipline in both lower and upper schools.
Since almost all academies and high schools required American
history, the average high school graduate in 1860 had at least three
years of history, some of it "world" or "universal" history, some
ancient history, and one-third or more of it American history.

During the post-Revolutionary years, most historical writing was
naturally concerned with the recent war. American historians accepted unreservedly the so-called "Whig" interpretation of the war,
developed by such British Whigs as Edmund Burke and Charles
James Fox, who had used it to discredit the party in power. In the
Whig view, the American colonies, forced into revolution by tyrannical Parliamentary leaders, fought not only for their own rights
but the rights of Englishmen and all mankind. Since the Revolutionary leaders had already used this particular version of events to
vindicate independence (as Jefferson did in the Declaration), the
postwar historians felt they needed no other justification. In addi-

48. "The Philosophy of History," *The American Magazine,* III (October, 1836),
14; "The Importance of the Study of the History of Our Own Country," *American
Magazine of Useful and Entertaining Knowledge,* II (March–April, 1842), 73–6.
Massachusetts, in 1827, was the first to require it in the schools.

49. David Van Tassel, *Recording America's Past* (Chicago, 1960) chapter IX;
Calcott, *op. cit.,* 55–66. Most of the school histories were supplied by New England
writers and publishers, so that many of the texts displayed a strong New England
bias. Charles Goodrich's *History of the United States* (1823), for example, taught
that "the free and licentious society" of Virginia produced an "unsteady and
capricious government" in contrast to New England's.

tion, they tended to see the conflict in Federalist terms—as the next-to-final act of national unity, followed logically by the adoption of the Constitution. The war "disseminated principles of union . . . ," wrote David Ramsay, "and a foundation was laid for the establishment of a nation." The Whig-Federalist point of view dominated American historical writing for the next century without serious challenge. Historians were also interested in histories of their own colonies or regions, as illustrated by Robert Proud's *History of Pennsylvania,* Samuel Williams's *Natural and Civil History of Vermont,* and Jeremy Belknap's *New Hampshire.*[50]

Few writers attempted to write a complete history of the United States, none successfully. No one was quite sure how to begin such an important undertaking. Benjamin Trumbull planned a three-volume work to be called *A General History of the United States from the Discovery in 1492,* but he completed only the first in 1810. Abiel Holmes, Oliver Wendell Holmes's father, brought out an outline of American history from Columbus's discovery to 1800, called *American Annals,* in 1805. Both Jedidiah Morse and Noah Webster put brief historical sketches into their school books, but curiously enough the earliest study of American history as a unit was Christopher Ebeling's, published in German in seven Teutonically thorough volumes in Germany between 1793 and 1816. Charles Botta, an Italian, and James Grahame, a Scotsman, both wrote popular American histories, but neither had real understanding of the American past or access to the necessary materials.[51]

Since some historical records were already scattered or lost, historians first turned their attention to collecting and organizing the remainder. Ebenezer Hazard's unfinished *Historical Collections* (1792–94) and Jedidiah Morse's *American Gazeteer* (1797) were early efforts to gather and publish primary materials, followed by those of Webster and Hezekiah Niles. Nonetheless, Jared Sparks in 1826 wrote that "nothing is more obvious than the loose and

50. For accounts of these early histories, see Michael Kraus, *A History of American History* (New York, 1937), chapters IV and V. Among Revolutionary histories were David Ramsay's *History of the American Revolution* (1790); Hannah Adams's *Summary History of New England* (1799); and Mercy Otis Warren's three-volume *History of the Rise, Progress, and Termination of the American Revolution* (1805).

51. Botta's history, which appeared in Italian in 1809, was translated in 1820; Grahame began his history in 1827. Timothy Pitkin's *Political and Civil History of the United States of America* was published in 1828.

scattered condition of all materials for history in the United States."[52]

Sparks himself made a great and permanent contribution to historical scholarship with his twelve-volume *Diplomatic Correspondence of the American Revolution* (1829–30). Jonathan Elliot's four-volume *Debates, Resolutions, and other Proceedings in Convention on the Adoption of the Federal Constitution* (1827–30), Peter Force's *American Archives* (1837–53), and Morse's *Annals of the American Revolution* (1824) were equally monumental. The Library of Congress began collecting source materials in the thirties, while diplomats, agents, and private collectors sent buyers and copiers into European archives. State and local historical societies gathered and published masses of materials; there were 111 such societies by 1860, most of them sponsoring some kind of publication. Genealogical societies and special-interest groups also collected information and published journals—the New England Society of New York, the Society of the War of 1812, the Philadelphia Religious Historical Society, the American Antiquarian Society, and others. Many states, by the fifties, had established agencies to collect, preserve, and publish records, while Congress in 1859 authorized the Public Documents Bureau in the Interior Department.[53]

The nineteenth-century reader asked certain things of historians. First, he expected them to deal with what Carlyle called "the history of living men," rather than "protocols, state papers, and controversies," simply "philosophy teaching by experience." Second, the era expected history to be dramatic. The historian gave the past form and structure, finding dramatic tension, climax, and resolution in chosen episodes of experience. History was the stage for a conflict of opposing elements. The encounter might be between the forces of progress and reaction, of liberty against authoritarianism, popular government versus absolutism, civilization versus barba-

52. Cf. Kraus, *op. cit.*, chapter V, *passim*, on record-keeping. Sparks's statement appeared in the *North American Review*, XXIII (October, 1826), 291.

53. Kraus, *op. cit.*, chapter VI; Van Tassel, *op. cit.*, 95–111; Calcott, *op. cit.*, 34–42. See also Leslie W. Dunlap, *American Historical Societies 1790–1860* (Madison, 1944). John Brodhead, for example, brought home eighty volumes of documents and transcripts from Europe in 1844; Bancroft had copyists at work in the national archives of Holland, France, Spain, Prussia, and Russia in addition to the British Museum and Records Office.

rism, order opposed to chaos, and so on, but whatever the forces involved it was essentially a dramatic conflict.

Third, to write history properly the historian needed a theme to bind events together, to give them focus and meaning. The historian thought of the past as an unbroken stream flowing toward some sea; beneath it lay those "pervading principles" which gave "continuity and vitality" to history. Such a principle might be, as Bancroft's was, the theme of man's progress toward liberty; or Parkman's of the conflict of Protestant and Catholic for mastery of the wilderness; or Motley's of the struggle of freedom with tyranny in Holland. Fourth, the historian, like the painter, composed and arranged his materials in artistic, vivid, and aesthetically pleasing fashion. Historians habitually used such terms as "portrait," "canvas," and "sketch"; gave careful attention to composition and arrangement of details; and quite deliberately set up "scenes" and "tableaux." Fifth, the historian must create in his work a precise sense of place, time, and immediacy. He must reconstruct the intellectual, social, and moral atmosphere of the times of which he wrote with what was labeled "the spirit of the age, the impalpable but necessary essence" of a society. Last, the historian had to write with taste, feeling, and art. "No man can dispense with excellence of style," said Prescott. "If this be wanting . . . a work cannot give pleasure or create interest."[54]

The historian was considered the equal of the poet, orator, and philosopher, possessed of the same aims and insights. "Of all the pursuits that require analysis," wrote Bancroft, "history . . . stands first. It is equal to philosophy . . . , [and] grander than the natural sciences, for its study is man." History addressed "the higher reason, equally with poetry, as an intuition of the spiritual, the universal, the eternal . . . , as a progressive, ever-unfolding verification of spiritual truths." Historians gave the past moral meaning and artistic order by "considering events in connection with one another . . . , observing the general principles by which that succession is controlled," using as their touchstone "the discovery, the diffusion, and the application of truths in the histories of man and

54. Levin, *op. cit.*, 3–49; Calcott, *op. cit.*, 140–50. An excellent summary of the contemporary view of the historian's task is in *The New England Magazine*, IV (January, 1833) 81, which asks that history be written "in a picturesque style of narrating, vivid delineations of character." "Instead of being a lifeless chronicle of events," it should "be animated by and warmed with a philosophical soul."

nature."[55] History was, then, quite clearly one of the literary arts. Historians read and wrote poetry, fiction, and criticism; they read and absorbed Wordsworth, Coleridge, Scott, Byron, Goethe, Carlyle, and many more. Bancroft, Motley, Prescott, Hildreth, Parkman, and other historians shared the intellectual society of Emerson, Everett, Holmes, Longfellow, Allston, and Channing; they belonged to the same literary and philosophical clubs, and were respected members of them.[56]

The first volume of George Bancroft's *History of the United States from the Discovery of the Continent* was hailed by the *Christian Examiner* in 1834 as "an instrument of Providence." Bancroft, educated at Harvard, Göttingen, and Berlin, tried his hand at teaching and criticism before choosing to write history. Strongly influenced by German historical theory, he chose as his theme "the necessity, the reality, and the promise of the progress of the human race" as it was exemplified in the history of the United States. History, Bancroft explained in his preface, must have some "great principle of action" to lend unity and significance to the narrative. He selected two. The first, stated concisely, was liberty—to trace how from small beginnings on an empty continent the United States grew to become the most free and just nation in history. The second was contained in his conviction that the United States was a creation of Divine Providence—everywhere in the American past he could find "the footsteps of Providential Intelligence." There was some truth to a reviewer's jest that Bancroft "wrote the history of the United States as if it were the history of the Kingdom of God," but it was exactly what his readers wanted to hear. His version of American history was eagerly accepted by the public as its standard, and his position as the most eminent of the Romantic historians went unchallenged through most of his long life.[57]

55. Bancroft, *Literary and Historical Miscellanies* (New York, 1855), 483 ff. Also "On Historical Composition," *Portfolio,* IX (January–July, 1820), 339–58; J. L. Dinan, Phi Beta Kappa Address, 1859, *Orations and Essays* (Boston, 1882), 96–7.
56. See Levin, *op. cit.,* "The Historian as Man of Letters," chapter I.
57. See Nye, *Bancroft,* "The Shape and Meaning of History." Bancroft completed his ten-volume *History* in 1875, immediately revised it in 1876–79, wrote two volumes of Constitutional history in 1882, and revised and republished the whole in 1883–85. For sketches of the nineteenth-century historians, see Harvey Wish, *The American Historians* (New York, 1960); Kraus, *op. cit.;* William T. Hutchinson, ed., *The Marcus W. Jernegan Essays in American Historiography* (Chicago, 1937); and H. Hale Belott, *American History and American Historians* (Norman, 1952).

Richard Hildreth, another New Englander, preferred to present the Founding Fathers, he said, "unbedaubed with patriotic rouge." Avoiding the dramatics and rhetoric of the Romantic school, he was among the first American historians to explore the influences of class interests and economic groups. Hildreth wrote anti-Texas editorials for the Boston *Atlas,* antislavery articles for Greeley's New York *Tribune,* and was attached politically to the conservative Whig party, although he did not always follow the party's line. He translated a French version of Bentham, wrote a brilliant abolitionist tract, *Despotism in America* (1840), and completed two volumes—*A Theory of Morals* (1844) and *Theory of Politics* (1853)—of a projected three-volume study of "the science of man." His *History of the United States of America* (1849–52) was strongly pro-Federalist, intellectually sophisticated, slightly iconoclastic, and never so popular as Bancroft's. George Tucker's *History of the United States* (1856) and John G. Palfrey's *History of New England* (1858–64) were distinguished histories, and Jared Sparks's *Gouverneur Morris* (1832) and *Washington* (1834–37) were sound biographies.

William Hickling Prescott worked seven years on *The History of the Reign of Ferdinand and Isabella,* which was enthusiastically received by public and critics in 1837. Prescott chose as his theme the drama of the Spanish conquest of South America and the death of the Indian empires. His *Conquest of Mexico* (1843) and *Conquest of Peru* (1847) were vividly dramatic histories, built about the figures of Cortez and Pizarro. John Lothrop Motley, who also wrote history in dramatic terms, found his theme in the Dutch rebellions against Spain, beginning with *The Rise of the Dutch Republic* (1856), in which he pitted William of Orange, representing liberty and Protestantism, against the Catholic absolutism of Philip II of Spain.[58]

After the *Oregon Trail* (1849), an account of a trip he made to the West, Francis Parkman turned to Cooper's theme—the clash of red man and white—in *History of the Conspiracy of Pontiac* (1851). He then resolved to write the history of France and

58. A useful introduction to Prescott is William Charvat and Michael Kraus, eds., *William H. Prescott* (New York, 1943). Motley wrote two more volumes in his series on Dutch history; a good introduction is Chester Higby and B. T. Schantz, *John Lothrop Motley* (New York, 1939).

England in North America, publishing the first volume, *Pioneers of France in the New World* in 1865, and the last, *A Half-Century of Conflict*, in 1892. Parkman's dramatic range and narrative drive rivaled that of Prescott and Bancroft, and, in the estimate of later critics, perhaps exceeded them. An aristocrat, Parkman tended to see history in terms of generals, governors, and nobles; a descendant of generations of New England Calvinists, he tended also to see the struggle for North America as a contest between the free, Protestant English and the authoritarian, Catholic French. But he was the first among American historians to grasp the feel of the great epic of the continent's conquest, and to catch something of the grandeur and wildness of Indian and forest life.[59]

The Boston-Cambridge monopoly of historical writing was soon challenged, and the tendency to treat all of American history as a gloss on New England's came under spirited attack. It became clear that other states and other groups had important roles in establishing the nation and that cultures other than Boston's and New York's had contributed to it. The South was especially sensitive to New England's claims of patriotic eminence; *The Southern Quarterly Review* in 1852 made a special plea for textbooks that treated Southern life accurately and justly. The historical division between North and South widened swiftly as the argument over slavery and disunion became more heated. Northern historians discovered the malevolent influence of Southern "agents of slavery and enemies of freedom" far back in the early colonies; Southerners also found there evidences of a Northern "conspiracy" to rob the South of its rights and subvert its institutions. The bitter divisions that led to war divided historical writing too.[60]

By the 1840s, there were critics who felt that the sweeping, nationalized histories of Bancroft and his school had submerged the identities of regions and states and that too few explored the histories of particular groups and cultures. Younger historians, disenchanted with the spread-eagle patriotism which infused much Romantic history, took closer looks at the legends, the documents, and the historian's method of using them. They pointed out that many incidents reported by historians seemed to have no basis in

---

59. Mason Wade, *Francis Parkman: Heroic Historian* (New York, 1942) is the best biography.

60. For a complete account, see Van Tassel, *op. cit.*, chapter 14.

fact, that too many historians repeated each other's errors. Some records were inaccurately transcribed; quotations were not always exact; contrary evidence was sometimes overlooked; most of all, many of the published records were poorly edited. During the mid-century years, a great body of historical material was re-edited and reassessed. The founding of *The Historical Magazine* in 1857, a scholarly journal devoted solely to historical research and criticism, was a sign of the new emphasis on accuracy, completeness, and factual accuracy in historical writing. It was no longer enough for history to be patriotic, philosophical, and literary.

CHAPTER 4

Poetry and the Public Arts

THE literary genres held in highest esteem in the first half of the nineteenth century were poetry, history, biography, and the essay; drama and fiction were accorded somewhat less prestige. Poetry was granted special eminence in the hierarchy of the arts, and the poet given equal rank with the philosopher and divine. Emerson called the poet "the sayer, the namer . . ." who "stands for the complete man"; it was he, wrote Bancroft, who, unlike other men, possessed that inward perceptivity which made him "the interpreter of Heaven . . . the receptor of messages from the infinite."[1] However, the contemporary image of the poet as egocentric individualist, alienated, impractical, even arrogant and immoral (deriving from the Byron-Shelley-Poe school), was also widely accepted, more so than perhaps the critics believed. It was Henry Wadsworth Longfellow, almost singlehandedly, over a quarter-century of effort, who did much to change that image, until gradually the picture emerged of the poet as man of wisdom and faith, with Longfellow himself as its symbol.[2]

1. Emerson's essay "The Poet" (1844) ; Bancroft's "Studies in German Literature," in *Literary and Historical Miscellanies* (New York, 1855) ; see Lowell's essay, "The Function of the Poet" (1855) .
2. William Charvat, *Literary Publishing in America* (Philadelphia, 1959) , 62–72. Longfellow's sales were phenomenal. His first collection, *Voices of the Night,* until absorbed into his *Collected Poems,* sold 40,000 copies. *Hiawatha's* advance sale was 4,000; it sold 11,000 the first month and 10,000 a year for the next ten years.

The poet, as the era saw him, had a specific, important position in society, and certain public obligations which derived from that position. While some elitist critics argued that poetry, like other arts, was really for "the favored few," the majority believed that to be effective the poet must speak to the many. It was "heart, not art," that made some poetry great.[3] The poet joined "the culture of art with the service of humanity," George Bancroft explained, combining art with moral direction. Since life involved a constant series of decisions, poets were conceived of as "guides" or "mentors" whose poems could help the reader to make them properly. James Russell Lowell, for example, reported in a letter to Longfellow his encounter with a shoe salesman in 1867, who told him:

I have a feeling of personal obligation to Mr. Longfellow. When I was in a state of deep personal depression, such as I have never experienced before or since, when everything looked dark and no chance of light, my daughter sat down by my bedside and read "Evangeline" to me, then just published. That gave me comfort, and sent light into my soul.

Readers also expected poets to celebrate and interpret public events of importance. Programs for special occasions—the laying of a cornerstone, the dedication of a monument, a college graduation, holidays like the Fourth of July and Washington's birthday—almost always included the reading of a poem. Famous poets like Longfellow, Bryant, Lowell, and Holmes contributed poems for such public events, but more often they were composed and presented by a member of the organization, the local schoolmaster, or a favorite newspaper versifier. After the occasion they were, as Holmes said, "something like the firework frames on the morning of July 5," but it was important to the nineteenth century that poetry be part of public life.

A great burst of poetic activity during the first half of the nineteenth century peopled the nation with bards. Poetry was the most

3. See, for example, the *Knickerbocker* reviewer, XLIX (1856), 22, versus the *United States Democratic Review*, XXVIII (1851); the *Knickerbocker* critic believed only "the favored few" could appreciate Shelley, while the other contrasted Shelley with Tennyson, who spoke for "all the people." The purpose of the poet is "to address and receive a response from the great majority of minds." See also the *Christian Examiner*'s review of Browning XLVIII (1850), 362; "The Taste for Poetry," *United States Democratic Review*, VI (September, 1839), 219-25; and A. P. Peabody, "The Intellectual Aspect of the Age," *North American Review*, LXIV (1847), 283-85.

widely practiced literary art between 1830 and 1870. Much of the poetry was lyric; poets tended to abandon the epic; dramatic verse was uncommon; formal poetry like the ode was reserved for special occasions. Lyric poetry, of course, suited best the Romantic's interest in nature, personal experience, and self-expression. Experimentation, freedom, openness was the order of the day; poets revived blank verse, experimented with the octosyllabic couplet, wrote sonnets again, imitated ballads, or did other things which pleased their fancy. Few poets specialized; Longfellow, for example, wrote everything from sonnets to drama, and during the course of his career worked in twelve different forms of verse.[4]

For all the American determination to be national, the poetry of the period was strikingly cosmopolitan. Wordsworth's preface to the *Lyrical Ballads* (1798) was the most important influence on American poets for the next half century, but they also knew Thomson, Akenside, Percy, and Ossian, and among the newer poets Coleridge, Scott, Byron, Shelley, and Keats. They learned about techniques and absorbed ideas from Goethe and the Germans, read Old Norse epics, Spanish drama, Oriental philosophy, and Neoplatonic criticism. And for all their determination to be original, American poets were quick to follow British fashions and emulate British favorites —Southey, Crabbe, Campbell, Leigh Hunt, Tom Moore, Mrs. Felicia Hemans, among others. Most imitated Scott and Byron; there were at least twenty imitations of *Lady of the Lake* and *Marmion*, while the Byronic pose was endemic among young American bards.[5]

The dominant figure in American verse over the first three decades of the nineteenth century was William Cullen Bryant,

4. Gay Allen, *American Prosody* (New York, 1935). For critical studies of the poetry of the period, see H. H. Clark, ed., *Major American Poets* (New York, 1936); Hyatt H. Waggoner, *American Poets from the Puritans to the Present* (Boston, 1968); and Roy H. Pearce, *The Continuity of American Poetry* (Princeton, 1961). Interesting and still useful is Edmund C. Stedman's *Poets of America* (Boston, 1885), chapter I, "Early and Recent Conditions," and chapter II, "The Growth of an American School."

5. James Fennell's *Hero of the Lake* (1813) put Commodore Perry into Scott-like metrics, while Joseph Hutton's *Field of Orleans* and Angus Umphraville's *Siege of Baltimore* were unblushing imitations of Scott's *Field of Waterloo*. John Neal cultivated Byron's style zealously, and so did R. H. Dana, E. C. Holland, James Gates Percival, and others. Fitz-Greene Halleck's *Fanny* (1819), based on *Don Juan*, was close to the original; even young Quaker Whittier affected the Byronic stance.

whose first collection was published in 1821 and his last in 1876. "Thanatopsis," "The Yellow Violet," and "To a Waterfowl," all of which appeared in his 1821 collection, established him at once as a major poet. "To the Fringed Gentian," "The Prairies," and "A Forest Hymn," published later, reaffirmed his reputation. On the one hand, Bryant's ability to find lessons in Nature (at his first reading of Wordsworth, he said, "A thousand springs seemed to gush up in my heart.") exemplified for his generation the Romantic's view of the world. On the other, he handled Romanticism's favorite theme of mutability and transience (learned from Blair, Collins, Young, and the British Graveyard School) with greater sensitivity than any of his contemporaries. His effectiveness rested in his ability to find meanings in Nature (always capitalized in his mind)—in a flower, a hurricane, the evening wind, and (most famous of all) the flight of a waterfowl across the sky. He believed firmly that poetry had didactic and public purposes, that it should have an active role in guiding people in the right path "by infusing a moral sentiment into natural objects, and bringing images of visible beauty and majesty to heighten the effect of moral sentiment."[6] Bryant's output was not large, but it reflected accurately the moods and attitudes of his times—the beauty and meaning of Nature, the hope of immortality, the quiet joys of contemplation, the Jacksonian era's faith in freedom and self-reliance. Although his style was superseded by more sophisticated poets by the fifties, his reputation remained.

In surveys of American literature made before 1840, Bryant and Irving almost always appeared as the nation's most eminent men of letters. In the forties and fifties supremacy passed to the New England circle—Emerson, Lowell, Whittier, Holmes, and especially Longfellow, the most famous American poet of all. Although no one ever displaced Longfellow in the public mind as the symbol of

6. See Tremaine McDowell's introduction to *Bryant* (New York, 1935) and Howard H. Peckham, *Gotham Yankee: A Biography of William Cullen Bryant* (New York, 1950). The interesting relationship between Bryant and others of the New York school and the painters of the period is traced in James T. Callow, *Kindred Spirits: Knickerbocker Writers and American Artists* (Chapel Hill, 1967). Bryant was also one of the nation's foremost newspaper editors, wrote essays and travelogues, and edited numerous popular anthologies. His *Library of Poetry and Song* (1871, 1876) was a standard home and library item, reissued over twenty times.

American poetry, James Russell Lowell's two-volume collection, which appeared in 1848, represented a second phase of prewar verse, a somewhat more intellectualized, formalized voice (except for his satires) which Lowell himself believed more representative of contemporary culture than either the public or critics realized. Whitman's *Leaves of Grass,* which burst upon the public in 1855, was greeted with praise and puzzlement; his "barbaric yawp" opened a third stage of nineteenth-century American verse and, in a sense, introduced the twentieth century as well.

Bryant's contemporaries, men such as Halleck, Joseph Rodman Drake, Nathaniel P. Willis, and James Gates Percival, were clearly not his equals.[7] Edgar Allan Poe, who clearly was, died in 1849 and never received sufficient attention from the critical journals to establish a major reputation.[8] His early verse (he was only eighteen when *Tamerlane* was published) reflected his enthusiastic reading of Byron, Shelley, Moore, and German theorists like A. W. Schlegel. He thought long and carefully about poetry, however, and evolved a poetic theory of his own which he hoped to embody in his verse. Poetry, Poe said, was "the Rhythmical Creation of Beauty," a "supernal beauty . . . the most intense, most elevating, and the most pure" of abstract pleasures, providing an effect of "intense and pure elevation of *soul,* not of intellect, or of heart. . . ." To create this effect, the poem must be brief, since intense emotion is transitory; and musical, since music is the most supernal and indefinite of the arts. It should also be (and here Poe severely limited himself) melancholy, for such is the legitimate mood of supernal beauty. But most certainly, poetry should have nothing to do with morality as such; he flatly rejected Longfellow and the whole New England school as practitioners of the "heresy of the Didactic."[9]

7. Other popular poets of the twenties and thirties were George Pope Morris, Richard Henry Dana, Charles Sprague, John Pierpont, Robert Sands, Charles Fenno Hoffman, Parke Godwin, J. G. C. Brainard, and two female poets, Lydia Sigourney and Maria G. Brooks.

8. *Tamerlane and Other Poems* (1827) attracted little attention. *Al Aaraaf, Tamerlane, and Other Poems* (1829), *Poems* (1831), and *The Raven and Other Poems* (1845) comprised Poe's collected output. For biographical and critical information see Arthur H. Quinn, *Edgar Allan Poe* (New York, 1941); Edward Wagenknecht, *Edgar Allan Poe* (New York, 1963); Edward Davidson, *Poe: A Critical Study* (Cambridge, 1957); and Vincent Buranelli, *Edgar Allan Poe* (New York, 1961). Robert Regan, ed., *Poe: A Collection of Critical Essays* (New York, 1967) is useful.

9. "The Poetic Principle" (1848) and "The Philosophy of Composition" (1846).

Much of what Poe said and wrote, of course, was simply Romanticism heightened and personalized—the pose of the lonely genius made of finer stuff; the interest in the dream and the occult; the Gothic emotionalism. His concept of poetry confined his talents to a relatively narrow range and set up ideal criteria which even he could only occasionally satisfy. Yet in a few poems, such as "El Dorado," or "Annabel Lee," or "The Sleepers," or "Ulalume," he reached his own standards, and even those in which he did not impressed a later generation. Meanwhile he served his era as its symbol of erratic, brilliant, isolated genius.

The presence in poetry of Henry Wadsworth Longfellow, whose first collection, *Voices of the Night,* came in 1839, overshadowed all others. No poet could have been more of New England—descended from John Alden and Priscilla Mullen; born in Maine, Bowdoin and Harvard educated—and his home at Craigie House (once Washington's headquarters) became a mecca for visitors from the world over. The most widely read poet in the United States during that century, he was the only one enshrined in Westminster Abbey, the only one whose birthday was celebrated by American schoolchildren as a national holiday, the only one whose face is still almost instantly recognized by millions of his countrymen.[10]

Believing that the poet's function was to guide, elevate, and cheer his society, Longfellow quietly accepted the responsibilities that his popularity brought. He took his role as poet seriously, producing verse when he sometimes had little to say—enough eventually to fill six volumes. To the American people he represented all that a poet should be—wise, lyrical, sensitive, understanding, a teacher and guide, an interpreter of common experience. And because Longfellow did his work well, "The Psalm of Life" ("Let us then be up and doing . . ."), "The Village Blacksmith," "The Old Clock on the Stair," "The Children's Hour," "Excelsior," "Paul Revere's Ride," "The Day Is Done," "The Wreck of the Hesperus," and a score of other poems became inseparable parts of the American poetic heritage, touchstones of the nation's cultural life.

10. For studies of Longfellow, see Edward Wagenknecht, *Longfellow: Portrait of a Humanist* (New York, 1965) ; Newton Arvin, *Longfellow: His Life and Work* (New York, 1963) ; and George Arms, *The Fields Were Green* (Stanford, 1953) , a study of the New England group.

The key to Longfellow's popularity was his consummate ability to draw meanings from common things—an hourglass, a fireplace, a snowstorm—and common experiences—the children's bedtime hour, the blacksmith at his forge. He had a genius for unwinding complexities; he could locate and express in artfully-done reflective verse all the homely, wholesome thoughts and feelings he shared with the great majority of men. "The secret of his immense favor," William Dean Howells wrote later, "will be found in the fact that he was so deeply, so entirely, of his time and place."

There was another Longfellow, however, the scholar who was Harvard Professor of Belles-Lettres and whose idols were Chaucer, Shakespeare, and Dante. He knew seventeen languages, wrote a sound history of Spanish literature, taught three generations of students, served his society as chief disseminator of cosmopolitan culture—and wrote highly skilled poetry for a sophisticated, discriminating audience. Beside "Hiawatha" must go "Michelangelo"; beside "Evangeline" must go "Christus" and "The Divine Tragedy." If "Excelsior" is a simplehearted verse, "The Belfry at Bruges," "The Tide Rises, The Tide Falls," and "Kéramos" are most certainly not. No poet of his time worked in a greater variety of forms with greater skill, for Longfellow was a master craftsman. His contributions to American prosody were so subtle and numerous as to be difficult to classify, but his influence on American poetry, in his search for form and his wide range of subject, was of major importance.[11]

John Greenleaf Whittier stood in sharp contrast to his New England contemporaries. He was a Quaker, not descended from Calvinist forebears, raised in rural Massachusetts by poor farm parents, self-educated, apprenticed to a shoemaker, a modest and retiring man who never considered himself a major poet and was content to be a minor one. He made his living as a journalist on small papers in troubled times—*The Essex Gazette, The Emancipator, The Antislavery Record, The Pennsylvania Freeman,* and a large one, *The National Era.* He was active in politics (the Liberty, Free-Soil, and Workingman's parties) and in the abolitionist movement as both editor and speaker. He was, he once said,

11. See Gay Allen, *op. cit.,* chapter VI, on Longfellow's prosody.

a "fighting Quaker," adding ruefully that he was "sometimes more fighter than Quaker."[12]

Whittier's early poetry, written in the thirties, was a blend of Ossian, Byron, Goldsmith, and the Graveyard School. Soon, however, the range of his interests broadened and he began to write more of the local color, regionalistic verse that made him famous— "The Barefoot Boy," "Telling the Bees," "Maud Muller," "Skipper Ireson's Ride," "Schooldays"—a strain that eventuated in *Snowbound* (1866), the finest regional poem of the times. He wrote literally hundreds of verses for the antislavery press, most of them earnest and mediocre, but when stirred by deep emotions, as in "Ichabod" and "Laus Deo!," his reform poetry had powerful impact. After the Civil War he returned to quieter, religious verse ("listening," he said, "to the whisper of an inward voice") such as "The Eternal Goodness" and "The Tent on the Beach."

Emerson's poetic output was not large; his poetry was another version of his essays, conveying the same messages of transcendental philosophy in different form. His famous "Brahma" (which says that God inhabits all creation) was simply an enigmatic, epigrammatic restatement of his essay on the Oversoul. The heart of Emerson's poetry lay in his transcendental view of knowledge, based on the doctrine of metaphor—that is, that the concrete symbolizes the abstract, the real exemplifies the ideal. To Emerson the interpretation of nature and experience was always poetic—both were symbolic of something that lay beyond and behind them. The influence of Coleridge, Wordsworth, and the Romantics permeated his thought, for, like them, he believed that poetry came by intuition, that the poet saw through the veil of matter and made the unseen visible in imagery and language.[13]

Because he conceived of poetry as organic and self-expressive, his poems tended to be free and individualized. He was perhaps incapable of writing a sonnet, since his muse could not be trapped within a form, and some of his better poems (such as "Days," "Bac-

12. There are at least three good studies of Whittier: John B. Pickard, *John Greenleaf Whittier* (New York, 1961); Lewis Leary, *John Greenleaf Whittier* (New York, 1961); and Edward Wagenknecht, *John Greenleaf Whittier: Portrait in Paradox* (New York, 1967).

13. In addition to his essay "The Poet" (1844), see also the "Language" section of *Nature* (1836) and the poem "Merlin" (1847).

chus," "The Snowstorm," "Give All to Love," and "Sea Shore") either partially or wholly abandoned rhyme. Emerson frequently used a rather loose blank verse (as in "Hamatreya") and occasionally what the age called an "ode," a relatively free-form verse. But whatever the form, the center of the poem was the image and the language.[14]

During the middle years of the nineteenth century female poets published in profusion—Frances S. Osgood, Elizabeth Kinney, Sarah Boyle, Anna Lewis, Sarah Helen Whitman—while the greatest of them, Emily Dickinson, wrote privately and unknown, sequestered in her Amherst home. Minor poets abounded, some with more than mediocre talents, others who had only the knack of striking the public fancy. Among the better ones were Richard Henry Stoddard, Thomas Parsons, George H. Boker the playwright, and Bayard Taylor. The best of the minor group, known even better for his essays, was Doctor Oliver Wendell Holmes of Boston, who published a volume of verse in 1836, others in 1862 and 1875, and two more in 1880 and 1887.

Holmes admired Pope, read Horace, and wrote witty, polished Augustan verse. A descendant of that group he named "the Brahmin caste of New England," his life centered on Boston. Except for a few "serious" poems (among them the famed "Chambered Nautilus") the bulk of his verse was "occasion" poetry, written for presentation at banquets, anniversaries, dedications, and public events. Much of it was quickly forgotten, but within his limited range Holmes was an excellent craftsman who could produce memorable lines. "The Last Leaf," "My Aunt," and "The Deacon's Masterpiece, or the Wonderful One-Hoss Shay," were known far and wide, and his metrical skill and incisive wit were often undervalued.[15]

14. Jean Gorely, "Emerson's Theory of Poetry," *Poetry Review*, XXII (July, 1931), 272–75; E. G. Sutliffe, "Emerson's Theory of Literary Expression," *University of Illinois Studies in Language and Literature*, VIII (Urbana, 1923); V. C. Hopkins, *Spires of Form: A Study of Emerson's Aesthetic Theory* (New York, 1951). The best biography is Ralph Leslie Rusk, *The Life of Ralph Waldo Emerson* (New York, 1949); studies of his thought are Stephen E. Whicher, *Freedom and Faith: An Inner Life of Ralph Waldo Emerson* (Philadelphia, 1953); and Sherman Paul, *Emerson's Angle of Vision* (Cambridge, 1952).

15. An excellent introduction and collection is S. I. Hayakawa and H. M. Jones, *Oliver Wendell Holmes* (New York, 1939), and the best biography is Eleanor Tilton, *Amiable Autocrat* (Boston, 1947).

James Russell Lowell's many-faceted career as editor, essayist, critic, scholar, and diplomat overshadowed his role as poet, though he began literary life as a poet and published two volumes of verse before 1850. He followed Longfellow in his Harvard professorship and, like Longfellow, believed the poet had civic as well as artistic functions.[16] But he was never, like Longfellow, a poet of the people, retaining always in his verse a formal, bookish quality. Except for his satires and critical pieces—as in *The Biglow Papers* and *A Fable for Critics*—he wrote either reflective, philosophical verse, or public, "occasion" poetry. In the first category belong poems such as "The Cathedral" and "The Vision of Sir Launfal," his reworking of Arthurian legend. Lowell's public verse may well have been his best. "The Present Crisis" (1845) was evoked by the Texas question; "Washers of the Shroud" (1861) came at the opening of the Civil War; in "Ode Recited at Harvard Commemoration" (1865), one of the finest poems to come from the war, he explored the meaning of the conflict and tried to fit it into the pattern of national experience. Most of Lowell's poetry was written between 1840 and 1870; from 1860 to 1890 his interests lay chiefly with prose and criticism. He felt, somewhat bitterly, that his poetry was not properly valued by his public and the critics, but in the decades dominated by Whitman's voice his verse seemed old-fashioned and academic.

Walt Whitman's *Leaves of Grass* (1855) irrevocably changed the course and tone of nineteenth-century poetry.[17] Although Emerson had called for a truly native, truly American poetry in "The American Scholar" and "The Poet," few critics were prepared for its dramatic appearance in *Leaves*. Emerson and others praised it and were puzzled by it; Whitman's prosody and his ideas seemed far too

16. The best critical introduction is that of H. H. Clark and Norman Foerster, eds., *James Russell Lowell* (New York, 1947). Biographical and critical studies are Leon Howard, *Victorian Knight Errant* (Berkeley, 1952), and Martin Duberman, *James Russell Lowell* (Boston, 1966). Lowell edited *The Atlantic Monthly* at its inception, was minister to Spain and England, and received honorary degrees at Oxford and Cambridge.

17. Gay W. Allen, *The Solitary Singer* (New York, rev. ed., 1967) is the best biography of Whitman. For studies of his verse, see James E. Miller, *A Critical Guide to Leaves of Grass* (Chicago, 1957) and Miller's *Walt Whitman* (1962); Roger Asselineau, *The Evolution of Walt Whitman* (Cambridge, 1960); Richard Chase, *Walt Whitman Reconsidered* (New York, 1955); and Howard Waskow, *Walt Whitman: Explorations in Form* (New York, 1966).

unrestrained and individualistic for contemporary tastes. Actually, Whitman's first thin volume contained the essence of his whole philosophy of life and art, and he continued to revise and supplement *Leaves* for the rest of his life.[18]

Whitman's art represented the culmination of American Romantic poetry. He read and reacted to Homer, Dante, Ossian, The Nibelungenlied, and Shakespeare; he was also the legatee of Scott, Rousseau, Wordsworth, and Emerson, of whom he recalled, "I was simmering, simmering, simmering, and Emerson brought me to a boil." In his celebration of subjective individualism, in his enthusiasm for direct, immediate experience; and in his open celebration of sensory and emotional experience, he summarized the literary trends of his era. He believed in progress, in science, in the common man, and he believed deeply in his country as the shape and hope of the future. Songs and rhymes of other lands and times, he felt, did not express the America of his day. Conceiving himself as the representative of all men, "the general human personality typified in myself," he called his major poem "Song of Myself," and made in it, he wrote, "an attempt to put a Person, a human being (myself in the latter half of the nineteenth century in America) freely on record." Thus he wrote, in an early version of the poem,

> I am your voice—It was tied in you—In me it began to talk.
> I celebrate myself to celebrate every man and woman alive.

To express this comprehensive, representative ego, Whitman believed it necessary to find new poetic forms. He did not want, he said, "old forms not fitted to a new age." Basing his theory of artistic creation on the organic principle, he allowed his poetry to shape itself. Perfect poems, he believed, grew like plants from natural laws and "bud from them as unerringly and loosely as lilacs or roses on a bush." "When Lilacs Last in the Dooryard Bloom'd," his elegy on Lincoln, and "Out of the Cradle Endlessly Rocking," among other Whitman poems, stand among the highest achievements of American verse. He used the line rather than the metrical foot as his thought-unit; he abandoned most of the formal rules of diction, using slang, adapted words, and neologisms. He took his imagery from all areas of experience (occasionally using frankly sexual references) and drew his metaphors from music, religion,

18. Editions appeared in 1856, 1860, 1867, 1871, 1876, 1881, and 1891–92.

politics, opera, labor, or wherever he found materials to fit his needs. Much of what he said about poetry was implicit in Wordsworth, Coleridge, and Emerson, but his distinctive "barbaric yawp" (as he called it) surprised and sometimes alienated his contemporaries. Nonetheless, Whitman's verse pointed the way in which American poetry went.

Nearly all serious music composed and played in the United States before 1820 was done by the foreign-born, and nearly all musical performers and teachers were either born or trained abroad, usually in England. Benjamin Carr and James Hewitt came from England in 1792, Carr to become a prominent teacher and publisher in Philadelphia and Baltimore, Hewitt to become organist at New York's Trinity Church. There were also other arrivals such as Raynor Taylor in Philadelphia, William Selby in Boston, Dutch Peter Van Hagen in Charleston, German Gottlieb Graupner in Boston, and Italian Lorenzo Da Ponte in New York. French and Italian artists came during the 1790s, coincident with the popularity of opera and ballad-opera. In the cities, where the foreign-born population was the largest, musical societies and academies sponsored dozens of public and private concerts—New York's Concordia Society, Euterpean Society, Sacred Music Society, and later its Philharmonic Society; Boston's Handel and Haydn Society, Academy of Music, and Philharmonic Society; Philadelphia's Musical Fund Society, "City Concerts," and so on.[19]

Though almost inundated by waves of European and British musical talent, a small stream of native American music nevertheless continued to flow. Francis Hopkinson of Philadelphia, a charming dilettante who could do many things well, directed a chamber music group, served as organist of Christ Church, and composed a number of songs and instrumental pieces. The first native American composer of any importance was probably William Billings (1746–

19. See John Tasker Howard and George K. Bellows, *A Short History of Music in America* (New York, 1957) chapter V; Gilbert Chase, *America's Music* (New York, 1966) chapter 8; and the early chapters of H. Wiley Hitchcock, *Music in the United States: A Historical Introduction* (Englewood Cliffs, 1969) for information on the music of the period. Da Ponte, banished from Italy, Austria, and England for "extreme profligacy," came to the United States in 1805, became professor of Italian Literature at Columbia College, and did much to introduce Italian concert and opera to New York.

1800) , a New England tanner who quit his vats to open a music shop in Boston. An unsophisticated, humorous, and self-taught musician, Billings published the first significant volume of music by an American, his *New England Psalm Singer* (1770) , and founded the oldest musical society in America at Stoughton, Massachusetts. Though his music was out of fashion soon after his death, it had an authentically native strength that made him, during his lifetime at least, an important figure in American music.[20]

American society exhibited, then, before 1830, a good deal of musical activity, including concerts, operatic productions, schools, and publishing, all of which required public support and a cultivated audience. New York, Boston, Philadelphia, and Baltimore were established musical centers; a study of New York newspapers in the 1830s, for example, revealed as many as seventy concerts in the city in a single year—ten of sacred music, ten instrumental recitals, fourteen vocal and instrumental concerts, and the rest ballad recitals.

As a nation without a distinctive musical tradition of its own, the United States was highly self-conscious about its lack of native composers and performers. American music, for obvious reasons, was dominated by Europeans and Englishmen, who had little awareness of, or interest in, native talent, and who simply transferred their own musical culture to American cities without appreciable change. The group that founded the New York Philharmonic Society in 1842, the first permanent American symphonic orchestra, had only one American-born member—Ureli Hill—and its first program presented Beethoven, Weber, Rossini, and Mozart, exactly as any European orchestra would have.[21]

Although the Philharmonic had a clause in its constitution requiring the performance of one American-composed work each season, it played only three pieces by Americans in its first eleven years. One of those was by George Frederick Bristow, who almost alone fought the European monopoly. The Philharmonic eventually performed four of his works; he also composed several oratorios

20. Raymond Morin, "William Billings, Pioneer in American Music," *New England Quarterly*, XIV (1941) , 25–34. See also J. Murray Barbour, "The Texts of Billings' Church Music," *Criticism*, I (1959) , 49–61.

21. The Philharmonic was a cooperative venture, in which the musicians paid the expenses and divided the profits. Still in existence, it is the third oldest symphonic orchestra in the world.

and his opera *Rip Van Winkle* (strongly reminiscent of Mendelssohn) played for four weeks in 1855.[22] However, the few American music critics there were often opposed such attempts at an "American" music. John Sullivan Dwight of Boston, who founded *The Journal of Music* in 1852—the only American periodical devoted to musical criticism—was a stern, serious critic who could not conceive of such a thing as "native" music. He inveighed against all such songs as Stephen Foster's, which, he said, were "whistled for lack of thought" and resembled "a morbid irritation of the skin."

During the forties and fifties, partly as a result of the European upheavals of those years, European musicians flocked to American cities, where audiences were eager to receive them and a good living could be made. Practically every American orchestra and choral society depended on European conductors, musicians, and teachers.[23] Each year touring artists flocked to the United States. Mr. and Mrs. Charles Edward Horn, British vocalists, toured the country from 1833 to 1839; so too did Anna and Arthur Seguin, London operatic singers, and a succession of Italian opera singers with names like Madame Albini, Signora Maroncelli, and Signor Rapetti. The Norwegian violinist Ole Bull found his first concert tour in 1843 so lucrative that he returned for four more over the next thirty years, playing more than a thousand concerts in the United States. Adelina Patti (who once toured with Bull), Henrietta Sontag, and Maria Malibran, all concert sopranos, were great successes, and so was Sigmund Thalberg, a pyrotechnical Viennese pianist. Louis Jullien (who possessed a magnificent moustache and conducted with a jeweled baton) brought a forty-eight-piece band from France to the United States in 1853, added a hundred American instrumentalists, and attracted tremendous crowds on tour. Louis Gottschalk, a New Orleans Creole pianist and composer who studied in Paris, returned to the United States after successful tours of Europe to give a series of concerts (eighty in New York City alone) in the mid-fifties and another in the early sixties. The sweetheart of the concert-going public, however, was "The Swedish

22. For accounts of these and other attempts at an "American" music, see Chase, *op. cit.*, 324–44; Paul Henry Lang, *One Hundred Years of Music in America* (New York, 1961), 25–35; and Irving Lowens, *Music and Musicians in Early America* (New York, 1964).

23. William Treat Upton, *The Art in America* (Boston, 1930); chapters III and IV cover orchestral music during these years.

Nightingale," Jenny Lind, who toured the country in 1850 under the auspices of P. T. Barnum, who paid her $150,000 for a single tour. A great artist and lovable person, she sang opera, lieder, ballads, and anything that pleased her adoring public, who would pay up to $225 a ticket for one of her performances.[24]

Though formal music in the United States was strongly European-oriented, the country also possessed a flourishing native tradition of sacred and popular music. The early colonists and later immigrants, of course, brought folksongs with them—from England, Ireland, Scotland, and Germany especially—and either retained them in fairly pure form or adapted them to American conditions. Of the three hundred so-called classic English folksongs, such as "Barbara Allen," "Lord Thomas," and "The Cruel Mother," probably the majority were still being sung in the nineteenth century; over a hundred of them, in fact, were collected in the twentieth. There were also work songs, native and imported. Lumbering was an important industry in New England by the mid-eighteenth century, and "shanty-boy" logging songs followed the camps westward. Sea chanteys (both words derived from the French *chanter*) were common to sailors of all nations. Except for work songs, which were sung collectively or in the traditional leader-response pattern, American ballad singing was usually solo, done in the plain British nasal style, accompanied, if at all, by a violin. The "fiddle" was as much a part of a pioneer's equipment as a rifle or an ax, and was usually the sole instrument for play-parties and country dances, which were made up of reels, jigs, minstrel tunes, and ballads, played in heavily rhythmic style.

Most of the folk music never got into the music books, but was transmitted instead from place to place and generation to generation by memory. There was much of it, for such music had a necessary function in an unsettled, immigrant, scattered society. It provided a way of maintaining stability and security, of keeping touch with one's ancestral roots; it also served to transmit moral precepts and social conventions; and it was also a way of summariz-

24. Carl Bode, *The Anatomy of American Popular Culture* (New York, 1959), 30–37; Howard and Bellows, *op. cit.*, 198–225; and Chase, *op. cit.*, 300–23. Gottschalk was equally popular in Central and South America, where he died on tour in 1869. Bull, who made over $400,000 on his first tour, returned in the fifties to found a communal society in Pennsylvania, which failed. He made tours again in 1869, 1873, and 1879.

ing social experiences in songs which told of "bad" girls, wild boys, wandering husbands and straying wives. Then too, this kind of music interpreted and reflected the new experiences of a new society—the railroad, the steamboat, the Indian, the emigrant trail, sea, forest, and plain.[25]

The most widely distributed American music in the eighteenth and nineteenth centuries was undoubtedly the hymn. Evangelical Protestantism made music an integral and central part of worship, both on the frontier and in the city. The religious revival was founded not only on the sermon but on the hymn, which provided a sense of group participation and a common fund of musical knowledge. Since people of every class and locality knew the same hymns and transmitted them from generation to generation, it is not surprising that poets such as Bryant, Emily Dickinson, and Longfellow used symbols and language derived from hymnody, as well as its metrics and metaphors. Many hymns came from England and Scotland (Americans knew Watts and Wesley by heart); many were composed by skilled hymn writers; and many were adapted from fiddle tunes, folk tunes, Scotch, Irish, and English "airs," as well as from popular ballads. Camp meetings roared with songs like "I Am Bound for the Promised Land," "Satan's Kingdom," and "The Old Ship of Zion," some of which were complex "dialogue" songs with intricate harmonies and interweavings of male and female voices. "Hymn meter" could be extremely complicated, with at least six major prosodic patterns and numerous variations. Writing lyrics for hymns required great skill and considerable linguistic sophistication; many hymnals had appendixes explaining the prosodic devices and illustrating the various meters.[26] There were at least fifty col-

25. Alan Lomax, *The Folk Songs of North America* (London, 1960) is an excellent collection with historical commentaries. See also W. T. Couch, ed., *Culture in the South* (Chapel Hill, 1935), A. P. Hudson, "Folk Songs of the South," 519–47.

26. See W. T. Marocco and Harold Gleason, *Music in America* (New York, 1964), 244–47 for a brief treatment. Some people were aware of the existence of Negro spirituals (many based on common hymn tunes) and of slave work songs, but were uncertain of where they belonged, if at all, in the musical tradition. Little attention was paid to them until after the Civil War, the first collection being *Slave Songs of the United States* (1867), by William F. Allen, Charles P. Ware, and Lucy McKim Garrison. In Couch, *op. cit.*, see Guy B. Johnson, "Negro Folk Songs," 547–70.

lections of hymns published between 1800 and 1850, not counting
the official hymnbooks of the churches themselves.[27]

Almost equally strong was a secular, popular ballad tradition,
drawn from both native and English sources, and well developed by
the close of the Revolution. Americans liked to sing, no less than
other people, and the "songster" or "miscellany," which included
patriotic and political songs, ballads, hymns, play songs, and comic
songs, was a fixture in many homes, with names like *The Musical
Cavacanet, The Virginia Warbler, The United States Songster,* and
The Missouri Songster (1808, which Lincoln remembered singing
from as a boy). Such collections proliferated from the 1790s well
into the nineteenth century, supplying the main source of American
popular music.[28]

The songbooks gave singable, simple songs to a wide public, songs
"well adapted to the family circle . . . tender, eloquent, and
chaste," as one editor said, suited to current tastes and every interest. There were sentimental "parlor songs" for family or individual
use—"Rosalie, the Prairie Flower," "Nobody's Darling," "Little
Nellie," "Amber Lee." There were songs about current events, like
Samuel Woodworth's lyrics for Jackson's campaign song of 1824,
"The Hunters of Kentucky," and James Hewitt's "Tammany
Quickstep" and "Lawrence the Brave." Woodworth, who wrote the
lyrics for "The Old Oaken Bucket," was one of the more successful
songwriters of the period. No American, however, approached the
popularity of Irish poet Tom Moore, who wrote lyrics for traditional Irish tunes. Moore's *Selections of Irish Melodies* (1807, 1813)
contained such favorites as "The Harp That Once Through Tara's
Halls," "Believe Me If All Those Endearing Young Charms," "Oft
in the Stilly Night," and "The Last Rose of Summer"; at least a
dozen of his songs sold steadily for the next twenty years. James

27. Edward S. Minde, *The Story of the American Hymn* (New York, 1921) remains an essential source of information. Timothy Dwight's collection of 1801
contained 263 hymns; other popular collections were Samuel Worcester's, Ashael
Nettleton's, Joshua Leavitt's, F. W. P. Greenwood's, and William Batchelder
Bradbury's.

28. Much of the singing was done by the "fasola" scale, which used four note
names repeated (fa, sol, la, fa, sol, la, mi) instead of the continental seven. These
were often printed as "shape notes," a system devised around 1800 as a method of
teaching harmony. By the forties the more sophisticated teachers had adopted the
continental system, though "shape note" singing remained popular for many years.

Hook wrote over two thousand ballad songs before his death in 1847, but the era's greatest hit was "Home, Sweet Home," written by John Howard Payne and Englishman Henry Bishop, introduced in the opera *Clari* in 1823. Not far behind in popularity was John Hill Hewitt's ballad "The Minstrel's Return from the Wars," published in 1827.

It was obvious in the 1830s that there was a large demand for popular music and that those who satisfied it stood to make substantial profits. For one thing, mass production of pianos and other instruments put music into the home in a new way. After James Chickering in 1823 developed a cast-iron piano frame and an improved method of stringing, other companies like Knabe, Stieff, and Steinway (originally Steinweg) entered the field. Violins and other instruments improved in quality and dropped in price; the melodeon, cheaper than a piano, cost less than a sewing machine. By 1860 there was a piano in the United States for every 1,500 people, while the industry produced 22,000 new ones each year. People now not only made music by singing, but took lessons and made their own music at their leisure.

The first composer to take full advantage of this great popular market was Lowell Mason, a musically-inclined banker whose hymnbook, published in 1822, returned him at least $60,000 profit. Mason became choirmaster of the Reverend Lyman Beecher's Boston church in 1827 and helped to found the music school of the Boston Academy of Music. He mostly wrote hymns, but they were good songs, four of them among the most popular of all time— "Nearer My God to Thee," "From Greenland's Icy Mountains," "Blest Be the Tie That Binds," and "Work, for the Night Is Coming." His collections illustrated his shrewd sense of the public's preference in music and his desire to improve it; he put together old and new hymn tunes, popular ballads, and melodies from Handel, Mozart, Palestrina, and Weber, along with familiar camp-meeting rousers and psalms.[29] William "Singing Billy" Walker's *Southern Harmony and Musical Companion* (1835), similar to Mason's collections, sold 600,000 copies over thirty years; Isaac Woodbury's *Dulcimer* collection sold 125,000 in two years.

29. Chase, *op. cit.*, 151–61, has a good estimate of Mason's musical importance. He established the first program for training music teachers and in 1840 helped to found the National Music Convention. The uniquely American "music appreciation course" was his invention.

Mason's and Walker's songbooks, however, though their audience was not exclusively religious, did not fully exploit the musical market. Henry Russell, an English concert baritone who arrived in the United States in the 1830s, immediately perceived the potential of the popular concert. Russell had a hand in more than eight hundred songs, which he promoted by singing them himself on tour. Working with good lyricists (especially George Pope Morris), he wrote direct, melodic songs, using a minimum of notes in a limited range, dealing with fundamental emotions and popular tastes—"Life on the Ocean Wave," "Woodman, Spare That Tree," "The Old Armchair" (the first "mother song" hit), "The Old Family Clock," "Baby Mine," and others which, he said, "made music the vehicle of grand thoughts and noble sentiments" precisely as his audiences desired. Others mined the vein that Russell uncovered— J. P. Knight with "Rocked in the Cradle of the Deep"; Thomas Bayley with "Long, Long Ago"; Frederick Crouch with "Kathleen Mauvourneen"—filling the songbooks with ballads to be sung around the parlor melodeon, in concert by touring tenors, by young ladies at singing schools, and in the minstrel shows.

Another medium for selling popular songs was the "singing family," in which everybody from grandfather to grandchild made up a chorus which toured as a unit, like the "singing Hutchinsons" of New Hampshire (Jesse Hutchinson, his eleven sons and two daughters), the Bakers, the Barbers, the Cheneys, the Blakeleys, and the Housers, among others. Such troupes were common in Europe; in fact, the successful tour of the Rainer family from the Austrian Tyrol in 1839–42 gave Americans the idea.[30] There were at least fifty such troupes on tour by the fifties, not all families, with names like The Harmoneans, the Alleghenians, and Father Kemp's Old Folks.

What they sang were hymns, comic songs, sentimental ballads and "story songs," which, like popular poetry and novels, dealt with home and family, love requited and unrequited, death and melancholy, hope and sorrow, designed for an audience quite different from that which bought the collections by Walker and Mason. Audiences heard them from the singing groups and then learned to play and sing them from hundreds of songbooks, designed specifically for the home, which appeared in the forties and fifties—*The*

30. Howard and Bellows, *op. cit.*, 173–76.

*Parlor Companion, The Forget-Me-Not Songster, The Great West-
ern Songster and Jovial Companion. The Universal Songster's* title
page illustrated their usual content, being

A General Collection of Comic, Negro, Sentimental, Patriotic, Military,
Naval, English, Irish, Scotch, and American Songs and Ballads; for All
Tastes and Occasions. Consisting of the Mirthful, Humorous, and Laugh-
Provoking; The Eccentric and Exquisite Ethiopian; Delicate and Beautiful
Love Songs; National and Heroic Lyrics—Hunting Songs and Sea Songs,
Duets, Glees, and Chordses. Including Several Hundred of the Most Ex-
quisite Songs, Choicest Melodies, and Divinest Harmonies of the World's
Minstrelsy.

Minstrel shows, the most popular form of musical entertainment
during the middle years of the nineteenth century, provided another vehicle for the performance of popular music. Not all minstrel
tunes (and fewer as time passed) were so-called darky songs,
although originally they formed the core of the show. Actually,
Negro-type songs such as "The Dinner Horn," "I Must Go to
Richmond," and "Way Down in Cairo" were only partly Negro-
based; Dan Emmett's great ballads and walk-arounds, "Old Dan
Tucker," "Blue Tail Fly," and "Walk Along John," were not really
Negro songs at all. Emmett, the most prolific composer and adapter,
wrote the most famous of them, "Dixie's Land," in 1859 for Bryant's
Minstrels. Minstrel shows drew songs from anywhere, using Irish
jigs, Scotch airs, parodies, humor songs, "girl" songs ("Baltimore
Belle," "Melinda May," "Angela Baker"), and many, many senti-
mental ballads like "Go to Jane Glover and Tell Her I Love Her,"
"Nora McShane," and "The Midshipman's Farewell."

The basis of the American popular ballad was the hymn tune,
out of the hymnbook and the long, powerful American churchly
tradition. Quite different from its European counterpart, the American ballad style can be clearly heard through all nineteenth-
century popular music—the thirty-two-bar hymn pattern, built of
harmonically related eight-bar phrases divided into introduction,
verse, and refrain.[31] On this model songwriters evolved a stand-

---

31. In common with most Western music, the ballad used the AABA song form,
that is, a musical statement, followed by its repetition with variation, followed by
a "release" or "bridge" forming a transition to a statement or conclusion. This
form can be easily discerned in such songs as "Swanee River" and "Old Uncle
Ned," since Stephen Foster did the popular ballad extremely well.

ardized tune pattern that was easy for an untrained voice to sing (within an octave range), easy to play (using the four principal chords and most familiar positions), and easy to remember.

The best-known American composer of the early ballad era was Stephen Collins Foster. Born in 1826 near Pittsburgh, Foster studied music, played guitar and flageolet (a kind of flute) with more than average skill, and published his first ballad, "Open Thy Lattice, Love," at sixteen. Since minstrel shows paid good money for songs, he began writing for them in the mid-forties, though he was more interested in music of a more genteel kind. When "Old Uncle Ned" was a great hit, and so was "Oh Susannah!," Foster found himself a success in what he called "the Ethiopian field." Though minstrel songs continued to stream from his pen, he received little for them and often allowed others (including minstrel leader E. P. Christy) to publish them under their own names.

Foster wrote nearly four hundred songs, including comic songs, "mother" songs, sentimental ballads, war songs, temperance songs, and (after he succumbed to alcoholism in the sixties) anything else that would bring him a few dollars. His best work came in the fifties. The great minstrel songs—"My Old Kentucky Home," "Old Black Joe," "Massa's in de Cold, Cold Ground" (his only dialect song), "Camptown Races"—were known everywhere. "Old Folks at Home" (or "Swanee River"), introduced by Christy's Minstrels in 1852, was such a hit that its publishers ran two presses around the clock for several days to satisfy the demand for sheet music. The majority of his songs, however, belonged in the sentimental ballad tradition and his best ones were almost as popular as his minstrel show tunes: the delicate "Jeannie with the Light Brown Hair," "Come Where My Love Lies Dreaming," "Beautiful Dreamer," "Gentle Annie," "Nelly Bly," "Our Bright Summer Days Have Gone."[32]

Foster's songs struck a responsive chord in the popular mind. Musically, he wrote a clean melodic line with simple harmonies— the tonic, dominant, sub-dominant pattern of the hymn and ballad—with interesting though uncomplicated variations. Beyond his really great talent for melody, Foster's effectiveness lay in the close

32. The best biography of Foster is by John Howard Tasker, *America's Troubadour* (New York, 1962).

integration of his lyrics with his music and in their content, which dealt with the verities of home, love, peace, security, and nostalgia.

There were other popular ballad writers, some nearly as good as Foster and most of them more financially successful.[33] Publishers recognized certain salable categories, usually classified as love, family, reform or moral ("The Drunkard's Child," "A Pack of Cards," "All That Glitters Is Not Gold"), religious, comedy ("Where Was Moses When the Lights Went Out?"), minstrel-type "darky," specialty (railroad, sports, etc.), tragedy ("A Faded Rosebud in Our Bible"), and topical. Writers and publishers joined in a business arrangement in which writers tried to locate public preferences and write for them, while publishers attempted to anticipate the market and supply it.

The most successful songwriter of the midcentury years was George Frederick Root, whose "Rosalie, the Prairie Flower" (1855) alone earned him royalties of $3,000. Henry Clay Work, who did "Father, Dear Father, Come Home With Me Now," the best-known of all temperance songs, and "Grandfather's Clock" (still a barbershop favorite), had an expert way with melancholy narrative ballads—"The Lost Letter," "The Mystic Veil," "Phantom Footsteps," "The Ship That Never Returned." Will S. Hayes wrote three hundred songs which sold 20 million copies; he published at least one 50,000 seller per year for twenty years, with names like "Write Me a Letter Home," "We Parted at the Riverside," and "Nobody's Darling."[34]

Oratory in the first half of the nineteenth century was recognized not only as a significant art, but one vitally important to a democratic society. The art of public address, wrote the editor of the *United States Literary Gazette* in 1826, "occupies a distinguished place among the departments of our literature, and contributes greatly to form the taste, guide the opinions, and increase the

33. For further information on the popular song, see Russel B. Nye, *The Unembarrassed Muse* (New York, 1970) chapters 13–15, from which this material is adapted.

34. The era was a golden one for songwriters. John Hill Hewitt wrote and sold over two hundred ballads. Others who hit the market right were Septimus Winner, "Listen to the Mocking Bird" (1855); Benjamin Russell, "My Darling Nelly Gray" (1856); George Johnson, "When You and I Were Young, Maggie" (1866); George Allen, "Bury Me Not on the Lone Prairie" (1850); Henry Tucker, "Sweet Genevieve" (1869).

information of our people." Oratory was considered kin to literature, the orator cousin to the poet. Although it was conceded that oratory must be heard to be fully effective (a handicap not placed on writers) it was also agreed that if arts of speech and literature were distinct they were not unequal, and that great orations had qualities which placed them among the masterpieces of art long after the voices that spoke them were silent.[35]

The nineteenth century was an oral age, accustomed to discussion and debate as a way of expressing its ideas and making its society work. Tocqueville noted that a love of talk seemed ingrained in Americans, that speeches were treated as forms of public entertainment—"An American cannot converse," he wrote, "but he can discuss. . . . He speaks to you as if he were addressing a society." The age abounded in talk—in court, legislature, and pulpit; at public meetings and private clubs; in schools, societies, and organizations. Since schoolchildren learned orations and declamations and spoke them on "elocution days," famous speeches were part of the cultural equipment of all literate Americans. Addresses like Henry Clay's "Evils of War," Edward Everett's "The Intelligence of the People," Daniel Webster's "Liberty and Union," and Robert Winthrop's "Bunker Hill Monument" were included among hundreds of others in dozens of school readers.[36]

People walked or rode miles to hear a famous lawyer plead a case, a well-known politician speak on campaign, or a famous minister preach a sermon. Daniel Webster's speech at the Bunker Hill Monument and his speech to the jury in the White murder case made him a national figure; Rufus Choate's defense summary in *Dalton v. Dalton* (1857), involving adultery and abortion, was a sensation of the times. Court days in rural communities served as showcases for forensic skills; members of state legislatures and of

35. *The United States Literary Gazette*, IV (September, 1826), 421–2. Oratory, wrote a critic in 1829, "is the combination of all arts and excels them all in their separate powers. It is not only the highest perfection of a human being (for an 'orator' must be a *good* man) but it is that perfection in act. It is sublimity, beauty, genius, power in their most glorious exercise." "Principles of Elocution," *North American Review*, XXIX (July, 1829), 38–67.

36. See, for example, C. W. and J. C. Sanders, *Sanders' School Reader, Fifth Book* (Chicago, 1848), J. W. Webb, *Normal Reader Number 5* (New York, 1856); and J. M. Watson, *Independent Reader* (New York, 1871). Such books had several chapters on rhetoric and the rules of elocution, with a hundred to two hundred selections for study and delivery.

Congress were ranked by newspapers and spectators in order of their talents. A visitor to a state capital or to Congress expected to hear polished, dignified oratory and usually did.[37] Important speeches by important men meant packed galleries and a dozen reporters. Henry Clay's Senate speech on the Compromise of 1850 took two days before overflowing crowds and sold 80,000 copies in pamphlet form within a week.

Political nominations and campaigns could be won or lost, of course, by oratorical skills; the Lincoln-Douglas debates of 1858 were examples of an oratorical art that had a century of develop- ment behind it. Funerals, holidays, picnics, and celebrations called out waves of oratory. Every hamlet had its Fourth of July cere- monies, while the death of a famous man elicited orations by the score. (The deaths of Jefferson and Adams, in July, 1826, brought forth almost a hundred.) Banquets were built about toasts and speeches, and so were town meetings on public issues like slavery, fugitive slaves, the Mexican War, secession, taxes.[38]

A speech of any kind, whether from pulpit or platform, was a public exhibition of a known and respected art. Audiences watched for, listened to, and evaluated such things as diction, allusions, modulations of voice, gestures, pauses, the uses of emphasis, and the organization of the whole—from introduction to peroration— wherein a speaker showed his mettle. Public addresses of all kinds were often reprinted for sale as pamphlets or extracted in the news- papers. Major speeches were regularly reviewed in the journals, equally with novels, poetry, and sermons, while collections of orations by famous speakers like Edward Everett were assigned to the better critics.[39]

37. One visitor, for example, jotted in his notebook that Clay was "warm, vehement, and headlong in his eloquence." William Pinkney was "lofty, expres- sive, elegant," and Lowndes of North Carolina "neither showy nor graceful, but his mildness and candour win the confidence." Quoted in William N. Brigance, ed., *A History and Criticism of American Public Address* (two volumes, New York, 1943) chapter I. A useful brief summary of oratory in the period is that of Allan Nevins, *Ordeal of the Union* (New York, 1947), I:83-6.

38. Banquet toasts followed specific rules and were judged by the speaker's skill and aptness. The St. Louis Guards' Dinner in 1820 had twenty-three toasts before the main speech; a Cincinnati businessmen's dinner in 1843 had seven- teen speeches spaced over six hours.

39. For example, see George Bancroft's review of Everett's orations, *New-York Review*, I (October, 1825), 333-41. *The American Quarterly Review, The North American Review, The Christian Examiner, The New England Magazine, The*

To a church-going society, the sermon naturally ranked high as a literary form. American critics took great pride in comparing America's preachers with England's; collections of sermons were reviewed in the major magazines; colleges and seminaries had Professors of Sacred Rhetoric; congregations, especially in the urban, nonevangelistic churches, demanded a high degree of sophistication and skill from their ministers. The Reverend Chandler Robbins, who replaced Emerson after his resignation from the pulpit in 1832, summed it up by saying that to the dedicated minister sermon-writing was[40]

an art, one of the highest arts. . . . Let him feel that it demands the exertion of all his highest faculties; that it affords scope for all his genius, all his knowledge, all his taste; for the play of imagination; for the expression of the most delicate shades of sentiment; for the exhibition of the utmost artistical skill.

The era's respect for oratory as a branch of literature and learning derived from the classical tradition, from British oratorical practices, and from the American's consciousness of the importance of public address in a democratically-conceived government. Speakers and audiences alike considered public speaking as a way of providing the public with information and considered it a medium of communication as effective as—or even more effective than—newspapers, magazines, and books. "I look upon the lecture room," Emerson said, "as the true church of today."

"Rhetoric" was defined as the art of speaking and "oratory" as the practice of that art. The aim of public speaking, in the classical definition, was persuasion, to be attained by "logical, pathetic, or

---

Democratic Review and other such journals usually reviewed a half-dozen or so in each issue. For examples, see "Eulogies on Jefferson and Adams," *American Quarterly Review*, I (March, 1827), 54–77; "Henry Clay as an Orator," *New England Magazine*, II (January, 1844), 105–13; or "Wharton's Discourse" and "Goddard's Address," *North American Review*, XCIV (November, 1837), 66–86. A good summary of nineteenth-century oratorical practice is Brigance, *op. cit.*, 55–111.

40. Quoted by Lawrence Buell, "The Unitarian Movement and the Art of Preaching in Nineteenth-Century America," *American Quarterly*, XXIV (May, 1972), 169. Two excellent contemporary articles are those by the Reverend George Shepard of Bangor Theological Seminary, "The Effective Preacher—Characteristics and Culture," *American Biblical Repository*, I (April, 1839), 346–56; and John G. Palfrey's "Pulpit Eloquence," *North American Review*, X (January, 1820), 204–17.

ethical appeal," and by "such disposition of materials, style, and presentation as would be conducive to moving the listener."[41] The principles according to which discourses were composed were held to be *invention* (the discovery of proper ideas), *disposition* (their arrangement), and *elocution* (the style in which they were expressed). The rules of rhetoric were drawn from the "three great masters, Aristotle, Cicero, and Quintilian," as reinterpreted for modern use by British rhetoricians like Blair, Campbell, Lawson, Priestley, Ward, and Whateley, whose books were familiar in American schools in the eighteenth century.[42]

During the latter decades of the eighteenth century, however, rebelling against the rigidity of classical theory, a group of so-called elocutionary rhetoricians developed sharp differences with the older school. Blair and his ilk, they believed, paid far too little attention to the manner of public address and far too much to the matter. Public speaking was akin to dramatic and musical art; manner, gesture, vocal cultivation, pronunciation, and even melody were as important as content. "Elocution" meant, said Thomas Sheridan, "the just and graceful management of the voice, countenance, and gesture in speaking. In voice, articulation, pronunciation, accent, emphasis, tones or notes, pauses or stops, key or pitch, and management of the voice."[43] The "elocutionary" school caught on quickly in the United States; there were twenty-five rhetoric texts of the type in circulation in England and America by 1810. Not only did

41. See Stephen Chambers and G. P. Mohrmann, "Rhetoric in Some American Periodicals 1815-50," *Speech Monographs,* XXXVII (June, 1970), 111-21, for oratorical theory.

42. John Quincy Adams's Boylston Lectures at Harvard, published as *Lectures Upon Rhetoric and Oratory* (Boston, 1810), remain the best single source of contemporary classically oriented rhetorical theory. Adams leaned heavily on Hugh Blair's *Lectures on Rhetoric and Belles-Lettres* (1783). Other influential books were John Lawson's *Lectures Concerning Oratory* (1752), John Ward's *System of Oratory* (1759), George Campbell's *Philosophy of Oratory* (1776), and Joseph Priestley's *Course of Lectures on Oratory and Criticism* (1777). An excellent study of British rhetorical theory is William P. Sandford, *English Theories of Public Address 1530-1828* (Columbus, 1931).

43. Thomas Sheridan, *Discourse Being Introductory to a Course of Lectures on Elocution and the English Language* (1763), a book widely reprinted in the United States. John Walker produced six books on elocutionary rhetoric; his *Elements of Elocution* (1781) listed sixteen rules governing pauses, thirty-one for voice inflection, and forty-two types of gestures. Gilbert Austin, *Chironomia* (1806), explained a system of charting bodily and facial movements and printed a hundred plates illustrating gestures.

the more popular British books sell exceptionally well to the American public, but nine American texts on the same pattern appeared between 1785 and 1827.[44] Oratory became a standard course in schools and colleges. Researches in voice, gesture, and oral effectiveness made elocution an exact art, something to be learned out of a book like William Russell's *The American Elocutionist* (1840), with rules and regulations by which a performance could be accurately judged.

The two great changes in rhetorical theory and oratorical practice which came as a result of the elocutionary emphasis were, first, that the oration became personalized expression instead of an exercise governed by fixed rules; and second, that it became an emotional and intellectual collaboration between speaker and audience. In the first instance, the new school of orators insisted that the classicist's concern for structure and arrangement, to use the words of a critic, placed "constraints on genius, fetters which confine and limit the free action of the soaring powers of the intellect." Instead of allowing the rules to inhibit "originality and vigor of thought and expression," speakers should, by involving themselves deeply in their materials, make each oration a separate, personal statement. "No man can be truly eloquent," said another, "who does not himself feel deeply." From this principle the elocutionary school conceived the speaker-listener relationship as a deep psychological rapport, for the great orator was one capable of "unlocking the heart" of the listener to release the "emotions and passions" held within. The power of true eloquence lay in establishing a relationship with an audience so strong and personal that it elicited "half-ejaculated expressions of delight and sympathy . . . raising men from their seats."[45]

44. Sandford, *op. cit.*, 169–83. Americans who published texts were Noah Webster, Joseph Dana, Caleb Bingham, Thomas Burch, Jonathan Barker, Samuel Newman, Ebenezer Porter, John H. Dwyer, and James Rush. Rush, who taught voice, and his followers dominated the teaching of oratory and debating in American colleges until late in the nineteenth century. His *Philosophy of the Human Voice* (Philadelphia, 1827) marked off thirty-seven separate vocal qualities and taught the student to produce them. See also Ota Thomas, "The Teaching of Rhetoric in the United States During the Classical Period of Education," in Brigance, *op. cit.*, I:193–213.

45. Quoted from "Eloquence and Eloquent Men," *New England Magazine*, II (February, 1832), 93–100; Henry Colman, "On Eloquence," *Ibid.*, II (April, 1832), 374–80; "Professor Newman's Remarks on Rhetoric," *Ibid.*, I (July, 1831), 83; the Reverend Daniel Dana, "Thoughts on Eloquence," *New Hampshire Repository*, I

In the context of Romanticism, great oratory thus joined speaker and audience in emotional union. The image of the great orator, in Romantic terms, was that of a man who, himself in a transported state of emotion, transmitted it to his hearer without diminution of effect. When the speaker himself, wrote William Cullen Bryant in *Lectures on Poetry* (1826), "is so affected with the feelings he would communicate that he becomes inspired," then the listener is similarly so affected that "he is chained in involuntary and breathless attention." Audiences waited for and analyzed this psychological sense of identification. Thus George Ticknor said that when he heard Daniel Webster in a particularly moving passage, "three or four times I thought my temples would burst with a gush of blood"; Clay, it was said, could utter the words "The days that are passed and gone" with "such melancholy beauty that no man heard him without a tear." Daniel Webster often served as the model for oratorical language at its best, the most frequently cited examples being the closing paragraphs of his reply to Hayne, or of his oration on the Plymouth Pilgrims, the latter much admired for its figurative blending of past, present, and future time:[46]

Advance, then, ye future generations! We hail you, as you rise in long succession, to fill the places which we now fill, and to taste the blessings of existence, where we are passing and soon shall have passed our own human duration. We bid you welcome to this pleasant land of the fathers. We bid you welcome to the healthful skies and the verdant fields of New-England. We greet your accession to the great inheritance which we have enjoyed. We welcome you to the blessings of good government and religious liberty. We welcome you to the treasures of science, and the delights of learning. We welcome you to the transcendent sweets of domestic life, to the happiness of kindred, and parents, and children. We welcome you to the

(July, 1846), 28–34, and II (October, 1846), 85–92; Edward G. Parker, *The Golden Age of American Oratory* (Boston, 1857), 5–6, 18–20. The five most important factors in oratorical eloquence, wrote Colman, were voice, gesture, language, sentiment, and passion, in contrast to what the elocutionary school considered classical rhetoric's overemphasis on invention and disposition.

46. "Eloquence and Eloquent Men," 96; Colman, *op. cit.*, 377–79; "Eulogies on Jefferson and Adams," 76. Textbooks such as Sanders, Webb, and Watson, *op. cit.*, are the best sources of information on elocutionary rhetoric of the period. Watson, for example, had seven chapters on voice training alone: Emphasis, Inflection, Modulation, Personization, Expression, Articulation, and the Uses of the Pause and Slur.

immeasurable blessings of rational existence, the immortal hope of Christianity, and the light of everlasting truth!

The "Great Triumvirate" of American political oratory, by virtually unanimous agreement, was Henry Clay, John C. Calhoun, and Daniel Webster. Clay was acknowledged to be the most persuasive man in the Senate, gaining his points by "the force of his magnetic personality." He was "forcible . . . using emphatic tones and gestures," yet "natural, never uncontrolled, with no appearance of acting." With Calhoun, remarked a critic, "rigidity of logic . . . took the place of brilliant oratory and personal charm." His speeches were marked by their "blunt earnestness of expression, and keen analytical powers of mind." Webster, called by some "the godlike Daniel," was usually granted first eminence by reason of "his overwhelming personality . . . , his perfect style . . . , simplicity and grandeur of expression." Webster delivered the Fourth of July Address at Dartmouth College when he was eighteen, and never until his death was he long absent from the public platform. He trained himself rigorously in the four classic categories of eloquence—memory, action, diction, and style—and attained fame in courtroom forensics, legislative debate, campaign oratory, and public address. E. P. Whipple called his style "perfect of its kind, being in words the express image of his mind and character—plain, terse, clear, and forcible; rising to the level of lucid statement and argument into passages of superlative eloquence."[47]

Edward Everett, who was essentially a literary man, was generally chosen as the finest combination of the older classical and newer elocutionary schools, and the nation's most eminent orator for public occasions. From his first public appearance as a young man when he gave Harvard's Phi Beta Kappa address (with Lafayette in the audience) to his death in 1865, he was constantly on the platform and known the country over for his eloquence. Everett considered each speech a work of art, to be evaluated by standards of logic, taste, unity, coherence, appropriateness, and "sublimity." His

47. For estimates of these and other orators of the time see Brigance, *op. cit.;* Parker, *op. cit.;* Warren Choate Shaw, *History of American Oratory* (Indianapolis, 1928) ; Robert T. Oliver, *History of Public Speaking in the United States* (Boston, 1965) , and Lorenzo Sears, *A History of Oratory* (Boston, 1895) . Examples of their oratorical art usually chosen were Calhoun's speech on the Force Bill (1833) ; Clay's speech on the Greek Revolution (1824) ; and Webster's reply to Hayne (1830) and his Bunker Hill Monument Speech (1825) .

skill was undoubtedly genuine, for even the most learned and sophisticated responded to his oratory; critics constantly spoke of "the symmetry, finish, and harmony of his discourse" and the "elegant, poetic nature" of his style.[48]

As Everett was noted for his literary eloquence, so Rufus Choate, of Boston, "the wizard of the courtroom" who spent thirty-five years in them, was acknowledged as first among lawyers. Choate served in the Senate, where he was praised for speeches on the tariff, the Texas question, and the Oregon boundary, and he was also in demand as a lyceum lecturer. But it was as a trial lawyer that he was best known; he handled juries, one of his opponents ruefully said, like a snake charmed birds. A superb legal scholar and an expert at cross-examination, Choate won his cases by meticulous preparation and a profound grasp of jury psychology. Although he was never concerned, as Daniel Webster was, with important constitutional cases, many lawyers thought him superior to Webster in the courtroom.[49]

Among ministers, there was little doubt of Henry Ward Beecher's oratorical eminence. Beecher, who made his reputation in the West, was called in 1847 to Brooklyn's new Plymouth Congregational Church, which held three thousand and never had an empty seat during his thirty-year tenure as pastor. Beecher had a mellifluous voice, an intense manner, and a strong, commanding presence; he spoke with what was described as "locomotive energy, charged with vivacity and fire." Among reformers, Theodore Parker and Wendell Phillips were considered to be especially effective. Phillips spoke in colloquial style, carrying his points, observers said, through "utter sincerity and irresistible logic"—his idea of oratory, he once said,

48. A good contemporary estimate is that of George Bancroft, in *The New-York Review*, I (October, 1825) , 333–341. Everett's appearance was guaranteed to draw crowds; in New York in 1856 over two thousand people were turned away from the Academy of Music on one evening alone. Everett had the misfortune, however, to be the other speaker at Gettysburg on November 19, 1863.

49. Oliver, *op. cit.*, 407–14; Parker, *op. cit.*, chapter IV. In the Tirrell case, Choate won acquittal for a man accused of murdering his mistress on the claim of somnambulism; in the Gillespie case he won the verdict from an all-Protestant jury for a Roman Catholic priest accused of statutory rape. There were those who thought that Sergeant Prentiss of Mississippi, the most famous trial lawyer in the South, was perhaps Choate's equal. Prentiss impressed all of New England when he shared the platform with Edward Everett at the Fourth of July dinner given in honor of Daniel Webster in Boston, 1838.

1. Celebration of the opening of the Erie Canal, The Battery, New York City, November 4, 1825

(The Museum of the City of New York)

2. "Sleighing in New York," a lithograph by Thomas Benecke, about 1855

(Library of Congress)

Der Staat „Michigan", Vereinigte Staaten von Nord-Amerika.

Endesunterzeichneter, von seiner Regierung angestellter Emigratio[ns] Commissär für Europa, ertheilt unentgeltlich Auskunft über obigen S[taat]. Auch übersendet derselbe Jedem auf Verlangen portofrei eine Broschüre [über] den Staat mit Special-Karte, sowie Probenummern des von ihm herau[s]gebenen „Michigan Wegweiser". Man adressire:

M. H. Allardt, Hamburg.

3. "Come-to-America" advertising for immigrants, 1840s

(Michigan State Historical Archives)

4. Crossing the Alleghanies, the first locomotive across the pass, about 1840

(Library of Congress)

5. Lockport, New York, on the Erie Canal, the gateway to the West, from a contemporary engraving

(Library of Congress)

6. Pioneer farm family and home, Michigan, 1850s

(Courtesy Clarke Historical Library, Central Michigan University)

7. Early Methodist circuit preacher on his rounds. Engraving from *Harper's Weekly*, 1867

8. Transportation in the backcountry. The Kalamazoo Stage Line in rural Michigan, 1850s

(Grand Rapids Public Library)

9. "Fur Traders Descending the Missouri." Painting by George Caleb Bingham

(The Metropolitan Museum of Art, Morris K. Jesup Fund, 1933)

10. "Laramie's Fort," one of forty-one watercolors done by Alfred Miller on William Stewart's expedition to the West, 1837

(Walters Art Gallery, Baltimore)

11. Shopenagon, chief of the Ottawas, with wife and child

(Michigan State Historical Archives)

12. Sioux boy, Little Crow's son, take prisoner by General Sibley's expeditio Fort Snelling, 1863

(Michigan State Historical Archives)

13. "Blackfoot on Horseback," 1840. Aquatint after Karl Bodmer

(Northern Natural Gas Company Collection, Joslyn Art Museum, Omaha, Nebraska)

14. "Rounding a Bend," Currier and Ives lithograph, 1866. The lead sidewheeler is the famous *Queen of the West.*

(Library of Congress)

15. "The Oxbow" (of the Connecticut River near Northampton), 1836. Painting by Thomas Cole

(The Metropolitan Museum of Art, Gift of Mrs. Russell Sage, 1908)

STOCKHOLDERS
OF THE UNDERGROUND
R. R. COMPANY
Hold on to Your Stock!!

The market has an upward tendency. By the express train which arrived this morning at 3 o'clock, fifteen thousand dollars worth of human merchandise, consisting of twenty-nine able-bodied men and women, fresh and sound, from the Carolina and Kentucky plantations, have arrived safe at the depot on the other side, where all our sympathising colonization friends may have an opportunity of expressing their sympathy by bringing forward donations of ploughs, &c., farming utensils, pick axes and hoes, and not old clothes; as these emigrants all can till the soil. N. B.—Stockholders don't forget the meeting to-day at 2 o'clock at the ferry on the Canada side. All persons desiring to take stock in this prosperous company, be sure to be on hand. By Order of the

Detroit, April 19, 1853. **BOARD OF DIRECTORS.**

16. Notice of meeting, Underground Railroad sympathizers, 1853

(Michigan State Historical Archives)

17. The escape of Henry "Box" Brown, shipped from Richmond to Philadelphia by the Adams Express Company on a 26-hour trip

(The Huntington Library, San Marino, California)

18. "A Slave Auction at the South," from a sketch by Theodore Davis, 1861

(Library of Congress)

19. Slave family of five generations, photographed at the J. J. Smith plantation, Beaufort, S.C., 1862, by Timothy O'Sullivan

(Library of Congress)

20. Work in the cotton fields

(Brown Brothers)

21. Stephen Collins Foster

(Foster Hall Collection, University of Pittsburgh)

22. Frederick Douglass, about 1850

24. Walt Whitman

(U.S. Signal Corps photo, Brady Collection, National Archives)

23. Daniel Webster

(Culver Pictures, Inc.)

25. "Kindred Spirits": Thomas Cole and William Cullen Bryant in the Catskills by Asher Durand

26. "Signing the Pledge," a temperance society lithograph of 1846

(Library of Congress)

27. Lampooning the feminist movement, a contemporary cartoonist's view of the Women's Rights convention of 1859

(Library of Congress)

28. Joseph Henry's electromagnet engine, 1837, the first type of electric motor

(Princeton University Library Archives)

29. The meeting of the Atlantic Cable, completed in 1858: an "electric current" joining all nations "in a spirit of love and justice"

(Library of Congress)

THE LAYING OF THE CABLE---JOHN AND JONATHAN JOINING HANDS.

30. The opera at Niblo's theater, New York, in 1855

(Library of Congress)

31. "Lyceum Lecture" by James P. Espy, Clinton Hall, New York, 1841

(The Museum of the City of New York)

32. "The Return of Rip Van Winkle," from *Scenes from Irving*. Painting by John Quidor

(National Gallery of Art, Andrew W. Mellon Collection)

33. "The Greek Slave," 1843, by Hiram Powers

(In the collection of the Corcoran Gallery of Art; Gift of William Wilson Corcoran)

34. "Indian Chief," figure for Senate pediment by Thomas Crawford

(Courtesy of The New-York Historical Society, New York City)

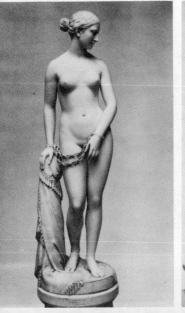

35. The "plantation Greek" style in the antebellum South: Belle Grove, Louisiana

(Library of Congress, F. B. Johnston photo)

36. Smith House, Grand Rapids, Michigan, 1853. Built on Orson Fowler's octagon plan, early cement block construction

(Grand Rapids Public Library)

was "animated conversation." Parker was more the student of classical rhetoric and a highly-trained thespian; his sermons drew as
many as three thousand, and he gave as many as a hundred additional lectures yearly.[50]

The forties and fifties, however, and the controversy over slavery,
secession, and states' rights, brought a new generation of speakers to
the fore, men such as Charles Sumner, Stephen A. Douglas (called
"the great persuader"), Ohio's Thomas Corwin, Abraham Lincoln,
Southerners like William Yancey and Robert Barnwell Rhett.
Yancey was no firebrand, despite his reputation, but rather "all
directness, all earnestness . . . unsparing logic." Most observers
remarked on Sumner's "fervor, vigor, and polish," while his diction
was deliberately high-style, classical, and allusive. Conscious of
gestures, he used his hands, Longfellow said, "like a cannoneer
ramming down cartridges." Classically trained as Everett was, Sumner was, like him, an essentially literary orator. Douglas, who often
spoke from a few notes, was a superb judge of his audience and,
according to observers, resembled more than anything else a good
lawyer pleading a case. Lincoln, who spoke in a high-pitched nasal
voice that was audible at a great distance, had studied elocution
books and was an expert trial lawyer. He used few gestures, apparently adopted few platform tricks, and spoke in a steady, deliberate,
conversational tone; listeners remarked on his deliberateness, clarity, and low-keyed style. His Second Inaugural, wrote one listener,
contained "no effort at oratorical display, no endeavour to be impressive, not the slightest mannerism of any kind whatsoever."

During the fifties it was evident that the elocutionary style was
passing, that the grandiloquence of Webster and the courtroom
rhetoric of Choate no longer impressed audiences of greater sophistication and literacy. The oratorical style of the twenties and
thirties was not a suitable vehicle for the arguments of the forties
and after; the "golden age," wrote Edward Parker, in compiling
The Golden Age of American Oratory in 1857, was already past.
The spread of newspapers, books, magazines, and the new medium
of communication, the telegraph, made the printed page a substi-

50. Parker, *op. cit.*, chapter III, treats Beecher. He spoke on a wide variety of
topics (his speeches filled twenty volumes) but was particularly famous for his
lecture on Robert Burns and his Fort Sumter speech of 1865. For Phillips and
Parker, see Brigance, *op. cit.*, I:740–857; and Oliver, *op. cit.*, 143–9, 155–80, 234–
8, *passim*.

tute for the spoken word. As Parker pointed out, people could read speeches more conveniently than hear them; how a man's thoughts looked in print became as important, or more so, than how they sounded in the lecture hall or the legislative chamber. Although the elocutionary style continued for another half century (reappearing noticeably in William Jennings Bryan) the change from old to new was made abundantly clear at Gettysburg when Lincoln and Everett shared the platform in 1863.

After the American Revolution playwrights and theater managers struggled to establish an American theater, but the going was difficult. However, the growth of an urban society, with the sophistication and the money needed to support the theater, was encouraging, and by the second decade of the nineteenth century the American stage showed signs of strength and independence. By the forties, the stage had developed popular support in all kinds of American communities and attracted audiences who were quite knowledgeable about repertory, acting styles, and actors.[51]

Traveling companies carried plays inland, down the Ohio and Mississippi and into the remote hamlets of the hinterland; amateur "Thespian" and "Aeolian" societies appeared in colleges and cities. As evidence of the growing popularity of the stage there was a boom in theater building—New York's Chatham Gardens, Park, Lafayette, and the popular Bowery; Philadelphia's New Chestnut Street, Walnut, Arch Street; Boston's Tremont, Federal Street, and Adelphi; Chicago's Rialto opened in 1837. In the fifties New York had at least ten major theaters, Philadelphia four, and Boston five. Theaters sprang up in smaller cities such as Buffalo, Louisville, Rochester, Cincinnati, and Pittsburgh, and in Southern towns from Baltimore to Savannah to New Orleans. A regular circuit developed for acting companies; touring groups in the forties and fifties might begin in New York, play Philadelphia, Baltimore, Washington, Alexandria, Charleston, Savannah, and Columbus, and swing back

51. Sources of American theatrical history are Glen Hughes, *A History of the American Theater* (New York, 1951); Oral Coad and Edwin Mims, Jr., *The American Stage* (New Haven, 1929); and Arthur H. Quinn, *The History of the American Drama from the Beginnings to the Civil War* (rev. ed., New York, 1943). T. Alton Brown, *History of the American Stage* (New York, 1870) is a mine of information on American actors, companies, and plays.

via New Orleans, Mobile, St. Louis, Cincinnati, Pittsburgh, Buffalo, and Albany.

The new buildings reflected changes in both the size and the character of audiences. They were much larger than before—the second Park Theater in New York held 2,500, with a pit, three rows of boxes, and a huge gallery; the Bowery, built not long after, held 3,500; the Broadway, constructed in the forties, held 4,000. Theater prices came down at the same time. The Park, which charged $2 for a box in 1800, now advertised a seventy-five-cent top, whereas others held to a fifty-cent top, twelve-and-a-half cents for the gallery. Producers appealed not to the elite or the select; although first-rate plays and actors drew large crowds, the emphasis was clearly on mass entertainment.

Still, few actors, managers, companies, or producers could be called prosperous. Actors were so poorly paid that managers were sometimes forced to hold "third nights" and "farewell tours" to augment the star's pay. Fees for playwrights were equally small; $500 for an original play was unusual, $100 for an adaptation generous. The plays themselves were often written in a matter of days, poorly rehearsed, badly acted; on the other hand, actors, stagehands, and producers developed considerable skill and many plays were well-produced and well-played.

One of the most difficult problems faced by the theater manager was that he had to try to please everybody; as a result, his theater might play Shakespeare one night, farce the next, and an equestrian-acrobatic troupe the next. (Edwin Booth once played *Richelieu* as half of a double bill with a rowdy farce called *The Double-Bedded Room*.) Serious plays had to have "afterpieces," a practice carried over from the eighteenth century, either after the play or between the acts, which entertained the crowd with pantomimists, trained animals, dancers, singers, and the like. The fact was that American society now possessed a large, affluent middle class which wanted its own kind of theater, neither Shakespeare on the one hand nor jugglers on the other, something that would entertain as well as reflect its tastes and values.

As a result, the nineteenth-century American stage developed two distinct theatrical traditions—an upper- and upper-middle-class "serious" theater; and a "popular" theater aimed at middle and

lower social and economic groups. In New York the Bowery Theater, the Peoples', the Windsor, the Third Avenue, the National,
the London—charging ten-, twenty-, and thirty-cent admissions,
"the People's own prices"—catered to the popular taste. Chicago
had a whole block of such theaters, and so did Philadelphia, St.
Louis, San Francisco, and other cities. An observer wrote in the
forties, "Opera (*comic opera*) and burlesque, the melodrama and
ballet, have literally swallowed up legitimate drama." So it may
have seemed, but such was not the case. What happened was that
the formal theater of Shakespeare and Sheridan, of classic opera and
symphony, continued to draw the same audiences who applauded
Forrest and Booth and Sir Henry Irving, while the other, popular
audience wanted and received something else—spectacles, dioramas,
comedies, and "living tableaux."

Although there were a great many plays written by American
playwrights (seven hundred in the period 1800–1860) few of them
could lay claim to literary distinction, nor did they attempt to
compete with the much more sophisticated British and European
theater. Some American plays were written as artistic productions,
of course, but the popular theater was meant to entertain and instruct, to deal with relevant issues and contemporary life. The
nineteenth-century stage, therefore, was used by Americans to explore their society, its past and present, its people and problems. It
followed the public taste and showed audiences what they wanted
to see in terms they could understand. It was not a drama of change
or protest (with a few notable exceptions, like *Uncle Tom's Cabin*)
but one which, a reviewer remarked, "must make the heart beat
responsively . . . and strike the chords of humanity . . . which
join all people as one."

The theatrical situation was clearly illustrated by the popularity
of Shakespeare and older plays. Shakespeare was tremendously
popular (in Philadelphia sixty-five performances in 1835 alone) but
his plays were either produced as vehicles for a popular star—like
Edwin Booth's Lear or Forrest's Macbeth—or treated as blood-and-
thunder spectacles, which accounted for frequent appearances of
Richard III, Othello, Julius Caesar, and *The Merchant of Venice.*
Actors tested themselves against these and other roles like Sir Giles
Overreach in Massinger's *A New Way to Pay Old Debts,* or Barabas

in Marlowe's *The Jew of Malta*.[52] Sheridan was popular, and so was Goldsmith; the Restoration wits were considered too strong for American audiences. Meanwhile, of course, adaptations of popular novels by Scott (six), Cooper, Bird, Bulwer-Lytton, the Brontës, and others filled the playbills. Since the majority of the plays were written to draw the largest possible audience for the longest possible time, playwrights searched for those kinds of materials which had the widest appeal.

The rapid growth of cities during the early nineteenth century provided large potential theater audiences and a demand for actors and plays that would satisfy it. James Nelson Barker, whose first success was *Tears and Smiles* (1807), a comedy of manners with music, found a new formula in *The Indian Princess, or La Belle Sauvage* (1808), the first of a long line of variations on the Pocahontas-John Smith-John Rolfe story. Barker's *Marmion* (1812), dealing with the Scottish border wars, was popular because of its anti-British sentiments. John Howard Payne, who began acting at fifteen, went to England, where he wrote or adapted sixty plays for American and British productions. Payne excelled at plays about persons of noble lineage and mysterious past, involved in a plot which included forged letters, birthmarks, false marriages, and fated love, such as *Mrs. Smith, or Wife and Widow* (1823) and *Thérèse, the Orphan of Geneva* (1821). Nathaniel P. Willis, better known as a Knickerbocker poet and essayist, wrote two romantic tragedies, *Bianca Visconti* (1837) and *Tortesa the Usurer* (1839), the latter a play based on the Romeo-Juliet theme and highly praised.[53]

Robert Montgomery Bird, a successful novelist, wrote fifty-four plays, among them *The Gladiator* (1831), a blank-verse tragedy featuring Edwin Forrest, who played the role over a thousand times. Based on the life of Spartacus, the slave who led a rebellion against Rome, the play was "as full of abolitionism as an egg of meat," Walt Whitman thought. Robert Conrad's *Jack Cade* (1835), deal-

---

52. David Grimsted, *Melodrama Unveiled: American Theater and Culture 1800–1850* (Chicago, 1968); Esther Dunn, *Shakespeare in America* (New York, 1939).

53. Quinn, *op. cit.*, chapters VI and VII. See also Paul H. Musser, *James Nelson Barker* (Philadelphia, 1929).

ing with peasant insurrections in fifteenth-century England, was another Forrest favorite. The most literary of the period's playwrights was no doubt George Henry Boker, who edited *Lippincott's Magazine* and wrote distinguished poetry. His romantic tragedies *Calaynos* (1849) and *Leonor de Guzman* (1853) concerned the Moorish wars in Spain; *Francesca Da Rimini* (1855), a blank-verse tragedy based on an episode in Dante's *Inferno,* was generally conceded by critics to be the best of its kind during the era.[54]

American theater managers tended to depend chiefly on British actors after the theaters opened following the War of 1812, since they knew that they attracted larger crowds. Edmund Kean, Charles Mathews, William Macready, Charles Keane, and Charles Kemble and his daughter Frances Anne, or "Fanny," were well known to American audiences. Some of these imported actors stayed—among them Junius Brutus Booth, Henry Wallack, George Barrett, Frances Weymss, and also John Brougham, who was also an expert playwright.

American actors learned their craft either in Britain or by working with visiting British actors and actresses. By the close of the eighteenth century the English theater had developed three rather distinct acting styles. The "classical" actor tended to follow rather closely the interpretation of the play as set by the author, striving for an accurate, effective imitation of the character. During the later eighteenth century, actors like Garrick and Macklin introduced what became known as the "romantic" style, based on the principle that actors must feel the emotions portrayed and live within the characters they acted. The actor, they assumed, was himself a creative artist, free to develop his own concept of his role. Brought to a high degree of skill by Edmund Kean and Junius Brutus Booth, the style led to exaggerated movement and passionate vocal interpretations. At the same time, another school emphasized the declamatory aspects of the actor's craft, in the belief that the theater was a rhetorical and oral art. Actors of course often combined elements of more than one style, but the "romantic" style was favored by the

54. For examples of and comments on many of these plays, see Richard Moody, *Dramas from the American Theater 1726–1909* (Cleveland, 1966). Clement Foust, *The Life and Works of Robert Montgomery Bird* (New York, 1919), remains a good source. Richard Moody's *America Takes the Stage* (Bloomington, 1955) is the best study of romantic drama during these years.

best English actors who appeared on American stages. American audiences learned to distinguish the various styles and to appreciate the actor's skill in using and adapting them.

Edwin Forrest, who was strongly influenced by Edmund Kean, was the best-known and most admired American actor of the middle decades. After his first great role as Othello in 1826, Forrest became the standard against which American actors were measured. A stocky, muscular man, he specialized in strong roles—Metamora, Brutus, Jack Cade, Coriolanus, Lear—and dominated American acting for thirty years. According to an observer,[55]

His acting was saturated with realism. . . . He could at all times be seen, heard, and understood; he struck with a sledge hammer. . . . In scenes of fury he panted, snorted, and snarled like a wild beast. In death scenes his gasps and gurgles were protracted and painfully literal. The bellows that he emitted almost made the theater walls tremble.

Edwin Booth, son of Junius Brutus Booth, was a graceful, slender man who stressed grace, control, and an intellectual approach to a role; critics called him a "poetic" actor, in contrast to Forrest. The pre-Civil War stage was filled with other excellent actors, among them Edward Davenport, James Murdoch, James Hackett, James Wallack, Joseph Jefferson, Henry Placide, Lawrence Barrett, and Charles Burke. American actresses, too, learned from Mrs. Siddons, Fanny Kemble, and their British cousins. Mary Ann Duff, who came from England in 1810, spent twenty-five years on the American stage and became known as "the American Mrs. Siddons" A beautiful woman, trained in classical ballet, she acted with Kean and Booth and gained the respect of both.

Charlotte Cushman, who played her first major role at nineteen in 1835, the year Mrs. Duff retired, dominated her roles as Forrest did his. A handsome woman with a magnetic personality and a striking, husky voice, she was best known for her tragic roles. Anna Mowatt, who starred in her own play, *Fashion* (1845), was an expert comedienne. Laura Keene, whom Wallack brought from England in 1852, replaced Charlotte Cushman as the reigning actress of the fifties and sixties. A woman of delicate charm and classic

---

55. Quoted in Margaret Mayorga, *A Short History of American Drama* (New York, 1932), 94.

acting style, she starred as Lady Teazle, Beatrice, Portia, and Rosalind.[56]

Playwrights soon discovered that certain plots attracted audiences more effectively than others. Practically every event of the Revolutionary War from the Tea Party to the Constitutional Convention was dramatized; André's capture, Arnold's treason, Marion's raids, and Washington's battles were favorite topics. William Dunlap's successful *Glory of Columbia* (1803) set the pattern, with cannon shots, martial music, marching armies, and patriotic declamations. There were at least thirty plays about the Revolution between 1820 and 1860. The naval war with the Barbary pirates produced eight plays, the War of 1812 a dozen or more, including Mordecai Noah's highly successful play about a girl masquerading in the army, *She Would Be a Soldier* (1819). The Mexican War furnished materials for a few more, while the Civil War went on the stage less than a month after First Bull Run.

Historical plays were naturally popular. Bird's *Gladiator* had much to say to an era already divided by the slavery controversy (ironically, Nat Turner's slave rebellion occurred in Virginia while Bird was writing the play), and so did David Brown's *Sertorius, the Roman Patriot* (1830), starring the elder Booth. Indian plays were especially durable. Major Robert Rogers's story of the fate of *Chief Ponteach* (1766, but not produced) introduced the "doomed savage" theme which early nineteenth-century playwrights repeated and amplified endlessly. Barker's revival in 1808 of the star-cross'd love of dusky maiden and English hero introduced another popular plot. Over fifty Indian plays, built about either or both plots, appeared over the next thirty years, among them George Washington Custis's *The Indian Prophecy* (1827) and *Pocahontas* (1830), Robert Dale Owen's *Pocahontas* (1838), starring Charlotte Cushman, and Charlotte Conner's *The Forest Princess* (1848). The greatest success was John Augustus Stone's play about King Philip's War, *Metamora, or the Last of the Wampanoags*, produced in 1829 with Edwin Forrest; it was still on the stage fifty years later, and evoked at least a dozen imitations.

The "half-horse, half-alligator" frontiersman, another native

56. A comprehensive study of acting is Garff B. Wilson, *A History of American Acting* (Bloomington, 1966).

product, appeared first in James K. Paulding's *The Lion of the West* (1831) as Colonel Nimrod Wildfire, a part written for actor James Hackett. Widely copied, the character of the rough, hearty Kentuckian, dressed in buckskin, appeared in many other plays. The "stage Yankee," or shrewd homespun Down Easter, created by Royall Tyler in *The Contrast* (1787), had a multitude of descendants. "Yankee plays," as they were called, were standard theatrical fare for another fifty years. Samuel Woodworth's Jonathan Ploughboy in *The Forest Rose* (1825) was a favorite vehicle for actors, while other "Yankees" named Solomon Swop, Jedidiah Homebred, and Solon Shingle vied for popularity. Irving's Rip Van Winkle, transformed into a stage Yankee, appeared first in 1829, played by Hackett, and again in 1833 and 1850. Joseph Jefferson, who played the role continuously for thirty-eight years, presented his version first in 1859.[57]

The cities, where the bulk of the theater audiences lived, attracted the attention of playwrights who, like their counterparts in London and Paris, recognized the dramatic possibilities of urban society. There was a play called *Life in New York* in 1829, and one could see *Life in Philadelphia* in 1833. *The New York Merchant and His Clerks, Fifteen Years in a Fireman's Life,* and other city plays appeared in the fifties. The era's greatest success in this genre was Benjamin Baker's *A Glance at New York* (1848), a potpourri of materials centered on the character of Mose the Bowery Boy, an Irish volunteer fireman played by Frank Chanfrau with a plug hat, red shirt, turned-up trouser bottoms, and plastered-down hair like a Bowery dude. Mose was such a hit that he soon had a series of plays to himself, such as *Mose in a Muss, Mose in China, Mose's Visit to Philadelphia,* and many more, mostly played by Chanfrau, the Bowery's favorite actor.[58]

57. George Handel Hill played so many such parts that he was known as Yankee Hill. Other well-known Yankee plays were Hackett's *Jonathan in England* (1829); C. A. Logan's *Yankee Land* (1834) and *The Vermont Wool Dealer* (1839); Joseph Jones's *Green Mountain Boy* (1833); and John A. Stone's *Knight of the Golden Fleece* (1834). There were also plays about Sy Saco, Industrious Doolittle, Sam Patch, and Curtis Chunk. Yankee specialists included actors Dan Marble, Joshua Silsbee, Henry Placide, and Hackett; Francis Hodge, *Yankee Theater: The Image of America on the Stage* (Austin, 1964).

58. For an excellent study, see Richard M. Dorson, "Mose the Farflung and Worldwide," *American Literature,* XV (1943–44), 288–300.

The popularity of Mose, impressive as it was, was less important than the fact that Baker and the Bowery plays opened a whole new vein of popular dramatic interest—the humor, joys, sorrows, people, manners, and society of urban America. Other plays quickly appeared, emphasizing not Mose but cross-sections of city life; among them *New York as It Is, The Mysteries and Miseries of New York, Philadelphia as It Is, Life in Brooklyn,* and others. Dion Boucicault, who based his play *The Poor of New York* (1857) on a current French success, took a realistic look at the world of Mose and produced a different and more meaningful play.[59] He peopled his stage with rowdy comics, virtuous heroines, and heroic heroes, but he also presented real people—policemen, seamen, bankers, street boys, shopgirls, clerks. Like the skillful writer that he was, Boucicault gave the audience rattling drama, sentimental love, and plenty of stage business. He also gave them a reflection of their own lives.

Social satire was a strong strain in American drama from its beginnings. Royall Tyler's contrast of true-blue American and Anglophile fop, in *The Contrast* (1787), stated a theme that never lost its appeal for American audiences. Satires of fashionable, pseudo-aristocratic society appealed to the American national spirit and to Jacksonian equalitarianism. James Hackett's masterful portraits of "high society" in *A Trip to the Springs* (1831) and *Scenes at the Fair* (1833) were repeated in dozens of plays and sketches which contrasted the pretensions of the upper class with the sound democracy of the common man. Anna Ogden Mowatt's *Fashion* (1845) became the classic of the type. Mrs. Mowatt took the old plot of the socially ambitious newly-rich woman, Mrs. Tiffany, and turned it into a clever study of social types, including the bogus French count, the worthless rich boy, the effeminate poet, the upstart clerk, and the honest American named Adam Trueman. *Fashion* inspired other satires, one of the most successful being British playwright Tom Taylor's *Our American Cousin* (1858) in which E. H. Sothern starred as Lord Dundreary, the comic monocled Englishman. Novels, of course, by Simms, Cooper, Kennedy, Charles Hoffman,

59. Boucicault, already successful as a playwright in England, came to the United States in 1853 and immediately began writing, directing, and acting. He collaborated with Jefferson on the final version of *Rip Van Winkle* (1865) adapted Dickens to the stage, translated and adapted French plays, and produced a series of Irish plays.

T. S. Fay, and others were quickly dramatized to capitalize on their popularity, and so were numbers of English and French novels.

Reformers were well aware of the power of the drama to instruct, and the nineteenth century had many messages to deliver. William Henry Smith's *The Drunkard, or the Fallen Saved,* which opened in 1844 (the first play in American theatrical history to run a hundred consecutive performances), combined sermon and stage with tremendous effectiveness. Smith's play, billed as "a moral lecture" and endorsed by every temperance society in the country, drew audiences that would never have entered a theater under any other circumstances. Though overwritten and poorly constructed, *The Drunkard* came across the footlights with undeniable power; the delirium-tremens scene, played hundreds of times separately as an actor's tour de force, was nearly as famous as Hamlet's soliloquies. Other playwrights imitated it—Timothy Shay Arthur's dramatized novel *Ten Nights in a Barroom; One Glass More; The Drunkard's Warning,* and so on.

But no play of the century equaled the impact of *Uncle Tom's Cabin.* After Mrs. Stowe's novel, which appeared in 1852, sold 300,000 copies within a year, it was of course inevitable that it would be adapted to the stage.[60] Two such adaptations, one in Baltimore and one in New York, appeared immediately without much success. In September, however, a version by a young actor named George Aiken began a phenomenal run in Troy, New York. The company then moved to New York City in 1853 for a run of two hundred consecutive days, toward the close presenting the play eighteen times a week, with the actors eating in costume between shows. Five other versions ran simultaneously in New York (one produced by P. T. Barnum himself) and others sprang up in other cities; it has been calculated that the play was staged an average of four times a week for the next seventy-five years.

Uncle Tom's Cabin exerted tremendous influence on the public

60. Henry Birdoff, *The World's Greatest Hit* (New York, 1947), is a study of the various "Uncle Tom" versions, companies, and actors. See also Moody, Quinn, and Hughes. Due to her publisher's failure to secure dramatic rights to the novel, Mrs. Stowe never received any royalties from the stage versions. By the late eighties there were at least four hundred "Tom companies" on the road. New characters were introduced and specialties added, such as steamboat races, jubilee singers, comic skits, panoramas, equestrian acts, or anything else which might draw a crowd.

concept of the pre-War South and the institution of slavery. The stage versions of the novel (which were responsible for many incorrect ideas about what the book said) presented to the nation the most widely disseminated and accepted picture of the slave-holding South. But from the theatrical point of view, the play, like *The Drunkard*, brought a new audience into the theater. Because the play was considered, its producers said, "a moral, religious, and instructive play," written by a lady of impeccably Christian views, respectable people could come to see it by the millions. These people, drawn from the middle class, provided a huge new kind of audience for the theater for the rest of the nineteenth century.

Melodrama, which dominated the popular theater from the middle to the close of the nineteenth century, was not a native form.[61] The Elizabethan "tragedies of blood" and the sensational English, French, and German Gothic plays (which inundated the American stage in the 1790s and early 1800s) popularized a new, full-blown dramatic type, free from rigid dramatic laws of cause and effect, characterized by coincidence and accident, intensified sentiment, and exaggerated emotionalism. Melodrama was especially well adapted to American audiences for its ability to present moral messages in easily-understood form while emotionally involving the audience, as *Uncle Tom's Cabin* and *The Drunkard* showed could be effectively done.

Techniques of melodramatic production were well-known in America when William Dunlap presented his adaptation of the German playwright Kotzebue's *The Stranger* in 1803. Within a few years American playwrights and producers developed their own melodramatic style, using native materials, in such plays as *Captain Kyd, or the Witch of Hell Gate; The Black Hound, or the Hawks of Hawk Hollow;* and Bird's *Nick of the Woods, or the Jibbenainosay,* whose closing scene featured twelve bloody corpses.

Melodrama was, despite its emotional excesses and its propensity to violence, fundamentally moral drama. In it virtue was rewarded, vice punished, justice done, evil defeated. The basic plot situation of the melodrama showed that faith and love—the essential elements of a Christian life—provided the right guides for moral action, encouraged a democratic society, and created happy homes,

61. The best study of melodrama is Grimsted, *op. cit.*

and triumphed over sin and wrong. Whether or not the world of melodrama accurately reflected the world in which the audience lived did not matter; what did matter was that it reflected their ideal of what the real world ought to be.

It would be difficult to identify the first American melodrama, but certainly the ubiquitous Dion Boucicault deserves to be recognized as a pioneer in the form. His *The Poor of New York* established much of the classic melodramatic pattern—a sensational plot, a dangerous villain, a brave hero, virtue rewarded, and evil foiled, all set in a familiar, semirealistic framework. His greatest success, *The Octoroon* (1859), which he adapted from a novel by Mayne Reid, *The Quadroon* (1856), combined the sentimental theme of tragic love (in this case between a white man and a free mulatto girl, a redoing of the Pocahontas story) with all the necessary melodramatic elements—a knife duel, a chase, a steamboat explosion, a slave auction, and two killings.

After Boucicault, other skillful playwrights took up the form, which reached its greatest popularity during the latter half of the century. But by this time the American stage had reached a much more sophisticated and mature level of development. The old days, when managers put on an extra night for poorly-paid actors, churchgoing people avoided the theater, and writing for the stage was regarded as a minor and unrewarding activity, were already gone. For the popular audience, a play like *Uncle Tom's Cabin* or *The Octoroon* represented one strong and flourishing strain of the American drama; for the elite, Boker's *Francesca da Rimini* represented the other.

CHAPTER 5

Painters, Builders, and Stonecutters

AMERICANS wanted, after the Revolution, a culture of their own, an original, authentically American art. Exhortations echoed through the journals of the early years of the nineteenth century, predicting the day, as Samuel Latham Mitchill did, "when the proficients in benign letters and arts . . . with crowns of glory on their heads," would adorn the new nation with its own great art.[1] Defining what this new art would be, and how to bring it into being, took up much of the energy of American artists and critics during these years. How to be great, and at the same time American, was the artist's problem.

No American artist in his right mind, of course, was willing to reject the great legacy of European and classic civilization; but on the other hand he did not want to be dominated by cultures foreign to his own. If the criteria by which art was judged were established by Britain and Europe, his problem was to create an American art within those boundaries, neither imitating nor rejecting too much, keeping a delicate balance between what was native and what was not. By the thirties, he seemed to have found it. Emerson's attack on "the timid, imitative, and tame" in American creative life, made in his address to the young men of Harvard in *The American Scholar*

1. *Discourse on the Nature and Prospects of American Literature* (Albany, 1821), Preface.

in 1837, wrote an end to American doubts. His ringing assertion that henceforth "we will walk on our own feet; we will work with our own hands; we will speak our own minds," marked the beginning of those years in which the distinctive configurations of an American art took shape.[2]

The creed for an American art, developed by artists, critics, and the informed public over the first half of the nineteenth century, was naturally based on current Romantic theory, strongly modified by American conditions and to suit the American style. The age assumed that art (not only painting but by extension all artistic creation) was a reflection and projection of God; it served a universal function, bringing to all men a sense of beauty, truth, and morality. Exactly what beauty meant was not always precisely defined, but it was usually characterized by its power to "elevate," to "stir the higher emotions," to illustrate the "ideal."[3] Lord Kames's statement in his *Elements of Criticism* (1762) that "an appreciation of the beautiful and true is closely allied to the moral sense" was repeated hundreds of times by American art critics over the nineteenth century.[4] It was an important function of art, therefore, wrote a critic in *The North American Review*, to develop "a great moral sentiment," and "to contribute to elevation of character."[5] To evaluate the beauty and truthfulness of art, man possessed (as one of the marks of his humanity) an inborn sense, present in equal degree in all classes and eras, of "aesthetic culture

2. Benjamin T. Spencer, *The Quest for Nationality* (Syracuse, 1957), is the most thorough study of American literary and artistic nationalism.

3. An excellent summary of contemporary thinking about the arts is "The Fine Arts in America," *The Christian Examiner*, XXXIX (November, 1845), 314–30. The author discusses the concept of beauty, 320–22, emphasizing it as "an element of the heart," "sensitivity," "warm and deep feelings, intense emotions. . . ." The sentiment of beauty "must be a prominent element in the individual and national character" to attain "any promise of excellence."

4. For an unusually explicit essay on this point, see Sydney Fisher, "Art: Its Meaning and Method," *North American Review*, LXXXI (July, 1855), 212–44. The "feeling of the beautiful," he wrote, "is produced alike by the moral and spiritual things contemplated by the mind and by the physical things which affect the senses." The beauty of scenery, or of human action, or of the human form touch the viewer with "the same emotions as the perception of intellectual truth or the contemplation of virtuous deeds."

5. "The Arts in America," *North American Review*, LII (April, 1841), 302. As "illustrator of moral subjects," the artist "can delight and strengthen the noblest feelings."

and taste . . . , the spring and source of beauty in the soul."[6] Judgments of art, therefore, could properly be based on this democratically distributed sense. "The great multitude," wrote sculptor Horatio Greenough,

deserves the best of everything, and in the long run is the best judge of it. . . . For art must be popular, enjoyed by the people, suggested by the people . . . , furnishing a deep foundation for the highest cultivation of popular taste.

The Romantic belief that beauty and truth could be found in the commonplace (a Wordsworthian idea that appealed strongly to Jacksonian America) led artists to seek them in ordinary life; thus Emerson, in *The American Scholar,* urged young Americans to find their inspiration and materials in "the meal in the firkin, the milk in the pan, the ballad in the street, the news of the boat," to "explore and poetize . . . the near, the low, the common." This kind of art would reflect American society and its ideals; it would be democratic, optimistic, moral, practical.

Since the United States was a practical, technological civilization, critics believed that technology and art should join to produce a utilitarian aesthetic of a uniquely American type. The essence of beauty, said Horatio Greenough, was the promise of function and the fulfillment of that promise in usefulness. "If there be any principle of structure," he wrote, "more plainly inculcated in the works of the Creator than all other, it is the unyielding adaptations of forms to functions," a sound pragmatic doctrine. Thus Greenough saw the beauty of peculiarly American things like the trotting wagon, the locomotive, and the clipper ship.[7] And in addition, to

6. See Greenough's two articles, "Remarks on American Art," *United States Magazine and Democratic Review,* XIII (July, 1843), 45–48, and "American Architecture," *Ibid.,* XIII (August, 1843), 206–10. See also John Neal's review of Jarves's "Art Hints," *North American Review,* LXXXI (October, 1855), 436–57. Arts, "appealing to the senses, and not to the reason, are felt when they are not understood." All men, concludes Neal, are art critics by nature, "without understanding the grounds of their judgments. It is enough for them that they feel. . . . They are qualified, if not by training or experience, at least by nature, which is far better, to enjoy and feel" the best in art.

7. For Greenough's ideas, see Sylvia Crane, "The Aesthetics of Horatio Greenough in Perspective," *Journal of Aesthetics and Art Criticism,* XXIV (Spring, 1966), 415–27; and James G. Fitch, "Horatio Greenough and the Art of the Machine Age," *Columbia University Forum* (Fall, 1959), 20–28. Cf. "The Fine Arts in America," 315–16. "Towards beauty all that is useful tends and

be effective, art must be not only useful but intelligible, "called out," as Emerson said, "by the necessities of the people" and comprehensible to them. Thus William Sidney Mount believed that a painting ought "to speak all languages . . . understood by the illiterate and enjoyed still more by the learned," while *The Christian Examiner's* critic called for art "that will faithfully and vigorously reflect the American character and life."[8] The contemporary aesthetic, therefore, rejected the esoteric and the private in favor of an authentic, understandable rendition of human, natural experience.

While the contemporary critical vocabulary was not always precise, *beauty* was understood to be that which was "marked by elegance, variety, harmony, and proportion," including "symmetry of parts . . . justness of composition." The *picturesque* was defined as "that peculiar kind of beauty which is agreeable in a picture, natural or artificial; striking the mind with great power or pleasure in representing objects of vision, and in painting to the imagination any circumstance as clearly delineated as in a picture." Most critics distinguished between the *grand* and the *sublime* in art. Grandeur "fills the imagination with its immensity," as in works of art or nature (the Pyramids); whereas sublimity "elevates the imagination" and is to be applied only to nature, such as a storm at sea. The artistic *imagination* was defined as "the power or faculty of the mind by which it conceives and forms ideas of things communicated to it by the organs of sense," *fancy* as "the faculty of the mind by which the mind forms images and representations of things at pleasure." The fancy, however, unlike the imagination, did not have the power of "combining and modifying our conceptions."[9]

Jacksonian America—patriotic, ambitious, vital as it was—placed much faith in the future of its arts. "Our Own Country," editorialized *The United States Literary Gazette* in 1826,[10]

---

strives . . . the utilitarian spirit is striving to blend itself always with the beautiful."

8. "The Fine Arts in America," 316.

9. See Webster's *American Dictionary of the English Language* (New York, 1844), and *Harper's Edition of Crabbe's English Synonyms* (New York, 1831) for these and other terms.

10. *The United States Literary Gazette*, IV (August, 1826), 388. An excellent survey of the arts in American society during these years is "Democratic Vistas," in Oliver Larkin, *Art and Life in America* (New York, 1949), 147-235.

seems to possess peculiar advantages for the cultivation of the Arts. There is the same spirit of competition, the same opportunity of free expression, allowed to every species of talent, as in the flourishing periods of the Grecian and Italian republics, when the glory of the Arts was at its highest.

Yet American artists of the thirties and forties faced, as their fathers had, the constant and inaccurate British and European claim that theirs was a "materialistic" culture, concerned only with "the mechanical arts" or "useful sciences." To refute this and similar criticisms, Americans hoped to create in their country both a native artistic tradition and a constellation of artists equal to any of England and Europe. The materials and the talents were there; art needed only recognition and encouragement. If the United States would but "give the Muses a cordial reception, and foster them with greatest care," the result would be "a superstructure of eternal honor to the American name, more pleasing, more refined, and more influential than that of classic Greece."[11]

That a great nation needed great art, whose existence in turn proved its greatness, was an accepted fact, but there were reasons beyond patriotism for its cultivation. Art, it was assumed, had social functions of real importance in the development of a stable, ordered, progressive community; according to Lord Kames, whose word on matters of aesthetics Americans accepted as gospel, art and the moral sense "went hand in hand." To one contemporary critic, the arts not only exerted "an elevating and softening influence" on society, but made men "more alive to the beauties of nature and truth"; a "Hall of Arts," said another, was as necessary to a community as "temples, marts, and the shops of toil." Thus the maintenance of a balanced, civilized, moral society required the creation of an American art. "The cultivation of the Fine Arts," wrote Benson Lossing,[12]

11. Benson J. Lossing, *An Outline History of the Fine Arts* (New York, 1840), 63.

12. See the discussion and quotations in Neil Harris, *The Artist in American Society: The Formative Years* (New York, 1966), 302–5; in Lillian B. Miller, *Patrons and Patriotism: The Encouragement of the Fine Arts in the United States 1790–1860* (Chicago, 1966), 213–15; and Lossing, *op. cit.*, preface iii–v. On the other hand, there were those who suspected the arts as "sensuous indulgence," recalling Rome and Babylon, and who wondered if art was more a luxury than necessity in a republic. See Harris, 33–35.

and a general dissemination of a taste for such liberal pursuits, are of the greatest importance in a national point of view, for they have a powerful tendency to elevate the standard of intellect, and consequently morals, and form one of these mighty levers which raise nations as well as individuals to the highest point in the scale of civilization.

Civic and cultural leaders joined to urge public and private support of the arts as necessary factors in national progress. Although there were a number of requests for national subsidies to artists and institutions, after the European practice, no direct assistance to the arts was forthcoming. The building of the national Capitol, the largest federal art project of the nineteenth century, provided employment to artists and artisans for sixty years, but neither federal nor state subsidies ever materialized. However, there were always government commissions to be had—federal, state, and local—and occasions and celebrations (like Lafayette's visit of 1824–25) which needed medallions, portraits, tablets, paintings, arches, and so on. Memorializing heroes like Washington and Jackson required statues; decorations of state capitols and public buildings required bas-reliefs, murals, and portraits. The growth of public parks and gardens alone created a great new market for sculptors.

When it seemed that a national policy on the arts would never appear from Congress, the cultural leaders of the nation appealed to its wealthy men to perform for their society through "liberal patronage" what the Renaissance princes had for theirs. The wealthy responded, and so did the less wealthy. Colleges, schools, libraries, literary societies, historical societies, "Young Men's" and "Young Ladies" Associations, and other groups gave exhibitions, bought paintings and sculpture, founded galleries, and hired artists for substantial fees. The public recognized the artist's importance to society and granted him a correspondingly important place within it, so generously that Horatio Greenough could truthfully say in 1852, "There is, at present, no country where the development and growth of an artist is more free, happy, and healthful than it is in the United States."[13]

Most large American cities had homes and galleries hung with paintings or adorned with sculpture, gathered by wealthy and

13. See Harris, *op. cit.*, 83–6, 162–4; Miller, *op. cit.*, chapters 13 and 14.

highly knowledgeable collectors. The fashionable thing to do in the twenties and thirties was to have one's own private gallery; James Jackson Jarves, who had one, wrote that collecting art "has become the mode of taste. Private galleries in New York are becoming as common as stables."[14] Wealthy collectors like Luman Reed, for example, gave lucrative commissions to Thomas Cole, Asher Durand, William Mount, and George Flagg. Thomas Perkins of Boston gave commissions to Washington Allston and Horatio Greenough. A survey in 1870 showed 150 major private art collections in the United States, not only in New York, Boston, and the Eastern cities, but in Cleveland, Milwaukee, Pittsburgh, Detroit, Louisville, and St. Louis.[15] The motivation behind them may have been partly personal pride, but it was partly too a sense of social obligation and genuine artistic appreciation.

A lingering Calvinist suspicion of "graven images" made sculpture somewhat suspect as an art in eighteenth-century America, but Americans were also heirs to a strong native tradition of woodcarving, stonecutting, and funerary sculpture, as well as to the English tradition of public monuments. In the 1790's sculpture began to attract the attention of American artists, for there was an obvious connection, of course, between sculpture and politics, and comparisons of the new American republic to Greece and Rome were commonplace. Since the United States had already "surpassed the Republics of Greece and Rome in our political institutions," wrote sculptor Thomas Crawford, there was no reason Americans should not "approach their excellence in the fine arts."

The Revolution and the War of 1812 gave the United States sets of heroes and events to be immortalized in stone (as Greeks and Romans had immortalized theirs) for statuary was a natural way of making the national heritage visible. The nation's most important

14. Lawrence V. Coleman, *The Museum in America* (three volumes, Washington, D.C., 1939) III: chapter I, contains a discussion of early art galleries. The Benjamin West exhibition, hung by the Pennsylvania Academy of Fine Arts, 1805–07, was probably the first major art exhibit of an American artist held in the United States.

15. Miller, *op. cit.*, chapter 14. There were five major private collections in New York alone, owned by Robert Livingston, Luman Reed, John P. Murray, Samuel Wood, and Philip Hone. Joseph Harrison and Robert Stuart of Philadelphia were also collectors of note.

public building, the Capitol then under construction, was an ideal sculptor's gallery. To "keep bright the fires of patriotism," Horatio Greenough believed, the Capitol ought to be surrounded "with the statues and monuments of illustrious men, who have devoted themselves to the glory of the country." There were also hundreds of other public buildings to be adorned—state capitols, banks, government offices, business buildings—which offered great new opportunities to sculptors and stonecutters.[16]

The demand for sculptors, however, was far greater than the country could supply. There was already a sizable body of sculpture in the United States, much of it by foreign artists who came to the country to accept commissions from wealthy Americans who wanted something more sophisticated than native stonecutters could provide. Also, for many years Americans had imported church and cemetery monuments from England. Though some artists, such as Joseph Wilton and Charles Willson Peale, executed a few pieces, most of the distinguished work of the early nineteenth century was done by Europeans—J.-A. Houdon from France, Richard Hayward and Robert Ball Hughes from England, Italians like Giuseppe Ceracchi, the Dane Christian Goldager. The first sculptors to work in the national Capitol were Italians, Giuseppe Franzeni and Giovanni Andrei, a fact which understandably wounded American artistic pride.[17]

American-produced or not, sculpture became an immensely popular art in the United States. Since its aesthetic was based on the human body, the greatest miracle of God's creation, it was among the holiest of arts. While sculpture could not match painting's comprehensiveness and range of execution, it had its own "peculiar excellencies" in its superior ability to depict "the grace and symmetry of the human form" and to "express reverence for a nation's

16. Albert T. E. Gardner, *Yankee Stonecutters* (New York, 1945), 4–9. For a good brief account of sculpture in America, see also Oliver Larkin, *Art and Life in America* (New York, 1949), 101–6, and his "Early American Sculpture," *Antiques*, LVI (1949), 176–79. Older, but still useful, is Lorado Taft's *History of American Sculpture* (New York, 1930).

17. Wayne Andrews, *Sculpture in America* (New York, 1968), chapter II, 46–71. Gardner, *op. cit.*, 59, lists twenty-one of fifty-four stonecutters at work in the United States in 1800 as foreign-born. In 1816, when asked advice about the proposed statue of Washington for the North Carolina Capitol, Thomas Jefferson said he did not know of a single American who could do it and recommended Canova at Rome.

heroes." It was visible and palpable art; the sculptor conceived "ideal representations of moral and intellectual qualities and perceptions," wrote one critic, and then presented them to the viewer in "tangible forms of beauty and grace, heroism and courage, and many others."[18] And since the sculptor translated his abstract vision into the most materialistic of materials, his art was a perfect symbol of the transcendentalist creative act; a statue, said Margaret Fuller, was "a bridge over the actual to the ideal."

Stone was a difficult and demanding medium, in which skill could be developed only slowly and after much work. Sculpture was an "honest" art, three-dimensional and therefore close to reality, offering little opportunity for tricks and deceptions. The challenge of sculpture as an art form, and the opportunities it furnished for both renown and profit, attracted dozens of young Americans to it.[19] By 1830 Horatio Greenough was studying in Italy, Hiram Powers at work in Cincinnati, and Thomas Crawford soon to leave for Italy himself. Others followed, by the dozens.[20]

Not all, of course, went to Italy. Some stayed home, developing their own brand of native realism, combining it with the fashionable European neoclassic style. John Frazee, who began as a stonemason, specialized in busts of famous men—Webster, Bowditch, Lafayette—as well as in statuary for public buildings, cemeteries, and home display. John H. I. Browere traveled about the country making life masks which he turned into busts; he opened a "Gallery of Busts" in 1828 which he hoped would become a national museum. Hezekiah Augur, a Connecticut woodcarver, and John Cogdell of South Carolina gained considerable reputations for busts, tablets, and memorials.

Most Americans seriously interested in sculpture, however, believed it necessary to go abroad. Few American academies taught

18. Lossing, op. cit., 115–16; Thomas T. Haines, The Royal Path of Life (Chicago, 1876), 368.
19. Margaret Thorp, The Literary Sculptors (Durham, 1965) lists over one hundred sculptors at work in the United States 1825–1875, more than at any time before or after in the century.
20. Van Wyck Brooks, The Dream of Arcadia (New York, 1958), chapter IX, counts at least a hundred American sculptors in Italy 1825–1861. Not until the seventies, when Augustus Saint-Gaudens chose Paris instead of Rome, did the migrations to Italy diminish. Brooks's account of these and other artistic expatriates is excellent.

sculpture; most Americans learned from woodcarving or tombstone cutting, or served apprenticeships as carpenters, painters, or silhouette cutters. The young American who wanted to study his craft had almost literally nowhere to go but abroad, to Italy, generally considered the world's center of sculptural art, where he could live in the midst not only of the past's great sculptural tradition, but in the shadow of the two men accepted by the age as Michelangelo's equals, Antonio Canova and Bertel Thorwaldsen, who dominated sculptural styles in the first half of the nineteenth century.[21] Canova, easily the most admired sculptor in the world and the leader of the classical revival, died in 1822 but his influence remained strong. After his death his native town of Possagno became a mecca for young sculptors, while his famous works—*Cupid and Psyche, Pauline Borghese, Perseus, The Three Graces,* and a dozen others—attracted millions to galleries over the next fifty years. Canova was a legend to the young Americans who arrived in Rome and Florence in the thirties and forties, but Bertel Thorwaldsen, who went to Rome from Denmark in 1797, was a powerful living presence.[22]

Public taste tended to follow Canova's idealized, heroically-styled white-marble manner, modeled on Roman emperors, Greek lawgivers, and mythological figures. Since sculpture represented persons and ideas of national significance—Liberty, Washington, the Republic, Union—the public wanted statuary which, to use Canova's own terms, was "pure, lucid, elegant, and dignified."[23] But whether the model was Canova or the more rugged and monumental

21. Edward Everett, "American Sculptors in Italy," *Boston Miscellany of Literature,* I (January–July, 1849) , 49–54. Everett explained that in Italy a sculptor could hire models for $10–$12 a week, work in "a salubrious climate," buy marble cheaply, and engage skillful workmen to cut and polish stone. Few sculptors did their own carving, hiring skilled assistants, so a sculptor's payroll was an important item. The great Thorwaldsen only once carved an entire statue with his own hands.

22. Canova's controversial *Washington,* done for the North Carolina Capitol with an inscription in Italian and depicting Washington as a Roman general, was destroyed in a fire in 1831. Small-scale reproductions of his *Psyche* or Thorwaldsen's *Lion of Lucerne* and *Vestal,* or of the latter's bas-reliefs *Night and Morning* decorated thousands of American mantelpieces. For an admiring contemporary essay on Canova, see "Canova and His Works," *North American Review,* X (April, 1820) , 372–86.

23. Canova's influence was strong on the adornments of the national Capitol, much of which was designed and executed by his pupils.

Thorwaldsen, the sculptor had small choice. His statuary had either to tell a story or call up associations with history, literature, or religion; it had to be done in the finest sheer white marble, smoothly polished; it had to depict an idealized human anatomy, covered, said Canova, "by a well-contrived veil of flesh and skin, presenting to the eyes only a gentle surface." Sculptors therefore dealt with such figures as Daphne, Cleopatra, Rizpah, and Hercules, or with incidents from the Greek wars, a stanza of Byron's, a dying Indian or gladiator.[24]

Not all, in fact only the lesser part, of nineteenth-century sculpture was made for gallery exhibition, public buildings, or civic display. The portrait bust had its own conventions. Unlike "ideal" sculpture, the bust was intended to provide both the subject's picture and his personality. Its aim was not to idealize, but to express a sense of the person, honestly and directly; the sculptor might drape his subject's shoulders with a Roman toga but both subject and sculptor wanted the result to be a "natural likeness." The artist, said Edward Everett, aimed[25]

to reproduce the man, in the best and most accustomed expression of his character. To attain this end, whatever is essentially characteristic in the original, must be preserved, whether it be great or small, feature or wrinkle. The consummate skill of the artist is shown in thus selecting what is thus characteristic—however seemingly inconsiderable—and still more in making these innumerable details work together, toward the uniform and appropriate expression and life of the whole.

A number of sculptors specialized in marble and plaster busts of the famous and wealthy and of others less so. Politicians, lawyers, merchants, bankers, manufacturers, and common folk could purchase a kind of three-dimensional immortality that the family portrait could never provide. There were thousands of such busts produced, so many that Nathaniel Hawthorne thought that "posterity will be puzzled" what to do with them. Prominent political

24. Thorp, *op. cit.*, chapter 7. See also Larkin, *op. cit.*, 177–79. The publication of Thomas Bulfinch's guides to mythology, *The Age of Fable* (1855) and *The Age of Chivalry* (1858), reflected and encouraged the popularity of this literary-minded sculpture. Horatio Greenough's list of ideas, contained in a youthful notebook, showed how strongly literature influenced sculptors—the death of Abel, David and Goliath, Medea, Eve startled by a bird, Perseus and Andromeda, and so on.

25. "American Sculptors in Italy," 53.

and military heroes were favorites, among them Washington, Sumner, Webster, and Jackson; Joel Hart made a career out of sculpturing Henry Clay, and Leonard Volk out of Stephen A. Douglas. A plaster bust by a journeyman sculptor could be had for $25; better sculptors charged $100 to $500; men like Crawford and Powers received at least $1,000 per commission. Shobal Clevenger, in addition to his widely reproduced busts of Jackson, Harrison, Clay, Van Buren, Webster, and J. Q. Adams, also did over a hundred of civic leaders in Boston, Cincinnati, New York, and Philadelphia. Edward Brackett, Nathan Baker, John King, and Henry Dexter were also well-known portrait specialists.[26]

Funerary sculpture for tombstones, memorials, and mausoleums was the most widely produced form of the art during the period. Tombstones, to nineteenth-century Americans, were especially important, since they held strong emotional and religious connotations of memory, grief, immortality, and divine guidance. Whereas the gravestones of the eighteenth century tended to be simple, with minimal symbolic decoration, the nineteenth century, under the influence of Romantic sentimentalism and the British-European memorial, preferred larger, more impressive funerary styles. The development of city cemeteries, beginning with Boston's Mount Auburn in 1831—followed by Baltimore's Green Mount, New York's Greenwood, and Philadelphia's Laurel Hill, among others—created a demand for stonework that was impressive, ornate, lavishly decorated, intricately symbolic. Famous cemeteries were considered by the public as statuary parks, and advertised as tourist attractions complete with admission charges, guidebooks, guides, and lectures. By the 1840s even rural cemeteries displayed smaller replicas of well-known tombstone styles, with marble angels, cherubs, broken lutes, weeping willows, and other symbols of death and immortality.[27]

Since the public was anxious to buy sculpture, and had the

26. Andrews, *op. cit.*, chapter VII; Gardner, *op. cit.*, 15–71.

27. Gardner, *op. cit.*, chapter 2. Cemetery commissions were highly lucrative. Hiram Powers received $15,000 for Daniel Webster's monument; W. W. Story $40,000 for his John Marshall memorial; Randolph Rogers $50,000 for one Civil War memorial and $75,000 for another. For contemporary attitudes toward cemeteries, see the Reverend J. Brazee's "Rural Cemeteries," *North American Review*, CXIII (October, 1841), 385–441, which included excerpts from Judge Story's address at Mount Auburn and John P. Kennedy's at Green Mount.

money to do so, dozens of dealers, galleries, and factories sprang up to accommodate the demand. A new method of casting statues was patented in 1842 and a "carving machine" in 1849, as well as a number of devices for sawing, cutting, and polishing stone. Thomas Blanchard's machine lathe, adapted to stonecutting, could reproduce a bust with absolute precision, day after day, in endless supply. Reproductions of famous sculptures to any scale could be easily and cheaply produced, both for galleries which wanted collections and for the housewife who wanted something for the parlor table. Sculptors usually made several copies of their work, some full-size and others reduced as models for plaster or metal replicas. Imported Italian workmen brought with them an improved method of plaster casting in the fifties, making possible mass-produced reproductions that were sold by the thousands in curio and souvenir shops and peddled from door to door.[28]

Possibly the best known—certainly the most controversial and articulate—of the American sculptors of the period was New England-born Horatio Greenough, who studied art, classics, and anatomy at Harvard and began by making portrait busts.[29] He went to Italy in 1825, where he studied briefly with Thorwaldsen and Bartolini, but he found the conventional voguish neoclassicism imitative and constricting. "I contend for Greek principles, not Greek things," he said, and he set out to develop his own version of the neoclassic style. *Chanting Cherubs,* a group commissioned by his friend James Fenimore Cooper, was his first famous piece, and additional commissions followed swiftly. His *Washington,* commissioned by Congress for the Capitol in 1832, caused a furore because of its treatment of the first President as a Roman senator, half-draped in a toga. It was not installed until 1841, moved out to the grounds in 1843, and finally given to the Smithsonian Institution. But *The Rescue,* begun in 1837 and placed in the Capitol in 1846, restored his reputation. Representing an avenging settler rescuing his wife and child from a marauding Indian, it was Greenough at his direct, realistic best. A thoughtful and perceptive man, he wrote a number

28. Powers, for example, made fifty copies of his *Proserpine* to sell at $500 each, and six of *The Greek Slave* at $4,000 each.

29. Thomas Brumbaugh, "Horatio Greenough, American Phidias," *Emory University Quarterly,* XVII (Spring, 1966), 24–34, is a good brief summary of his ideas. The best biography and critical study is Nathalia Wright, *Horatio Greenough: The First American Sculptor* (Philadelphia, 1963).

of essays on aesthetics and sculpture, collected in *Travels, Observations, and Experiences of a Yankee Stonecutter* (1852), which seemed to Emerson to embody "the most magnificent theory of art and artists I have ever chanced to hear from one of themselves."[30]

Hiram Powers, another Yankee stonecutter, made his reputation in Cincinnati. Moving to Washington in 1835, he made a bust of Jackson that attracted notice, and then busts of Marshall, Calhoun, Webster, and Van Buren. He went to Italy in 1837, continuing to accept commissions for busts at $1,000 each and completing 150 more. Since the real test of a sculptor was not portrait work but the "literary" piece, expressing an "ideal," sentiment, or story, Powers began a series of busts of this type—*Ginevra, Proserpine, Diana, Psyche, Eve*—justly acclaimed by critics as the finest of their kind. His naked *Fisherboy* (1841) caused comment, and in 1842 he began work on *The Greek Slave*, depicting a nude Christian slave girl put at auction by her Turkish captors. It drew crowds wherever it was displayed—in London, Boston, New York, Cincinnati, New Orleans, and elsewhere. Marking the first important appearance of nudity in American sculpture, *The Greek Slave* decorated millions of mantelpieces in plaster reproductions and became the nineteenth century's most widely known statue. The girl's nudity, Powers explained, was beside the point:

As there should be a moral in every work, I have given to the expression of the Greek slave what trust there could be still in a Divine Providence for a future state of existence, with utter despair for the present, mingled somewhat of scorn for those around her. . . . It is not her person, but her spirit that stands exposed.

A man of great charm and energy, Powers worked in a variety of styles for another thirty years, influencing a whole generation of younger Americans before he died in 1873.[31]

Thomas Crawford, who learned his craft as a woodcarver and stonecutter, went to Rome in 1835 to study with Thorwaldsen,

---

30. The Greenough family included two sculptors, a painter, an architect, and a writer. Andrews, *op. cit.*, 100–44 contains an excellent estimate of Greenough's ideas and work.

31. Andrews, *op. cit.*, chapter IV; Larkin, *op. cit.*, 180–82. Powers and W. W. Story served Hawthorne as models for the sculptor Kenyon in *The Marble Faun* (1860) and furnished him with much of the information about sculpture in that novel.

anxious, as most sculptors were, to test himself with an "ideal" subject in "the spirit of the ancient Greek masters." His *Orpheus,* exhibited in Boston in 1843, had everything the public expected a major work to have—sentimentality, narrative, classic proportions, literary reference. Having found his metier, Crawford continued to produce similar works, among them *Hebe and Ganymede, Cupid,* and *Sappho,* but as his style developed, Crawford moved away from classic subjects toward romantic narrative and a realistic style. After reading Prescott's histories, he did *Dying Mexican Princess;* later he made the famous *Indian Chief* for the Senate gallery. Through his friendship with Senator Charles Sumner and other political figures Crawford received a number of choice commissions, among them (with Randolph Rogers) the bronze doors of the Capitol, an equestrian *Washington* for the City of Richmond, and the design for *Freedom* atop the national Capitol.

Greenough, Powers, and Crawford formed a triumvirate, Americans believed, who equaled any other group of sculptors in the world. There were others, of course, not quite so well known but, in Edward Everett's opinion, many of them so skilled that the United States could rightfully claim artistic eminence equal even to "Greece in the golden age of her prosperity." Boston-born William Wetmore Story, the most literary of the expatriates and friend of the Brownings, Hawthorne, and Henry James, sent his *Libyan Sibyl* to the London Exposition of 1862, where it made a sensation. Harriet Hosmer, a talented and strongminded woman, executed a much admired bronze of Thomas Hart Benton; William Rimmer's *Dying Centaur* and *Falling Gladiator* were famous "story pieces."

Some sculptors did not go to Italy and rejected the Canova-Thorwaldsen style. Henry Kirke Brown visited Florence, did not think much of it, and convinced of "the folly of studying the works of others," repudiated the whole classic-Italian school. Unlike many of his contemporaries, he drew on the American frontier for meticulously researched, realistically detailed studies such as *Aboriginal Hunter, Dying Tecumseh,* and *Indian and Panther.* Erastus Palmer, a woodcarver and cameo-cutter, turned to native subjects for his sculptures; his wife, in fact, read Cooper's novels aloud to him while he worked. His *Indian Girl,* holding a cross to signify her conversion to Christianity, and his *White Captive* (modeled on his own daughter), a nude white girl kidnapped by Indians, were nearly as famous as Powers's *Greek Slave*. Clark Mills developed a new method of taking life masks and after his *Calhoun* (1845) did a series of portrait busts. In 1848 he accepted a Congressional commission for an equestrian *Jackson*, unveiled with great ceremony in 1853, and continued to make heroically sized statuary based on American history.[32] John Rogers specialized in "picture" or "situation" statuary groups. His first, *The Checker Player* (1859), was an immediate success, followed by *The Slave Auction* (1859), *The Village Schoolmaster* (1860), and dozens more. Reproduced in metal and plaster, "Rogers groups" appeared on thousands of parlor tables for the next forty years. Rogers had sixty workmen in his New York studio and sent out yearly catalogs listing the sizes, subjects, and prices of his reproductions. Done with great care from photographs and live models, Rogers's pieces were, in effect, three-dimensional local-color stories, told with extraordinary skill.

American painting during the early years of the Republic was most strongly influenced by nationalism and Romanticism—that is, by the desire to develop an *American* art; and by the prevailing interest in Romantic aesthetic theory sweeping England and Europe. Despite Samuel Miller's apology for the lack of first-rate painters in the United States, he could nonetheless point with some pride to portrait painters like Copley, Stuart, and Peale; historical painters like West, Trumbull, and Vanderlyn; and to an energetic native landscape school, transferred from England by such men as Francis Guy, Thomas Beck, and William Winstanley.[33]

The "high style" painting that prevailed during the latter decades of the eighteenth century and the early nineteenth emphasized the painting as a tableau whose aim was to teach and influence the viewer. The painter's implicit model was statuary—polished, idealized, and generalized, arranged with attention to group relation-

32. Andrews, *op. cit.*, 144–74; Taft, *op. cit.*, 160–87; Larkin, *op. cit.*, 180–88. Brown was also known for his *Washington*, put in place in New York in 1856. Palmer's *Washington Irving* was displayed at the Philadelphia Exposition in 1876. Mills's *Jackson* is in Lafayette Park, opposite the White House, and Brown's *Washington* is in Union Square, New York City.

33. Samuel Miller, *A Brief Retrospect of the Eighteenth Century* (New York, 1803) blamed Americans' interest in "the pursuits of more immediate utility and profit." For summaries of painting in the United States to 1820, see Virgil Barker, *American Painting* (New York, 1950), 300–389, and Larkin, *op. cit.*, 109–185.

ships and classically columned backgrounds, while emphasizing the narrative or "story" quality of the picture. Designed to impress the viewer with "grandeur," "sublimity," or another lofty emotion, the painting was intended to appeal to the taste and reason, rather than to the "sensibilities." Color, since its appeal was sensual, was subordinated to form and content; since painting ought to have "timeless" or "universal" value, subjects of national or contemporary interest were considered too impermanent. Genre painting was too local and too current to qualify as significant art; landscape too pictorial and insufficiently intellectual. The painter should study the Masters, avoiding those who were too colorful and sensual (Titian) and imitating those (like Raphael) whose work was most exemplary of the rules.[34]

Not all painters, of course, Americans included, scrupulously observed the rules. The thrust of Romantic painting—its high regard for color, contemporaneity, individualism—was too strong to be restrained by the older conventions. The West was opening up; the American was discovering his national past; and most of all the pull of the great sweeping panorama of American nature was too strong for poets, novelists, and painters to resist. The painters who worked after 1812 were also for the most part native-born Americans, to whom England was no longer home nor London the capital of the world. They might go abroad to study but not to stay; Washington Allston, generally regarded as the country's most eminent painter, came back from London, as Benjamin West had not.

The new generation of painters, therefore, felt themselves part of a new culture that had a usable past, a visible present, and an exciting future, placed in natural settings unmatched by any. To explore its resources and find its meanings was the aim of painters like Cole and Allston, as it was for poets like Freneau and Bryant and writers like Irving and Cooper.[35]

Romantic painting, of course, like Romanticism in the other arts, was not solely an American phenomenon; artists everywhere were in revolt against the formalized classicism of the eighteenth century.

34. For a good brief exposition of the Romantic aesthetic in painting, see James Soby and Dorothy Miller, *Romantic Painting in America* (New York, 1943), 6–10.

35. See Edgar Richardson, *American Romantic Painting* (New York, 1944) on which much of this discussion depends; James T. Flexner, *That Wilder Image* (Boston, 1962); and Barbara Novak, *American Painting of the Nineteenth Century* (New York, 1969).

The word, applied to painting, had numerous (and sometimes contradictory) meanings, but in general it implied a vigorous assertion of the importance of the individual artist, and a changed relationship among him, his audience, and the world. The *painter's* view of the world took on new importance; his record of what *he* saw and how *he* felt became paramount; a painting was a subjective impression of *his* mind, to which the viewer responded and in which he shared. The emphasis in painting shifted from a consideration of how expertly the artist handled his materials within the conventions to what was "peculiar, original, and creative" in his product.

Second, Romanticism emphasized the emotional content of painting. How the artist responded emotionally to his materials, and how the viewer responded emotionally to the painting, became important factors in judging its effectiveness. The viewer, for his part, judged the painting by his own standards while William Ware, writing in 1852, even went so far as to deny that there existed any unanimously accepted standards of beauty at all. Though "there are certain forms on which the greater part would agree," he said, "there is no fixed standard of the beautiful, but it varies and changes with the individual. . . . Each has his own conception of what is beautiful." Color, because of its emotional impact on the viewer and because it expressed the painter's own inward state, took on major importance. Feeling became as important as taste, the appeal to the imagination more important than the appeal to the norm, the "passions" (as aroused by color, shape, and sensory impression) more important than the message.[36] Romanticism thus set up a new and complex chain of relationships among painter, subject, painting, and viewer.

Third, Romantic painting made large new areas of subject matter available to the painter and encouraged him to deal differently with the traditional ones. The commonplace, the contemporary, and the popular became directly relevant as not before; on the other hand, so did the Gothic, the otherworldly, the subconscious. Thus William Sidney Mount could paint a barn dance and Rembrandt Peale *The Court of Death,* both within the Romantic rubric. Romantic painters, striving for a high degree of emotional

36. For an astute discussion of aesthetics in painting, see William Ware, *Lectures on the Works and Genius of Washington Allston* (Boston, 1852) , X, especially 8–10, 19–20, 63–65, 94–5.

communion with their audience, were especially attracted to three areas of subject matter: scenes from literature and mythology which would elicit preconditioned responses from the viewer; subjects drawn from common experience, which would evoke basic human emotions such as fear, pity, loneliness, happiness, and so on; and subjects which would appeal to one's sense of the nostalgic, exotic, sublime, or historical.

Fourth, the Romantic painter was intensely involved with Nature in a new and personal way. He saw Nature as parallel to human nature, as a projection of human states of mind; to him it was a valid source of moral, emotional, and aesthetic truth, a manifestation of beauty and divinity in the visual world. "The volume of Nature," wrote William Sidney Mount, is "a lecture always ready and bound by the Almighty." The affinity between Cole the painter and Bryant the poet, or Allston the painter and Emerson the philosopher, was not accidental. All used Nature—particularly American nature—in the same way.

Fifth, the Romantic painter established close relationships with contemporary society. In a society that was optimistic, fluid, nationalistic, and pragmatic, so was painting; it took in a wider range of values than before, described things, told stories, reported current events, depicted real situations. He felt no division between his emotions and those of his fellowmen, and none between his interests and society's. At harmony with their times, the painters sought to observe, clarify, and interpret them. Thomas Eakins, speaking to young painters, advised them to "remain in America, to peer deeper into the heart of American life," if they wished to become great. These men were at one with their world.

Romanticism, inchoate and complex mass of ideas that it was, guided American painting in two directions—toward the "picturesque" (emphasizing the pictorial quality of the subject) and toward the "naturalistic" and "real" (an imitation of nature, visually accurate). One road led toward William Sidney Mount, George Bingham, and eventually to Currier and Ives—to genre painting of the native, "true," everyday experience. The other led toward Thomas Cole, Asher Durand, Henry Inman, George Inness —to the "Hudson River" and landscape painters.[37]

37. See the discussion by Alan Gowans, "Painting and Sculpture," in Wendell Garrett, *et al.*, *The Arts in America* (New York, 1970), 177–80, *passim;* and by Richardson, *op. cit.*, 20–23.

Washington Allston, who tried throughout his life to combine the modes and techniques of the earlier neoclassical tradition with the newer Romantic attitudes and style, served as a transition. Although Allston died in 1843, his influence on his own and the next generation was considerable. He studied with Benjamin West in London, stayed four years in Paris and Rome (where he met Samuel Coleridge), and returned to Boston in 1818 to stay. He was enthusiastically welcomed as "America's greatest painter" by the influential Boston-Cambridge circle of poets, critics, and preachers, and though he never quite found his own style or painted the great picture his friends expected of him, he became the spokesman for the painter's world. As Allston addressed himself more and more to issues of artistic theory in the twenties and thirties, he turned more to the philosophy of art than its practice. Partially, no doubt, through his admiration for Coleridge, and partially by reason of his exposure to the New England climate of ideas, he evolved a theory of art resembling the Emersonian system, summarized in his *Lectures on Art*, written between 1832 and 1845, published after his death.[38]

Because Allston never became the great master that his age expected him to be, it was easy to label him a failure. However, Allston was important to American painting for other reasons. He was one of the first American painters to explore a wide range of art—portraits, landscapes, history, still life—verging beyond art into poetry, sculpture, fiction, and philosophy. Though never systematic in his thought, Allston touched upon in one way or another most of the primary problems of the artist in his times. He was the only painter of his era who tried to evolve a set of new concepts instead of imitating and varying the old or the European.[39]

---

38. The best critical study and biography is Edgar P. Richardson, *Washington Allston* (Chicago, 1948). A useful article is John R. Welsh, "Washington Allston, Cosmopolite and Early Romantic," *Georgia Review*, XXI (Winter, 1967), 491–502. The function of the artist, Allston believed, was to perceive and present the organic relationship between Art and Nature, Idea and Matter, as "life to life responding." See his *Lectures on Art and Poems*, ed. R. H. Dana, Jr. (New York, 1850), 210–15. For analyses of Allston's theories, see Regina Soria, "Washington Allston's Lectures on Art," *Journal of Aesthetics and Art Criticism*, XVIII (March, 1960), 329–44; and George P. Winston, "Washington Allston and the Objective Correlative," *Bucknell Review*, XI (December, 1962), 95–109.

39. Van Wyck Brooks, *The Flowering of New England* (New York, 1936), 159–65, has a sensitive discussion of Allston and his society. For another view, see

Genre painting was an attempt to catch the appearance and behavior of people at revealing moments in place and time. It focused on an anecdote or incident, always with a narrative or "story" quality, suggesting action that begun before, and would continue after, the moment of the painting—which might be comic, tragic, melodramatic, sentimental, or simply "picturesque." Such painting, of course, had long lineage behind it—to Hogarth and Brueghel and beyond—but it had especial appeal to the times. Jacksonian America was deeply interested in itself and its people; genre painting was an excellent way of finding out about how Americans looked on election day, or at militia muster, or appearing in court, or spearing eels, hunting bears, racing horses, or playing cards. "A painter's studio should be everywhere," said Mount. "Wherever he finds a scene or a picture, indoors or out, the painter should look for materials everywhere, in the blacksmith shop, the shoe-maker's—the tailor's—the Church—the tavern."

William Sidney Mount was one of the best of them. A Long Islander, he found his subjects on neighboring farms and in the villages. *Dancing on the Barn Floor, Bargaining for a Horse, Raffling for a Goose, The Banjo Player,* and other paintings transcribed segments of contemporary life honestly and without sentimentality. Believing with Jacksonian firmness that art was about people and for people, he advised others to "paint pictures that will take with the public—never paint for the few, but the many," which was to him a matter of principle rather than commercial opportunism.[40]

George Caleb Bingham, a native Missourian, was as well attuned to the boisterous life of the West as Mount was to rustic Long Island. He painted the society he saw around St. Louis, he said, so that "our social and political characteristics . . . will not be lost in the lapse of time for want of an Art record." Like Mount, Bingham

---

Richardson, *supra. cit. Belshazzar's Feast,* on which Allston worked for twenty years, was never finished; had it been, it might have been less successful than his *Thunderstorm at Sea* (1804) or *Moonlit Landscape* (1826) in which he caught beautifully that "poetical treatment of pigment" for which he strove.

40. Bartlett Cowdrey and Herman W. Williams, *William Sidney Mount* (New York, 1944); see also Allan Burroughs, *Limners and Likenesses* (New York, 1965), 128–35 for Mount and other genre painters. Some painters, influenced by contemporary European genre fashions, also did Italian street boys, Turkish girls, Arab peddlers, and the like.

was a superb craftsman, skilled at handling light, mood, and pattern. Most of all, he had great sensitivity to the feel of Western places and people. *Fur Traders Descending the Missouri, Raftsmen Playing Cards, Daniel Boone Coming Through Cumberland Gap,* and other Bingham paintings were effective evocations of the Western spirit, while paintings like *The Verdict of the People* and *Country Elections* caught visually the rowdy vitality of Jacksonian politics. Bingham's *Stump Orator* is an entire essay on nineteenth-century American political life.[41]

Since genre painting was particularly popular in the forties and fifties, many tried their hands at it. Richard Woodville, had he not died young, might have equaled Mount or Bingham. His *War News from Mexico* and *Politics in the Oyster House* were Bingham-like scenes of public life; *Sailor's Wedding* was a tour de force of character painting. John Weir, Frank Blackwell Mayer, Henry Inman, and John Neagle also did genre painting, while Eastman Johnson studied at Düsseldorf and came home to produce *Old Kentucky Home* (1859) and *Corn Husking* (1860), ranked among the best of the type.

The West, naturally, attracted a number of painters, since it presented a whole new society—Indians, miners, hunters, emigrants, and the like. Indians were especially fascinating, both to painters and a public whose interests had been whetted by plays like James Nelson Barker's *Indian Princess* and John A. Stone's *Metamora.* George Catlin, who lived with both Eastern and Plains tribes at various times between 1832 and 1837, made over six hundred detailed and accurate paintings of Indian life; he saw Indians through Romantically colored glasses as "knights of the forest" whose culture was a kind of wild Greek. Western landscapes also stirred Catlin to emotion—the sight of the Missouri River raised in him "a sweet delirium" and the prairies seemed to him so beautiful that "a Divine would confess he had never fancied Paradise" before. Karl Bodmer, a German, traveled among the Sioux; Alfred Miller, a Baltimore society painter, joined an Army exploring party to Oregon; Seth Eastman lived with the Sioux and Chippewas and made illustrations for Henry Rowe Schoolcraft's six-volume work on Indians. John Mix Stanley of Detroit traveled the Southwest in the

41. Albert Christ-Janer, *George Caleb Bingham of Missouri* (New York, 1940), is an excellent study.

forties, accompanied Colonel Stephen Kearny's expedition to San Diego, and explored the Columbia River with paintbox and rifle. These and others captured in paint the people and life of the West, from portraits of chiefs to buffalo hunts, rice harvests, camp scenes, and trappers' weddings.[42]

Allied to genre painting, but with different aims, were paintings of reveries and fantasy which attempted to capture a mood, vision, or mystery. The strong imaginative and introspective element of Romanticism encouraged some painters to try to capture on canvas those subjective moods that "play across the surface of the mind." Intended to stimulate the viewer's fancy, these "dream" paintings had much the same purpose as the Gothic and Oriental pictures then popular in Europe and England. American artists tended to treat them as allegories. Thomas Cole's *Voyage of Life,* a set of four commissioned by banker Samuel Ward of Boston, depicted Childhood, Youth, Manhood, and Old Age. Asher Durand's *Morning of Life* and *Evening of Life* allegorized life and death, youth and age. There were dozens of similar paintings, engravings, and lithographs interpreting the course of life in terms of the weather or the seasons, or as vision, idyll, and dream, which hung on parlor walls in thousands of homes. Some had literary associations; Allston's *Florimell* derived from Spenser's *Faerie Queene,* Rembrandt Peale's *Court of Death* from Dante. John Quidor, who began painting in 1823, was an eccentric and self-trained artist who put together literary incidents—Irving's headless horseman or Cooper's forest chases—in a Gothic, semihumorous style of utter fantasy. Quaker Edward Hicks's *Peaceable Kingdom,* an authentic American primitive, is still the best-known example of this blend of allegory and fantasy that nineteenth-century painting produced.

The second major category of nineteenth-century American painting, the "naturalistic" or Nature school, represented a continuation of the landscape tradition already strong in America. American nature appealed powerfully to the Romantic mind, which treated this new country as a rugged, vast, and innocent Arcadia. European and British painters were drawn to nature too, of course, but the American scene fitted Romantic ideology much better, since, as Thomas Cole said, "All nature here is new to art . . ., primeval forests, virgin lakes, and waterfalls." Landscape

42. Larkin, *op. cit.,* 208–10.

painting appealed to the American; there was so much of the land, and it was so fascinatingly varied, that he wanted to see all of it he could on canvas. It was also *his* land, with bigger and better falls, higher mountains, wider rivers, and more enchanting vistas than Europe's. The "majestic" and "grand" qualities of American nature led landscape painters to paint it differently than Europeans painted theirs. The French Barbizon School believed that a landscape ought to be perceptible at a single glance, to be taken in as a whole. The Hudson River painters, and other American landscapists as well, saw the scene as a large horizontal stage, to be "read" by the viewer as his eyes traveled across it in "panoramic" style.[43]

Landscape painting had deeper connotations as well. Since Nature was assumed to have relationships with moral and emotional sentiment, painting it was a moral as well as an artistic act. Nature was no toy, remarked Emerson, but reflected man's "wisdom of his finest hour"; "the true and beautiful in art," wrote Cole, "are one and inseparable." Falls, mountains, valleys, and fields gave painter and viewer aesthetic pleasure, but both knew there were deeper meanings beneath it. The groves might seem "sublime" or "picturesque," yet, as Bryant reminded his readers, they were also "God's first temples." Then too, while historical painting required certain intellectual preparation of both painter and audience, landscapes appealed directly to all men, whether they had training and education or not. Landscape painting was, then, a truly democratic art, more valuable than others, for, as the *North American Review*'s critic wrote in 1855, it "excites and gratifies the intellectual desires, cultivates a love of nature and of beauty, and surrounds life with charm and elegance."[44]

Since the Hudson Valley was the most spectacular and easily available landscape to artists and poets and nature-lovers, it featured largely in work of the thirties and after. The so-called Hudson River school was not restricted to the Hudson (it included the Catskills, the White Mountains, New Jersey, and other areas as well) and the painters related to it looked for the same things in nature as the poets did—that is, beauty, truth, morality, and deep emotional feeling. Thomas Doughty, who worked out of Newburgh,

43. See Wolfgang Born, "Sources of American Romanticism," *Antiques*, XLVIII (November, 1945), 276.

44. Sydney Fisher, *op. cit.*, 220.

New York, made a career out of painting the area; his canvasses sold for $500 and up in the thirties and forties, until his formalized style lost popularity in the fifties.[45]

The most thoughtful painter of the Hudson River school was Thomas Cole. An English-born immigrant, Cole made a good living as a portrait painter until 1823, when he saw an exhibition of landscapes in Philadelphia. Challenged by this new kind of subject, he turned his attention to landscapes. Cole never painted scenery for its own sake, but always with the landscape's moral and aesthetic suggestions in mind. Scenery to him had a moral force; it was a message from God, an emotional experience. Paintings like *The Oxbow* and *Crawford's Notch* were sermons of a sort, and the story was that he always spent a few moments in prayer before picking up his brushes. He felt a personal identification with Nature, "the standard by which I form my judgment," and he observed it closely in every detail so that he could not only imitate it but understand it. Because of his philosophical bent, he was much admired by the poets and critics of the day and was a close friend of William Cullen Bryant.[46]

After Cole, landscape painting moved gradually away from message toward description, from ideology toward the pictorial. For one thing, the rise of engraving taught both public and artist to look carefully at detail and technique. Asher Durand, who began as an engraver and turned to landscape in the thirties, approached Nature differently from Cole. He regarded a landscape as a formal composition, a combination of scenes that had a unity and beauty of its own, whether or not it was controlled by meaning or idea. A landscape, he once said, was not so much a message as "a sort of dramatic scene in which a particular tree or aspect of nature may be called the principal figure." He urged painters to work outdoors

45. Virgil Barker, *op. cit.*, 417–45 has a useful chapter on landscape painting of the period. See also Wolfgang Born, *American Landscape Painting* (Yale, 1908) and Frederick W. Sweet, *The Hudson River School* (Chicago, 1945) .

46. Soby and Miller, *op. cit.*, 16–19, provide a good summary of Cole's ideas and career; see also Walter Nathan, "Thomas Cole and on Romantic Landscape" in George Boas, ed., *Romanticism in America* (Baltimore, 1940) . Cole also had a strong strain of the allegorical, and painted sermonic canvases like *The Voyage of Life* and *The Cross and the World*.

and to paint what they saw, rather than work from sketches in a studio, as Cole did.[47]

Others, like Durand, moved away from content toward form in landscape painting—James and William Hart, John William Hill, Jasper Cropsey, David Johnson. John F. Kensett, who studied engraving as Durand had, worked with larger canvasses and in a much more poetic mood, so much so that critic James Jackson Jarves called him "the Bryant of painters." George Inness owed debts to Turner, Constable, and the French, as well as to Cole and Durand. For those who found the Hudson and the Catskills insufficiently dramatic, the West provided scenery of a quite different kind. German-trained Albert Bierstadt, who accompanied General Landers's surveying party over South Pass in 1859, was nearly overwhelmed by the immensity and grandeur of the Rockies, qualities he caught admirably in his heroically sized *Mount Corcoran, Yosemite Valley,* and *Hetch Hetchie Canyon.*[48]

History painting did not disappear in the flood of genre and landscape painting that inundated the era, though it was less evident. The completion of the national Capitol and the construction of new state capitols, courthouses, banks, and public buildings furnished a good market for filio-pietistic art. The public, accustomed to West, Trumbull, and the British school, preferred the traditional grand style; John Chapman, Robert Weir, and William Powell, who completed the paintings for the rotunda of the Capitol, continued it without change. Emmanuel Leutze's *Westward the Course of Empire Takes Its Way,* which covered six hundred square feet of Capitol wall, was typical of the overblown historical school; it was matched in popularity, however, only by his *Washington Crossing the Delaware,* painted in Düsseldorf without much regard for either American history or landscape.[49]

Daguerre's "sun pictures," made on copper plate in 1837, were

47. See Durand's *Letter on Landscapes* (1855). "Go first to Nature to learn to paint landscapes," Durand wrote, "and when you shall have learned how to imitate her, you may learn to study the pictures of great artists with benefit." His Catskill scenes, his painting of Cole and Bryant contemplating a forest, *Kindred Spirits,* and *First Harvest* are good examples of his sense of form and eye for detail.

48. Larkin, *op. cit.,* 209–10; Burroughs, *op. cit.,* 148–50.

49. See Charles Farman, *Art and Artists of the Capitol* (New York, 1927).

being produced in the United States in 1839. The process of making a paper positive from negative, perfected in England in 1840, was imported equally as fast. Photograph studios flourished in the cities in the late forties and fifties; the New York *Tribune* in 1855 calculated that the city's photographers took three million pictures that year. Although much impressed by what a camera could do, painters were not certain how it concerned them. Clearly, it reproduced details with a realism no brush could match; if photography made Nature herself the painter, what remained for the painter to do? Paul Delaroche's remark that henceforth "painting was dead" seemed overly pessimistic, however, to Americans; photography might even be a substitute for sketch pad and model, an aid rather than a competitor. Because they required long exposure times, photographs seemed useful only for landscapes; since the painter could work in his studio from photographs of places he had never seen or could hope to see, photography furnished him with a kind of freedom he never had before. However, the camera missed the whole range of color, nor did it have a painter's selectivity, his ability to deal with abstractions, imaginings, and intuitions. Later, of course, as photography changed, so did its relationship to painting.[50]

Although photography doomed miniature painting, it paradoxically stimulated portrait painting. While the small, colored "tintype" developed by Daguerre easily replaced the delicately drawn miniature as a souvenir, it was never considered a substitute for the portrait. The Romantic era was intensely interested in people, and the photograph, though it might be accurate in detail, was nonetheless too impersonal. Portraits, in fact, provided painters with the best way to make a living—and in some cases a fortune—until the seventies. The market for official portraits of governors, mayors, councilmen, army and navy officers, and the like was consistently good, that for family portraits even better.[51] From polished profes-

50. Flexner, *op. cit.*, 210–12. Samuel F. B. Morse, for example, was much interested in photography and taught it to Matthew Brady, among others.

51. John Wesley Jarvis, for example, charged $300 for a full-length portrait, $60 for a half-length that included the hands, and $40 for heads alone. In one stint in New Orleans he averaged six portraits a week, week after week. Thomas Sully averaged thirty-seven portraits a year and produced 2,600 canvases in his career. Rembrandt Peale, who painted in other genres, did thirty to fifty portraits a year; George F. A. Healy did over six hundred in his career, and Charles Loring Elliott over seven hundred.

sionals to self-taught amateurs, portrait artists traveled from town to town taking commissions, while the better-known maintained studios in the major cities and let sitters come to them. There were so many of them that Gilbert Stuart in his old age grumbled that if "you kick your feet against a dog kennel, out will start a portrait painter." Each had his specialty of style or technique; at the same time, the buyer wanted a firm, realistic likeness, perhaps somewhat idealized, without too much fancy variation.

American portrait painters, however, approached their subjects in a slightly different manner than their British and European contemporaries. In the foreign tradition, the portrait was seen not only as an individual likeness but also as an arrangement of form and color, emphasizing decorative elegance. Americans, following the powerful native tradition of Stuart (who died in 1828), concentrated on the person behind the portrait, considering it primarily a study in personality. Early portraits like Thomas Sully's *Captain Jean David* (1813), Samuel Waldo's *Jackson* (1817), and Rembrandt Peale's magnificent *Washington* (1824), when compared with current British portrait work, clearly illustrated the differences. Some well-known painters (like Sully) specialized in portraits, others (like Peale) painted them in addition to other works. Peale, of the Philadelphia "painting Peales," studied with West, exhibited at London's Royal Academy at twenty-five, and after returning to the United States replaced Trumbull as president of the American Academy of Fine Arts. Samuel F. B. Morse, who studied with both West and Allston, was one of the best American portraitists until his interest in telegraphy displaced his art. His *General John Stark* and *DeWitt Clinton,* among others, were honest, direct, and craftsmanlike. Thomas Sully of Philadelphia studied with Stuart and also with Sir Thomas Lawrence in London. His portrait of Edgar Allan Poe, the most revealing ever done of that doomed man, was perhaps his finest. John Wesley Jarvis, an English-born engraver, studied anatomy and phrenology to prepare himself for portrait painting and turned out dozens of likenesses. A rough, colorful, blustering man, Jarvis painted the heroes of the War of 1812 for an admiring public; his portrait of young, heroic Oliver Hazard Perry was one of the most popular of the times. John Neagle, Francis Alexander, and Henry Inman were also among the more competent craftsmen. Samuel Waldo and William Jewett formed a painting partnership in 1816 and took commissions for the next fifty years. Chester Harding, a peddler and saloonkeeper before he taught himself to paint, painted till the age of seventy-four, and once painted eighty portraits—good ones—in six months.[52]

Painting, like sculpture, enjoyed greater prestige and support among the arts during the years 1830–1860 than at any other previous period in American history. To Anna Jameson, an Englishwoman who traveled in the United States in 1837, "the country seemed to swarm with painters"; collectors spent thousands on paintings, the market was good, sales high. The records of one New York gallery from 1839 to 1851, for example, showed an annual attendance equal to 50 percent of the city's population.[53] Organizations in the major cities such as the National Academy of the Arts of Design and the Academy of Fine Arts in New York, the Boston Athenaeum, the Philadelphia Academy of Fine Arts, and the Cincinnati Academy organized yearly exhibitions and sales; private dealers sold works for both American and European artists. Painters themselves, through "art unions," developed new marketing methods via the raffle. The New York American Art-Union bought paintings and engravings, issued lottery tickets to members, and held annual drawings for winners. The American Art-Union had 19,000 members in 1850, while the Cosmopolitan Art Union, its successor, counted 38,000 before it dissolved in 1861. Boston, Cincinnati, Philadelphia, and other cities had similar organizations. Their purpose might have been primarily commercial, but the art unions were quite conscious of their role in "diffusing among the people a love of Art, refinement of taste, and general aesthetic culture." They understandably exhorted painters to avoid European styles and subjects, and hoped, said the American Art-Union, "to advance the cause of *American* art . . . , to develop talent and encourage taste" in an American context.[54]

52. Burroughs, *op. cit.*, 118–33; and Larkin, *op. cit.*, 123–7, 193–5. Other contemporary portraitists were Mather Brown, Nathaniel Jocelyn, James Lambdin, William Powell, Jacques Aman, Elijah Metcalf, Jacob Eichholtz, Matthew Jouet, James Frothingham, Daniel Huntington, Henry P. Gray, George P. H. Healy, Charles Loring Elliott.

53. Richardson, *American Romantic Painting*, 6; Flexner, *op. cit.*, xi–xii.

54. *Annual Reports* of the American Art-Union, 1844, 1849, in Carl Bode, ed., *American Life in the 1840's* (Garden City, 1967), 229, 232. See also Barker, *op. cit.*,

The introduction of new printing techniques made possible good reproductions in quantity for the mass market. An artist could make prints for general sale, or for magazine and book illustrations, or for straight fees and royalties. Some worked directly for this market (George Harvey; Felix Darley, who illustrated Irving; William H. Bartlett), while others sold reproduction rights to their pictures. The use of steel plates for engraving instead of copper meant that the plates were practically indestructible; mezzotints and line engravings on steel could be used thousands of times. Lithographs on stone were also popular, as was chromolithography in different colors. Gift annuals like *The Token* and *The Diadem* and magazines like *Graham's* and *Godey's Lady's Book* paid high fees for the finest examples of the engraver's art; later, magazines like *Leslie's* and *Harper's* employed artists like Winslow Homer and George Waud.

Nathaniel Currier and James Ives, who did for American art much what John Rogers did for sculpture, became the most successful merchants of popular art in American history. Currier founded the business in 1834 and formed a partnership with Ives in 1852 to produce lithographs for home decoration. These lithographs were intended to serve not only as substitutes for paintings which the average homeowner could not afford, but as a kind of journalistic record of important events like elections, steamboat races, battles, disasters, horseraces, and the like. Employing several hundred artists and technicians, Currier and Ives published three prints a week for years, selling them at 15 cents to $4.00 each through peddlers, mail orders, and stores. Best-selling prints sometimes sold upwards of 100,000 copies. Covering every aspect of American life from the fifties on, Currier and Ives prints were important agents in expanding America's knowledge of itself and in developing a national identity. They still provide—together with prints from competitors like Sarony and Major, the Kelloggs, and J. Baillie—an irreplaceable social and cultural record of their times.[55]

362–5, and Bode, *The Anatomy of American Popular Culture* (Berkeley, 1959), chapter 5, "Paint for the Public Eye," for an excellent discussion of the art unions and public taste. The diffusion of paintings, of course, also created interest in art criticism and body of critics, among them Henry Tuckerman, Charles Lester, James Jackson Jarves, and art magazines like John Durand's and William Silliman's *Crayon*, founded in 1855.

55. See Harry T. Peters, *Currier and Ives: Printmakers to the American People* (New York, 1942).

From Trumbull to Currier and Ives, tintype to Sully, or *Greek Slave* to cheap plaster *Venus*, the art of the times was a democratic art that had, as the American Art Union described it, "an American aspect, in the subjects, in the landscapes, in the treatment, in the sentiment, and in various other particulars." It included "healthfulness and purity of sentiment," avoiding "the false and affected . . . or an enchanted, sensual atmosphere," displaying instead "truth and purity . . . , originality, beauty, and power," so that while it might provide "elegant ornament" for the American home, it also furnished "refined enjoyment" that was "American to the heart's core."[56]

Until the 1830s, American architecture was dominated by two styles inherited from the eighteenth century—the federal, or "Adam" style, developed from British Georgian; and the classical, developed from the Palladian-European tradition. The first, as practiced by Samuel McIntire and Charles Bulfinch, moved westward with the population; the second, whose most eminent practitioner was Thomas Jefferson, moved south and west with plantation culture.[57] Since both were essentially foreign traditions, however naturalized by usage, some architects felt that neither was really suitable to a democratic, open society.[58] What America needed was an architectural style of its own, which expressed the national purpose and exemplified the national character. The era found it, curiously enough, in a revival of Greece.

The reasons were understandable enough. Certain other choices were automatically eliminated; Georgian was too British, the current Napoleonic use of Roman models had unpleasant imperialistic connotations. Greek classicism, however, had obvious parallels to America's image of itself, reflected in the Greek love of liberty, restraint, discipline, simplicity, and commitment to beauty. Fur-

56. Bode, *American Life in the 1840's,* 323–4.
57. For currents in American architecture 1770–1830, see Russel B. Nye, *The Cultural Life of the New Nation* (New York, 1960), 268–75; Marcus Whiffen, *American Architecture Since 1780: A Guide to the Styles* (Cambridge, 1969), 21–31; and Wayne Andrews, *Architecture in America* (New York, 1960), chapter I.
58. Much late-eighteenth- and early-nineteenth-century American building was based on imported architectural handbooks, while a number of prominent architects—among them James Hoban, Joseph Mangin, Maximilian Godefroy, William Jay, and Benjamin Latrobe—were foreign-born.

thermore, the United States, like Europe, was fascinated by the ancient world. Recent excavations at Pompeii and Herculaneum, the transfer of the Elgin Marbles to London, and France's collections of classic antiquities for the Louvre all focused attention on the classic past. The same impulse that scattered names like Troy, Athens, and Syracuse across New York and Ohio and built wooden copies of the Parthenon beside log cabins in Western towns, also built banks and state capitols to look like Greek temples. The United States hoped to draw out of the pure sources of classicism a unique American style that would suit its own greatness—not necessarily a wholly new architecture, but a dignified, eclectic tradition founded on those models which, as Jefferson had said, had "the approbation of thousands of years."

There were practical reasons too. The Greek style was an uncluttered, unadorned style that could be translated into wood, brick, or stone by the ordinary workman, and it was fitted to both public and domestic use. Greek Revival was a safe style, suggesting learning, taste, and decorum; it could also be varied and adapted in a number of pleasing ways. Although American architects did things with it that were hardly Greek, it remained the most characteristic national architectural style for the next half century and, in one guise or another, is still a familiar tradition in American building.[59]

Benjamin Latrobe, born in England and an émigré to the United States in 1796, did much to mold the character of early Greek Revivalism. His Bank of Philadelphia building, completed in 1801 and the first important Greek Revival public building in America, was so widely copied that a dozen years later Latrobe could truthfully say, "I have changed the taste of a whole city." Latrobe was an engineer, and while serving as engineer for the Philadelphia water system he designed a Greek Revival waterworks building—the first American structure to combine classical style with technological function.

"I am a bigoted Greek," Latrobe wrote Jefferson. "My *principles* of good taste are rigid in Grecian architecture." Roman architec-

59. Talbot Hamlin, *Greek Revival Architecture in America* (New York, 1944) is still the basic study. See also remarks in Larkin, *op. cit.*, chapters 13–14; Alan Gowans, *Images of American Living* (Philadelphia, 1964), 257–67; and James Marston Fitch, *American Building* (Boston, 1966, rev. ed.), chapters III–IV.

ture, in his opinion, was much too overblown and grandiose to fit
the United States, and as the product of an empire hardly democratic in character, it was quite out of key with the spirit of American institutions. Greek art and Greek democracy, and American art
and American democracy, he felt, both grew from the same roots.[60]
After him came the Greek Revival that left Greek post offices, railroad stations, banks, capitols, and homes in every corner of the
land, designed by such men as Robert Mills, William Strickland,
Ithiel Town, Thomas Walter, and many others.[61]

Magazines, builders' catalogues and handbooks, and carpenters'
design books carried the Greek Revival everywhere. An architect
simply needed to show his workmen the book and let them follow
it. By the fifties, the Northwest and South were studded with Greek
Revival buildings of all descriptions and functions.[62] Nevertheless,
popular as it was, the Greek style did not permanently satisfy the
demand for a native American architecture. Robert Mills told his
contemporaries to "study your country's tastes and requirements
and make classic ground here for your art"; Thomas Walter warned
his fellow builders that American structures ought to "conform to
the local circumstances of the country, and the republican spirit of
its institutions."

Although it was by no means played out, the Greek style soon
began to seem mannered and artificial to younger architects. It was,
they felt, too formal and inflexible to express the spirit of the times,
too restrictive of the architect's creativity. To an age enthusiastic
over science and technology, the classic style seemed outmoded; to a

60. The best source of Latrobe's ideas is his own journal, J. H. B. Latrobe, ed.,
The Journal of Latrobe (New York, 1905) ; the best biography is Talbot Hamlin,
Benjamin Latrobe (New York, 1955). Latrobe left buildings scattered through
several states, among them the Baltimore Cathedral, Christ Church in Washington, and the Louisiana Bank in New Orleans. He drew plans for rebuilding the
national Capitol in 1815, and designed the Bank of the United States in Philadelphia, his last major work before his death. He also, as engineer for the
Chesapeake and Delaware Canal, designed the first drydocks in the United States.

61. Examples are Strickland's Second Bank of the United States in Philadelphia
and his Tennessee State Capitol; Walter's Girard College buildings; and Mills's
United States Treasury, Ohio State Capitol, and Kentucky State Capitol.

62. The more influential guides were Asher Benjamin's *Practical House Carpenter, Being a Complete Development of the Grecian Order of Architecture*
(fourteen editions, 1830–57) ; Minard Lefever's *The Beauties of Modern Architecture* (five editions by 1855) ; and Edward Shaw's *Civil Architecture* (eleven
editions, 1830–70).

society increasingly wealthy, sophisticated, and diversified, it seemed inadequate to express the contemporary feel. Andrew Jackson Downing's *Treatise on the Theory and Practice of Landscape Gardening* (1841) was one of the first serious attacks. Whatever its usefulness in public buildings, Downing concluded, the Greek order had little relevance to American domestic architecture. If one believed, as he did, that the "two leading principles" of architecture were "fitness and expression of purpose," then the Greek style "makes a sad blow at both these established rules." Sculptor Horatio Greenough, who also wrote on architecture, thought that a Greek temple, used as the model for a bank, "makes a pile that stands like a stranger among us . . . , a make-believe . . . , not the real thing." In the meantime, Romanticism was already saturating American artistic thinking with a wholly different set of aesthetic aims and principles.[63]

The new trend in architecture represented a response to three powerful impulses, all derived from Romantic literary theory and influenced by contemporary British and European aesthetic theory and practice.[64] The Romantics rediscovered and fell in love with the past—not only Rome and Greece, but the Middle Ages, China, India, Egypt, Renaissance Italy, and everywhere else. Romantic architecture "revived" the past not only to transmit a sense of history, but to excite emotional response by giving a building a literary and historical frame of reference with which the viewer was familiar. American architects, with only shallow and tentative roots, discovered that by adopting others' traditions they could add historical dimensions to their own. In keeping with the Romantic spirit, architects assumed that the viewer would respond intuitively to a building which represented the past, as he did to a poem or painting which (like Keats's medievalism) similarly drew upon it. As a result there was a wild proliferation of "revival" styles, since architecture was one of the most effective visual means of recapitulating history.

Second, Romantic theories of the "organic" in art seemed as

63. Fitch, *op. cit.*, 59. For a discussion of the new Romanticism in Architecture see Richard P. Adams, "Architecture and the Romantic Tradition," *American Quarterly*, IX (Spring, 1957), 46–63.

64. See the discussion of Romantic theory in Don Gifford, ed., *The Literature of Architecture* (New York, 1960), 17–23.

applicable to buildings as to poems or sculptures. Organicism, as the nineteenth century explored it, implied in architectural terms a number of things—that form and materials were integrally related; that there were "natural" bonds between building and environment; and most clearly that form and function were but two sides of the same identity. "Instead of forcing the functions of every sort of building into one general form," wrote Horatio Greenough, "let us begin from the heart as a nucleus and work outward," so that "the connection and order of the parts . . . cannot fail to speak of their relation and uses."[65]

A building ought to be planned, therefore, to fit its use, with due regard for the needs of its occupants and the requirements of the site.[66] T. C. Clarke, writing in 1850, explained architectural functionalism clearly and thoroughly. The first purpose of a building, he wrote, is "that it should entirely answer the purpose for which it is built"; its second that it should be built "with the least possible outlay of labor and material"; its third that it should "delight as a work of art in proportion . . . , truthful expression . . . , and finish." Instead of "attempting to breathe life into the dry bones" of outmoded styles, the architect should "make his buildings subservient to the uses and wants of today . . . and boldly express their purpose on their fronts."[67]

Third, according to the Romantic aesthetic, organicism meant that in any art the outside form and the inside thought should be one. "Surface" was the symbolic embodiment of inner "idea"; they

65. The phrase "form follows function" seems to have first appeared in a letter from sculptor Horatio Greenough to Ralph Waldo Emerson in 1852. Greenough, as early as 1849, believed that the basis of architecture was "the adaptation of the forms and magnitudes of structures to the climate they are exposed to, and the offices for which they are intended." He did distinguish, however, between "organic" buildings which were "formed to meet the needs of their occupants" and public, monumental buildings which were to exemplify "the sympathies, the faith, and taste" of a people. See his statement of the organic doctrine in "American Architecture," *The Democratic Review*, XIII (August, 1843). For further discussion see Gifford, *op. cit.*, 27.

66. Architecture must be aimed at "the production of a WHOLE," wrote Samuel Sloan in *Homestead Architecture* (1861) and James Jackson Jarves repeated, in *The Art Idea* (1864), that architecture "grows naturally out of the wants and needs of a people."

67. "Architects and Architecture," *Christian Examiner*, XLIX (September, 1850), 278–86. The law of adaptation to use, said Greenough, "is the fundamental law of nature in all structure."

were inseparable, the one a translation into concrete terms of the other. Emerson expressed this relationship through the metaphor of "language," with the artifact serving as a kind of word to embody the artist's idea. All art was, in a sense, verbal; a painting or a poem or a sculpture "spoke." To the Romantic architect, therefore, a building said something to the viewer. Each style had its own cluster of meanings—Greek Revival (liberty and order), Egyptian (exoticism, permanence), Romanesque (power and grandeur), Gothic (religious fervor, imaginative freedom), Renaissance (splendor, wealth, sophistication), and so on. This concept of architecture of course also reinforced historical revivalism, since it meant that the architect could search history for styles that expressed what he wanted to say and then use them in his own way. An architect, since he had to know the past and to translate abstract concepts into material form, was considered to be a creative scholar and artist co-equal with philosopher or poet.[68]

American architecture, between 1820 and 1870, therefore exhibited a remarkable variety of styles, since the Romantic aesthetic could find a place for everything.[69] To the Romantic artist—architect or sculptor or painter—personal taste and personal expression counted for all; the individual statement was far more important than rules and traditions. In building a house, in fact, said Andrew Jackson Downing, the architect must make it his own unique creation, in harmony with its setting, expressing its purpose, and reflecting the personality of its owner.[70] As a result, architectural styles simply exploded—Philadelphia by 1850 could display an Egyptian jail, a Greek bank, medieval cottages, and Moorish churches, while New York had a Jewish synagogue with a Gothic tower and Greek columns. Architects were expected to be able to work in any style the client wished (Alexander Jackson Davis listed fourteen he was prepared to build), though most specialized in their favorites.[71] Of all nonclassical styles, the most favored, the most prolific, and the most varied was the Gothic.

68. See Gowans, *op. cit.*, 287–92.

69. An excellent survey of the profusion of styles is Whiffen, *op. cit.*, 37–87.

70. A good explanation of Downing's ideas is George B. Tatum, "The Beautiful and the Picturesque," *American Quarterly*, III (Spring, 1951), 36–51.

71. Davis listed, in 1867, American Log Cabin, Farm House, English Cottage, Collegiate Gothic, Manor House, French Suburban, Swiss Cottage, Lombard Italian, Pliny's Tuscan, Ancient Etruscan, Suburban Greek, Oriental, Moorish, and Castellated.

The great impetus for Gothic came from England, where it was one of the most popular styles of the early and middle years of the nineteenth century. Though it appeared on both sides of the Atlantic in many variations, common to all—whether in wood, stone, or brick—were its pointed arches, pinnacles, battlements ("castle" style), window tracery, and elaborate decorations.[72] American builders took to it gladly, both as a relief from the discipline of Graeco-Roman and as a declaration of Romantic independence. Critics claimed that classic architecture was too self-contained, limited, and conventionalized, whereas Gothic was open, untrammeled, based on "the right of free growth as of nature itself . . . , flexible and infinite in character, affording working room for every intellectual and spiritual faculty."[73] It was an imaginative, bold, and varied style in which a builder could show off his taste and an owner his wealth in profusions of frets, curlicues, finials, chimneys, colors, glass, patterned brick, or carpentered wood. And as critics pointed out, Gothic was much more functional than classical, which used more materials and led to inefficient interior planning.

Gothic buildings had already appeared in the United States before the twenties (Latrobe, in fact, built a Gothic house in Philadelphia in 1799) when builders' handbooks and English architects brought the style across the ocean. Kenyon College's buildings (1827–29) were among the first important examples; Richard Upjohn, who came from England in 1830, accepted a number of important commissions, among them New York's Trinity Church (1839–46); while Alexander Davis was already designing New York University's Washington Square buildings on the Gothic plan. The partnership of Davis and Ithiel Town scattered Gothic structures across half the states; meanwhile Andrew Jackson Downing's *Cottage Residences* (1842), his *Architecture for Country Houses*

72. The works of the English architectural writer Augustus Dugin, *Specimens of Gothic Architecture* (1822) and *True Principles of Pointed or Christian Architecture* (1841), were especially popular in the United States. Also influential was Georg Moller, *An Essay on the Origin and Progress of Gothic Architecture* (1824). Agnes Addison, *Gothicism and the Romantic Revival* (Staten Island, 1967) is a useful study.

73. Wayne Andrews, *Architecture, Ambition, and Americans* (Glencoe, 1964), 103 ff. and Gowans, *op. cit.*, 303–15. John Ruskin's influence on American architectural thinking was strong, and his plea for a return to the "magnificently human" Gothic style, in "The Nature of Gothic," *The Stones of Venice* (1853), reassured many American readers.

(1850), and his partnership with Calvert Vaux, whom he brought from Europe, had equal effect on the popularity of the Gothic style. Gothic churches, because of their connotations of mystery, spirituality, and medieval piety, were especially popular; so too was so-called Collegiate Gothic, a reminder of the medieval university; and so too were Gothic villas, cottages, banks, post offices, and business buildings.

The reaction against neoclassicism took other forms as well, occasionally bordering on the eccentric, with Swiss chalets, Indian pavilions, Chinese pagodas, and other exotic borrowings. The contemporary fascination with Egypt and the Middle East, partly the result of the Napoleonic campaigns and partly of recent archaeological discoveries, elicited an Egyptian revival in France and England as well as in the United States during the twenties and thirties, the best-known example being New York City's Hall of Justice, or The Tombs. There was a burst of interest in the Italian villa, derived from the Italian farm home; many plans for villas were in the builders' books by the forties—Davis, in particular, excelled in it. The Italian Renaissance palace inspired another Italianate style, popular in city architecture after the fifties; A. T. Stewart's famous department store in New York, built in 1847 and the wonder of the decade, was designed to resemble a five-story Florentine palace. Architects in the fifties and sixties revived Romanesque (called also Norman and Lombard), recalling the round-arched castle with towers and massive walls, as in James Renwick's spectacular Smithsonian Institution group (1846–55). A favorite for church architecture into the seventies and eighties, Romanesque was also favored for railroad stations, armories, banks, and libraries.[74]

The most quoted architectural theorist of the era was no doubt Andrew Jackson Downing, whose ideas on landscape gardening and domestic building helped to make Gothic the most widely popular of the new revival styles. His first important book, *A Treatise on the*

74. The octagonal house was uniquely American, however. Introduced by Orson Fowler, phrenologist, inventor, diet faddist, philosopher, and engineer in his book *A Home for All or the Gravel Wall and Octagon Mode of Building* (1848), dozens of them appeared over the midcentury years. Made of wood, brick, or concrete, a material whose use Fowler pioneered, it provided 20 percent more floor space than the conventional house, allowed much better heating and ventilation, and was much more efficient in its interior arrangements.

Theory and Practice of Landscape Gardening Adapted to North America (1841, and still in print in 1921), by emphasizing the relationship of building to environment, altered the prevailing concept of the connection between structure, builder, and Nature. If Nature were "naturally" free, growing, irregular, and constantly changing, the building set within it must reflect those qualities. Its ornamentation—gables, turrets, frets, and finials—must be set against the trees, ivy, hedgerows, shrubs, and plants around it. Nature and building thus joined, man's work and nature's growth were organically related. His *Cottage Residences* (1842) and *Architecture of Country Houses* (1850) were equally influential, not only for the Gothic plans and suggestions they incorporated, but for their exposition of Downing's architectural philosophy. A building, he wrote, must be useful ("adaptation to the end") and expressive of "its single and definite use." It must use its components honestly, "frankly avowing the materials," and must fit "the character of the scenery itself."[75] Downing, however, drowned at thirty-seven. His most successful successor was Alexander Jackson Davis, who, like Downing, worked enthusiastically in Gothic and Italianate styles. He and Ithiel Town, who joined him in partnership in 1829, built banks, churches, villas, hospitals, and capitols everywhere in a variety of styles. On his own after the forties, Davis specialized in Grecian and Gothic town houses, moved into Romanesque and Moorish, and had more wealthy clients than he could handle.[76]

Professional architects did little home building until the forties; more often than not, carpenters, bricklayers, and masons designed houses with the owner's assistance, following plans and methods laid out by handbooks like Asher Benjamin's and Minard Lefever's. However, by the forties new and better handbooks were appearing—dealing with landscape, location, new materials, colors, and decorations—which had immediate impact on home building. Andrew Jackson Downing's *Hints to Young Architects,* edited from an English book in 1847, and others like *The Modern Home Builder, The American Cottage,* and Vaux's *Villas and Cottages* (1857) introduced owners and builders not only to newer designs, but to

75. *The Architecture of Country Houses* (1850), 205–13. See also the discussions of Downing's aesthetic by George Tatum, *op. cit.,* 40–45.

76. Gowans, *op. cit.,* 293–6.

the wide array of materials and techniques that had been developed over the last decade.

Taking full advantage of the new technology, American building was swiftly industrialized. Laborers developed specialized skills and a new class of building engineers appeared in the cities; the architect, who previously had done much of his own engineering and on-the-job supervision, became designer and consultant. One reason for this division of labor was the rapid development of new building techniques and the introduction of new materials as well as the adaptation of old ones to new uses. The construction industry, which had little time to train specialists, took advantage of every technological innovation that would save time and cost or would allow the use of semiskilled labor. The adaptation of the bridge truss to large buildings, the use of poured concrete and cast iron for walls, the development of machine saws for complicated woodwork, the introduction of the iron supporting column, standardized lumber sizes (especially adapted to balloon-frame construction, itself a major advance), the invention of nailmaking machines—these and other innovations irrevocably changed the building industry between 1830 and 1870. Taken together, they meant that the architect need not be bound by the conventional; he could ask builders to do things that less technologically oriented British and European workmen could not; he could plan his buildings in a new way. Certainly one contributing factor to the proliferation of architectural styles over the nineteenth century was the freedom that American technology gave the architect to experiment.[77]

Forty years of freedom left American architecture, in 1870, uncertain of where it was to go next. Architects recalled old styles, tested out new ones, and experimented with the new technology and materials. They toyed with French chateaus and Second Empire, Queen Anne and Elizabethan, developed so-called High Gothic, and experimented with Spanish. H. H. Richardson's powerful

77. See Gifford, op. cit., "The New Technology," 289–98. James Bogardus's use of cast-iron walls in 1848 forever doomed old-style building. The truss allowed large areas of uninterrupted floor space which could also support great weight; the iron column could (unlike wood or stone) support heavier loads without corresponding increase in size; the concrete wall was not only strong but inexpensive to construct; the iron wall and girder were practically indestructible and simple to put into place.

Romanesque dominated the scene for a time, but Richardson died in 1888. Charles McKim, William Mead, and Stanford White, who incorporated in 1879, used neoclassic, Renaissance, and Gothic with restraint and imagination. The future of American architecture, however, belonged to the group of young men reaching maturity in the seventies and eighties—Richard Morris Hunt, John Wellborn Root, Louis Sullivan, and others like Sullivan's eighteen-year-old assistant, Frank Lloyd Wright, who joined the firm in 1888 as an apprentice draftsman.

CHAPTER 6

The Other Americans

ANTHROPOLOGICAL theories of race were not well developed until the eighteenth century, when continued close contact with Indians and Negroes forced Englishmen and Europeans to examine their opinions about different kinds of men and their origins. Eighteenth-century scientists, arranging life forms into systems, considered man a *species* and the separate races as *varieties* of that species. Though color was not a wholly satisfactory criterion for classifying men in groups, it provided the most visible and logical basis for identifying those varieties. Beginning with the Biblical account of the creation of Adam, they postulated that though at one time all men were alike, different environments had changed them into related races who differed in color, size, hair, and other physical attributes. There were also those who believed—with Biblical support—that different races were the result not of environmental influences but of a *second* creation; later, others suggested that each race originated in a *series* of separate creations, arranged in descending order of importance. Whatever the theory, however, it was generally agreed by nineteenth-century scientists that there were five biologically identifiable groups of men: Caucasian or white; Mongolian or yellow; Malay or brown; "American" or red; and Ethiopian or black.[1]

1. For summaries of early racial theory, see John S. Haller, Jr., "Concepts of Race Inferiority in Nineteenth Century Anthropology," *Journal of the History of Medicine and Allied Sciences*, XXV (January, 1970) , 40–52; Oscar Handlin, *Race*

Anthropologists attributed certain characteristics to each race, asserting that each had inherent intellectual, cultural, social, political, and religious traits that could be isolated and identified. The races were not equal in abilities; most authorities ranked them in descending order as white, yellow, brown, red, and black. Josiah Clark Nott, who collaborated with George Gliddon on *The Types of Mankind* (1854), summarized in the book most of the accepted principles of contemporary racial theory—resting on the assumption that the white race was superior, all others inferior. Nott and Gliddon's book went through nine editions over the next fifty years and its principles dominated American popular thinking about race well into the twentieth century. Nott's ideas received powerful support from the nation's best-known scientist, Louis Agassiz of Harvard, who agreed that "the different races do not rank upon the same level" and assigned the lowest racial orders to the Indian and Negro.[2] Darwinism, of course, provided what seemed to be the final proof, by suggesting that differences in races were the result of different adaptations to environment and that natural selection determined the superiority of some races over others.[3]

Nineteenth-century ideas of race, therefore, helped to shape and to justify national policy toward Indians and Negroes. Although Jefferson once expressed the guarded hope that the Indian might merge into white American society, it seemed clear by the thirties that such was not going to be the case; Indians were no more

and *Nationality in American Life* (Boston, 1957), 76–92; and William Gossett, *Race: The History of an Idea in America* (Dallas, 1963), chapter I. For contemporary essays on anthropological theory, see "The Various Races of Man," *United States Magazine and Democratic Review*, XI (August, 1842), 113–40; "The Natural History of Man," *Ibid.*, XXVI (April, 1850), 327–45; and XXVII (July, 1850), 41–8; and "Varieties of the Human Race," *Ibid.*, XXIX (September, 1851), 246–57. Samuel G. Morton, *Crania Americana* (Philadelphia, 1839) divided the five races into twenty-two "families" or subdivisions.

2. See Josiah C. Nott, *Two Lectures on the Natural History of the Caucasian and Negro Races* (Philadelphia, 1844); and Louis Agassiz, "The Diversity of the Origin of the Human Race," *Christian Examiner*, XLIX (July, 1850), 141–5. The most effective counterstatement is Frederick Douglass's eloquent oration, "The Claims of the Negro Ethnologically Considered," in Philip F. Foner, *The Life and Writings of Frederick Douglass* (New York, 1950–55), II:289–309.

3. The racial theories of the Frenchman Arthur de Gobineau expounded in his *Essays on the Inequalities of the Human Races* (1853) were also influential in the United States through the one-volume edition published by Nott and Henry Hotz in 1856.

civilized than before, nor were prospects of improvement at all bright. Something, certainly, would have to be done with the red population, since his racial characteristics made it unlikely that the Indian could ever be assimilated or even adapted to a separate but equal existence with the white. The situation of the Negro was even clearer. If the black race were inherently and incontrovertibly inferior, slavery was therefore the proper system by which to govern him. As Chancellor William Harper of South Carolina explained, since "the African negro is an inferior variety of the human race . . . , his distinguishing characteristics are such as peculiarly mark him out for the situation he occupies among us."[4]

The great majority of Americans, North and South, believed in the innate superiority of the Caucasian race and in the natural inferiority of the African race.[5] Lincoln, one of the more enlightened politicians of the era, accurately represented contemporary opinion when he explained in 1858 that he believed there was "a physical difference between the white and black races which . . . will forever forbid the two races from living together on terms of social and political equality." While antislavery supporters would grant the Negro civil rights, few would grant him equal political rights until he was ready to assume them, and very few would grant him full social equality. At the same time, they argued, as Lincoln did, that the Negro's inferiority gave no one the right to enslave him. Whatever his subordinate place in the scheme of things, said William Seward, the black man "is still your brother, and mine

<hr>

4. Arthur Y. Lloyd, *The Slavery Controversy* (Chapel Hill, 1939), 227–43. See also Louis Ruchames, "Sources of Racial Thought in Colonial America," *Journal of Negro History,* LII (October, 1967), 251–73; and Charles H. Wesley, "The Concept of Inferiority of the Negro in American Thought," *Ibid.,* XXV (October, 1940), 540–61. For contemporary views, see John H. Van Evrie, *Negroes and Negro Slavery: The First and Inferior Race, The Latter Its Normal Condition* (1853), and "The Black Race in America," *Southern Literary Messenger,* XXI (November, 1855), 676 ff.

5. Informative studies of attitudes toward race in the United States are Frederick M. Binder, *The Color Problem in Early National America as Viewed by John Adams, Thomas Jefferson, and Andrew Jackson* (The Hague, 1968); and particularly George M. Frederickson, *The Black Image in the White Mind* (New York, 1971). Vincent Freemark and Bernard Rosenthal, eds., *Race and the American Romantics* (New York, 1971), treats the racial ideas of Poe, Melville, Emerson, Cooper, and others. Lowell's 1845 essay, "The Prejudice of Color," is the most judicious and sophisticated treatment of the complexities of the question during the pre-Civil War years.

. . ., and bears equally with us, the present inheritance of our race—the image of our Maker."[6]

Furthermore, the acceptance of theories of white superiority and black inferiority was reinforced by the Jacksonian period's emphasis on egalitarianism. The concept of racial inferiority became an equalizer among *white* Americans, North and South, for it allowed the unsuccessful poor man to accept the doctrine of "natural equality." Jacksonians like John L. O'Sullivan argued that artificial distinctions of class had been eliminated in American society, but nonetheless distinctions of race remained to create natural distinctions which society could never erase.[7]

From 1775 to about 1815 both America and Europe were so entangled in wars that it was difficult for immigrants to leave Europe and equally difficult for them to enter the United States. A few came (about a quarter million during these years) but postwar inflation and depression discouraged others for several years after the peace of 1814. The prosperity of the twenties and thirties, however, and the swift growth of the American economy, turned the stream of arrivals from abroad into a torrent.

The United States offered dazzling prospects to the immigrant. Europe's increased population—which doubled between 1790 and 1830—had nowhere to go; depression, unemployment, epidemic, and famine plagued every country. There were near-revolutions in France, Germany, Belgium, Poland, and Ireland in the late 1820s, ruthlessly put down but not extinguished. On the other hand, in the United States labor was scarce and wages were double or more the European rate; good land cost about one-fourth of what poor land cost in Europe. Fare to the United States was not expensive (£4 to £6 from England) and there was plenty of work and plenty to eat. "Tell Miriam," one immigrant wrote back to his family, "there is no sending children to bed without supper, or husbands to

6. William and Jane Pease, "Antislavery Ambivalence: Immediatism, Expedience, and Race," *American Quarterly*, XVII (Winter, 1965), 682–95. For Northern attitudes, see V. J. Vogeli, *Free But Not Equal* (Chicago, 1967), chapter I.

7. An excellent study of racial theory and American society, which develops this and other points, is George M. Frederickson, *op. cit.* See especially "Slavery and Race," "Science, Polygenesis and the Proslavery Argument," and "Uncle Tom and the Anglo-Saxons."

work without dinner in their bags." Furthermore, America had no military conscription, no overbearing aristocracy, nor did a workman call his employer "Master." Gottfried Duden, who settled in Missouri, wrote home to Germany of his relief at the "absence of overbearing soldiers, haughty clergymen, and inquisitive tax collectors."[8]

Europeans knew little about America, but what they did know was romantic and attractive, compounded out of Cooper's wilderness, Jefferson's agrarian empire, Jackson's kingdom of the common man, and tall tales of miles of virgin trees and acres of fertile soil. Travelers reported the beauties of the new land, newly arrived settlers wrote home about it, and land companies advertised it tirelessly. States passed legislation favorable to immigrants, especially in the new Western country, and frontier communities promised, as the Western Pennsylvania Emigrant Society did, "advantages which are not to be found in Europe nor in any other quarter of the globe."[9]

Enough of it was true to draw hopeful immigrants across the Atlantic by the hundreds of thousands. The statistics were revealing. During the 1830s immigrants arrived at the rate of 60,000 a year, then 80,000, then 100,000, and by the late forties 150,000 a year. In 1851 400,000 arrived, and in 1854, the peak year, 427,833, a number gradually reduced to 144,000 in 1858 (after the panic of 1857) and 141,000 in 1860. By far the largest number entered through New York, which established a processing center at Castle Garden in 1855 (replaced by Ellis Island in 1890), but others entered at New Orleans, Boston, Philadelphia, and Baltimore.[10]

8. The most comprehensive study is Marcus Hansen, *The Atlantic Migration, 1607–1800* (Cambridge, 1940) and his *Immigrant in American History* (Cambridge, 1940). See also Edith Abbott, ed., *Historical Aspects of the Immigration Problem* (Chicago, 1926) and George Stephenson, *A History of American Immigration 1820–1924* (Boston, 1926). John Higham, *Strangers in the Land* (New Brunswick, 1955), though concerned with a later period, is valuable reading.

9. Hansen, *The Atlantic Migration*, 145–71 ff. and Carl Wittke, *We Who Built America* (New York, rev. ed., 1967), 101–16. A traveler in Ireland in 1837 reported that "there were handbills on every corner, tree, and pump and public place in the city of Dublin, and for forty or fifty miles around, that the people were fools not to leave the country . . . , and that work was plenty in America and wages high."

10. *Statistical History of the United States* (Stamford, Conn., 1947) tables under "Migration: International," 59–63.

Although the majority were workers and farmers, the flood swept up people from all classes. Some were mechanics, shipbuilders, shoemakers, printers, metal workers, and other craftsmen. Abortive European revolutions of 1820, 1830, 1848, and 1852 sent liberals and intellectuals like Carl Schurz and Francis Lieber. Utopian and religious groups came (as the Puritans had) seeking freedom for experiment and toleration—communities like Zoar, Amana, Bishop Hill, Icaria, New Harmony, and various Fourieristic phalanxes. Of course, when they could scrape together the fare, the poor came in droves, and with them the landless, the displaced, the victims of war, depression, and famine. But most were laborers, who for the first time formed a distinctive and different American working class, with its own special needs and its own class and cultural outlooks—not a "working class" in the European sense, for it had too many rights and too much mobility for that, but a working class nonetheless.

The largest immigrant groups were Irish and German. During the thirties, arrivals from Ireland made up 44 percent of the total and those from the German states about 30 percent; in the forties the Irish rate reached 49 percent, with the German rate about the same. There were already enough Irishmen in New York in 1812 to form a regiment called the Irish Greens, but the number more than doubled over the next twenty-five years. Ireland, in a chronic state of depression after 1790, offered nothing to keep Irishmen at home. They began to stream out of Ireland toward Australia, Canada, and the United States after 1830, and after the potato rot epidemics of 1845 and 1846 destroyed nearly one-half the crop, the Irish economy collapsed, bringing poverty, starvation, and suffering. One hundred and five thousand Irish entered the United States in 1847, 221,000 in 1851, and the rate continued to rise for another five years.

Although they were chiefly agricultural workers, Irish tended to stay in the Eastern port cities, for few had money for travel, land, or even seed; accustomed to small holdings, few knew how to work the big, diversified American farms as the Germans and Scandinavians did who settled the West.[11] The Irish too tended to cluster about their Catholic churches, which provided stability and security in the

11. In 1860 Minnesota's and Iowa's populations were 20 percent immigrant, and Wisconsin's 30 percent, mostly Germans, Scandinavians, and British, including Welsh, Scots, and Canadians.

big, strange American cities. Not easily assimilated into a Protestant, industrialized, urban culture, the Irish usually worked as servants and laborers and lived in the city's worst slums. Since they brought with them the European workman's tradition of violence and drunkenness, the stereotype of the brawling, drinking, Irish Paddy developed early. They were regarded, wrote one observer, as "a great rabble, who because of their tendency to drunkenness, their fighting, and their knavery, made themselves commonly hated." Yet they were ambitious, hardworking, energetic people, and aggressively patriotic, as the number of Irish Civil War regiments showed. As a people long accustomed to dealing with rent collectors and oppressive landlords, they knew the advantages of organization and took to American politics with skill and enthusiasm. No immigrant group made its influence felt in political life more effectively and quickly than the city Irish.

There were fewer Germans who came before 1860, but they had equal influence on American life.[12] Though the rate increased after the revolution of 1848, Germans were already arriving in sizable numbers during the thirties. There were scholars, educators, reformers, and musicians among them—Karl Follen, who taught at Harvard; journalist Francis Grund; and Gustav Korner, who became Minister to Spain—but the great majority were artisans and farmers. Usually financially better off than the Irish, they moved westward into New York State, Pennsylvania, Ohio, and Illinois, to cities like Albany, Buffalo, Cincinnati, Milwaukee, Chicago, and St. Louis.[13] Better farmers than the Irish, they brought considerable agricultural knowledge to the American West and were responsible in large part (with the Scandinavians and Scots) for the great boom in pre–Civil War agriculture. Less combative than the Irish, and less monolithically Protestant than the Scandinavians, Germans brought too a socially sophisticated tradition of food, drink, recreation, and entertainment. Beer gardens, vineyards, athletic games, dances, theaters, and feasts followed them wherever they went,

12. During the fifties, German immigration slightly exceeded Irish; the 1860 census showed 1,300,000 German residents. The peak year for German immigration was 1854, when 101,000 Irish and 215,000 Germans came. From that point German immigration exceeded Irish.

13. Hansen, *The Atlantic Migration*, chapter VII. Studies show that the average German arrived with about $125. The 1860 census showed over 100,000 Germans in New York, Pennsylvania, Ohio, Illinois, and Wisconsin.

sometimes to the scandal of the native American population. Great believers in education, they founded schools; great musicians, they organized orchestras and singing societies. Germans, in fact, dominated classical music in the United States over the next half century. Adaptable, ambitious, and strongly patriotic (there were German regiments in the Civil War too), they were a powerful cultural force in nineteenth-century America.[14]

Scandinavians, again mostly farmers, came in numbers during the fifties; between 75,000 and 85,000 arrived during the decade. Dutch, Scots, Welsh, and English continued to come, as they had since the early eighteenth century. Jews, treated harshly in Germany after 1815, began to migrate in larger numbers in the twenties. There was already in the United States a small, influential group of Jews in the Eastern cities, and while anti-Semitism was not unknown in American life, it was much less virulent than the European variety. Usually urban people, possessed of education, capital, and business skills, Jewish immigrants scattered into the cities and larger towns where they quickly took over important roles in banking and merchandising.[15]

Some Americans welcomed the immigrant. Ralph Waldo Emerson, reflecting what many felt, believed that

the energy of the Irish, Germans, Swedes, Poles and Cossacks, and all the European tribes—and of the Africans, and of the Polynesians—will construct a new race, a new religion, a new state, a new literature, which will be as vigorous as the new Europe which came out of the smelting pot of the Dark Ages. . . .

Others were not so pleased, and still others were apprehensive about the effects on American society of large groups of people whose language, manners, morals, and life-styles contrasted so sharply with the native culture. Poverty-stricken slums, filled with foreigners, meant rising welfare costs; in New York in 1852 half the state's paupers were Irish, and in 1858 about half of those convicted of crimes in New York were also Irish. Since many immigrants retained their ties with Europe, there was fear that this would mean

14. Henry A. Pochmann, *German Culture in America 1600–1900* (Madison, 1957) is the definitive study.

15. Hansen, *The Atlantic Migration*, 139–42. Scandinavian entries exceeded Irish in 1869 and continued to increase, witth the largest number, 105,000, coming in 1882.

involvement in Europe's troubles. Frequent visits to the United States by European revolutionaries—such as Louis Kossuth's in 1851—did little to quiet such apprehensions. Some Americans suspected a plot by European enemies of democracy to inundate the country with criminals and radicals; thus one speaker warned against "the ravenous dregs of anarchy and crime, the tainted swarms of pauperism and vice that Europe shakes on our shores from her diseased robes." Others perceived a Catholic plot behind it all. Samuel F. B. Morse published two books presumably proving it—*A Foreign Conspiracy* (1834) and *Imminent Dangers to the Free Institutions of the United States Through Foreign Immigration* (1835). Bloc voting by ethnic groups in the cities created new kinds of political problems, while the competition of unskilled cheap labor angered the workingman.[16]

Hostility to the immigrant was based less on racial than on religious and economic grounds. It consisted of four elements, emphasized in various proportions: anti-Catholicism; fear of foreign entanglements; fear of economic competition; and, less frequently, concepts of racial inferiority. Preaching a kind of inverted nationalism, the nativists of the forties and fifties wanted to keep America Protestant, isolated, competitively open, and predominantly Anglo-Saxon in culture.[17] Predictably, the opposition to these "foreign elements" in American society took political form, beginning with secret societies like the Order of the Star-Spangled Banner in the forties and the society known as the Know Nothings, a name taken from the reply members supposedly gave to questions. The "Know Nothing" movement emerged in 1852 as a political force in state and local elections, and then as the American Party in 1854. Millard Fillmore was its presidential candidate in 1856, but its alliance with pro-slavery groups alienated much of its support and it disappeared.[18]

What the nativist organizations wanted to do was to eliminate the immigrant from the political process, fearing that if the foreign-born took control of local, state, and even federal government, the

16. Cf. Nelson Blake, *A Short History of American Life* (New York, 1952), 212–28; Wittke, *op. cit.*, 490–3; Stephenson, *op. cit.*, chapter X; and Ray A. Billington, *The Protestant Crusade 1800–1860* (New York, 1963).

17. See John Higham, "Another Look at Nativism," *Catholic Historical Review*, XLV (July, 1958), 147–58, for an interesting discussion of these components.

18. See Billington, *op. cit.*, for detailed discussion.

whole style and character of American life would change. Thus the Know Nothings demanded that Catholics and "foreigners" be excluded from public office, and that the period for naturalization be extended from five to twenty-one years. The reason was not simply bigotry, but rather an attempt to maintain the quality and values of American culture as it had developed within the context of the Jeffersonian-Jacksonian, Protestant-Anglo-Saxon heritage. Know Nothingism, however, disappeared in the larger issues of the fifties, while the ardent support of immigrant groups of the Union Cause in 1861 erased much hostility toward them for another generation.

The wave of immigration that swept into the United States over the middle years of the nineteenth century permanently altered the content and style of American life. The orderly development of American culture from eighteenth into nineteenth century was sharply diverted by the arrival of large groups of people who carried with them differing sets of intellectual, emotional, and aesthetic attitudes. The influx of immigrants fixed forever in American life the principle of religious diversity. The immigrant might be asked to change his dress, speech, and manners, but never his religion; though the native-born American might resent the Catholic church or the Jewish synagogue, he never attempted to eradicate it. As a result, American Catholicism and American Judaism became the most powerful branches of their faiths in the world. The wide range of ethnic, economic, and religious groups who came to the United States provided America with a pool of cultural traditions, in extent and variety characteristic of no other recent civilization. American life was, as a result, marked by a combination of eclecticism, flexibility, and responsiveness unique in the world. The constant renewal of cultural energy, through continuous infusions of new and old ideas from elsewhere, provided nineteenth-century American life with great vitality as well as great variety.

The relationship between red and white man during the nineteenth century rested on two hundred years of conflict. The history of English settlement in America was one of continuous warfare between Indian and white, beginning with the disappearance of Raleigh's Roanoke Colony in 1586. Except for infrequent peace, the seventeenth and eighteenth centuries were years of constant combat between Indians and settlers, fought with ferocity on both sides;

King Philip's War (1675–76) took the lives of one white New England male in ten, which New England did not forget.

During the French and Indian War, the French had powerful Indian allies, who by accident or design were allowed to commit atrocities, leaving a legacy of hatred, especially on the frontier, after the peace in 1763. During the Revolution Americans hated the British army's Hessian and Indian allies with equal fervor; memories of the massacres at Cherry Valley, in New York, and Wyoming Valley, in Pennsylvania, by British-controlled Indians remained fresh for a long time. After the Revolution, of course, British assistance to the recalcitrant tribes of the Ohio-Indiana-Michigan country rankled deep, and names like Tecumseh and Little Turtle and The Prophet stirred anger in American hearts. Although the battles of Fallen Timbers (1794); Tippecanoe (1811), and Thames (1813) broke Indian power in the Northwest, and Jackson's slaughter at Horseshoe Bend (1814) in Florida in the Southeast, it was a long time before frontier families felt safe from depredations.[19]

By the 1820s, then, the United States had a tradition of Indian fighting that stretched over two centuries. Pacifying the Indian, if indeed he could or ought to be pacified, was a perennial—and, some believed, an insoluble—problem. The nation inherited two incompatible policies from British rule: one, to conciliate, domesticate, and trade with the tribes; the other, to open their lands to white settlement and remove them elsewhere. The tremendous pressures of westward movement meant that the first was simply unacceptable (as the 1763 Proclamation Line had already proved) and the second mandatory. Nor was it ever fully clear in the early years of the Republic where the responsibility for Indian policy lay—in the courts, the Congress, the Executive, the states, or elsewhere. After the Revolution, federal and state governments obtained land for expanding settlements from Indians by force, treaty,

19. A useful source is William N. Fenton, *et al., American Indian and White Relations to 1830* (Chapel Hill, 1957). English and French attitudes toward the Indian are well handled in Lewis Saum, "Frenchmen, Englishmen, and the Indian," *The American West*, I (Fall, 1964), 4–10 ff. Two excellent historical and anthropological studies are Alvin F. Josephy, *The Indian Heritage of America* (New York, 1968) and Peter Farb, *Man's Rise to Civilization* . . . (New York, 1968).

and bribe, not without feelings of guilt, but under necessity to do so by any method.[20]

Most enlightened Americans of Jefferson's generation agreed that dealing with the Indian simply by force was morally wrong and that an honest attempt had to be made to integrate him in some way into American society. Men like William H. Crawford, for example, who became Secretary of War in 1815, sincerely believed that the government must civilize the tribes out of respect for Christian morality. Believing that environment and education were decisive influences in shaping culture, they were convinced that the tribes could be quickly transformed from savage hunters to peaceful yeoman farmers and thus culturally amalgamated into white society. Not realizing that such attempts to change a primitive culture into an advanced one without real knowledge of it or preparation were more likely to shatter and demoralize it, they simply hastened the disintegration of red culture in a well-intentioned effort to preserve it.[21]

On the other hand, the majority of settlers in Indian country, less concerned with abstractions than with land, considered the Indian a removable obstacle. Men like President Monroe believed that since "the earth was given to mankind to support the greater number of which it is capable . . . , no tribe of people have a right to withhold from the wants of others, more than is necessary for their support and comfort." It also seemed clear by the twenties that acculturation of the Indian was not working. Missionaries, philanthropists, government agents, and teachers admitted that they could see little progress in trying to civilize tribes who seemed to be as recalcitrant—or as degraded by liquor—as ever. Support for the assimilation of Indians waned rapidly after 1820, except from a few missionary groups, for, as Calhoun pointed out, it seemed unlikely that any state of the Union would accept such assimilation willingly.[22]

20. A good source of information is Reginald Horsman, *Expansionism and American Indian Policy 1783–1812* (East Lansing, 1967).

21. See Bernard W. Sheehan, *Seeds of Extinction: Jeffersonian Philanthropy and the American Indian* (Williamsburg, 1972) for an extended study of Indian-white relations in the later eighteenth and earlier nineteenth centuries.

22. See Jack D. Forbes, *The Indian in America's Past* (Englewood Cliffs, 1964), 98–105, for a summary of early Indian policy; also Wilcomb Washburn, "The Moral and Legal Justifications for Dispossessing the Indians," in James E. Morton,

Removal of the eastern Indian tribes to land west of the Mississippi was announced as official federal policy by Monroe and carried out energetically by Andrew Jackson, himself an old Indian fighter. Congress passed the Indian Removal Bill in 1830, voided hundreds of old treaties or made new ones, and moved the tribes westward to the newly created Indian territories—not without resistance, however, from Sacs and Foxes under Black Hawk in 1832–37 and from the Seminoles, 1835–43. By 1846, the removal of all major Indian populations from the old Northwest Territory and the Southeast was virtually complete.[23]

American attitudes toward Indians in the first half of the nineteenth century were thus shaped partly by long experience, partly by the expediencies of the moment, and partly by the racial theories of contemporary anthropology. Seventeenth-century Englishmen, who had little previous contact with primitive peoples, knew little about Indian society and culture, and found much of what they learned repugnant—personal habits, warfare, sexual customs—nor could they comprehend Indian attitudes toward such things as property rights, ownership of goods, labor, and political organization. Unable to judge Indian culture by any other standards and values than their own, they could only find it different and inferior.[24] The early colonist assumed that the Indian, since he lived a life of violence and worshipped strange and bloody gods, was quite literally either a beast or a devil; Governor Bradford found them "savage and brutish men, which range up and down, little otherwise than wild beasts."

Eighteenth-century philosophers were divided on the question of

---

ed., *Seventeenth Century America* (Chapel Hill, 1958) ; and the accounts reprinted in Washburn, *The Indian and the White Man* (Garden City, 1964) Part III. A good study of motivation is Reginald Horsman, *The Origins of Indian Removal* (East Lansing, 1970) .

23. F. P. Prucha, "Andrew Jackson's Indian Policy: A Reassessment," *Journal of American History*, LVI (December, 1969) , 527–40, is a recent treatment. The Bureau of Indian Affairs was established in 1836 within the War Department, and transferred in 1841 to the Department of the Interior. Federal policy, said Commissioner Luke Lea in 1851, was "their concentration (*on reservations*), their domestication, and their ultimate incorporation into the great body of the citizen population."

24. Roy Harvey Pearce, *The Savages of America* (Baltimore, 1953) , is the best study of the Indian, savagism, and the American mind. See also David Levin, *History as a Romantic Art* (Stanford, 1959) , 126–36.

the Indian's adaptability to improvement. Montesquieu believed him incapable of civilization; Locke, more optimistic, thought he could be educated and eventually absorbed. Jefferson thought that no matter what was done, Indians would "always relapse into barbarism and misery," as he told John Adams in 1812. But scientists such as Benjamin Smith Barton, arguing from the premise that human nature was the same everywhere, believed that since differences in culture came from environment, the Indian nature could be changed by changing his environment.[25] Romanticism provided still another view of the Indian, as "child of nature" and "noble savage" whose innocent, primitive virtues were threatened by civilization. Thus Mrs. Sarah Wentworth Morton's novel *Ouabi, or the Virtues of Nature* (1790) contrasted the corruptions of civilization with the simplicity and goodness of Indian life, a theme often treated in plays of the period, among them William Dunlap's *Cooloo: An Indian Tale* (1793) and Josiah Arnold's *Warrior's Death Story* (1797).

The search by admirers of Scott for native literary materials and a national past guided them to the forest and the red man; the cult of natural nobility, inherited from the eighteenth century, led in the same direction; the sentimental concern of the Romantics for this "vanishing race" settled on the Indian too. The publication of a number of important works about the Indian during the early nineteenth century drew further attention to his position in the American past and present. Father Heckewelder's *Indian Nations of Pennsylvania* (1818), which proved invaluable to Cooper; Albert Gallatin's pioneer study of Indian ethnography, *Synopsis of the Indian Tribes* (1836); McKenney and Hall's three-volume *History of the Indian Tribes of North America* (1836–44); Schoolcraft's *Algic Researches* (1839) and his *Oneóta* (1844–45); George Catlin's *Manners, Customs, and Condition of . . . the Indians* (1841); Benjamin Drake's *Life of Tecumseh* (1841) —these and other publications captured the interest of artists and scholars throughout the period.

25. Paul Honigsheim, "The American Indian in the Philosophy of the English and French Enlightenment," *Osiris*, X (1952), 91–108. An excellent treatment of American racial theory and the Indian is Gossett, *op. cit.*, chapter X. An interesting and suggestive essay is Alfred I. Hallowell, "The Backwash of the Frontier: The Impact of the Indian on American Culture," in Walter Wyman and Clifton Kreeber, eds., *The Frontier in Perspective* (Madison, 1957).

The newly founded state and local historical societies of the 1820s and 1830s produced hundreds of articles on Indian languages and customs. The discovery of Indian mounds in the West encouraged Romantic speculations about a lost "golden age" and led to the belief, popular in the thirties and forties, that a great "lost race" had once roamed the land. Caleb Atwater, investigating the Ohio mounds, identified forts, temples, altars, racecourses, watchtowers, monuments, and other remains of a highly advanced civilization, no less distinguished, perhaps, than that of the Romans or Egyptians. On the basis of the archaeological remains, wrote Marcus Willson, one might conjecture that "empires flourished here that would vie in power and extent with the Babylonian, Median, and Persian, and cities that might have rivalled Nineveh and Tyre."[26]

Only a minority of Americans probably accepted either the "noble savage" or the "lost race" theory. To the settler who faced the Indian directly, finespun theories were nonsense; at the cutting edge of the frontier the Indian was at the very least a hindrance and at the most a terrifying menace. The frontiersman who lost his wife and children in an Indian raid was not likely to consider the Indian a noble savage. Scientific study of Indian life was far in the future; cultural pluralism did not exist within current anthropology. Henry Rowe Schoolcraft, who served as Indian agent at Sault Sainte Marie and married a half-Indian girl, knew more about Indian culture and society than any other man of his time; but even Schoolcraft could only conclude that the solution to the problem lay in converting the Indian to a farmer and confining him to reservations. Schoolcraft, Cass, Andrews, and a few others who knew Indian life were the exceptions. The first scientifically sound study did not appear until 1851, in Lewis H. Morgan's *League of the*

26. Marcus Willson, *American History: Comprising Historical Sketches of the Indian Tribes* . . . (New York, 1847), 93. See *The Writings of Caleb Atwater* (Columbus, 1833); Josiah Priest, *American Antiquities and Discoveries in the West* (Albany, 1833); and E. O. Randall, "The Moundbuilders and the Lost Tribes," *Ohio Archaeological and Historical Quarterly*, XVII (April, 1908), 208–18. Some speculated that these were the lost tribes of Israel, or Malays, Tartars, Egyptians, or since it was reputed some Indian languages resembled Gaelic, lost tribes of Welshmen. An excellent brief survey of theories is that of William O. Stanton, *The Leopard's Spots* (Chicago, 1960), chapter I. Not until the publication of E. G. Squier's *Ancient Monuments of the Mississippi Valley* in 1848, which proved the remains were Indian, did the "lost race" theory begin to decline.

Iroquois, and it was not until the seventies that further advanced work on Indian culture appeared.

Yet to the earlier nineteenth century, the Indian was undeniably *there,* the problem of his existence ever present and unsettled. Savage or not, primitive innocent or not, assimilatable or not, thousands of Indians lived within the boundaries of the United States without being part of it. The anthropology of the times assumed that race was a determining factor in people's destiny; color, character, and intelligence went together; certain traits were inherent in certain races, nor could they be substantially altered by either education or environment. Some races were better than others, the Indian and Negro being lowest in the scale. Anthropologists, however, endowed the Indian with a different set of qualities than they did the black man. He could not be made a slave, or so it was thought; he had fortitude, courage, and certain primitive codes of honor.[27] It was agreed that though the Indian's color marked him as inferior to the white man, it was for reasons different from those which made the Negro inferior—chiefly because he was savage in a way that the black man was not.

The idea of the Indian as irremediably savage was the commonly accepted basis for thinking about him for the first half of the nineteenth century. The article "America," written by Jedidiah Morse for the *Encyclopaedia Britannica* in 1793 and widely reprinted over the next fifty years, noted the Indian's "propensity to violence," the "surprising contrasts" of his nature, his "perfidy combined with cruelty," and his "weak understanding" and morality. Whether such primitives could ever be raised from their savage state, whether they possessed sufficiently strong mental and spiritual qualities ever to be absorbed into civilized society—these were debatable questions throughout the first half of the century. Henry Schoolcraft believed that they could, with education and discipline, improve themselves—in reporting to the federal government on Indian affairs in 1850, he claimed to have observed measurable "progressive improvement in the Indian character." Anthropologist Lewis Morgan, in writing his study of the Iroquois, believed too

27. Cooper ranked the Indian above the Negro in the hierarchy of races, comparing an Indian chieftain to a Negro slave in *The Redskins* (1846), while scientist Louis Agassiz contrasted the "indomitable, courageous, proud Indian" with the "submissive, obsequious, imitative Negro" and the "tricky, cunning, and cowardly Mongolian." See Gossett, *op. cit.,* 242–4.

that Indians could progress toward civilization if given the proper means.[28]

The opposition, however, had stronger arguments. It was generally agreed that the Indian's racial inheritances made it impossible to civilize him. It followed, then, that if he could not improve and be integrated into civilized life, he would therefore disappear. Joel Poinsett of South Carolina, who made a thorough investigation of the issue in his *Inquiry . . . on the Natural Progress of the Human Race from Barbarism to Civilization* (Charleston, 1834), concluded that the Indian would "have to retreat before the advance of civilization, or perish." Josiah Nott, studying Indian phrenology, felt that the Indian did not possess the mental equipment for civilization, and that "a full-blooded civilized Indian is a contradiction in terms." Andrew Jackson, in his *Second Message to Congress,* could see no reason to bemoan the red man's departure:[29]

Humanity has often wept over the fate of the aborigines of this country, and Philanthropy has been long busily employed in devising means to avert it, but its progress has never for a moment been arrested, and one by one have many powerful tribes disappeared from the earth.

Experience and observation seemed to substantiate this. Josiah Nott's edition of Gobineau's work (1856), called *The Moral and Intellectual Diversity of Races,* showed that neither Indians nor Negroes had ever progressed over the centuries, despite changes of education and environment. Frontiersmen like Timothy Flint took a simpler view, that the Indian was naturally "organized to the love of the horrible excitement of war and murder for their own sake."[30] It was "common opinion," wrote the Commissioner of Indian Affairs as late as 1860, that "there are such inherent obstacles in the Indian's character that he cannot become a peaceable, industrious, and humane citizen."

28. See Arthur Ekirch, *The Idea of Progress in America* (New York, 1951), 44–6.

29. James Richardson, *Messages and Papers of the Presidents* (Washington, 1896–99), II:520–1. Nott's *Types of Mankind* (Philadelphia, 1856) found Indian skulls showed overdeveloped organs of "animal propensity" and underdeveloped organs of intellect.

30. See Stanton, *op. cit.,* 174–6; Gossett, *op. cit.,* 73–5; Flint, *Indian Wars of the West* (Cincinnati, 1833), 37. Western traders agreed that Indians were "childlike, lazy, selfish, dishonest, and inferior," incapable of civilization; see Lewis Saum, *The Fur Trader and the Indian* (Seattle, 1966).

Tragic as the prospect appeared, it was thus inevitable that the Indian seemed doomed to perish as a race. The historian George Bancroft came to this conclusion thoughtfully—and sadly—when in the writing of the third volume of his *History of the United States* in 1839 he considered the Indian's past and future. Drawing on the best contemporary anthropological scholarship, he gave over an entire chapter to a history of the Indian in North America, concluding with the question: How could the elimination of the Indian and the displacement of his culture by the American settler be explained and justified within a reasonable historical and philosophical framework?

In providing an answer Bancroft resorted to a double solution. On the one hand, he adopted the prevailing sentimental view of the Indian, given its greatest popularity by Cooper and the Romantic historical novelists, of the Indian as "child of nature," the "last of a mighty race" who "came into the presence of a race more powerful than his" and was doomed to vanish. At the same time, Bancroft turned to contemporary anthropology for a quite different answer. The Indian was doomed because although he possessed the same faculties as the white man, he did not have the power of using them in such a manner as to become truly civilized. The Indian possessed "the moral faculty which can recognize the distinction between right and wrong," but he was unable to use it; he possessed reason, but he followed instead "the promptings of undisciplined instinct"; he possessed imagination, but he was "limited to the external world in its application" and "nearly destitute of abstract moral truth." In other words, the Indian was hopelessly savage, dominated by instinct, and could not adapt to civilization—he must, therefore, disappear.[31]

Bancroft's chapter reflected the views of the majority of thoughtful Americans of the period. The "doomed race" concept appealed to the Romantic mind, echoing its favorite themes of mutability

31. In the 1879 edition, this was expanded to three chapters in Volume II, covering the languages, history, manners, polity, religion, and origins of the Indian. Parkman, in *The Conspiracy of Pontiac* (1851), came to much the same conclusions; the extinction of the Indian, wrote Jedidiah Morse, was inevitable "by the unavoidable operation of natural causes." See Russel B. Nye, "Parkman: Red Fate and White Civilization," in Clarence Gohdes, ed., *Essays on American Literature* (Durham, 1967), 152–64. Morse is quoted in *The North American Review*, XVI (January, 1823), 30–5.

and transience. Bryant and Freneau caught some of this sense of loss
in poetry, James Fenimore Cooper in his novels, and so did the
paintings of George Catlin, who spent many months capturing
moments of the colorful, savage life, so soon to disappear, on canvas.
The "vanishing American" theme, treated at varying levels of
sentimentality, permeated the literature of the period. Between
1824 and 1834 there were thirty-nine novels about Indians, and
between 1820 and 1860 over fifty plays. John A. Stone's *Metamora:
or the Last of the Wampanoags*, written in 1829, played for twenty-
three consecutive years in Philadelphia alone and was still on the
boards in 1889. Cooper's Uncas, the last of the Mohicans in the
novel of the same name (1829), became one of fiction's most famous
characters; Longfellow's *Hiawatha* (1855) sold 50,000 copies in its
first four months and became the century's best-selling poem. The
Pocahontas story of star-crossed lovers, which first appeared in
James Nelson Barker's play *The Indian Princess* (1808), reappeared at least thirty times in literature before the close of the
century.[32]

In direct contradiction was another body of literature, drawn
from an older tradition, which treated the Indian as barbaric
savage, the legacy of years of raids and massacres. The "captivity"
story, relating the terrors of Indian cruelty, had been a staple in
American literature since the seventeenth century; over five hundred such accounts were published during the colonial period,
while Mary Rowlandson's (second edition, 1682) after thirty editions was still in print in 1860. Her story of life among "these
atheistical, proud, wild, cruel, barbarous, brutish (in one word)
diabolical creatures" set a pattern for a kind of popular literature
that persisted for two hundred years, repeated in the nineteenth
century in such books as Samuel Drake's *Indian Captivities* (1839),
and *The Narrative of the Captivity and Sufferings of Isaac Knight*
(1839). Robert Montgomery Bird's brutal novel of revenge and
Indian killing, *Nick of the Woods* (1837), provided a violent anti-
dote to Cooper's noble Mohicans and a model for thousands of
dime novels in which thousands of rascally redskins bit the dust.

32. See Pearce, *op. cit.*, chapter VI; Albert Keiser, *The Indian in American
Literature* (New York, 1933); Paul A. W. Wallace, "Cooper's Indians," *New York
History*, XXX (1954), 423-46.

The situation of the Negro was quite different. There were many more Negroes than Indians; they lived in close proximity to white society; and they had been an integral part of the American social and economic system for over a century.[33] The Negro had (it was assumed) no culture of his own, and he had for the most part adopted white ways and values. As a slave he performed essential services and contributed substantially to the national wealth. He was not nomadic, his entire life was carefully controlled by custom and law, nor had there ever been (as with the Indian) the slightest thought of assimilating him into the mainstream of American society. Large as it was, the black population never posed a direct danger to public or individual safety, nor had the Negro—unlike the Indian—any tradition of war or resistance. The white population (as it did not of the Indian) knew a great deal about Negro society, which was not an uncomplicated one. There were free Northern blacks and free Southern blacks; domestic, skilled, and field slaves; urban slaves and rural slaves; uneducated and educated blacks—all judged by current anthropological racial theory to be inferior to all other races.

Nevertheless, the question of the black man's place in an American society founded on the natural rights of free and equal men was not entirely settled, racial theory to the contrary. Enlightened men, Northern and Southern, were well aware of the anomaly of slavery in a free country. Strong opposition to slavery and to racial discrimination ran deep in religious groups such as the Society of Friends; that slavery did not fit into the natural rights ideology had long bothered such men as Franklin and Jefferson; there were more than a few Southerners of distinction and power who disliked the system and were disturbed by its presence. After the Revolution Negroes like minister Lemuel Haynes of New England, mathematician Benjamin Banneker, and Paul Cuffe, the Massachusetts shipowner, fought for the right to vote and almost obtained it. But no

33. In 1830 there were 2,328,042 Negroes counted in the census, of whom 2,010,043 were slaves. In 1840 there were 3,638,808, of whom 3,204,313 were slaves; in 1860 4,441,830, with 3,953,760 slaves, out of a total population of 31,513,000. Indians were not counted by the census until 1860, and then only those on reservations or resident in Indian Territory. The definition of "Indian" was never clear, and persons of mixed blood were counted either way. The 1860 census showed only 440,021 Indians. *Statistical History of the United States* (Stamford, Conn., 1947), 9.

one had satisfactory answers to the questions raised by Negro slavery, while the rise of the South's cotton economy made criticism of the system more difficult and the subordination of the black man seemingly more necessary.[34]

The Northern Negro's life was quite different, obviously, from that of the Southern Negro, free or slave; yet there were similarities. Northern society believed in white supremacy and black inferiority, sanctioned social and economic discrimination, and segregated the Negro in jails, hospitals, churches, schools, parks, and public accommodations. Racial restrictions applied in burial grounds, trade and employment, and residency; the pattern of the racially-segregated city was firmly established in the North before 1850. After the opening of the aggressive phase of the abolitionist movement, there were serious anti-Negro riots in cities like Philadelphia, New York, Pittsburgh, and Cincinnati, while individual Negroes who defied custom, as Frederick Douglass and David Ruggles and Charles Remond determined to do, were beaten or humiliated.[35]

Yet the Northern Negro could organize and protest as the Southern Negro could not. His life was a constant struggle against prejudice and injustice, and he continually demanded those rights to which the Declaration and the Constitution said he was entitled. Black leaders read the documents of American history carefully and knew them in detail; in sermons, editorials, orations, and pamphlets they reminded white men that they did not have them. The statement adopted by the National Negro Convention of 1853 was typical:[36]

34. August Meier and Elliott Rudwick, *From Plantation to Ghetto* (New York, 1966), chapter I, is a useful summary of slavery in American life to 1830. John Hope Franklin, *From Slavery to Freedom* (third ed., New York, 1967) is an essential source, while excellent documentary collections are Leslie H. Fishel and Benjamin Quarles, *The Negro American* (Glenview, Ill., 1967) and Gilbert Osofsky, ed., *The Burden of Race* (New York, 1967).

35. Leon Litwack, *North of Slavery* (Chicago, 1961); see Meier and Rudwick, *op. cit.*, chapter III, for further accounts. Chester A. Arthur served as attorney for a Negro woman who was ejected from a New York streetcar in 1854 and collected substantial damages.

36. Quoted by Earl E. Thorpe, *The Mind of the Negro* (Baton Rouge, 1961), 358. Such declarations should be read in light of the fact that in 1840 only five states allowed free Negroes to vote, that they were banned from jury duty in all states except one, that the Indiana Constitution of 1851 banned Negroes from the state for purposes of residency. See Franklin F. Ferguson, *The Negro American: A History* (Ann Arbor, 1969), 51–6.

We declare that we are, and of right we ought to be, American *citizens*. We claim this right, and we claim all the rights and privileges, and duties, which properly attach to it. By birth, we are American citizens; by the principles of the Declaration of Independence we are American citizens; within the meaning of the United States Constitution we are American citizens; by the facts of American history . . . we are American citizens.

The Northern free Negro was well aware of what prejudice meant—he could not learn some trades, he could not participate in social or business life, he was constantly subjected to experiences which, as Charles Remond said, "demean and embarrass."[37] Black leaders emphasized that they were "native Americans, children of the soil," that they were born in the United States, had contributed much to its progress, and deserved to share in its benefits. No speaker put the case more eloquently than Frederick Douglass, who told his fellow Americans in 1841 that the existence of slavery in the country "brands your republicanism as a sham, your humanity as a base pretense, your Christianity as a lie."[38]

The greatest obstacle in the path of the black man, every Negro knew, was his color. On this depended the white man's conviction that the Negro was inherently alien, forever set apart. If the Negro were to find an equal place within American society, he would have to establish his black identity as an equal and have it accepted by the white majority. He could do this, his leaders reasoned, first by taking pride in his race, its accomplishments, and its potential; and second by proving the validity of his own American past by establishing his own historical roots. Negro leaders constantly proclaimed their belief in themselves as *black* men, equal to men of any other race, and protested the use of "nigger" and other racial slurs. "We shall ever cherish our identity of origin or race," resolved the National Emigration Convention in 1854,

37. For a powerful statement of Negro feelings, see the speech of the Reverend Theodore S. Dwight to the New York Antislavery Society, 1837, in Carter C. Woodson, ed., *Negro Orators and Their Orations* (New York, 1969) .

38. Robert Ernst, "Negro Concepts of Americanism," *Journal of Negro History* XXXIX (July, 1954) , 206–20. Quotations are from Herbert Aptheker, *A Documentary History of the American Negro* (New York, 1951) , 217, and Thorpe, *op. cit.*, chapter III. Douglass's speech is from *The Liberator,* November 19, 1841. His speech at Rochester, New York, July 4, 1852, is a powerful statement of this issue, "What to the Slave Is the Fourth of July?"

as preferable, in our estimation, to any other people; that the relative terms Negro, or African, Black, Colored, and Mulatto, when applied to us shall ever be held with the same respect, and pride; and synonymous with the terms Caucasian, White, Anglo-Saxon, and European, when applied to that class of people.

Negroes tirelessly reminded the white public that if their race seemed to have accomplished less in terms of white values, the reason lay not in color but in the black man's lack of preparation and opportunity; given these, he could achieve equally with any race. As one group of Ohio Negroes put it in 1856,[39]

The assumption that we are ignorant is untrue; but even if it were true, it really affords an argument for the removal of our disabilities that cramp our energies, destroy the feelings of self-respect, so essential to form the character of a good citizen.

To refute the doctrine of black inferiority and to show that Negroes "by their genius, capacity, and intellectual development" could surmount all the hindrances which slavery and prejudice had placed in their way, the Negro press and pulpit reported the black man's accomplishments in whatever field they could, emphasizing his contributions to American life.

Northern Negroes fought the slavery system in the South with every weapon they could. The movement to abolish slavery by colonizing the Negro in Africa or some other land aroused their unremitting opposition. Since they believed the United States their native and proper home, any attempt to remove slaves to some "barbarous, savage land" they considered a monstrous denial of their rights. Conventions of Afro-Americans held in 1830 and 1832 condemned the scheme roundly; the second featured a debate between William Lloyd Garrison, who opposed colonization, and R. R. Gurley of the American Colonization Society, which Garrison won easily. After that the support of Northern black leaders like Douglass went overwhelmingly to the abolitionists, although some black militants, convinced that slavery would never be abolished and that the Negro's case was hopeless, proposed to emigrate to

39. See Thorpe, *op. cit.*, 39, 65, 102; Fischel and Quarles, *op. cit.*, 138. Douglass, a powerful, imposing, and handsome man, used to step to the edge of the speaker's platform and say quietly, "Am I a man?"

Africa or to some other part of the world to form a free Negro nation.[40]

Meanwhile the Northern Negro organized his community life for his self-protection and advancement. Beginning in 1830, when the first Convention of Free Men of Color met in Philadelphia, Negro organizations sponsored state and national conventions—among them the Annual Convention of Afro-Americans, the Citizens' Union of Pennsylvania, and the American League of Colored Laborers—to discuss, protest, and memorialize; the National Council of Colored People was formed in 1853 to coordinate their efforts.[41] Negroes founded newspapers not only to agitate for black rights but also to establish the identity of the black community. There were twenty-four Negro newspapers published between 1827 and 1861, many irregular and ephemeral, with names like *The Mirror of Liberty, The Genius of Freedom,* and *The Alienated American;* others, like the African Methodist Episcopal Church organ, *The Christian Recorder,* were soundly financed and well-edited. Douglass's *North Star* (later called *Frederick Douglass' Paper*), published at Rochester, was perhaps the most famous and certainly one of the most effective.[42]

The mutual benefit society also served as an agency for maintaining stability and cohesion within the black community. The African Union Society, founded in 1780, recorded births, deaths, and marriages, supervised burials, and assisted the needy. Similar societies sprang up through the early years of the nineteenth century, sponsoring schools, libraries, apprentice programs, and insurance; during the thirties there were 106 such groups in Philadelphia alone. City Negroes also formed chapters of fraternal societies

40. Led by Martin Dulany, whose book, *The Condition, Elevation, and Destiny of the Colored People of the United States Politically Considered* (1852), provided the impetus for the movement. Dulany, a Harvard graduate in medicine, served in the Civil War and was the first black soldier to be commissioned to field rank by Lincoln.

41. See Howard Bell, "National Negro Conventions," in August Meier and Elliot Rudwick, eds., *The Making of Black America* (New York, 1969), 315–26; Franklin, *op. cit.*, 236–38; and Bella Gross, *Development of the Negro Peoples' Convention Movement* (New York, 1947).

42. Irving Garland, *The Afro-American Press and Its Editors* (Springfield, Ill., 1891) and Frederick Detweiler, *The Negro Press in the United States* (Chicago, 1922).

(obtaining charters from England) like the Masons and Odd Fellows. Other orders, whose rites and oaths appealed as much to black men as they did to white, appeared with names like The Nazarites, The Seven Wise Men, and The Galileans. These were valuable sources to the community of organization and leadership.[43]

The free black man was acutely aware of the importance of education, for he knew that so-called Negro ignorance was both a major factor in propagating the myth of racial inferiority and a device for keeping the black man under control. White church groups, abolitionist societies, and philanthropic organizations maintained schools in some cities, but many public schools in the North were segregated, unequal, and inadequate. In Ohio, Michigan, Wisconsin, and Iowa there were no public school funds for Negro schools until the fifties, nor in Illinois and Indiana until the late sixties. Massachusetts established separate public schools for black children in the twenties, New York in the thirties and forties. Negro churches, societies, and conventions constantly asked city and state governments for more and better schools, believing with Douglass that to educate the Negro was "to invest him with a power that shall open to him the treasures of freedom."

The center of Northern black society was the church. Although the Negro had been accepted into white churches in the North and into some in the South during the colonial period, it was clear to Negroes by the late eighteenth century that resistance to racial integration within the churches was growing stronger and that a separate, independent black church was the only answer. Although this meant segregation, it also meant that the Negro would have some refuge from white prejudice and control, and that he might find in his own church opportunities for self-expression and self-respect. Richard Allen and Absalom Jones organized the African Methodist Episcopal Church in 1794; an African Baptist Church was formed in Philadelphia in 1809 and another in Boston the same year. By 1816 there were a sufficient number of African M. E. congregations to warrant a national organization, while by the twenties there were black churches in all major cities. In New York City a group led by

43. Meier and Rudwick, *Plantation to Ghetto*, chapter II; Franklin, *op. cit.*, 226–7. Prince Hall and fourteen other Negroes were raised to Masons by British officers in Boston in 1775. Negro Odd Fellows did not appear until 1843.

Peter Williams founded the African Methodist Episcopal Zion Church in 1796 and elected their first bishop in 1822.[44]

These churches and societies furnished the acknowledged leaders of Northern black intellectual life, men like Pennsylvania's James Forten and William Whipper. Forten was active in almost all state and national Negro organizations, and his *Letters of a Man of Colour* (1813) was one of the influential documents of the early antislavery movement; Whipper was an organizer of the American Moral Reform Society that same year. In New York Peter Williams, an Episcopal clergyman, and Theodore S. Dwight, a Presbyterian minister, were especially effective leaders. David Ruggles, the secretary of the New York Committee of Vigilance (formed to protect Negroes from seizure as escaped slaves), served as spokesman for the militant wing of the city's black antislavery element; Henry Highland Garnet, son of a slave and educated at Oneida Institute, was also a New York minister. Charles Lenox Remond was a powerful leader in the Boston black community; Samuel Ringgold Ward, a Presbyterian minister in New York State, spoke in every hamlet and city in the East against the Fugitive Slave Law. There were others of equal or lesser fame who used the platform, press, and pulpit to advantage.

Southern slaves, the oldest and largest American minority, constituted about 15 percent of the population by the early decades of the nineteenth century. Because of the Southern Negro's legal and racial situation, his culture developed separately from that of the Northern black, but it was no less American, nor less indigenous. As Margaret Butcher has pointed out, the slavery system "planted the Negro deep into the subsoil of American life and made him culturally a basic American" who assimilated, while adapting it to his own situation, the whole cultural apparatus of American life. The slave system, however, also erected a barrier between him and

44. Carter G. Woodson, *The History of the Negro Church* (Washington, 1921); and Franklin, *op. cit.*, 162–5, 226–8. In 1787 a group of slaves led by Richard Allen started the independent black church movement in America, establishing the Free African Society and two churches. Allen later rose to the office of bishop. See Carol Ann George, *Richard Allen and the Independent Black Church Movement 1760–1840* (New York, 1973).

American life which forced him and his culture into a parallel current, rather than the mainstream, of that life.[45]

Southern slave society was more complex than it seemed. There were about a quarter-million free Negroes (free either by manumission or self-purchase) concentrated in the cities. Occasionally quite prosperous, the urban free Negro tended to model his manners and values on white middle-class society. Since slavery was predicated on the assumption that the Negro could not take care of himself, and since the free black was also assumed to be a potential source of trouble by the very fact of his existence, his life was ringed with restrictions. Despite such controls, a number of free blacks attained relative security and prosperity; by 1860, for example, in Virginia blacks were working at fifty-four different kinds of jobs.[46]

Their lot, however, was not much better than that of the urban slave, who often enjoyed considerable freedom. "A city slave," Douglass recalled, "was almost a free citizen." Many were skilled workmen—carpenters, tailors, shoemakers, weavers, mechanics, seamstresses, and so on—who earned substantial profit for their masters and who sold for three or four times the price of a prime field hand. House slaves, whether urban or rural, shared the manners, style, and life of white masters, to whom they might even be related by blood. From this group of slaves came the clerks, artisans, cooks, and servants who kept the plantation economy running, in return for which they were granted considerable privileges, even literacy and cultivation. "Mammy" or "Auntie" or faithful "Old Ned" occupied a special position within the slave system, oversentimentalized by slaveholders but nonetheless real.[47]

45. Margaret Butcher, *The Negro in American Culture* (New York, 1957), 1–9, contains an excellent discussion of the Negro's cultural situation in American society.

46. Ferguson, *op. cit.*, 51–3. Depending on the state, a free black man could not own firearms, purchase liquor, move about freely, testify in court, hold meetings, leave his county of residence, sell corn or tobacco, work as a clerk, buy on credit, set type, or send his children to school, but he could buy and sell property.

47. Southern city slaves numbered about 400,000 in 1850; the number of non-urban slaves was about 2,800,000, of whom between 1,800,000 and 2,000,000 were farm and plantation workers. For descriptions and analyses of the slave system, see Franklin, *op. cit.*, chapter XIII; and Kenneth Stampp, *The Peculiar Institution* (New York, 1956); and for urban slavery, Richard C. Wade, *Slavery in the Cities: The South 1820–40* (New York, 1964). About 25,000 Southerners owned half the slaves.

The culture of the field slave was least influenced by white culture and thus tended to retain far more of its African heritage. Those elements which the slaves adopted from white culture—in music, religion, social patterns, and the like—became clearly Negrified, neither white nor African, but with distinctive American and black identity of their own.[48]

The social and cultural institution at the base of Negro slave life was the church, which served the master as a device for control and acculturation, and the slave as a means of adjustment and self-expression. The Negro lost in the journey from Africa nearly all his social bonds—his language, religion, kinships, folkways, values, and his sense of group cohesion. The church and Christianity gave him a foundation for a wholly different kind of Westernized life. Throughout the seventeenth and early eighteenth centuries some slaveholders thought converted slaves were easier to control, while others took seriously the Biblical injunction to bring salvation to the heathen.[49] During the later eighteenth century, however, Methodists and Baptists began intensive missionary work among the slaves. The creed that their missionaries preached was simple and direct; its emotionalism attracted the oppressed; the camp meeting's revivalistic atmosphere, which encouraged group participation, gave black people a feeling of collective identity they sorely needed. More important, evangelical Christianity's emphasis on the Bible furnished the slave with a whole new set of gods, doctrines, myths, tales, and folk heroes to replace those he had lost. The story of Jewish slavery and deliverance had special significance to the slave; David's conquest of Goliath held great symbolic meaning to him; "old Pharaoh" provided him with a villain, Joshua with a warrior-hero, Daniel in the lion's den with an inspirational allegory. The Bible formed the heart of much of black thought and art. The church became in the South, as in the North, the focal organizing point of black life, and the black missionary or preacher the closest thing to a leader that slave society had.[50]

48. Butcher, op. cit., 20–26. The Methodist hymn became the spiritual, which was neither African nor white; the Biblical account of Daniel or Moses, in the course of adaptation, turned into something quite different in quality and purpose than the white version.

49. See E. Franklin Frazier, The Negro Church in America (New York, 1964).

50. There were famous preachers like "Black Henry" and Harry Hosier, both of whom once traveled with Bishop Asbury; John Jasper, who preached in Virginia for sixty years; and others with wide reputations like "Virginia Jack," Harry

In some cities there were separate Negro churches, but in others slaves attended their masters' churches but were seated separately. The reactions of owners to the Negro church varied considerably; some paid little attention to the slaves' religious life, some suspected churches as sources of trouble, others encouraged them. Actually, the version of Christianity the church gave to the slave was quite orthodox, emphasizing those doctrines that applied to his lot. The slave should obey the Biblical injunction to serve his master; God was just, belief in Him would be vindicated, and the Negro who kept the faith would be freed in the hereafter. "The deeper the piety of the slave," said one Southerner, "the more valuable he is in every respect."[51]

As the abolitionist crusade mounted in intensity Southern states and communities established tighter control of black churches, ministers, and meetings; the fact that Nat Turner, who led the Virginia revolt of 1831, was a deeply religious lay preacher was not lost on Southern minds. Black preachers, it was suspected, did not always preach submission, nor did slaves always believe it. Bible stories could work both ways. The children of God, after all, fled from Pharaoh's land, as Samuel Ward, William Wells Brown, Josiah Henson, Henry "Box" Brown, and dozens of others fled North toward Canaan.[52]

It is practically impossible to reconstruct the mind of the slave or to find out what his attitudes really were. Since slaves were generally illiterate, they left few written records, nor did they reveal themselves to white persons. Accounts written by escaped slaves were not always typical or trustworthy; often edited or written by white men and women, these "narratives" or "memoirs" very likely represented the white reformer's idea of how it felt (or should feel) to be black and a slave. Over many generations the slave developed techniques of deception that were, for the white man, virtually impenetrable.[53]

Evans, and George Sharp. See William Pipes, *Say Amen, Brother!* (New York, 1951) and Ruby Johnson, *The Development of Negro Religion* (New York, 1954) .

51. See Benjamin Mays, *The Negro's God as Reflected in His Literature* (Boston, 1938) , and Frazier, *op. cit.,* chapter V.

52. Thorpe, *op. cit.,* 24–5. See also Vincent Harding, "Religion and Resistance Among Antebellum Negroes," in Meier and Rudwick, eds., *Black America,* 179–99.

53. Mrs. A. M. French, who went South to teach Negroes, observed that the slave dissembled in the presence of the white man at all times. "He is never off ·

Relationships between slaves and masters quite early developed stable, rigidly observed patterns. Blacks were considered as workers or children, depending on their proximity and situation. Close relationships between house slaves and master families were not unusual and quite authentic, but masters often had little contact with or feeling for field slaves. A slaveholder might grieve at the death of a faithful servant, as one South Carolinian did, and record the death of two field hands and a mule in the same sentence. Some slaves were special pets, given comic names like Caesar or Venus or Pompey and treated with "that maudlin tenderness," wrote Fanny Kemble, "of a fine lady for a lapdog"; others were simply cattle, as articles on slave keeping in *DeBow's Review* showed year after year. Whatever the relationship, it could never be of equals. The ideal relationship, slaveholders constantly reiterated, was as parent to child.[54]

The tribal family-life pattern of African society was completely disrupted by the transfer to America, while the pattern of white family life was not available to the Negro as a substitute. Marriage among slaves was casual and had no legal standing; the sale of children or parents broke the family unit. Negro family life was matriarchal—the child had economic value and the practice of breeding slaves for sale gave the father little importance or responsibility. At the same time, relations between white owners and slave women produced a different kind of family, which existed parallel to, but not part of, the white family unit.[55]

guard. He is perfectly skilled at hiding his emotions. . . . His master knows him not." Quoted in Fischel and Quarles, *op. cit.*, 117. Some concept of what the slave thought about his situation may be gained from Stanley Feldstein's study of slave accounts, *Once a Slave: The Slave's View of Slavery* (New York, 1971) ; and Charles H. Nichols, *Many Thousands Gone: The Ex-Slave's Account of Bondage and Freedom* (London, 1963) .

54. Stampp, *op. cit.*, 324–7. The most delicately controlled master-slave relationship was sexual, despite laws forbidding miscegenation. Sexual relations between black men and white women, though rare, apparently did occur. Those between white men and black women were tacitly approved, concubinage fairly common. The fact that the census of 1860 showed about one in ten of all Southern slaves was classified as mulatto testifies to widespread racial intermingling. See Thorpe, *op. cit.*, 135–7; Stampp, 350–57; and James H. Johnston, *Miscegenation in the Antebellum South* (Chicago, 1939) , and *Race Relations in Virginia and Miscegenation in the South 1776–1860* (Amherst, 1970) .

55. For a comprehensive treatment, see E. Franklin Frazier, *The Negro Family in the United States* (New York, 1948) .

Even under good masters, slavery was a dehumanizing system, against which any overt protest by the slave was immediately doomed. "Black codes" governed his life down to the smallest detail, with punishments and deprivations imposed by regular courts, slave courts, and the master. No slave could take a case to court without a white sponsor, and most justice was meted out at home.[56] Any slave protest, therefore, was of necessity covert. Slaves feigned stupidity and humility, lost or broke tools, pretended illness, damaged crops, sabotaged machines, set fires, hid or ran away, and did other things against which white masters had no defense. Fooling "Ole Marster" was a favorite slave game.[57] Self-mutilation and suicide were rare, actual uprisings infrequent, but some were violent—Gabriel Prosser in 1800, George Boxley in 1815, Denmark Vesey in 1822, Nat Turner in 1831. There were disturbances among slaves of one kind or another almost monthly through the forties, until by the fifties parts of the South lived in paranoid fear.[58]

Whatever the Southerner's belief that most slaves were "contented," there is little trustworthy evidence to support it. Obviously there were wide variations in how slaves were treated; obviously, too, fear of punishment made slaves docile and willing to bear hardship. Some plantations had vicious and sadistic overseers and owners, others mild and humane ones. On the other hand, celebrations, dances, feasts, and holidays (ironically, the Fourth of July) were part of the slave's life too. Punishments and hardships could break some slaves' wills and frighten others into subjection. It toughened men such as Douglass and Remond, who never

56. Stampp, *op. cit.*, chapter IX, "To Make Them Stand in Fear." Franklin, *op. cit.*, 187–9 is a good summary of laws and punishments. Branding and whipping were the most common punishments, with imprisonment and death for capital crimes, which included rape, arson, and conspiracy to revolt. For studies of specific cases see Helen T. Caterall, *Judicial Cases Concerning American Slavery* (Washington, 1939).

57. See Stampp, *op. cit.*, 109–24, *passim*; Ferguson, *op. cit.*, 44–6; and Raymond and Alice Bauer, "Day to Day Resistance to Slavery," *Journal of Negro History*, XXVII (October, 1942).

58. J. W. Coowell, "The Aftermath of Nat Turner's Insurrection," *Journal of Negro History* (April, 1920), 208–35; Harvey Wish, "The Slave Insurrection Panic of 1856," *Journal of Southern History*, V (February–November, 1939), 206–91. Comprehensive but not trustworthy is Herbert Aptheker, *American Negro Slave Revolts* (New York, 1943). See also Marion Kilson, "Towards Freedom: An Analysis of Slave Revolts in the United States," in Meier and Rudwick, eds., *Black America*, 164–78.

gave in, and every locality had its "bad" slaves who fought the system every inch of the way. Despite variations in treatment, and despite the existence of good and bad masters, no Negro after emancipation ever looked back at slavery with anything but fear of it and hatred for it.[59]

Black culture was essentially American culture, for most African elements brought to American shores were soon eliminated by slavery. The cultural life of the Negro was thus almost wholly fashioned from the materials of and within the forms of the majority culture of the master class; the black artist perforce worked within that context, for he had no other. Denied education, assumed to be incapable of creative expression, early black writers—few in number—understandably wrote in imitation of the white tradition.[60]

The dearth of Negro writing, of course, did not mean that the black man had nothing to say, but rather that it was extremely difficult for him to say it. Few blacks had either the training or time for writing, and since the only kind of writing the public would accept was its own, any Negro who wrote was judged in terms of how well he could imitate white art.

The growth of antislavery feeling in the early nineteenth century helped to encourage black writing, gave it a medium for expression, and, more importantly, provided a motive to write.[61] Memoirs, autobiographies, and slave narratives appeared in profusion after the thirties, dealing with life under slavery, escapes, conversions to Christianity, and the like. The majority were edited by, or in some cases written by, white reformers who emphasized their value as propaganda. They were also, of course, interesting and exciting stories in their own right, resembling the Indian captivity tales already popular for more than a century; they too dealt with the

59. Cf. the discussion in Thorpe, op. cit., chapter IV, and in G. M. Frederickson and C. Lasch, "Resistance to Slavery," Civil War History, XIII (December, 1967), 315–30.

60. For accounts of early Negro writing, see Benjamin Brawley, The Negro Genius (New York, 1969); and Vernon Loggins, The Negro Author in America (New York, 1964). The best critical introduction to earlier black poetry is the collection edited, with a useful bibliography, by William H. Robinson, Early Black American Poets (Dubuque, 1969).

61. Cf. Alain Locke, "The Negro in American Literature," New World Writing (New York, 1952), 18–33: "If slavery molded the emotional and folk life of the Negro, it was the antislavery struggle that developed his intellect and spurred him to disciplined, articulate expression."

triumph of determination and fortitude over danger and adversity, with the victory of faith over oppression. Fugitive slave narratives became a recognized genre of popular literature, with heroes and villains, escapes, pursuits, and moral meanings; they played an important part in the debate over slavery by introducing into it a new image of the slave—as martyr, as hero, as inspirational model.[62] John Greenleaf Whittier edited one of the earliest and most popular, *The Narrative of James Williams*, in 1838. William Wells Brown's *Narrative* (1847) and Frederick Douglass's books, *Narrative of the Life of Frederick Douglass* (1845) and *My Bondage and My Freedom* (1855), had wide sales. At least sixty such narratives were published between 1830 and 1860.[63]

Negro fiction was small in amount and imitative in its inspiration; William Wells Brown produced an unusual amount and variety of work, often stilted and melodramatic, but nonetheless vital. He tried his hand at essays, a play called *Escape* (1858), and a novel, *Clotel, or the President's Daughter* (1853), based on the rumor that Jefferson had a mulatto daughter whom he sold. Chiefly self-educated, a fluent and articulate speaker, he made his reputation as a lecturer for the Western New York and the Massachusetts antislavery societies.[64]

62. See the introduction and narratives in Robin Winks, ed., *Four Fugitive Slave Narratives* (Reading, Mass., 1969). Winks's study, *The Blacks in Canada* (New Haven, 1971) is an invaluable source of information on fugitives, settlements, etc.

63. Among the more important were *The Narrative . . . of Charles Ball* (1836); *The Adventures and Escape of Moses Rogers* (1837); Charles Lester, *Chains and Freedom* (1840); *The Narrative of Lunsford Lane* (1842); *Narrative of the Sufferings of Lewis Clarke* (1845); *The Narrative of Henry "Box" Brown* (1849); *The Life of Josiah Henson* (1849); *The Narrative and Adventures of Henry Bibb* (1849); *The Narrative of Sojourner Truth* (1850); Samuel Northrop, *Twelve Years a Slave* (1853); Samuel Ward, *Narrative of a Fugitive Negro* (1855); Austin Steward, *Twenty-two Years a Slave and Forty Years a Freeman* (1857); and J. W. Loguen as Slave and Freeman (1859). Harriet Beecher Stowe urged Henson (whom she used in her novel) to expand his short account into a longer autobiography, *Truth Stranger Than Fiction* (1858), which he published in two versions in 1876 and 1878. For the relationship between Uncle Tom and Henson, see Winks, *Blacks in Canada*, 185–93.

64. Brown's book, *The Black Man, His Antecedents, His Genius, and His Achievements* (1862), went through ten editions in three years. Composed of sketches of fifty-three Negroes to show "their genius, capacity, and intellectual development," it had great influence among both black and white readers. His *Negro in the American Rebellion* (1867) placed the black man in the stream of liberty by showing his contributions to the Revolution, the War of 1812, and

The abolitionist controversy called forth responses from a number of Negro poets, Northern and Southern. George Moses Horton, a self-educated janitor at the University of North Carolina, published in 1829 (with white sponsorship) a book of poems, most of them previously published in newspapers, called *The Hope of Liberty,* reprinted in 1837 and 1838. In 1865 he published more poems under the title *The Naked Genius,* primarily topical pieces interspersed with light or sentimental verses. Daniel Payne, a bishop in the A. M. E. Church, wrote religious verse, collected as *The Pleasures and Other Miscellaneous Poems* in 1850. There were a number of other black poets, among them Charles Reason, Elymas Rogers, George B. Vashon, and James Madison Bell (who helped raise volunteers for John Brown). One of the more interesting was James Whitfield, who sent poems to the newspapers for over a decade before collecting them in *Poems* (1846) and *America and Other Poems* (1853). Whitfield was among the most militant of the group and his poem "How Long?" had the authentic ring of a Douglass:

> How long, O gracious God! how long
>   Shall power lord it over right?
> The feeble, trampled by the strong,
>   Remain in Slavery's gloomy night . . ?
> O Lord! In vengeance now appear
>   And guide the battles to the right,
> The spirit of the fainting cheer,
>   And nerve the patriot arm with might!

While much black poetry was cast in the conventional tradition of Scott, Byron, Pope, and the rest, it was often written to be heard rather than read; meant to be declaimed in public, it lost some of its effectiveness on the printed page. Allied to the Negro's oral literary tradition—to the sermon, hymn, and oration—such poetry assumed the form of a public dialogue between poet and audience; some of it never appeared in print, while some of it was not published until it was already familiar to audiences as spoken verse. Mrs. Frances E. W. Harper, for example, toured for a number of

"the late War of the Rebellion." *The Rising Son, or the Antecedents and the Advancement of the Colored Race* (1874) was intended to be a complete history of the American Negro from his African origins down to Brown's own time. The best study is William Edward Farrison, *William Wells Brown* (Chicago, 1969).

years on the lecture platform, but the effectiveness of her verse did not carry over into her *Poems on Miscellaneous Subjects* (which reached its 20th edition in 1874). Whitfield, Payne, Bell, and Rogers were among those better known for their platform recitations than for their published verse; Rogers's famous "Fugitive Slave Law," for example, published in 1855, reveals in its written form little of the fire that made it one of the best-known poems of the fifties.

Some Negroes were moderately successful in the fine arts. Ira Aldridge, a ship's carpenter who worked as a stagehand for Edmund Kean, joined Kean's company when it left for England and played on English and continental stages for thirty years. His star role was Othello, naturally, but he was famous too for his Lear and Macbeth. Daniel and Eugene Warbourg, of New Orleans, were sculptors who established reputations in Europe, as did Robert Duncanson, who studied painting in France. In the 1840s Frank Johnson's Negro military band made highly successful tours of the United States and England—Queen Victoria, in fact, presented him with a silver trumpet. Justin Holland, a self-trained guitarist, had a national reputation as a performing artist and published two best-selling instruction books. The Luca family was one of the better known "singing family" groups; Edward Dede, from New Orleans, toured as a concert violinist and became eventually conductor of the Bordeaux Municipal Opera; Elizabeth Taylor Greenfield was a talented concert soprano. The most spectacular black musician of the day, however, was Thomas Green Bethune, or "Blind Tom," whose perfect pitch and prodigious musical memory fascinated audiences for years. A well-trained, talented artist, Bethune was, however, treated more as a freak than as a musician.[65]

Such Negro artists, however, were exceptions. Black men and women, no matter how talented, had limited opportunities to create or perform in the arts, for to recognize artistic creativity or excellence in the Negro, of course, implied doubts about black inferiority. As a result, the Negro developed a powerful, subterranean artistic tradition of his own, confined to those forms allowed to him as outlets for creative expression. Slaves brought from Africa a strong folktale tradition, including fables, jests, quests, history, legends, and so on. Adapting their African originals to the Ameri-

65. Alain Locke, *The Negro and His Music* (rev. ed., Washington, 1968).

can situation, they developed cycles of animal tales, trickster tales, and indigenous tales like those dealing with "Ole Marster" and his favorite slave. These tales, plus "runaway" stories and "tragic mulatto" stories (themselves a variant of the Indian-white theme), became the basis for more formal Negro fiction later in the century, serving as resources for writers like Charles Chesnutt, Paul Laurence Dunbar, and James Weldon Johnson.

The African's religious art came with him to America, a powerful tradition based on bone and wood carving, metal sculpture, weaving, and pottery making. A disciplined, formalized, symbolic art of surface decoration, it was quite different from anything the West knew and had no meaning within the context of slavery. It continued to exist, however, in those arts and crafts to which the Negro had access and over which the master did not care to exercise control—ironworking, fabrics, masonry, gardening, carpentry, carvings, household utensils, and the like. White masters put the slave's talents to use very early. The Negro supplied the manpower for much of the South's building and manufacturing, and while there is no way of determining how much of the country's artifacts were designed and produced by blacks, it must have been a considerable amount. Certainly much of the ironwork in New Orleans, for example, was the work of Negro craftsmen. Black cabinetmakers made a great deal of the South's furniture; Tom Day's shop in Milton, North Carolina, was famous through the South. A number of Negroes seem to have worked as engravers and lithographers, and there must have been thousands of skilled, anonymous slave craftsmen among the builders and bricklayers of the South.[66]

African music, like African art, simply did not fit into any Western artistic pattern. The slave brought with him, nonetheless, a well-developed musical tradition, both vocal and instrumental, that served him as a medium for transmitting history, preserving custom and morality, and interpreting daily experience. Music had strong social and religious functions in tribal life—there was music for birth, courtship, marriage, initiation, war, and death. Its complex rhythmical structures were more or less incomprehensible to Western ears, its pattern of recitative and response unfamiliar to the white master. While the slave retained some elements of African

66. See Lindsay Patterson, ed., *The Negro in Music and Art* (New York, 1967); and Cedric Dover, *American Negro Art* (New York, 1960).

music, he also adopted much of what he heard of white music. Lacking his own instruments, he made simple ones out of bone, reed, wood, and metal; forbidden the use of drums (which could be used for signaling), he clapped his hands and stamped his feet. As memories of his African heritage faded, he adapted white music in his own way. Listeners could identify portions of Scotch and Irish airs, revival hymns, and popular ballads in Negro songs. If a white listener often found the words unintelligible, he ascribed it to the slave's ignorance—however, it is not difficult in retrospect to identify the Promised Land as the North, or God's children in slavery as the Negro, Old Pharaoh as a hated overseer or master, and so on.[67]

Since none of those who heard and commented on Negro music had any knowledge of African music, all tended to hear in it only those elements of Western music they could recognize. White listeners very probably heard, for that matter, only that portion of Negro music which slaves allowed them to hear. Whites knew Negroes sang hymns, "spirituals," and recreation songs; the great body of black music they probably never heard. It is difficult, then, to reconstruct what Negro music was really like, and it was not until the 1840s that it began to be notated and collected at all. The first authentic collection, *Negro Slave Songs of the United States,* did not appear until 1867.[68]

67. Miles M. Fisher, *The Negro Slave Song in the United States* (Ithaca, N.Y., 1953) and Butcher, *op. cit.,* chapters III and IV. See also Maude C. Hare, "Spirituals" and "The Source" in Patterson, *op. cit.,* 3–31, for an analysis of slave music. Minstrel show songs were written by white men for white performers and audiences and had nothing to do with black music.

68. Bernard Katz, *The Social Implications of Early Negro Music in the United States* (New York, 1969) is a good study. Overseers, who believed that "a singing slave is a happy one," thought that songs helped slaves work harder; sad or slow songs, however, were usually forbidden on work gangs. Slaves, of course, used songs as carefully coded satire, protest, and communication.

CHAPTER 7

Nature as Law and Machine

THE development of science in America over the middle decades of the nineteenth century must be considered within the context of British and European science, for American scientists were, after 1820, very much a part of the worldwide scientific community. Most of the basic discoveries that were to dominate research for the rest of the century were made by 1820—concepts of the structure of matter, of chemical reaction, of the nature of electricity, of heat and energy, of cellular structure. Faraday, Davy, Liebig, Helmholtz, Lamarck, and others were as well known in the United States as in Europe. Many of the tools of modern science—improved microscopes, measuring devices, mechanical apparatus—were in the final stages of development. Scientists were experimenting with theoretical techniques, such as the construction of theoretical models against which to test hypotheses, and were developing new and much more accurate systems of classification and arrangement. Meanwhile, there were swift advances in supportive fields, especially in statistics and mathematics.

Nearly all of the major scientific achievements of the years 1820–70 were British or European, of course, but to view American science of the time as naïve or inept is to do it injustice. That a young, undeveloped scientific culture could produce such men as Joseph Henry, Asa Gray, Matthew Maury, and James Dwight Dana, given the conditions of the period, was in itself significant. Although they made no scientific breakthroughs of major importance, the contributions of American scientists to the sum of scientific knowledge were not inconsiderable.[1]

Science in the United States had its real beginnings with the generation of men who came to intellectual maturity after 1820. The country's scientific education was admittedly weak, but Americans were confident that their scientists would soon surpass those of the Old World, for American society provided for them, as Europe could not, greater freedom from constraints, nor were there Europe's "scientific rivalries and contentions" to hinder them. The era had a deep Baconian trust in science as man's great deliverer and regarded the scientist as the chief architect of social and moral progress. Now, in the nineteenth century, science, said Thomas Cooper, could "enter every workshop, every factory, every home," to do all that was needed "to render human existence more desirable."[2] The study of science, and its application to human affairs, furnished man's best guarantee of wealth, comfort, knowledge, and faith.

First, science furnished the public with reassuring evidence of God's existence and of his infinite beneficence. The doctrine of design (that everything in nature had its purpose, fixed by God, and that the purpose was benevolent) was ingrained in contemporary belief; Bishop Paley's *Natural Theology: or Evidences of the Existence of the Attributes of the Deity, Collected from the Appearances of Nature* (1802) was such standard reading for educated Americans that references to him need never be explained. Students were constantly reminded that science and religion went hand in hand, for both "studied the thoughts of God."[3] Professor Edward Hitchcock in his lectures at Amherst used the catalytic process in

1. For a discussion of science in Europe and the United States in this period see Edward Lurie, "Science in American Thought," *Journal of World History,* VIII (1965), 642–4; and David Van Tassel and Michael Hall, *Science and Society in the United States* (Homewood, Ill., 1966), 1–17.

2. John W. Oliver, *A History of American Technology* (New York, 1958), 147.

3. See Walter and Mabel Smallwood, *Natural Science and the American Mind* (New York, 1941), 232–5; and George Daniels, *American Science in the Age of Jackson* (New York, 1968), 52. "There cannot be a design," wrote Paley, "without a designer, contrivance without a contriver," and since nature showed design and order in all its parts, it proved the existence of a "Great First Cause," or "Great Designer." Paley's book was imported by shiploads and endlessly adapted and revised for the American market in works such as John Mason Good, *The Book of Nature* (1826), and Josiah Priest, *The Wonders of Nature and Providence Displayed* (1825).

chemistry to make a point about Christian morality; Benjamin Peirce at Harvard once stopped a lecture on celestial mechanics to exclaim to his class, "Gentlemen, there must be a God!"[4]

Second, science "conquered" or "harnessed" nature for man's service and profit. If God created the world for man's use, science showed him how to use it; through it man might find that good life God planned for him. Of this the era had no doubts. Judge Job Durfee, Chief Justice of Rhode Island, told the young men of Brown University in 1843 that the future of the human race, because of science, was "as boundless and inexhaustible as the universe." He mused on the meaning of his visit to an iron foundry, and when the twenty-foot bar of metal emerged from the furnace, "ready for the hand of the artisan," he saw in it

the unquestionable proof of the existence of a law of progress, carrying on its grand process through the whole humanity by a logical series of causes and effects, from its earliest premises, in far distant antiquity, to its latest result.

Science, wrote a correspondent to *Scientific American* in 1847,[5]

develops, enlarges, and strengthens the powers of the mind; it sets free the intellect, and puts the whole machine in active motion. . . . Of all the discoveries yet made by men which has any tendency to ameliorate the condition of the human race, none are so noble in their character or happier in their results.

There were warnings, too. To some the great burst of scientific endeavor in American society seemed to symbolize the advance of an insidious materialism that was slowly eroding humanistic, religious values. Thoreau resented the intrusion of the tracks of the Fitchburg railroad into his Walden; Emerson, who suggested that his society trusted steam engines more than Divine Causes, thought that "things are in the saddle, and ride mankind." Some thought science needed to be kept in its place lest it displace moral theology

4. Joseph Blau, *Men and Movements in Philosophy* (New York, 1952) , 78–9; Dirk Struik, *Yankee Science in the Making* (Boston, 1948) , 334–5.

5. Durfee's oration is reprinted in Joseph L. Blau, ed., *American Philosophic Addresses 1700–1900* (New York, 1946) , 381–415; the second quotation appears in "The Utility and Pleasures of Science," *Scientific American,* II (August 21, 1847) , 381.

as man's spiritual guide. Robert Winthrop, speaking at Harvard in 1852, cautioned scientists not to go too far:[6]

Let them not think by searching to find out God. Let them not dream of understanding the Almighty to perfection. Let them not dare to apply their tests and solvents, their modes of analysis and terms of definition, to the secrets of the spiritual kingdom. Let them spare the foundations of faith.

Nevertheless, such doubters were a minority, and the majority put its confidence in the Baconian method. What the age understood by Baconian science was not always clearly defined (Newton and Bacon were often interchangeable) but in the main it assumed that science was empirical, avoiding speculation and hypothecation. In general, science meant taxonomy, the creation of systems; it aimed primarily at discovering, identifying, and classifying information. "All science," said Samuel Tyler, "is classification," and since botany exhibited the clearest and most usable taxonomy, it served as the scientist's favorite model. But by the fifties, as George Daniels has pointed out, science suffered from a "deluge of facts," so much new information that it could not be fitted into the Baconian taxonomical framework. No one really rejected Bacon, but arguments over scientific methodology, begun in the fifties, persisted for another quarter century.[7]

One of the important characteristics of American science in 1820 was its increased trend toward organization, reflecting the growing sense of scientific community. The age believed in the efficacy of "association," and quite realistically, scientists recognized that by acting together they could attract public support more efficiently than singly—this was, at least in part, the purpose of the short-lived Columbian Institute, organized in 1816 as an advisory body to Congress. The rate of proliferation of scientific societies after 1840 was swift. From 1785 to 1845, a total of 107 societies were founded; however, the twenty-year span 1845–65 brought 318 more. Many, of course, were ephemeral, but their numbers reflected scientists' organizing zeal. The most developed fields of science naturally established professional societies first. The Chemical Society of Philadelphia, the Columbian Chemical Society, and the Pittsburgh

6. Robert Winthrop, *An Address to the Alumni of Harvard University* (Cambridge, 1852), 63.

7. See the excellent exposition of early nineteenth-century scientific method in Daniels, *op. cit.*, chapters II–IV.

Chemical Society were all founded before 1820; they did not last long, but chemists played a major part in founding other societies until the formation of their own, the American Chemical Society, in 1876.

Among other early societies were the American Geological Society (1819), the Linnaean Society of Philadelphia (1806), and the Washington Botanical Society (1817). Agricultural societies (which emphasized chemistry and botany) were oldest of all, beginning with the Philadelphia Society for Promoting Agriculture and the South Carolina Agricultural Society in 1785. With the opening of Western farm lands after 1830, societies for the study of agriculture appeared in every new state and territory. In 1858 the Commissioner of Patents published a list of 912 state and local agricultural societies, five-sixths of them founded after 1849.[8] The result was that by the fifties there existed a flourishing scientific community, organized into professional societies which sponsored a growing number of publications.

These societies and their journals provided American scientists with channels of communication hitherto unavailable. The American Philosophical Society (organized in 1743) first published its transactions in 1771 and the records of its proceedings in 1838. The American Academy of Arts and Sciences, the other original from the eighteenth century, published its *Memoirs* from 1785–1821, and reinstituted them in 1833. The most important of the early journals was Benjamin Silliman's *American Journal of Science,* which, founded in 1818 to print "communications on MUSIC, SCIENCE, ENGINEERING, PAINTING, and generally on the free and liberal, as well as the useful Arts," endures to the present day.[9]

Scientists of the Jacksonian era were aware that in organization lay strength and support, and that their greatest need was an organization to operate on a national level, especially with Congress. The position of the scientist in American society, whatever the public's faith in him, was not at all clear. Was he to be only a servant to society and to religion? Was he expected to increase the

8. See Van Tassel and Hall, *op. cit.,* 26–29; Ralph S. Bates, *Scientific Societies in the United States* (New York, 1945), chapter II; and Daniels, *op. cit.,* chapter II.

9. Edward S. Dana, ed., *A Century of Science in America* (New Haven, 1918), 28–29. For Silliman's life, see John F. Fuller and Elizabeth Thomson, *Benjamin Silliman* (New York, 1947).

national wealth by applying his knowledge to useful projects? Was his place in society above or below the lawyer, the engineer, the minister, the politician? American scientists envied the exalted role assigned to their counterparts in the older societies of Europe; Jacksonian America did not feel this way. Since the small but encouraging successes of the Columbian Institute showed how potentially effective such a society might be, a number of leading scientists (among them Joel Poinsett, currently Secretary of War) formed the National Institution for the Promotion of Science in 1840 (incorporated as the National Institute in 1842) which asked for "the support of all, with a view to the general diffusion of knowledge and the advancement of American science." The first *national* scientific organization, the Institute included Congressmen, military officials, and interested laymen in its membership, as well as scientists.[10]

The National Institute sponsored the first country-wide scientific congress held in the United States in 1844, but languished thereafter and expired in 1847. However, good fortune and a philanthropic Englishman combined to give the American scientific community a much better national organization. James Smithson, who died in 1829, had left his fortune to found an institution in the United States for "the increase and diffusion of knowledge." In 1846 Congress finally chartered the Smithsonian Institution to fulfill the terms of his will and appointed a board to govern it. For the first Secretary of the Institution the board chose the eminent American physicist Joseph Henry, who over the next thirty years made it the nation's most powerful and prestigious scientific society.[11]

The Smithsonian served as the base of operations for the leaders of the scientific community—Henry; Alexander Dallas Bache of the United States Coast Survey; Benjamin Peirce, Harvard mathematician; chemist Oliver Wolcott Gibbs; Harvard's Louis Agassiz, and

10. Bates, *op. cit.*, 69–80; A. Hunter Dupree, *Science in the Federal Government* (Cambridge, Mass., 1957), 20–90.

11. Nathan Reingold, ed., *Science in Nineteenth Century America* (New York, 1946), 155–60, *passim*. The standard brief biography of Henry is James G. Crowther, *Famous American Men of Science* (New York, 1937). Henry gathered the nation's best collection of scientific books and journals, and involved the Institution in original research, expeditions, and international exchanges, but under political pressure in 1857 finally established a national museum.

others. Bache, who took over the Coast Survey in 1843, made it the country's largest employer of physicists, mathematicians, and astronomers. (Henry nominated Bache for the Coast Survey post, and Bache nominated Henry for the Smithsonian secretaryship.) Calling themselves the *lazzaroni* (after the beggars in Naples), these men formed a powerful inner circle that virtually controlled the allotment of university and government posts, federal funds, and officerships in professional organizations. In 1848 they organized the prestigious American Association for the Advancement of Science, to serve as a means of expressing the scientific community's views on public policy—or, as Bache put it bluntly, "to guide public action in scientific matters." Bache, Agassiz, and Peirce served in succession in the Academy's presidency, and those who did not fit the *lazzaroni*'s model were not invited to membership.[12]

The AAAS ruled the American scientific scene for the next twenty years. There is no doubt that its dedication to the public advantage and the progress of science was sincere; at the same time, the *lazzaroni* considered themselves a scientific elite and acted like one. However, Henry, Bache, and Agassiz wanted an even more professionalized, disciplined organization than the AAAS, so after some shrewd maneuverings by their political allies, Congress passed and Lincoln signed a bill in 1863 creating a National Academy of Sciences, modeled on British and European precedents. The Academy was limited to one hundred members—fifty incorporators chosen by Congress were to choose fifty more—who would for the next half century control the channels of communication with Congress.[13]

12. See Bates, *op. cit.*, 75–80; Reingold, *op. cit.*, 126–29. Among the conspicuous absentees were Asa Gray, the nation's most eminent botanist, and Matthew Maury, the country's best oceanographer. Merle M. Odgers, *Alexander Dallas Bache* (Philadelphia, 1947) is the best biography of this important man. See also Nathan Reingold, "Alexander Dallas Bache: Science and Technology in the American Idiom," *Technology and Culture*, II (April, 1970), 163–78.

13. Reingold, *op. cit.*, 200–2. Lurie, *op. cit.*, 331–5, is an excellent account of the Academy's founding. Lurie points out that the bill was sponsored by Senator Henry Wilson of Massachusetts, a close friend of Bache, and that its wording was worked out in discussions in Bache's home. George Bond, the Harvard astronomer; James Dwight Dana, the nation's foremost geologist; John Draper, the eminent New York chemist; and others were left off the list. Troubled by internal divisions, the Academy lost momentum and funds, until by the end of the century membership was more honorary than financially useful.

A second important characteristic of American science over the middle years of the nineteenth century was that it tended to be applied rather than theoretical, aimed at social usefulness. Jacksonian America needed to know many things science could tell it—where to build a factory; where to find coal or iron or copper or gold; how to find the best route for a railroad; where the arable lands and forests and rivers were; where to put a dam or dig a canal; what the weather was going to be; what were the best weapons and ship designs. The country needed locomotives and steam engines and tools and power sources and ways to communicate; it needed the best seeds to plant, the best plows and fertilizers, and a thousand other things that only science could tell it. The public wanted results from its scientists. Zachariah Allen, writing in 1829, put it succinctly by saying that "Instead of indulging in abstract and profitless investigations, once so common," scientists should find "delight in researches into nature for the purpose of making discoveries applicable to the useful arts." The application of science to society, a writer in *The American Review* reminded his readers, was a matter of national survival, for "without the useful arts, no nation can prosper."[14]

The United States needed all the information it could get about the land, to be gained from surveys and explorations that only government could afford to finance and that only government could organize. Jefferson started this, with Sibley's Red River expedition in 1803, Lewis and Clark's historic expedition (1804–6), Pike's in 1807, and others. For forty years, from 1820 to 1860, state and federal governments provided funds to survey, catalogue, and map half the continent acre by acre. The federal government, for example, authorized Henry Schoolcraft's expedition in the upper Mississippi River country in 1817–19, Lewis Cass's to Lake Superior (1820–23), John C. Frémont's to the West (1843), David Dale Owen's geological and geographical survey of the Superior country (1839–40), and Charles Jackson's of upper Michigan (1847–48) among others. Six parties surveyed six separate routes for a transcontinental railway between 1850 and 1857, submitting twelve volumes of reports about the western country that scientists mined for years afterwards. Similarly, the army's expeditions through the

14. Quoted by Struik, *op. cit.*, 238; "Sketch of the Rise, Progress, and Influence of the Useful Arts," *The American Review*, V (January, 1847), 88.

West (over fifty between 1850 and 1890) were as much scientific as military in purpose. The Army Engineers, which attracted the best of West Point's graduates, served as manager and escort to numerous civilian expeditions and made many of its own. Lieutenant Warren's expedition into the Dakotas in 1856–57, for example, carried a topographer, an astronomer, and a geologist in addition to surveyors and engineers.[15]

Since the practical values of such sciences as astronomy, navigation, and meteorology were quickly recognized by a maritime nation, the federal government eagerly assisted scientific research in these and related fields. The United States Coast Survey, reorganized in 1832 by Ferdinand Hassler, a Swiss scientist, was expanded and developed to a high degree of efficiency by Alexander Dallas Bache (a great-grandson of Benjamin Franklin), who served as its director from 1843 to 1867. The United States Naval Observatory, established in 1842, grew out of the navy's Department of Charts and Instruments. In meteorology, William C. Redfield's studies of winds and storms (1842, 1846) and James Espy's *Law of Cooling of Atmospheric Air* (1843) were major contributions. Weather records were kept in scattered fashion by a number of civilian and military agencies, until Espy, at Franklin Institute, organized a national network of meteorological reports. Joseph Henry at the Smithsonian, in 1849, using the telegraph, put together a national service that, combined with Espy's, provided a country-wide weather map based on five hundred daily observations. Henry's maps became the basis of the United States Meteorological Service in 1870.[16]

The most elaborate scientific effort of the pre-Civil War period was the navy's Polar and Pacific Expedition, under the command of Lieutenant Charles Wilkes, which left the United States on August, 1838, and spent four years in the Pacific, visiting the Cape Verdes, eastern and western South America, the Pacific islands, Australia, New Zealand, the Philippines, and Singapore. Although it took Wilkes and his small staff nearly twenty years to publish the results, the voyage taught the federal government, the military, and the

15. For further discussion, see Dupree, *op. cit.*, 91–115. For an estimate of the impact on the public mind of such expeditions, see Donald Jackson, "The Public Image of Lewis and Clark," *Pacific Northwest Quarterly*, LVII (January, 1966), 1–8.

16. Reingold, *op. cit.*, 128–30; Dupree, *op. cit.*, 44–66; Bernard Jaffe, *Men of Science in America* (New York, 1944), 202–7.

scientific community a great deal about working together. The navy continued to send out expeditions to lesser-known areas of the world, among them Lieutenant W. F. Lynch's to the Dead Sea, Lieutenant James Gilliss's to Cuba, and Captain John Rodgers's to the Arctic. Commodore Perry's staff, when he visited Japan in 1853, included several scientists.[17]

The most active collaboration of government and science occurred at the state level.[18] Although North Carolina commissioned a catalogue of the state's resources in 1823, the model for subsequent state surveys was Edward Hitchcock's of Massachusetts, completed in 1833. Hitchcock's commission summarized all the pertinent information about the state's natural resources for the use of scientist, businessman, and farmer; it included much local history, and a tourist guide so that "the man of taste" would know, he wrote, "where he will find natural objects calculated to gratify his love of novelty, beauty, and sublimity." Between 1833 and 1865, when Nevada's appeared, twenty-three states published similar surveys, many done by distinguished scientists like William and Henry Rogers (Virginia and Pennsylvania), Zadoc Thompson (Vermont), and James Gates Percival (Connecticut and Wisconsin), and written by groups that included geographers, geologists, mining engineers, foresters, chemists, and zoologists.

These state surveys, in combination with the military and naval expeditions, weather services, railroad surveys, and the like, furnished the nation with a pool of trained scientists who knew how to work together in teams. (David Dale Owen's survey of the upper Mississippi, for example, employed 139 assistants organized into 24 field parties.) Science, scientists were learning, was not only an individual working in a laboratory, but a cooperative venture, with each discipline and specialty playing its part. In addition, the public was learning the cash values of applied science; it was not difficult to convince laymen and legislators that investments in science yielded good returns.

17. Reingold, op. cit., 109–11; and Dupree, op. cit., 58–62. Nathaniel Hawthorne hoped to accompany the Wilkes expedition as "historiographer." Other important expeditions were Lieutenant Pase's up the La Plata River, Lieutenant Strain's to Panama, and Lieutenant Henderson's crossing of the Andes.

18. Walter B. Hendrickson, "Nineteenth Century State Geological Surveys: Early Government Support of Science," Isis, LII (1961), 357–71.

American science in the prewar years was not only being organized and nationalized, but it was also being popularized and specialized. Never before (and seldom since) has American science enjoyed such public interest and support. "A thirst for natural science," wrote Professor Amos Eaton at the time, seemed "to pervade the United States like the progress of an epidemic." Museums sprang up everywhere, exhibiting "curiosities of nature"; itinerant showmen and pseudo-scientific "professors" crisscrossed the country doing experiments with electromagnets and chemicals. The lyceum system, organized in the 1820s, furnished an excellent medium for the diffusion of scientific knowledge. *The American Lyceum*, published in 1829, advertised magic lanterns and demonstration guides for lectures on geometry, astronomy, geology, chemistry, and "natural philosophy," as well as equipment like levers, wedges, flasks, retorts, axles, wheels, inclined planes, and a portable orrery. Not all lecturers were competent, of course—some were "petty swindlers," as Eaton called them—but many of the nation's best scientists appeared on the platform, among them Benjamin Silliman, Thomas Nuttall, Louis Agassiz, and the English geologist Charles Lyell. Lectures by scientists attracted thousands; Boston, in the 1837–38 lyceum season, had twenty-six lectures on science which drew a total of 13,000 listeners.[19]

The years 1840–60 marked the final stages of the scientific specialization that began a half century earlier. During early years of the century, there was a place in science for both amateurs and professionals, for the generalist and the specialist. Holiday collectors and trained scientists worked side by side; the local minister who collected plants and the skilled botanist were kin. By the thirties, however, there was so much to do and so much to know in every field of science that the old-fashioned scientist who took all knowledge as his province, or the "natural philosopher" who studied "nature," could no longer grasp it all. By the fifties it was impossible for any single scientist, as Edward Hitchcock had done only twenty years before, to lecture with authority on chemistry, geology,

19. See Struik, *op. cit.*, 207–12; and Oliver, *op. cit.*, 151. Amos Eaton, a Williams College professor of chemistry and geology, was one of the most famous lecturers. He gave over six thousand scientific lectures in his career and boasted he could hold any audience spellbound with no more apparatus than "a dish, a bottle, a warming-pan, and a cheese press."

mineralogy, and zoology at Amherst; or, as Joseph Burnett did at Norwich, to hold simultaneously professorships of botany, chemistry, and mineralogy. The older generation of scientists were rapidly passing (Mitchill, Say, Bowditch, Maclure, Cooper, and Rafinesque all died before 1840) and the men who replaced them were specialists.

The new scientist narrowed his interests, limited his objectives, concentrated on smaller segments of knowledge; better to specialize in one field and share information with others, he believed, than to attempt mastery of several at once. The trend toward specialization reflected fundamental changes in the attitude of scientists themselves toward science. The eighteenth-century concept of knowledge as unified and finite was fast disappearing, and with it the Paley-Newtonian picture of the universe as a complex but orderly system whose parts could be discovered and organized into a design. Instead, as scientists viewed the universe, they tended to see it as a place of modification and change. The flood of information that swept over the sciences in the preceding century led scientists to suspect that beneath Nature there was perhaps no single, fixed, unchangeable design, but rather continuous and infinite development. No one scientist in any one field, or even several, could master Nature; only a community of professional scholars, working together and combining information, could eventually, perhaps, comprehend something of her plans. It was significant that the American Association for the Advancement of Science in 1848 divided its membership into Physics, Mathematics, Chemistry, Civil Engineering, Applied Science, Natural History, Geology, Physiology, and Medicine, in tacit recognition of the departmentalization of knowledge.

The most "useful" sciences, understandably, attracted the most attention and the most funds. This did not necessarily mean that American science was dominated by the practical as opposed to the theoretical, for American scientists, like Europeans, recognized the vital relationship between pure and applied research. But scientists—and the public—also recognized the value of science in improving life and contributing to progress.[20] Naturally, therefore,

20. See Daniels, *op. cit.*, 19–33, on the relationship during the period between pure and applied science.

those researches in "natural history" most directly concerned with finding and applying knowledge of the earth, air, sky, and sea to social needs received more emphasis. Mathematics was considered an invaluable tool for astronomers, engineers, navigators, and the like; chemistry contributed to agriculture, mineralogy, and industry; physics was useful for the study of electricity, for heat and power sources, and for applied engineering.

No branch of science (with the possible exception of astronomy) had as yet developed a tradition of pure research. Government, science, and the public agreed that scientific knowledge was to be used in some way, nor could the pragmatic American find much use for the useless. Jacksonian society understood and valued science as it contributed to society—better medicine, bigger crops, new sources of power. Otherwise, most Americans could see no reason to finance research that produced no visible benefit. When John Quincy Adams, a man of sound scientific training, proposed to establish a national observatory, Congress jibed at his "lighthouses in the sky." (Later, when the practical value of astronomical observations was clearly demonstrated, Congress and private sources poured funds into observatories.) Science was fully secularized. It might, as Paley's "evidences" once claimed, show God, but it was much more important that it show men how to use nature's resources to their advantage.[21] The idea that pure research might have ultimate value was not yet part of either the scientist's or the public's equipment. Although Joseph Henry's researches in electricity pointed toward Samuel F. B. Morse's telegraph, the federal government would subsidize Morse, but not Henry.

The sciences that received most support, therefore, in the first half of the nineteenth century were those of most direct utility. Since mathematics was regarded as a necessary tool for astronomy, surveying, engineering, navigation, statistics, and the like, few if any mathematicians thought of doing theoretical research. Mathematics was so closely associated with astronomy that at many colleges it existed only in conjunction with it; at major universities the professor of mathematics was usually also professor of chemistry, or astronomy, or natural philosophy. Benjamin Peirce of Harvard,

---

21. Excellent discussions are Richard Shyrock, "American Indifference to Basic Science in the Nineteenth Century," *Archives Internationale d'Histoire des Sciences* (1948) #5, 50–65; and Dupree, *op. cit.*, 44–65.

the nation's leading mathematician, edited journals, wrote texts, trained most of the country's younger mathematicians, and served as consultant to practically every scientific venture of his time, but he did little research. Robert Adrian, an Irish emigrant who taught at Pennsylvania, Princeton, Rutgers, and Columbia, trained nearly as many younger men as Peirce but, like him, was primarily a teacher. With the great advances in mathematics of the nineteenth century—non-Euclidean geometry, noncommunicative algebra, the arithmetization of analysis—Americans had little to do.[22]

Chemistry was one of the most advanced of the physical sciences, and American chemists were well abreast of European researchers. Lavoisier's destruction of "phlogiston" and Dalton's suggestions of atomic structure opened the way for the development of a great body of chemical knowledge, finally systematized in the sixties. The stabilization of atomic weights, the introduction of the theory of valence, the development of analytic chemistry, and improvements in instrumentation were important factors in the rise of what became, by the seventies, modern chemistry.[23] American chemistry, however, was almost wholly applied. Few chemists did research in specialized fields. Prior to 1850, a chemist could do competent work in any area—he could study minerals, organic substances, do analysis, or work with agriculture, and what he did was presumed to have some social or industrial use. For example, chemists like Thomas Gleason and Parker Cleaveland at Bowdoin, and John Torrey at West Point, were primarily mineralogists; Gleason, in fact, discovered diamonds in North Carolina. John Gorham of Harvard was an agricultural chemist, interested among other things in the sugar content of corn. James Freeman Dana experimented with batteries and pharmaceuticals; Samuel Luther Dana did research on fertilizers; Denison Olmsted, professor of chemistry at North Carolina, headed the state's geological survey.

Although the majority of American chemists taught in colleges and universities, several of the most influential industrial chemists set up their own laboratories for commercial research. James Booth of Philadelphia studied in Germany and returned to establish the

22. Howard Eves, *An Introduction to the History of Mathematics* (rev, ed., New York, 1964), 351 ff.; David E. Smith and Jekuthiel Ginsburg, *A History of Mathematics in the United States Before 1900* (Chicago, 1934) chapters III and IV.
23. See Aaron J. Ihde, *The Development of Modern Chemistry* (New York, 1964) chapter II.

country's first successful commercial laboratory; he did consulting work for the iron industry and also for the United States Mint. More important, he trained over fifty students who founded laboratories of their own or entered industry. J. Lawrence Smith did experimental work with coal, emery and other abrasives, agricultural nitrates, and perfected a process for the commercial production of silicates. Frederick Genth, a German refugee of 1848, specialized in mineral analysis and served as consulting chemist to the Pennsylvania Board of Agriculture.[24]

Physics, like chemistry, tended to be practical. Physicists were still working out the implications of Newton's laws of motion and gravitation when the sudden breakthrough in electricity opened up new fields of research. Volta developed his battery in 1800; Oersted in Denmark, Ampère and Arago in France, and Sturgeon in England spent the next thirty years exploring electromagnetism, the most challenging aspect of electrical physics. Joseph Henry, a mathematics teacher at Albany Academy, in 1831 hung a steel bar between the poles of an electromagnet and swung it against a bell by the force of a current sent through a mile of wire. By thus translating current into power and sound by electromagnetic induction, Henry opened a path toward dynamos, meters, the telegraph, and electrical production. Working independently, Faraday in England did much the same experimentation, and both published papers in 1832; then, in 1834, Thomas Padgett built a small electric motor from Henry's descriptions.[25]

Telegraphic systems, based on research in electromagnetics, were worked out in Britain and France, but Samuel F. B. Morse's instrument, demonstrated to an amazed presidential cabinet in 1838, was the most practical. The full development of electrical technology, however, had to wait until all the necessary components were combined. Electrochemistry, used in electroplating, appeared quite early. Electricity was used to produce light as early as 1808. The

24. Horace Wells and Harry Foot, "The Progress of Chemistry During the Past Hundred Years," in Dana, *op. cit.,* 288–335; Edgar F. Smith, *Chemistry in America* (New York, 1914) chapters X–XII; and Henry M. Leicester, *The Historical Background of Chemistry* (New York, 1961).

25. Leigh Page, "A Century's Progress in Physics," Dana, *op. cit.,* 335–90; Jaffe, *op. cit.,* 183–202; Struik, *op. cit.,* 262–4. Henry also did research in astronomy, optics, and metallurgy. He did not patent any of his work, since his aim, he said, was "only to add to the sum of human knowledge."

battery, and the electric motor were perfected by the 1850s. However, better means of electrical production and distribution were needed before electricity could be widely used as a source of power; the generator, transformer, and dynamo were still to come.[26]

One of the best-known American scientists was Matthew Fontaine Maury, whose work in oceanography and navigation was a major factor in developing the country's maritime trade. Virginia-born and self-educated, Maury entered the navy at nineteen and found that he had unusual mathematical talent. Struck by the paucity of information about sea currents and winds, he began research which led to his appointment as Superintendent of Charts and Instruments in the Navy Department. Here he undertook one of the most awesome tasks in scientific history—the study of thousands of log-books kept by sailing captains over every mile of the world's seas—and after five years of studying the records he published *A Wind and Current Chart of the North Atlantic* (1847). Ships using his charts cut from ten to twenty days from the run to Rio de Janeiro; his revised charts, published in 1855, reduced the New York–San Francisco voyage by forty to fifty days; his *Lanes for Steamers Crossing the Atlantic* (1853)—later including the Pacific—took forty days off the passage from London to Australia. Maury and his staff at the Naval Observatory also catalogued 100,000 stars for navigational use; he compiled from soundings a topographical map of the North Atlantic floor that helped make the transatlantic cable possible in 1866; and his *Physical Geography of the Sea* (1855) became one of the classic documents of modern oceanography. Few American scientists made more significant use of their knowledge to society's benefit than Henry and Maury.[27]

Astronomy, however, still reigned as queen of the physical sciences, and much of the period's scientific effort was directed at the establishment of observatories which served not only as research

26. W. James King, "The Development of Electrical Technology in the Nineteenth Century," *Contributions from the Museum of History and Technology of the Smithsonian Institution* (Washington, 1963), Bulletin #228, papers 28, 29, 30, 231–406.

27. Jaffe, *op. cit.*, 207–31 provides a good sketch of Maury's career. A good earlier biography is John W. Wayland, *The Pathfinder of the Seas* (Richmond, 1930); the best recent study is Frances Williams, *Matthew Fontaine Maury* (New Brunswick, New Jersey, 1963). Maury was Commander of the Confederate Navy and later taught at Virginia Military Institute.

laboratories, but as proof that American science, if not equal to European, was well on the way. The earliest were privately funded. Yale had a large telescope in 1830, Williams an observatory in 1836, Harvard in 1839, West Point in 1840, Michigan in 1853. The United States Naval Observatory, after much maneuvering, was established in 1844. Observatories were expensive, but since astronomical research had immediate practical effects, it was somewhat easier for them to obtain public and private funds. The appearance of the great comet of February, 1843, which could be seen in daylight and lit the sky at night, fascinated the public and helped astronomers the nation over in soliciting funds. Because observatories could often find support where other scientists could not, they attracted physicists, mathematicians, and other scientists who added substantial strength to astronomical research.[28]

The biological and earth sciences in the early nineteenth century had not yet completed their task of collecting, describing, and classifying materials. The country was filled with plants, animals, and rocks, all to be identified, studied, and arranged. It had taken nearly a century to do it, but workable systems of nomenclature and classification were almost finished by the thirties. The tools of research were ready to be used.

American zoological study, until the forties, was primarily descriptive, concerned with the classification and the habits of animals. Zoologists had only faint concepts of the cellular structure that formed the basis of plant and animal life and no way of studying it accurately until the adaptation of the compound microscope to the purpose in the mid-thirties.[29] Usable theories of cell structure and cell function did not appear for another decade, marking—when they did—a complete redirection of research. American zoologists were therefore still chiefly naturalists, in the tradition of the Bartrams, Silliman, and Barton. Thomas Gay's *American Entomology* (three volumes, 1824–28), John Godman's *North American Mammals* (three volumes, 1826–29), Thomas Nut-

28. For a survey of astronomical research in the nineteenth century, see the early chapters of Bessie Z. Jones, *Lighthouse of the Skies: The Smithsonian Astrophysical Observatory, Background and History* (Washington, 1965).

29. For a discussion of the significance of the improved microscope in botanical and zoological research, see Walter and Mabel Smallwood, *op. cit.*, chapter VIII.

tall's *Manual of Ornithology* (1832–34), and James De Kay's *Natural History of New York* (1842–44) were excellent examples of traditional systematic zoological work.[30]

During the forties American zoology entered another stage, that of morphology and embryology, partly as a result of improved laboratory instruments and techniques, but most of all the effect of European influences. Although zoologists still described and classified animals, their major interest was now in studying their structures, developmental histories, and relationships among them. Much of this was the result of the arrival in the United States in 1846 of Swiss-born (Jean) Louis (Rodolphe) Agassiz. A student of Cuvier's, already well-known for work in ichthyology, Agassiz came to lecture at Lowell Institute in Boston and stayed to occupy the Chair of Natural History at Harvard's new Lawrence Scientific School.[31] Agassiz lectured in comparative embryology, a field of specialization almost unknown in the United States, established a Museum of Comparative Zoology at Harvard, and trained dozens of students who dominated American zoological classrooms and laboratories for the next half century.

Professionally, Agassiz's influence was felt immediately. His textbook, *Principles of Zoology* (1848, with Augustus Gould), remained standard for years; his *Methods of Study in Natural History* (1863), a summation of his methodology, powerfully influenced the research for three generations of zoologists. Agassiz published four hundred books and papers, lectured tirelessly, and played a role in the organization of most of the major American scientific societies. His enthusiasm made science exciting to the layman; his dedication to the pursuit of knowledge made him a model for the scientist. He was also deeply concerned with the philosophical and theological implications of science. To him the living organism was evidence of great natural laws; the structure, habits, and development of animal forms were parts of a pattern of life which, when fully understood, would reveal the meaning of all Nature. It was this belief in the existence of God behind the natural world that led him, ulti-

---

30. Older studies, but still useful, are William A. Lacy, *Biology and Its Makers* (New York, 1928) and R. T. Young, *Biology in America* (Boston, 1922).

31. The definitive biography is Edward Lurie, *Louis Agassiz: A Life in Science* (Chicago, 1960).

mately, to oppose the Darwinian hypothesis and to delay for a decade American zoology's acceptance of it.[32]

Pre–Civil War botany, like zoology, remained for a time chiefly in the collecting and classifying stage. The work of Colden, Garden, the Bartrams, Cutler, Ellis, and others, in gathering and cataloguing plants left a strong systematic tradition, continued by such men as Mitchill, Barton, and Hosack, all of whom founded journals, trained students, and organized societies. Amos Eaton, who studied with Mitchill and Silliman, was a distinguished product of this early botanical school. In addition to his influence as a popular lecturer, his *Manual of Botany* (1817) went through eight editions before 1840; it was safe to assume that nearly every person in the United States who studied botany between 1820 and 1848 (when Gray's *Manual* appeared) used Eaton.[33]

Two American scientists, beginning work in the 1830s, exerted a decisive influence upon botanical research. John Torrey, a student of Eaton's, in 1833 edited for American use John Lindley's *Introduction to the Natural System in Botany,* a book which replaced the Linnaean system of classification. Linnaeus' method of botanical classification was an "artificial" system, that is, one which classified plant life on the basis of a limited number of arbitrarily selected characteristics. Lindley, an English botanist, proposed a "Natural" system, one which classified plants on the basis of as many characteristics as possible. While Lindley's system was not wholly satisfactory and was itself later modified, its introduction into American botany helped to redirect botanic systematization. Torrey himself did pioneer studies of the flora of the Northern and Middle states in 1824, while the two-volume *Flora of North America,* published with Asa Gray between 1838 and 1843, was a major contribution to scholarship.[34]

The dominant figure in American botany over the middle years of the nineteenth century was undoubtedly Asa Gray. Born in

32. A. S. Packard, "A Century's Progress in American Zoology," *The American Naturalist,* X (1876) , 591–99; Wesley R. Coe, "A Century of Zoology in America," Dana, *op. cit.,* 391–438.

33. See G. L. Gondale, "The Development of Botany," Dana, *op. cit.,* for a survey of botanical studies to 1870. Ethel M. McAllister, *Amos Eaton: Scientist and Educator* (Philadelphia, 1941) is a good biography.

34. For a biographical study, see Andrew D. Rodgers, *John Torrey* (Princeton, 1942) .

upstate New York, trained as a physician, Gray turned to botany under Torrey's influence and in 1836 published the first of his influential texts, *Elements of Botany*. His *Manual of the Botany of the Northern United States* (1848) (known to generations of students as "Gray's Manual") was still in print in 1972. Gray's work in systematic botany and his editorship of the *American Journal of Science* were important enough; more important was the fact that he moved from collecting and classifying to theoretical botany, that is, to the consideration of the origin, development, and nature of plant life. His speculations led him toward an evolutionary theory of botanical development, so that at the appearance of the *Origin of Species* in 1859 Gray was ready to accept Darwin's hypothesis. His review of the book in *The American Journal of Science* caused a stir in the American scientific community, particularly since Louis Agassiz had rejected it. Gray's review, and his subsequent defense of Darwin, were of undeniable importance in gaining the English scientist an American hearing.[35]

Geology was easily the best developed and most sophisticated of the earth sciences. There were more geologists than any other kind of scientist, and much better prospects of employment for them. Geological research had easily perceived economic value, and since it dealt with the earth's creation and God's most tangible works, it had religious connotations as well.[36]

The second generation of geologists—men like James Hall, Edward Hitchcock, James Gates Percival, Denison Olmsted—had the sound work of previous scientists (Maclure, Silliman, and others) to build on. Geologists were professionally organized quite early (the American Geological Society was founded in 1819) and were strongly represented in the major scientific societies. The long argument between Neptunists (who believed rocks were formed by chemical precipitation from the original oceans) and the Vulcanists

35. Joseph Ewen, *A Short History of American Botany* (New York, 1969), 1–49, provides an account of botany during this period. Harry B. Humphrey, *Makers of American Botany* (New York, 1961). A. Hunter Dupree's *Asa Gray* (Cambridge, 1959) is an excellent study of Gray and of contemporary science.

36. Out of 92,000 pages of text published by *The American Journal of Science* during its first century, over 20,000 dealt with geology. State and federal surveys and expeditions usually had more geologists than other scientists—the New York State Survey, for example, had four geologists, one chemist, one zoologist, and one botanist.

(who believed they were of igneous origin) was settled in favor of the Vulcanists, so that with a theory to work from, geologists could now fill in the theoretical framework with research. Much of the country lay unexplored, so that there was still plenty of basic data to be gathered and classified; at the same time, there was the problem of fitting geology into the pattern of worldwide research. Did the geology of Indiana, for example, agree with the geology of Wales? Were American mountains the same as European, and what information would emerge from a comparison of the Ohio River Valley with the Thames?[37]

As Agassiz dominated American zoology and Gray botany, so James Dwight Dana at Yale dominated the study of geology during the middle years of the century. He studied with Silliman (whose daughter he married) specializing in mineralogy; his *System of Mineralogy* (1837) and his *Manual of Geology* (1862) were as standard in the field as Gray's in botany. Dana, however, soon turned from systematic to historical geology. Geology, to him, embodied the story of the earth's origin and development; the geologist was the decipherer of the past. Rocks, he once wrote, were "records of successive events . . . actual historical records," and he set himself the task of imposing a chronological pattern on all the flood of facts available to the geologist. What Dana hoped to do was to see the earth as a whole, with a unified history of organic development, set into the sequence of time. He therefore assigned time periods to the earth's geological history, beginning with the Archezoic and continuing to the Pleistocene, thus subdividing the time scheme of the history of the North American continent. Though his own studies conditioned him to the idea of evolutionary development, his reaction to Darwin's book was less positive than Gray's. He told Darwin that he wanted to wait until all the facts were in, and finally, in the last edition of his *Manual of Geology*, printed shortly before his death in 1895, he accepted the evolutionary hypothesis with the reservation that he still believed there was

37. George E. Merrill, *The First One Hundred Years of American Geology* (New York, 1964, rev. ed.) is an extended account. Chapter XV, "How Old Is It?" gives an excellent review of various theories of the origin and age of the earth. Mineralogy and paleontology also developed rapidly as supportive sciences; see W. E. Ford, "The Growth of Mineralogy," and R. S. Will, "The Development of Vertebrate Paleontology," in Dana, *op. cit.*, 216–47, 268–83.

behind Nature, whatever its processes, "the will and enacting power of the Divine Being."[38]

Dana's doubts exemplified the great dilemma that faced earth scientists during the first half of the nineteenth century, for all their observations and generalization had direct and sometimes disturbing theological implications. The Mosaic account of the creation lay at the very base of nineteenth-century science. The Bible said God made the earth and all things in it in six days, and while scientists no longer accepted arbitrary dates (like Bishop Ussher's 4004 B.C.), they found themselves forced either to provide evidence to support the Biblical account or else to find some way to accommodate it to contradictory evidence. Paley's view, expressed in his *Evidences of Christianity* (1794) and *Natural Theology* (1802), that science showed the perfection of God and the truth of the Bible, was still that held by the majority of the public and probably by most scientists. On the other hand, many scientists were not satisfied with the Biblical account of the earth's origins, nor were they satisfied with such things as Paley's explanation that the slight inclination of the earth's axis was God's plan for the change of seasons.

Geologists were in a particularly difficult position, since they dealt directly with theories of earth's creation. Edward Hitchcock, in his popular and influential text *Elementary Geology* (1840), added, after his account of the origin of the earth, another chapter titled "The Connection Between Geology and Revealed Religion" to reassure his readers that there was one.

It was obvious that the making of the earth required more than six days, or for that matter, more than 4,004 years. Benjamin Silliman suggested that a Biblical "day" could be a figure of speech used to describe a geological period of several million years, but there were other scientists who felt this left too much unexplained. If one accepted the "catastrophic" theory of geology (that the earth was formed by a series of catastrophes, the Flood being the last) he could reconcile it with the Bible's. But if the earth was the product of a long and slow evolutionary process, as Lyell's *Principles of Geology* rather convincingly argued, then the Biblical version was invalid. Meanwhile, paleontology, a swiftly developing corollary science, found simple life forms in older rocks and more complex

38. A sketch of Dana's life is in Jaffe, *op. cit.*, 266–78. The standard biography is Daniel C. Gilman, *The Life of James Dwight Dana* (New York, 1899).

ones in later ones—which tended to support not only Lyell but Darwin too.

Biological scientists were having equal difficulties. The Lamarckians presented evidence that species evolved on the basis of physiological needs, deriving from a change in conditions of environment, a theory which if true denied the old fixed-species version of Divine creation. The anonymous publication in 1844 (the first American edition in 1845) of *The Vestiges of the Natural History of Creation* (probably by Robert Chambers) not only suggested a relationship between the lower order of animals and man, but postulated "a progressive development" of species from lower to higher orders, creating an uneasy stir among scientists and laymen. Zoologists and botanists were also speculating about why and how some species developed, and why some survived and some did not. Darwin, at the time Chambers's book appeared, had already spent a number of years gathering data and speculating about these questions. In 1855 he opened correspondence with Asa Gray, who had published some interesting papers about changes in plant structures, and in 1857 Darwin outlined to him the essentials of his theory. When his book appeared in 1859, not even Agassiz could hold back the tide, and American science, like that of the rest of the world, changed direction drastically and permanently.[39]

Science is commonly defined as the systematic arrangement of a body of facts or truths from which are derived general laws dealing with the operation of the physical world. *Technology* describes the application of that knowledge for practical ends, particularly in the industrial arts, the uses of machinery, and the processes of production. Jacob Bigelow, who was Rumford Professor at Harvard and one of the first to use the word in this sense, defined *technology* as "the applications of science . . . which may be considered useful, by promoting the benefit of society together with the emolument of those who pursue them." The dollars-and-cents value of technology was very much a part of Bigelow's—and the era's—conception of it. Equally important to its meaning was the fact that technology was

39. See the accounts of the evolutionary controversy in American science in Lurie, *op. cit.*, 290–301; and Struik, *op. cit.*, 304–16. Agassiz never conceded defeat, and at his death in 1873 left an article, published posthumously, attacking the theory.

applied science, science made relevant to society.[40] To an emergent nation, in the process of arranging and developing an industrial society, words like Bigelow's had great appeal. Born into the midst of the Industrial Revolution, the United States knew no other cultural environment; since the steam engine, the iron industry, the chemical revolution, and the discovery of electricity all preceded Yorktown, the nation began its life with a well-defined industrial consciousness and full acceptance of the facts of a technological society.[41]

Science and technology were considered to be separate fields until the nineteenth century in both America and Europe. With notable exceptions (Joseph Henry in physics, Maury in navigation and oceanography), American scientists made few substantial contributions to scientific theory. But so far as engineering and mechanics were concerned, the picture was quite different. Where science and technology came together—in mining and metalworking, navigation, agriculture, mechanical production, the generation and transmission of power—Americans were daring, imaginative, and easily among the most technologically advanced in the world.[42] Henry Howe, when he compiled a roster of American engineers and inventors in *Memoirs of the Most Eminent American Mechanics* (Boston, 1840), could include in his list some men of real accomplishment.[43]

Howe drew up his list in the midst of America's most active period of technological development. After the War of 1812 manufacturers and businessmen competed directly in world markets with the highly developed European technological societies. To cut the cost of production, or to produce a better product, or to get it more efficiently to the buyer, meant instant and substantial profit. Tech-

40. Jacob Bigelow, *The Elements of Technology* (Boston, 1829), preface.
41. See Samuel Resnick, "The Rise and Early Development of Industrial Consciousness in the United States, 1760–1830," *Journal of Economic and Business History*, IV (April, 1932), 784–811. Brooke Hindle, *Technology in Early America* (Chapel Hill, 1966) is the best source for the colonial period.
42. I. Bernard Cohen, "Some Reflections on the State of Science," *Proceedings of the National Academy of Science*, XLV (1959), 666–77; Kendall Birr, "Science in American Industry," Van Tassel and Hall, *op. cit.*, 35–81.
43. Howe named Fitch and Fulton (steamboat), Franklin (battery), Evans (production engineering), Slater (textile machinery), Whitney (cotton gin, arms), Bushnell (submarine), Whittemore (carding machine), Perkins (metallurgy, nail-making machine), Blanchard (lathe), Eckford (naval architecture).

nological innovation in American industry was thus an utter necessity as well as a matter of national pride. Speakers extolled the names of Franklin, Rittenhouse, and Jefferson; what the nation needed, they said, was a second generation to build on and to exceed the accomplishments of the first.[44]

To encourage American technological skill, Congress in 1836 created the office of Commissioner of Patents, who was responsible for testing inventions and judging their patentability on the basis of novelty and utility. "Who can predict the results," the Congressional Committee asked, "even in a few years, of that spirit of enterprise which pervades the Union, when, aided by the Genius of Invention, and propelled onward by powers which she alone can bring into exercise?" Henry Ellsworth, the first Commissioner, realized the importance of his office and considered it to be the focal point for a great national scientific effort. The results that Congress hoped for were reflected in the Commissioner's yearly reports; in 1837 he issued 436 patents; in 1850, 993; and in 1860, 4,778, a tenfold increase.[45]

Americans seemed to have, observers agreed, an inherent interest in and skill with machines. Thomas Cooper in 1794 found Americans "ingenious in the invention, and prompt and accurate in the execution of machinery and workmanship." Frederika Bremer, a Swedish lady who visited the United States in 1849–51, noted that American schoolboys who drew pictures on their slates nearly always drew steamboats, engines, or some piece of "locomotive machinery." Many other travelers remarked on the national interest in machinery, and so did Americans. William Seward believed that the American's sense of economy and efficiency meant that he

44. See Perry Miller, *The Life of the Mind in America* (New York, 1965), 271–87, on science, technology, and nationality; and Hugo A. Meier, "American Technology and the Nineteenth Century World," in Henning Cohen, ed., *The American Culture* (Boston, 1968), 191–200. A typical contemporary document is "A Sketch of the Rise, Progress, and Influence of the Useful Arts," *The American Review*, V (January, 1847), 87–95.

45. Dupree, *op. cit.*, 47, 63–65; Frederick J. Kilgour, "Technological Innovation in the United States," *Journal of World History*, VIII (1965), 742–68; Peter C. Welsh, "United States Patents, 1790–1870," *Contributions from the Museum of History and Technology*, Smithsonian Institution Museum Bulletin #241, Paper #48 (Washington, D.C., 1965); C. J. Hylander, *American Inventors* (New York, 1934); and Roger Burlingame, *Machines that Built America* (New York, 1953) are useful popular studies of inventors and inventions.

"examined every instrument, and engine . . . and often improved it or devised a new and better one." Seward's analysis of some of the reasons for American mechanical ingenuity was particularly shrewd. The European and British workman did not have, he remarked, the same urgent need for technology; the American is "required to subdue nature through a broad range quickly, and to bring forth her resources with haste and yet with having numbers inadequate and capital quite unequal to such labor."[46]

There were a number of practical reasons for the sudden burgeoning of American technology in the decades 1830–70. The United States had a chronic labor shortage and an unparalleled abundance of natural resources for labor to turn into industrial products. For this reason, American labor offered practically no resistance to technological innovation. American workmen had no entrenched craft or guild tradition, nor did they feel that machinery threatened their jobs; instead, it created more. To the farm or small-town boy who came into the factory the machine was an ally; he grew up with machinery, understood and respected it.

Nearly all American inventions were in response to a direct, immediate need. The textile industry needed and got the cotton gin, the improved loom, rug-weaving machinery, the sewing machine (which created another industry, clothing), and others. The steamboat, the American locomotive, lattice-truss and suspension bridges, and the stone-crusher helped the nation conquer distance. The demands of mushrooming cities brought the balloon-frame house, the steam shovel (called "the Yankee geologist" by the British), and the steam drill. Opening the Western lands to farming required the reaper, the steel plow, the hayrake, the harrow and disc. Mass factory production called for machines that could produce parts at a speed and with precision never before dreamed of—hence the copying lathe, the milling machine, and the turret lathe. An increasingly literate public required things like new typesetting machines and power presses; typewriters, which appeared in the forties and fifties, were finally perfected in the sixties. Iron manufacturers even developed a way of using hard coal, of which the United States had virtually unlimited supplies, in the smelting process. All these technological innovations and improvements

46. Welsh, *op. cit.*, 110; Marvin Fisher, *Workshops in the Wilderness* (New York, 1967), 39–40, 73; Seward, *Works* (Boston, 1884), IV:173–4.

fitted into the economy, filled urgent needs, and had instant commercial value.[47] To the man or industry that could find a way of harnessing technology to production, the rewards could be and often were tremendous.

Americans hailed the machine, then, as an engine of hope. James K. Paulding predicted that technology would bring

a greater revolution in the habits, opinions and morals of mankind than all the efforts of legislation. Machinery and steam engines have had more influence on the Christian world than Locke's metaphysics, Napoleon's code, or Jeremy Bentham's codification.

Jacob Bigelow's *Elements of Technology* (1829), the first important consideration of the relationships of technology and society, expressed in glowing terms what Americans felt about the future. The application of mechanical knowledge to the affairs of living, Bigelow believed, would infinitely accelerate social, economic, and moral progress. By the proper use of mechanics, men would acquire "dominion over the physical and moral world" as the ancients never could. "The application of philosophy," he wrote, "to the arts may be said to have made the world what it is at the present day."[48]

The key to industrial and technological development in the early and middle nineteenth century was transportation.[49] The United States faced problems both of distance and terrain to which solutions were crucial. The size and span of the country forced American technology to improve older means of communications and to develop new ones quickly. During the turnpike era, from the Cumberland Road to the thirties, transportation was swifter and easier than before, but better roads alone could not sufficiently

---

47. Dupree, *op. cit.*, 48–64; Kilgour, *op. cit.*, 750–65.

48. James K. Paulding, *A New Mirror For Travellers* (New York, 1828) preface; Jacob Bigelow, *Elements of Technology* (Boston, 1829), 5. Bigelow gave a series of lectures and published them in book form; he explained the properties and uses of materials—stone, timber, metals, etc.—and the technologies of such things as printing, modeling, casting, building, heating and ventilation, illumination, locomotion, solids, hydraulics, dyeing and coloring, timekeeping, vitrification, and storage. In 1840 he published *The Useful Arts*, a two-volume revision and expansion of his 1829 book. Bigelow's books comprise the most useful and important compendium of technical knowledge published before 1860.

49. The definitive study is George Rogers Taylor, *Transportation Revolution, 1815–1860* (New York, 1951).

increase the rate of horsedrawn vehicles. American coaches and wagons were good ones, well designed to American needs, and they gave excellent service. The network of canals, built from the twenties to the fifties, covered much of the country east of the Mississippi and provided a valuable supplement to the road system, but canal travel, too, depended on horsepower.

River and lake traffic on flatboats, keelboats, barges, and steamboats was heavy and moved much of the nation's goods and many of its people. The Ohio-Mississippi-Missouri river system alone furnished 6,000 miles of waterway, though there were also great landlocked areas where boats could not penetrate. American ocean packets, designed for world commercial trade, dominated the seas. The American clipper, the ultimate in sailing ship design developed in the forties by men like John Griffiths and David McKay (who designed 160 ships), could carry more cargo faster over long distances than any other ships of the time. Steam power and iron hulls came rather slowly, but in the fifties the transition from sail to steam was nearly complete. There were by that time fifteen companies operating sixty-three steamers out of New York.[50]

The railroad changed it all. Few other technological innovations have had such immediate and far-reaching effects on society. The basic technology was British, but the railroad was obviously so important to the United States that American technicians soon caught up and surpassed the English. The T-rail, the rail spike, and the "fifth-plate" connector were American improvements on tracks, while American locomotives—with swivel trucks, equalizing beams, hollow iron wheels, "cow catchers," and advanced high-pressure boilers—were superior to any in Britain and Europe.[51]

The American economy needed locomotives and cars by the hundreds, and manufacturers applied mass-production methods to their manufacture to fill the demand. The Baldwin Works alone

50. John Oliver, *op. cit.*, chapter XIII. A well-handled clipper could average fifteen miles an hour, day in and day out. The *Lightning* once logged 436 miles in twelve hours, the *Flying Cloud* 433, the *Sovereign of the Seas* 495.

51. Oliver, *op. cit.*, 192–6. See also Roger Burlingame, "Railways and Steamships," in Melvin Kranzberg and Carroll Pursell, eds., *Technology in American Civilization* (New York, 1967), II:425–30; John W. White, Jr., *American Locomotives: An Engineering History, 1830–1860* (Baltimore, 1968); and Albert Fishlow, *American Railroads and the Transformation of the Antebellum Economy* (Cambridge, Mass., 1965).

built 1,500 engines between 1832 and 1860. By the fifties New England and the upper South were covered with rails; in 1851 the Erie reached Lake Erie, in 1852 the Pennsylvania reached Pittsburgh, and the Baltimore and Ohio entered Wheeling. The railroad at once gave a center to American economic life. Mails, freight, and people moved over the country more swiftly than ever before, tying regions and localities into a natural economic unit. To the public, the railroad represented the triumph of a beneficent technology. Thus in Edward Everett's apostrophe to the locomotive, an oration given in 1852, he saw it as the symbol of technology's power and future—"a miracle of science, art, and capital, a magic power . . . by which the forest is thrown open, the lakes and rivers are bridged, the valleys rise, and all Nature yields to man."[52]

The spread of railroads meant thousands of new bridges. American bridge builders, accustomed to working in a land of innumerable bays, creeks, rivers, and lakes, were already highly competent in the use of wood; builders like Timothy Parker in Massachusetts and Theodore Burr in Pennsylvania had already made bridge construction a skilled art. Improvements on the truss meant longer spans, so that by 1860 there was scarcely an American river that bridges could not cross. Ithiel Town patented his lattice-truss method of construction in 1820, Stephen Long his "assisted truss" in 1830; William Howe's improvements on Town (1841) dominated techniques for the next half century, while bridge builders substituted iron girders for wooden beams. The invention of a machine to make powerful wire cables, which replaced chains, made possible longer and stronger suspension bridges, culminating in John and Washington Roebling's Brooklyn Bridge, 1869–83.[53]

Next to the locomotive, the technological wonder of the age was the telegraph, which opened vistas to the imagination almost too wonderful to contemplate. Samuel F. B. Morse, an excellent painter, became interested in electricity in the thirties, and following Joseph Henry's experiments with electromagnets, had constructed a workable telegraph and devised a code in 1838. In 1843,

52. *The Railroad Jubilee* (Boston, 1852) , 171–4.
53. Charles Elliott's Wheeling Bridge (1846–49) was the first American bridge with a thousand-foot span. John Augustus Roebling, who came to the United States from Germany, and his son Washington dominated bridge building over the later nineteenth century. See Carl Condit, *American Building Art: The Nineteenth Century* (New York, 1960) , chapter III.

Congress, after repeated rejections, appropriated $30,000 to finance a line from Washington to Baltimore to be built by Morse, which he successfully completed in 1844.[54] Telegraph lines went up quickly. Within two years Washington, Baltimore, Philadelphia, Newark, New York, Boston, Buffalo, and Pittsburgh were linked by wire; in 1852 there were 23,000 miles of line, and in October, 1861, the telegraph reached California. Thousands of orators and editorialists hailed this new technological triumph, while Ralph Waldo Emerson, speaking in 1857, probably expressed what the majority of people felt when he expressed pity for all those born too soon to profit from the new technology,

pity for our fathers for dying before steam and galvanism . . . and before we borrowed the might of the elements. These forces now serve us day to day, and cost us nothing.

Because of them, he wrote, "life seems made over new."

Perhaps less visibly spectacular, but equally as important, were changes in techniques of building and in the uses of building materials. American builders in the seventeenth and eighteenth centuries, for the most part, simply followed traditional British and European methods. The customary pattern of framed wooden construction—joist, beam, and rafter—was in ordinary use until the early nineteenth century, with roof trusses adapted from shipbuilding. American workmen, long accustomed to handling wood, used it with great skill, but during the first half of the nineteenth century, changes in technology and the use of materials influenced American building more powerfully than at any time during the previous two hundred years, reflecting the needs of swiftly changing society.[55]

First of all, the nation needed new kinds of buildings—factory buildings, which had to be larger than any constructed before; office buildings; freight terminals; warehouses; hotels; pumping stations; and so on. The railroad alone demanded buildings which could handle huge equipment, crowds of people, and mountains of goods —all in motion—and which involved complex arrangements of tracks, platforms, walkways, and loading docks. Second, there was a

54. Carleton Mabee, *American Leonardo, Samuel F. B. Morse* (New York, 1943) is the best biography. Although Congress subsidized Morse, it refused to purchase his invention, so Morse formed his own company, which made millions.
55. The indispensable study is Condit, *op. cit.*, from which this section derives.

tremendous need for homes to house a growing and highly mobile population. Third, there were technological innovations which had to be absorbed into the building industry, with such things as the improved truss, arch rib and cantilever construction, wire cable, nail and spike machines, a perfected circular saw, and many others. Fourth, the introduction of two new materials, iron and concrete, demanded a whole new building technology.

The critical fact of American building during the first half of the century was its clear division into two types: serious (or monumental) and commercial (or utilitarian). The former—which included public structures like banks, government buildings, memorial structures, and the like—tended to use traditional materials such as brick and stone in traditional ways. For commercial buildings, builders used wood, which was cheap, easy to work with, and allowed large areas of unobstructed space, as masonry did not. (Later, they transferred their techniques to iron and concrete.) Textile mills, for example, needed five or six stories of open space with floors capable of supporting heavy machinery. American carpenters used broad-framed post-and-beam construction (though iron began to appear in the forties) that could be multiplied without change to make larger and larger structures.[56] A great change, of course, came with the introduction of a new building material—iron. Iron had been used in bridge construction in England during the later eighteenth century, and iron beams and columns appeared after 1800. Disastrous fires led to its use in city buildings in the twenties and thirties, while James Bogardus and Daniel Badger, who worked out its essential techniques in New York, made that city the center of iron building construction in the fifties.[57]

American domestic architecture was forever changed by the invention of balloon-frame construction, first used by Augustine Taylor in building St. Mary's Church in Chicago in 1833. Instead of the usual heavy beam-and-post construction, Taylor built his frame of light studs and joists, cleverly arranged to distribute load and stress. A balloon-framed house was actually a cage of light boards

56. The most impressive example of American building technology in wood is the Tabernacle of the Church of the Latter-Day Saints in Salt Lake City, built 1863–68.

57. Condit, op. cit., chapter II. Portland cement was not adapted to building construction until the later nineteenth century, although both "natural," or hydraulic, and Portland cement were used to make building blocks.

nailed together with diagonals to provide rigidity. The absence of heavy posts and beams gave such houses open, light interiors, more free space, and made them adaptable to prefabrication. Combined with the invention of nail-making machines and light power-driven saws, balloon-frame construction helped to make the swift growth of the American city possible.[58]

Technology altered the shape and style not only of the American home but of the domestic life within it. A severe servant shortage, as factories drew off the supply of labor, together with feminist demands for female independence outside the home, created a need for labor-saving devices and methods in day-to-day household life. The American home was a food-processing and residential plant of considerable size and complexity; the woman who superintended it and did a major share of the labor recognized that it involved a number of complicated tasks. Catherine Beecher's *Treatise on Domestic Economy* (1841) made it clear that housework was to be considered a technical process, to be done with skill and efficiency. The dozens of such "domestic economy" books that appeared over the next generation (the phrase itself reflected a new attitude toward household work) emphasized the need for efficient use of space, introduced the concept of the kitchen as a production center, and emphasized the values of labor-saving tools and work methods.[59]

Changes in the quality of domestic life between 1830 and 1870, due to technology, were enormous. The iron "Betty lamp" was replaced by the gas jet, the outhouse by the indoor toilet, the well pump by pipes and plumbing, the woodstove by the coalstove, the fireplace by the furnace, the tub by the washing machine. The cast-iron stove, a much more efficient instrument for cooking and heating, entered the home in the forties. Robert Mason's canning jar (1858) changed the nation's food-buying and storing habits; the improved icebox made refrigeration of perishables available in

58. A good treatment is Daniel Boorstin, *The Americans* (New York, 1965), 147–53.

59. See Siegfried Giedion, *Mechanization Takes Command* (New York, 1948), 512–82. Catherine Beecher and Harriet Beecher Stowe, *The American Woman's Home* (1869) is an excellent example of the nineteenth-century domestic economy manual. Walter Buehr, *Home Sweet Home in the Nineteenth Century* (New York, 1965), points out that the well-equipped kitchen in 1860 had over thirty small machines for food processing, from sugar cutters to cherry stoners to oyster crackers, not including heavier machines like churns, cheese presses, meat cutters, and coffee roasters.

every home. Washing machines appeared in the forties; the sewing machine permitted cheap and quick production of clothes. All these gave women more freedom, more time, more independence from household labor.[60]

Since balloon-frame construction allowed the builder to enclose more space more cheaply, houses began to have specialized rooms for sleeping, eating, bathing, cooking, and relaxation. After 1840 most houses for middle-class and upper-class families had several specially designated rooms—parlor, library, living room, dining room, bedrooms, bathrooms—giving an opportunity for privacy hitherto available only to the very wealthy. The application of mass production and distribution to home furnishings made good furniture, rugs, dishes, and decoration available in quantity at moderate prices. The arrangement of domestic life in 1870 bore little resemblance to that of the 1830s. Technology changed it all.[61]

The growth of the factory system and the industrialization of the American economy after 1814 emphasized the country's great need for industrial technology. In mass production, the replacement of manually operated tools by machines was the vital factor; the New England textile mills, Whitney's and North's arms factories, and Eli Terry's clock factories were early examples of successful industrial use of the machine. Continuous operation, interchangeable parts, the assembly line, and automatic machine operation all appeared in factories by the 1820s.[62] High labor costs, by reason of labor's scarcity, an abundance of raw materials, and the need to compete with British and European products made constant technological innovation mandatory for American industry. To survive, American manufacturers had to reduce the cost of production, increase its quality, and—whenever possible—find and develop new products

60. Between 1790 and 1847 there were 600 patents issued for "machines and implements for domestic purposes," from bedbug repellents to washing machines, for which there were 228 alone. See Welsh, *op. cit.*, 115.

61. See Anthony N. B. Garvan, "Effects of Technology on Domestic Life 1830–1880," Kranzberg and Pursell, *op. cit.*, II:546–59.

62. For discussions of mechanization in industrial production see Struik, *op. cit.*, 47–51, 79–96; and Kilgour, *op. cit.*, 746–50. Roger Burlingame, *Backgrounds of Power* (New York, 1949) is a useful popular study of mass production. New England clock factories could make one clock every four minutes in 1854; at the Seth Thomas factory three men could cut movements for fifty clocks a day at fifty cents each.

or change old ones to fit new needs.[63] As one manufacturer put it bluntly, "Handwork don't pay." For that matter, economist Henry Carey pointed out that by using machinery the factory owner could avail himself of unskilled and female labor—an English male textile operator handled two looms, whereas a New England girl could operate four.[64]

The New England textile mills became the technological models for other industries; between 1814 and 1840 there were fifteen major improvements in textile production alone. The boot-and-shoe industry, based on new machines, showed spectacular productive increases—in the period 1830–60 it increased the value of its yearly products over sixty times. Elias Howe's sewing machine (1846) with Isaac Singer's (1850's) quickly transformed both shoe and clothing industries; Washburn's wire-drawing machine, originally intended to make wool cards for the textile mills, was adapted to make nails, screws, bolts, chains, buttons, tacks, and so on. The story was repeated again and again throughout the century— machines developed for one industry quickly revolutionized production in others. The impact of technological invention and adaptation was clear in the statistics. From 1812 to 1850 the amount of available industrial labor doubled, but the volume of manufacturing increased twelvefold. The textile industry provided the most spectacular example—by 1860 it had increased the number of spindles in operation four times over, but it employed not quite twice the number of operators as in 1830.[65]

The chemical industry furnished another example of a technologically-based industry that now only dramatically increased its production, but created new products and new markets. The technology of industrial chemistry had been in existence for at least a century, in industries like brewing, glass, soap, fertilizers, dyes, and

63. An excellent study is W. Paul Strassman, *Risk and Technological Innovation in American Manufacturing Methods During the Nineteenth Century* (Ithaca, 1959).

64. Carey is quoted by Ray Ginger, "On an American Technology: 1810–1860," *American Quarterly*, X (Winter, 1953), 369. H. J. Habbakhuk, *American and British Technology in the Nineteenth Century* (Cambridge, England, 1962) is a comprehensive study of the differences.

65. Courtney R. Hall, *The History of American Industrial Science* (New York, 1954), chapter I; Oliver, *op. cit.*, 157–68; Kendall Birr, "Science in American Industry," Van Tassel and Hall, *op. cit.*, 35–81.

pharmaceuticals. Processes for bulk production of basic chemicals—salt, sulfur, quicklime, gypsum, soda, saltpeter, acids—were well known by 1800. Rapid developments in chemical theory, however, led to new understanding of such things as the nature of compounds, oxidation, and the nature of chemical reactions, all of which supported research and development. The clearest example of a technologically based chemical industry was the manufacture of rubber, founded on vulcanization. Rubber goods of limited usefulness were made in the 1820s, but Charles Goodyear's process (1839), which treated rubber with sulfur under heat, created a wholly new industry almost overnight. Within twenty years the American rubber industry employed 10,000 workers and produced $5,000,000 worth of rubber products per year. Similarly, the perfection of coal-tar dyes in the forties and nitrocellulose in the fifties (celluloid in 1863) opened new industrial opportunities. At mid-century the chemist, like the engineer, was an integral part of a factory's personnel, and names like Grasselli, Dow, and Mallinckrodt became as familiar in industrial circles as Du Pont.[66]

Technology transformed American agriculture, before the close of the century, into a different kind of economic venture. In 1820 the farmer operated on a small scale, dealing with a relatively limited and adjacent market; a half century later, except in remote or newly settled regions, he was a commercialized, semi-industrialized business. There were a number of reasons for the change—the opening of new lands, improved means of transport to markets, growing cities demanding more agricultural produce—all of which demanded changes in agricultural production. The farmer had to know how to produce the largest crops best suited to his land, and how to market them at the lowest labor cost, which meant using machinery to replace manual and animal labor on the one hand, and on the other using scientifically sophisticated methods to increase yields.[67]

66. Hall, op. cit., 263–9; Robert Multhauf, "Industrial Chemistry in the Nineteenth Century"; Kranzberg and Pursell, op. cit., I:468–89.

67. For further information, consult Reynold Wik's excellent essay, "Science in American Agriculture," Van Tassel and Hall, op. cit., and George Borgstrom, "Food and Agriculture in the Nineteenth Century," Kranzberg and Pursell, op. cit., II:408–24. The refrigerator car, the ice refrigerator, and new food-preservation processes like condensed milk and pressure canning also had great effects on

American agriculture, until the thirties, had been singularly lacking in technological imaginativeness, but after the opening of the Western lands, new machines appeared every year. In 1830 the Patent Office issued thirty agricultural patents, a number which reached 503 in 1863. Harvesting, the most laborious and expensive farm task, attracted the interest of many inventors, and Cyrus McCormick patented his version of the reaper in 1834, almost simultaneously with Obed Hussey's.[68] In 1840 the time required to harvest one acre of grain had dropped from 37½ hours to 4½ hours. John Deere's steel plow (1837), like the plows of Jethro Wood and James Oliver, was an important tool in turning over the tough sod lands of the West. While the horse remained the primary power source for agricultural machinery, steam engines were quickly put to use for grinding, sawing, and milling. Obed Hussey demonstrated a steam-powered plow at the Indiana State Fair in 1856 and steam was used for threshing not long after the Civil War, but the engine did not replace the horse as the farmer's chief power source until the gasoline engine arrived on the farm in the twentieth century.[69]

The development of American technology depended on three factors: an abundance of natural resources; the imaginative use of materials and of new power sources; and the development of a machine tool industry. Of natural resources—wood, coal, water, minerals—the nation had large and easily available supplies. Until the early nineteenth century industrial activity everywhere depended on four sources of power—manual, animal, wind, and water. American factories developed sophisticated waterpower systems quite early, so that by the early nineteenth century, water

---

the market for agricultural products. The impact of the steam engine on agriculture is considered in Reynold Wik, *Steam Power on the American Farm* (Philadelphia, 1953).

68. Preceding McCormick's, there were thirty-three English reapers, twenty-two American, two French, and one German, but his worked best. When binders were added to the machine in 1872 and 1878, hand work was virtually eliminated from the process. See Fred Kohlmeyer and Floyd Herum, "Science and Engineering in Agriculture: A Historical Perspective," *Technology and Culture*, II (1961), 368–79.

69. Charles H. Danhof, *Change in Agriculture: The Northern United States 1820–70* (Cambridge, Mass., 1969). See also Robert Ardrey, *American Agricultural Implements* (Chicago, 1894) and Stewart L. Holbrook, *Machines of Plenty* (New York, 1955).

provided by far the cheapest power source. In 1840 the Blackstone River, a minor stream between Worcester and Providence, powered 150 industrial plants—94 cotton mills, 22 woolen mills, and 34 machine shops and ironworks. Though it continued to run the majority of American machines (especially in New England) for another quarter-century, waterpower had its limits. Its potential was restricted by the number of available streams, and if American industry were to expand, some new power source—one that delivered large amounts of energy per unit and need not be near a stream—had to be found. The answer, of course, and a particularly fortunate one for a nation with tremendous beds of coal, was steam.[70]

The low-pressure steam engine had developed into a highly effective power unit by the early nineteenth century, well adapted to use by steamboats, locomotives, and stationary engines. The steam engine was a mobile, efficient, consistent, and almost unlimited power source. Since the New England textile industry found waterpower quite satisfactory for its needs, steam engineering took hold slowly. However, farsighted men like Zachariah Allen, who saw the advantages of steam as early as 1827, warned Americans to pay close attention to European steam technology, and he used a picture of a double-acting steam engine as the frontispiece of his book, *The Science of Mechanics,* which he published in 1829. Events bore him out. The demand for steam engines in the thirties and forties was tremendous; the Secretary of the Treasury reported in 1838 that there were 3,010 in the country, powering 350 locomotives, 800 steamboats, and 1,860 factories.[71]

The steam engine was the great wonder of the age and the great hope of its future. Steam power, applied to human needs, became the symbol of technology's triumph, a sign of God's beneficence to man, the motive power of a new paradise. It was, said George Burnap, "the mightiest agent that man has ever enlisted [in] aid of his labors." "By the side of this tremendous energy," wrote Salmon P. Chase, "every other power becomes insignificant."[72]

70. *Hall, op. cit.,* 14–16.
71. A comprehensive recent treatment is Carroll W. Pursell, *Early Stationary Steam Engines in America* (New York, 1969).
72. G. W. Burnap, "The Influence of Machinery . . . ," *American Magazine of Literature and the Arts,* II (May, 1839), 349–64; S. P. Chase, in *The North*

If the nineteenth century was the Age of Steam, it was equally the Age of Iron. Eighteenth-century technology used iron only when wood or a more easily wrought metal would not do, but improved methods of smelting iron produced a cheaper and more useful metal that fitted any number of uses. The steam engine provided power for mining and metalworking machines; steam engines drove hoists, blast furnaces, forge hammers, and rolling mills. The demand for steam engines stimulated the market for iron (an iron boiler cost about half as much as copper) and required new kinds of tools to use it; the creation of new tools increased the usefulness of iron for a whole new range of purposes. Steel remained essentially a special-purpose metal until the Bessemer method in the fifties made it possible to produce low-carbon steel cheaply and quickly. By 1860 the industry was producing large quantities of steel for rails, ship hulls, tools, and other uses in place of iron.[73]

To use metals in industry required tools to work it; to use machines meant that other machines and tools had to be developed to make them. The steam engine, for example, required an accurately bored cylinder, the locomotive needed a huge drive beam tooled to delicate balance. The center of machine-tool technology from 1750 to 1850 was England, where boring and planing machines and (more important) the engine lathe were designed in the eighteenth century. American machine tools at first were mostly imported or adapted from British and continental models. There were three American adaptations of imported machines, however, that later proved particularly important: Thomas Blanchard's "stocking lathe," a duplicating machine used in making rifle stocks; Stephen Fitch's improved turret lathe that replaced four less efficient ones; and Frederick Howe's universal milling machine, a cutting machine for metals.

Most factories set up their own machine shops and, as the demand for machines and tools increased, might sell to other firms or become independent producers themselves. Meanwhile, as industrial technology became more complicated, new shops appeared to fill the need for more complex machines. The earliest machine-tool

---

American Review, XXXIV (January, 1832) , 240. While workable electric motors existed in the forties, the means of cheap production and transmission of electrical power (the generator and transformer) were still to come.

73. C. S. Smith, in Kranzberg and Pursell, *op. cit.,* II:349–67.

shops were attached to the two most technically advanced industries—textiles and arms. Since the first needed general-purpose
machinery like lathes and planers, and the latter needed lighter,
high-speed precision tools—grinders, milling machines, and the
like—a balanced industry developed rather swiftly. The Lowell
Machine Shop, for example, which began by making textile machinery, later turned to making locomotives; the great Baldwin
Locomotive Works also grew from a textile shop. The larger shops
produced a variety of machines and tools—a British observer in
1851 noted that a single American firm made spinning machines,
mill gears, hydraulic presses, and marine engines as well as smaller
tools. The result was the creation of an entirely new American
industry, fitted to the needs of a machine age.[74]

It required more than machines, of course, to make an industrial
society, for they needed engineers to design and run them. The
supply came from three main sources. There were a number of
English and European engineers who came to the United States and
stayed, finding employment in industry, on the railroads, and on
canal-building projects. James Francis, whose water-powered machinery helped lay the basis for the textile industry, was an Englishman; John Roebling, who pioneered in the building of suspension
bridges, came from Germany. Other engineers came from the
United States Military Academy at West Point (itself influenced by
the French École Polytechnique) which provided most of the engineers for government projects over the thirties and forties. Many
West Pointers, after serving out their military obligations, went
directly to civilian jobs with railroads or factories. A few colleges
taught engineering—Rensselaer Polytechnic Institute was founded
in 1824—but professional engineering training did not appear in
most colleges until the fifties, and later in those Morrill Act institutions founded after 1862 for the study of "agriculture and the
mechanic arts."[75] Much more influential were the "mechanics insti-

74. Nathan Rosenberg, in Kranzberg and Pursell, op. cit., II:524–7; Carroll
Pursell, ed., Readings in Technology and American Life (New York, 1969),
392–440.
75. Engineering was introduced at Harvard in 1847, and Yale in 1850; Massachusetts Institute of Technology was founded in 1861. Brooklyn Polytechnical
Institute came in 1854, Cooper Union in 1859, and Stevens Institute of Technology in 1871. Meanwhile, land-grant colleges instituted engineering in their

tutes" which flourished in the thirties and forties, half-educational, half-professional societies patterned after British models which offered mathematics, science, surveying, hydraulics, simple metallurgy, and other studies.[76]

By far the largest number of engineers, mechanics, and technicians learned on the job. Canal building taught techniques that could be transferred to dams, waterworks, power systems, and drainage projects. The three Baldwins—Loammi Sr., Loammi Jr., and James—whose specialty was harbor and river engineering, served their apprenticeships on the canals. Young men who entered factory work learned to repair and build machines, then left for other factories as machinists or to found their own shops. Railroads produced hundreds of men who knew something about metallurgy, steam engineering, surveying, topography, bridge building, soils, and other skills. Engineers soon recognized the need for professional training, standards, and organization; professional societies sprang up in the forties, leading to the establishment of the American Society of Civil Engineering in 1852. By that time, American engineers were equal to the world's best. Salaries rapidly reached professional levels, and by the seventies engineers were moving into executive and managerial positions in industry and transportation.[77]

The speed and extent of technological progress, however, raised doubts about its benefits among some American intellectuals. There was a strong impulse, rooted deep in American Calvinism, to suspect that industrial society assigned too much value to material achievements. Critics of technological progress drew from both

---

curricula. See John B. Rae, "The Invention of Invention," Kranzberg and Pursell, op. cit., II:325–33; and R. S. Kirby and P. G. Laurson, The Early Years of Modern Civil Engineering (New Haven, 1932).

76. Cincinnati's, founded in 1828, was typical. The Institute had its own library and scientific apparatus, offered formal instruction by faculty recruited from Cincinnati College, held annual trade fairs, and was the city's center for trade and technical education for thirty years. Charles Crist, Cincinnati in 1841 (Cincinnati, 1841), 128–32.

77. Raymond H. Merritt, Engineering in American Society, 1850–75 (Lexington, Kentucky, 1969). Matthias Baldwin's locomotives, for example, were no doubt the best in the world; Major George Washington Whistler (whose son, James McNeill, did not do well at West Point) built the St. Petersburg to Moscow railway for the Russians; George Corliss's four-valve steam engine dominated engine design for a half century. It was a single huge Corliss engine that powered all eight thousand machines at the Philadelphia Exposition of 1876, and so impressed Henry Adams.

European and domestic sources for their warnings. Some English and continental thinkers had already found the implications of the Industrial Revolution disturbing, and thoughtful Americans wanted none of the "dark satanic mills" that William Blake inveighed against. Thomas Cole, the painter, feared too much progress: "What is sometimes called improvement in its march makes us fear that the bright and tender flowers of the imagination shall be crushed beneath its iron tramp." Washington Irving, in 1842, was much more forthright, wanting to "blow up all the cotton mills . . . and make picturesque ruins out of them." For all the comforts and prosperity of a machine age, some Americans felt, the price might be too high.[78]

But whereas European critics of industrialism drew support from an aristocracy whose cultural and social values were threatened by the new technology, there was no such class in America. Since probably most American workers shared the ambitions and attitudes of businessmen and skilled workmen, labor gave little support to critics of the system. Timothy Walker of New England, for example, in reply to Thomas Carlyle's attack in 1829 on "that malevolent spirit, Mechanism," wrote in 1831 an impassioned "Defence of Mechanical Philosophy." "In plain words," he said, "we deny the evil tendencies of mechanism."[79]

So far from enslaving, it has emancipated the mind, in the most glorious sense. From a ministering servant of matter, mind has become the powerful lord of matter. Having put myriads of wheels in motion by laws of its own discovery, it rests, like the Omnipotent Mind, of which it is the image, from its work of creation, and calls it good.

But in a machine-dominated civilization, its critics believed, material values must necessarily outweigh spiritual; the chief aim of the whole industrial system was simply to make money, to gain reward for the pocket instead of the soul. When machines finally did all of man's work, they warned, all the old values would disappear under a flood of affluence. The United States, Henry David Thoreau warned in *Walden,* was becoming "an unwieldy and overgrown establishment, cluttered with furniture and trapped by its

78. See Morrell Heald, "Technology in American Culture," *Stetson University Bulletins,* LXII (October, 1962) # 3; and Leo Marx, "Two Kingdoms of Force," *The Massachusetts Review,* I (October, 1959) , 62–95.

79. *North American Review,* XXXIII (January, 1831) , 122–36.

own traps"; civilization was threatened by the machine just as his own forest retreat was threatened by the neighing whistle of that "devilish Iron Horse," the Fitchburg Railroad. Melville thought he saw something of this in the textile mills and dealt with it in his half-veiled allegory, "The Tartarus of Maids." To Hawthorne, as to Thoreau, the locomotive symbolized the threat of technology. The "startling shriek" of its whistle, he wrote in his notebooks, was an intrusion by "a noisy world into the midst of our slumbrous peace." While Emerson, in his lecture "Works and Days," delivered in 1857, hailed the "mechanic arts" as a truly liberating force for mankind, he also warned that tools had "questionable properties."

They are reagents. Machinery is dangerous. The weaver becomes the web, the machinist the machine. If you do not use the tools, they use you. All tools are in one sense edge-tools, and dangerous.

Almost to a man, American intellectuals feared technology and its twin, industrialism, and searched for strategies to defeat them. The roots of the issue, of course, lay in the old American dream of America as an agrarian Arcadia. The ideal of America as pastoral Eden appeared to be threatened by industrialism and technology; the machine in America's garden seemed destined to destroy it.[80]

The more enlightened American manufacturers were well aware of some of the undesirable consequences of the Industrial Revolution. They did not want to repeat Europe's errors; many came from rural backgrounds—the Lowells, Appletons, Lawrences, and Jacksons of textile industry fame were all small-town or farm boys—and the European and British brand of industrialism was not what they envisioned. Daniel Webster, who understood the entrepreneurial mind as thoroughly as anyone, wanted no "close and unwholesome workshops" or "Birminghams and Sheffields" in his New England.[81] Instead of a recaptured Eden, there were Americans who had another image of their land as a workshop in the wilderness, a technological utopia in which the machine, far from being man's adversary, was harnessed to his needs. There was reason to believe—

80. The most complete exploration of this is Leo Marx, *The Machine in the Garden: Technology and the Pastoral Ideal* (New York, 1964), to which this discussion is indebted.

81. Charles Sanford, *The Quest for Paradise* (Urbana, 1961), 155–60; and Clarence Mondale, "Daniel Webster and Technology," in Hennig Cohen, ed., *The American Culture* (Boston, 1968), 191–206.

and evidence to support it—that the United States, through wise use of its tremendous resources and aided by a beneficent technology, could become a paradise of a different kind.[82]

The contemporary enthusiasm for technology also had a nationalistic bias; the opportunity for Americans to use machines properly, as Britain and Europe had not, appealed to their patriotic instincts. Instead of bringing black factory towns and ghettoes of urban poor, Americans saw technology bestowing its benefits on all men and not only the wealthy, aristocratic few. Benjamin P. Johnson, who reported on the 1851 London Exhibition as New York State's agent, noted that the American exhibits showed how "we worked for the masses" in contrast to the French, Russians, and Austrians, whose exhibits consisted chiefly of "the most costly articles, wrought with exquisite taste, silks, statuary, diamonds, jewelry, etc." By contrast, the Americans made "articles of utility and comfort . . . for the advantages of the middling classes."[83]

Whatever Thoreau, Melville, or Emerson thought of it, the majority of Americans believed that the American technology, which put machines to man's service, was the crowning glory of American society. Names of inventors and industrialists were always high in lists of "great Americans"; it was the American industrial system, Edward Everett thought, that made "the difference between the savage of the woods, and civilized, cultivated, and moral and religious man." John Pendleton Kennedy, when he saw "the vast engineering, this infinite complication of wheels" in a factory, was "lost in admiration" for the genius who designed it. To the era the inventor and the engineer became a kind of hero.[84]

Progress in technology, the age assumed, was closely associated with the progress of democracy. Technology provided the nation with the practical means of achieving political, social, and economic equality; by giving men wealth and leisure, it gave them time to cultivate themselves. Benjamin Hallett of Massachusetts, speaking in the thirties, made it abundantly clear that as a Jacksonian he

82. For a discussion of this concept as Europeans saw it, see Marvin Fisher, *op. cit.*

83. Carroll W. Pursell, *op. cit.*, 97–98.

84. A series of engravings, popular in the fifties, called *Men of Progress,* included Samuel Colt, Cyrus McCormick, Charles Goodyear, Samuel F. B. Morse, Elias Howe, Richard Hoe, Joseph Henry, and many others.

considered the development of science and technology the best safeguard against tyranny, revolution, and division:[85]

We have no populace, no rabble, but free and independent citizens. What has made them so? The development of our resources. . . . Develop the resources of the country, place the means of wealth within the reach of industry, and you produce the happy medium in society. All will then move forward evenly, as on the level of a railroad, with occasional inclined planes and elevations.

Salmon P. Chase felt that machinery represented "a new and almost infinite power brought to bear on the action of the social system . . . taking from none, yet giving to all, producing almost unmingled benefit. . . ." Writers and speakers, one after another, testified to the conviction that technology was a great liberating force, democracy's greatest ally. The most fulsome tribute perhaps, one not untypical, was that of philosopher F. H. Hedge, who told the citizens of Bangor in 1838:[86]

The time shall come, when new inventions, lightening labor and redeeming time, shall remove from the lot of the poor, those obstructions which have hitherto checked the free circulation of social privilege and brotherly love. The desert will gush with new resources. The very rock on which their feet now stumble, some kind prophet shall smite to healthful issues. For them, too, shall be opened the everlasting fountains of intellectual life. The laboring man shall wipe the sweat from his brow, and steep his bread in the cooling wave; the meanest shall drink thereof, and be filled. In those days, a more extended mechanism shall take from the overtasked their heavy load, and abridge the hours of manual service. Wood and iron shall serve for sinews and for bones. The gases shall steam up from the bowels of the earth and relieve the toilworn hand. Unseen powers shall labor and drudge . . . . The sacred frame of man shall no longer be bent and seamed with servile tasks. Different functions shall no longer have different spheres of privilege and honor. Moral worth shall constitute the only distinction.

Americans were so busy exploiting the machine during the first half of the nineteenth century, and doing it so successfully, that

85. A good discussion is Hugo A. Meier, "Technology and Democracy, 1800–1860," *Mississippi Valley Historical Review*, XLIII (March, 1957), 618–40. Hallett is quoted by Henry Howe, *Memoirs of the Most Eminent American Mechanics* (New York, 1840), chapter I.

86. F. H. Hedge, "An Oration Before the Citizens of Bangor . . . ," *Western Messenger*, VI (November, 1838), 36. S. P. Chase, "Effects of Machinery," *North American Review*, XXXIV (January, 1832), 220–46.

they were much less concerned than British or Europeans with the philosophical implications of the new technology.[87] Having embraced machinery as an essential ingredient of their culture, they were interested in fitting it into existing patterns of thought—as part of their nationalism, their democratic society, their belief in progress—and into the Christian design of the world they lived in. The philosophy of technology the era developed was one of hopeful acceptance; it assumed that machinery—from steam engine to apple parer—was by God's decree beneficial to mankind. This theme appeared in dozens of essays and orations, suggesting that somehow the "mechanic arts" belonged within the pattern of progress decreed by the Creator. The beneficial resources of machinery, one commentator wrote in 1857, were as yet hardly tapped, the technological golden age lay yet in the future, where "within the machine shop and laboratory, are wonders that shall throw the old magic in the shade." Technology, by "its arts of building, drawing, watering, lighting, ventilating, and clothing, has done for the wretched and miserable the very deeds pronounced blessed by our Lord." What lay ahead was an American society "beyond the theorist's dream, in the progressive order decreed by the God of Ages."[88]

The impact on American culture of technological development over the first half of the nineteenth century was so decisive and pervasive that its implications are difficult to assess precisely.[89]

87. In England men like J. R. McCulloch, Charles Babbage, Andrew Ure, and of course Karl Marx, all wrote thoughtful treatises on the technology and society. Not until W. G. Moody (1878), Carroll Wright (1882), and David Wells (1890) did comparable American studies appear. See Richard S. Rosenbloom, "Some Nineteenth Century Analyses of Mechanization," *Technology and Culture*, V (1964), 489–511.

88. See Peter Welsh, *op. cit.*, 109–11, for a discussion of this idea. Thomas Ewbank's *The World a Workshop* (1855) represented best the relationship his times assumed between the machine and society. Ewbank made a fortune in metallurgy and manufacturing and was appointed Commissioner of Patents in 1849. Since God was "the chief of artificers" and constructor of the world, "What is the world but one of workshops, and the universe a collection of inventions?" The human technician was, in making machines, only copying God and making His wisdom available to mankind. See his report as Commissioner of Patents, 33rd Congress, 2nd Session, Executive Document 65, Part I (Washington, 1853), 16 ff. See "The Destiny of the Mechanic Arts," *Harper's Monthly Magazine*, XIV (April, 1857), 696–9.

89. An invaluable source of information on technology is Appleton's *Dictionary of Machines, Mechanics, Engineworks, and Engineering* (two volumes, New York, 1852).

Clearly, the swift acceptance of the machine allowed American industry to use the country's resources more quickly and efficiently than would have been otherwise possible. Productivity, in all sectors of the economy, and per-capita output increased at an amazing rate over these years and continued to do so through the century. The rate of economic growth over the two decades 1840–60 was 57 percent each decade, a swifter rate than for any other decade in the century. By the best estimates, the gross national product rose at the rate of 1.55 percent per year from 1830 to 1880, while the population quadrupled, which meant the American society was getting richer at a rate unequaled elsewhere in the world. True, Americans were blessed by a country rich in natural resources—in contrast to England and Europe—but it was also true that their mastery of a sophisticated technology enabled them to utilize those resources swiftly and efficiently. Whereas in 1839 17 percent of the national commodity output originated in manufacturing, in 1879 the figure stood at 47 percent and was still rising. American wealth, and there was much of it, came from machinery.[90]

Steam, iron, and their technological applications made the growth of the nineteenth-century American city possible by providing housing, transportation, markets, and employment; it also made it inevitable by placing factories in cities and making cities out of towns. Westward settlement would have been difficult, if not impossible, without railroads, reapers, windmills, pumps, and a dozen other machines. Without technology the factory system and the industrial system that enclosed it could not have developed as it did—the factory depended on the machine, and nothing else mattered so much. The effect on domestic life of machinery was enormous. It altered rural life by making it possible to farm larger and larger areas and allowed more efficient use of both labor and land. On the other hand, the spread of technology created millions of new specialized jobs within the emergent industrial society— engineers, mechanics, machine operators, skilled technicians. The railroad alone brought into being, within a single generation, a whole new labor system involving thousands of jobs that had never

90. Rosenberg, *op. cit.*, 518–20. For discussions of economic growth in the nineteenth century, see Walter W. Rostow, *The Stages of Economic Growth* (Cambridge, England, 1960) and Robert Gallman, "Commodity Output 1839–1899," in W. N. Parker, ed., *Trends in American Economy in the Nineteenth Century* (Princeton, 1960).

existed before. Technology brought increased wealth, hours of released time, needs for education, even better foods and clothes. And on a broader scale, technology made the American economy genuinely independent of Europe; by annihilating distance, it bound the country together internally in one vast, unified society. A decade before the Civil War, the technological revolution had already made disunion impossible.

CHAPTER 8

The Life of the Soul

AMERICAN Protestant churches and American Protestant theology had by the nineteenth century developed their own unique characteristics.[1] First, by reason of the decision made at the Constitutional Convention, no agency of government, federal or state, took responsibility for the religious life of the citizen. The Constitution assumed that religion was beyond the government's jurisdiction.

Second, a church was considered to be an association of individuals who joined it by choice; it was responsible to no civil authority and equal to all other churches. "Voluntarism" meant that any person was free to join or not to join any church, and that the church was free to accept or reject him. It meant that matters of theology and polity were decided within the group, by the group,

1. For general considerations of nineteenth-century American religion, see Kenneth Latourette, *A History of the Expansion of Christianity* (New York, 1937–1945) IV:424–26, *passim;* Sidney Mead, *The Lively Experiment: The Shaping of Christianity in America* (New York, 1963), chapters VII, VIII; and Winthrop Hudson, *The Great Tradition of the American Churches* (New York, 1953) on voluntarism. Useful brief histories are W. W. Sweet, *The Story of Religion in America* (New York, 1939) and his *Religion in the Development of American Culture* (New York, 1952); Winthrop Hudson, *American Protestantism* (Chicago, 1961). Major historical treatments are Edwin E. Gaustad, *A Religious History of America* (New York, 1966), William A. Clebsch, *From Sacred to Profane America: The Role of Religion in American History* (New York, 1968); and Clifton Olmsted, *A History of Religions in the United States* (Englewood Cliffs, 1960) to which this chapter owes a substantial debt. Gaustad's *Historical Atlas of Religion in the United States* (New York, 1962) is an excellent statistical source.

and only there. Voluntarism meant stability; change tended to be gradual, extremes to drop away. Too, voluntarism meant a greater lay control within the church, more authority in nonclerical hands.

Third, American Protestantism was denominational; that is, its churches were organized according to belief in, or emphasis on, certain doctrinal differences. New denominations could be formed, or old ones merged or discarded, by consent of their members on the basis of common beliefs and objectives. The denominational organization was a practical way for churches to handle problems of internal control and finance, and it was also a way for them to coexist peaceably in a pluralistic society. Denominations recognized each other's differences, yet all were Americans and all members of the same body of Protestant Christianity; no American church ever made war on another over such differences. There was therefore no American church but American churches.[2]

Fourth, although any church had the right to make its own interpretations of Christian theology, all American Protestant denominations agreed on a central body of doctrines. Man was sinful, but capable of regeneration through the saving grace offered by God, and by his own efforts. He was a free agent—more or less—responsible for his sins as for his salvation, which would be granted if he worked sufficiently hard for it and lived so as to merit it. This theology was rooted in love—God's love for man, man's love for God, man's love of fellowman—for "pure love," John Wesley had said, "is the whole of scriptural perfection." This basic creed was Bible-based, derived from the individual's direct comprehension of the Scriptures. It was also deeply evangelical, derived from "Awakening" theology of the eighteenth century as developed by the nineteenth. It accepted the validity of the individual's own emotional revelation and granted him the right (within reasonable limits) to act as his own judge. All major American denominations in the nineteenth century turned away from the reasoned, "natural religion" of the Enlightenment toward a "romantic" religious faith in the internal and intuitive.[3]

2. The largest in 1850 in order were Roman Catholic, Methodist, Baptist, Presbyterian, Congregationalist, Lutheran, Christian Disciples, Episcopal, and the Latter-Day Saints.

3. Cf. the discussions in Mead, *op. cit.*, and Stow Persons, *American Minds* (New York, 1958), chapter 9.

Fifth, American Protestantism of the period was missionary Christianity. The evangelical mood was activist—once saved, it was one's duty to save others, to win converts as one had himself been converted. "The Presbyterian Church," its General Assembly said in 1847, "is a missionary society, the object of which is to aid in the conversion of the world," a sentiment with which other American denominations fully agreed. If individuals were converted, the regeneration of society would follow in due course; American Christianity was thus socially conscious, participatory, reformist, perfectionist. If moral perfection were possible through individual salvation, then the social perfection of a wholly moral society was possible too. The churches were, then, not to be set apart from the dust and heat of life, but involved in change and progress.[4]

The result was a confederation of American Protestant churches, fitted to the American situation in the nineteenth century, bound together by a distinctively American theology, polity, and purpose. Unique in the world, the American system provided for religious unity and allowed variety; it gave apparatus for control and opportunity for freedom. It was admirably suited to a fluid, relatively classless society, living under a loosely centralized government, a society in the midst of an era of expansion and social change.

The most important fact about American religion during the first half of the nineteenth century was that it was evangelical, revivalist Christianity. Revivals, wrote the Reverend Calvin Colton in 1830, "have become the grand absorbing theme and aim of the American religious world," and they remained so for another generation. The wave of evangelism that swept the nation from 1780 to 1810 receded for a time, returned in the twenties and thirties, receded once more, and reappeared with renewed vigor in the fifties.[5]

The center of evangelism lay in its belief in the need for "instan-

4. Cf. the discussion in Perry Miller, *The Life of the Mind in America* (New York, 1965) Book I, "The Evangelical Basis." The list of church-sponsored societies dealing with public issues is very long, among them such groups as the American Colonization Society, the American Education Society, the American Seamen's Friend Society, the American Tract Society, the American Temperance Society.

5. A useful recent study of the "Second Great Awakening" of the late eighteenth century is John B. Boles, *The Great Revival: Origins of the Southern Evangelical Mind* (Lexington, Ky., 1972).

taneous, conscious conversion, preceded by an overwhelming sense of personal guilt, and followed by a joyous assurance of acceptance" by God. Put another way, as Charles Grandison Finney defined it, conversion moved through three stages—"conviction, repentance, and reformation." A revival was a special religious service or services at which attempts were made to convince the unconverted of their sinfulness, thus beginning the process of regeneration that would lead to repentance and conversion.[6]

Evangelism cut across sectarian lines, occurring particularly in Congregational, Presbyterian, Methodist, and Baptist churches— that is, in those which were least ritualistic and which most emphasized the role of the individual in seeking his salvation. It was, additionally, powerfully reinforced by the parallel Romantic movement in philosophy and literature, which also stressed the role of the individual in finding truth and the validity of his inner, intuitional convictions. Ralph Waldo Emerson's idea that man had connections through his mind and Nature with an Oversoul and the camp meeting conversion's burst of inward joy were expressions of the same articles of Romantic belief. "Nearer, My God, to Thee" (1859), with words by Sarah Adams and music by Lowell Mason, was a perfect summation of the era's Romantic, evangelistic faith:[7]

> There let the way appear,
> Steps unto heaven;
> All that thou sendest me
> To mercy given;
> Angels to beckon me,

6. Evangelism is the term generally applied to those beliefs held by orthodox Protestants which emphasize the sinfulness of man's nature, his personal relationship with God, his salvation through faith, and the need for his conversion through inward grace. See Vergilius Ferm, *Encyclopaedia of Religion* (New York, 1945). A good contemporary essay is Charles G. Finney, "What a Revival of Religion Is," in William C. McLoughlin, ed., *The American Evangelicals, 1800–1900* (New York, 1968), 86–101.

7. W. W. Sweet, *Revivalism in America* (New York, 1944) is a good historical study. Charles C. Cole, *The Social Ideas of the Northern Evangelists 1826–1860* (New York, 1954) is a key study of persons and trends; as is McLoughlin, *op. cit.;* Bernard Weisberger, *They Gathered at the River* (Boston, 1958) is a study of the great American evangelists. McLoughlin's *Modern Revivalism: Charles Grandison Finney to Billy Graham* (New York, 1959) continues the historical narrative. Perry Miller, "The Evangelical Basis," *op. cit.,* is an excellent survey; Ralph H. Gabriel, "Evangelical Religion and Popular Romanticism in Early Nineteenth Century America," *Church History,* XIX (1950), 34–47 is a key interpretative article.

Nearer, my God, to Thee,
    Nearer to Thee . . . ,
Or if on joyful wing,
    Cleaving the sky,
Sun, moon and stars forgot,
    Upwards I fly;
Still all my song shall be
Nearer, my God, to Thee,
    Nearer to Thee.

The evangelistic movements of the thirties and after met stiff opposition at first from conservative clergymen, who opposed their methods more than their theology. Probably more than anything else, the public display of emotionalism that often accompanied revivals offended taste; some of the aggressive, strong-willed revival preachers alienated their better-mannered brethren. Revivals, some clergymen believed, diverted energy and attention from more fundamental religious matters; furthermore, evangelists preached what scholarly clergymen regarded as an oversimplified doctrine, one that avoided or gave emotionally loaded answers to difficult questions. The connections between evangelism and reform were quickly noted by the socially conservative. Revivalists and their followers tended to get mixed up with unsettling matters like abolitionism, women's rights, and prohibition. Nonetheless, the opposition was simply buried by evangelism's sweep across the nineteenth century.[8]

By 1860 the spirit and doctrines of evangelical Christianity had been adopted to some degree by all major Protestant denominations. It was accepted that revivalism, or "a state of continuous awakening," was and should be the normal condition of American religious life, while revivalistic attitudes were reflected in parts of the customary church services. Some churches, in fact, added the word "Evangelical" to their official names. The main thrust of the movement was toward interdenominationalism. The trend was to de-emphasize doctrinal differences, to consider the spirit of faith more important than doctrine. There was room for everybody, said *The New Englander* in 1860, "on a broad and comprehensive platform of Evangelical Faith."[9]

8. For contemporary estimates, see Charles A. Johnson, "The Frontier Camp Meeting: Contemporary and Historical Appraisals," *Mississippi Valley Historical Review*, XXXVII (June, 1950), 91–111.

9. Timothy Smith, *Revivalism and Social Reform* (New York, 1965), 80–81.

In the East, evangelism during the twenties was dominated by the Reverend Lyman Beecher. A Connecticut blacksmith's son, graduated from Yale in 1797 and ordained by President Timothy Dwight himself, Beecher was called to Litchfield, Connecticut, in 1810, where he preached such powerful sermons that when the Hanover Street Church was organized in Boston in 1826 he was chosen for its pulpit. He was active in a number of reforms—antislavery, anti-dueling, temperance, among others, and when Lane Seminary was opened in Cincinnati in 1832 to train young ministers for the conversion of the West, Beecher was chosen as its president. However, his kind of Calvinism was too moderate for the West; although he was against slavery, his views were attacked as too weak by student abolitionists, many of whom rebelled against the seminary's rules and withdrew to Oberlin College. Beecher stayed at Lane until 1850, when he returned to Boston and retirement.

Among Baptists, a leading figure was Jacob Knapp of New York, who for twenty-five years battled sin and stirred up controversy by his aggressive preaching which, he claimed, had converted over a hundred thousand sinners. Peter Cartwright, who spent sixty-five years in the Methodist ministry in the West, gave over fourteen thousand sermons in his career. Fearless, physically tough, making up in fervor what he lacked in learning, Cartwright was probably the best known of the frontier exhorters. Albert Barnes, a product of Princeton, was well known among Eastern Presbyterians; Congregationalist Joshua Leavitt joined the antislavery movement and became one of the more effective abolition journalists.[10]

Of all the evangelists, the most prominent—not only because of his popularity but because of his theology—was Charles Grandison Finney, born in Connecticut in 1792. He taught school and worked in a law office before deciding on the ministry after being converted in 1821. He prepared for the Presbyterian pulpit by private study and was licensed to preach in 1824. Within two years he was well known as a revivalist, with a trail of successful meetings behind him in New York State and multitudes of conversions to his credit. There were doubts among the orthodox about his theology—he preached "a free and full salvation" that was almost Methodist—

10. McLoughlin, *The American Evangelicals 1800–1900* is an excellent anthology with useful introductions.

and further doubts about the "new measures" he introduced into his meetings.[11]

In 1832 Finney accepted a call to New York City, where the wealthy Tappan brothers built a church for him, the Broadway Tabernacle. Chafing at what he felt were the restrictions of his Presbyterian Synod, he turned Congregationalist and began training young ministers in his own way of thinking. Meanwhile he spoke out strongly on social issues, particularly on slavery. He was at the same time working out a theology of his own, a combination of older Calvinism with newer evangelical doctrines. Given the general title of "perfectionism," Finney's creed emphasized God's perfection as its ideal and unselfish love as its central principle. All the converted, he said, "should aim at being holy and not rest satisfied till they are as perfect as god." Sin, said Finney, is selfishness; virtue is selflessness, disinterested benevolence. Conversion or "sanctification," the first step toward perfection, is accomplished exchanging selfishness for selflessness, imitating Christ and fulfilling God's decree.

Having once attained conversion, the ex-sinner must help others. Salvation was not the end but the beginning of a useful life; the converted must "have the determination to aim at being *useful* in the highest degree possible" by improving the world in which he lived. Finney's doctrines seemed to violate practically every tenet of orthodox Congregational and Presbyterian creed—sin, salvation, election, good works, predestination.[12] Nevertheless, his supporters far outnumbered his critics.

In 1835 Finney was called to Oberlin College in Ohio, where dissident students from Beecher's Lane Seminary had withdrawn

11. Finney advertised in the papers and used a large tent with banners inscribed "Holiness to the Lord!" He used the "protracted" meeting, lasting from three days to a week; he instituted an "anxious seat" where applicants for conversion sat in front of the audience; he used his newly converted disciples as helpers and lecturers; and he allowed women to pray and testify in public.

12. Charles G. Finney, *Memoirs* (New York, 1876), 135. These *Memoirs* are the best source of information on Finney's life and theology. See also his *Lectures on Revivals of Religion* (1835) and his *Lectures on Systematic Theology* (1846). *Lectures on Revivals of Religion* is a virtual handbook on promoting and conducting revivals, based on Finney's observations and experiences. Finney's doctrine of benevolence is explained in "How to Change Your Heart," in *Sermons* (New York, 1835), 41-9. An informative article is James C. Johnson, "Charles G. Finney and a Theology of Revivalism," *Church History*, XXXVIII (September, 1969), 338-59.

earlier. He taught there for the next forty years and made this small school into a nationally famed training school for ministers of what became known as the "Oberlin Theology." His influence and that of his followers had more than theological significance. Like transcendentalism and Unitarianism, perfectionism stressed individual ability, equalitarianism, and self-reliance couched in terms that the ordinary man could easily grasp. The perfectionist ideal was in essence another affirmation of the contemporary belief in optimism, progress, and democratic individualism. In particular, Finney's idea of "usefulness" reinforced the numerous humanitarian-reform movements of the time. Many of Finney's followers were attracted to abolitionism, which was gaining ground in the thirties, simply transferring revivalistic techniques to this new and different crusade.

While the revivalism of the thirties and forties might have seemed at first a rural, Western phenomenon, it was equally strong in the cities. Saving the West was urgent, the churches believed, but it was also plain that the city dweller, were he not also brought to grace, would become a threat to stability and morality. A "godless working class," said Lyman Beecher, could be a source of serious trouble; in fact, he preached a whole series of sermons on the issue, published in 1835 as *Lectures on Political Atheism.* The city, evangelists knew, was a great new field for saving souls. "What can save our large cities," asked the Reverend Henry Clay Fish, "but a powerful revival of religion?"[13] It was obvious that the sins of the cities were increasing as swiftly as their population, and something had to be done about it.

The second wave of evangelism of the pre–Civil War years, then, came in the cities. In 1857 Jeremiah Lanphier, a popular evangelist, began holding prayer meetings for New York businessmen. The movement spread swiftly into other cities, where people jammed into prayer meetings by hundreds, traveling evangelists held street-corner revivals, and well-known preachers like Finney and Knapp

13. Quoted by Smith, *op. cit.,* 49. Cf. also W. H. Hudson, *American Protestantism,* chapter VI; and especially A. I. Abell, *The Urban Impact on American Protestantism* (Cambridge, 1943). In 1800 there were only six cities of more than 8,000, in 1860 there were 141. The urban religious crusade was supported by the popularity of books about city corruptions, such as the Reverend E. H. Chapin's *Moral Aspects of City Life* (1853) and a number of semifictional exposés, among them George Lippard's and E. Z. C. Judson's.

received more invitations to speak than they could even acknowledge. Urban revivalism swept across sectarian lines and out of the big cities into the smaller ones, into the industrial towns of New England and the growing cities of the West. Temporarily stopped by war, the urban evangelistic movement reappeared immediately afterwards and remained a powerful religious force—Moody and Sankey, the Salvation Army, and Billy Sunday were its heirs.[14]

The revivalistic movement that characterized popular Protestantism over the first half of the nineteenth century left lasting imprints on the national character. Most directly, of course, it reinforced and reinvigorated the reform movements of the times, providing theory and motive for everything from dietary reform to utopian communities. The commitment to "usefulness" and "benevolence" that conversion brought, when translated into practical terms, changed the style of American reform. As *The Christian Spectator* had said in 1832, "Piety grows by the operations of benevolence, and the operations of benevolence acquire new strength by the growth of piety." American Protestant Christianity gained from the revivalistic movement—and never lost—a social consciousness and sense of obligation that still remains one of its major characteristics.[15]

Paradoxically, there was little doubt that evangelistic religion tended to strengthen the populistic drift of Jacksonian democracy. It encouraged church members to participate in politics and taught them how to act effectively as groups. The insistence of the evangelical congregations on lay participation in decision; the strong equalitarianism implicit in the movement; and its emphasis on the ability of the ordinary man to make choices—these reinforced the political tendencies of the times. Peter Cartwright, looking back at his long career in frontier revivalism, half seriously remarked that he had spent his life in "incessant warfare against the world, the flesh, the devil, and all the enemies of the Democratic party." Similarly, in the cities, the allegiance of the evangelized workingman

14. Olmsted, *op. cit.*, 350–52 provides a useful summary.
15. The example set by British churchmen helped to encourage this. John Howard, a Baptist, worked in prison reform; Anglican William Wilberforce was an antislavery leader; Robert Hall, a Baptist, worked with trade unions; Thomas Chalmers, a Presbyterian, worked among the urban poor.

and clerk was more than likely to go to "the party of the people."[16]

Generally, in ways influential but difficult to document, the evangelistic era helped to set the mood of the times—confident, dynamic, individualistic, deeply involved with the work of making the nation better and the world someday, perhaps, perfect. If America were to fulfill its mission, said the Reverend David Riddle in 1851, "it must be a holy people as well as a great one."

Evangelical Christianity, of course, was always missionary-minded; by Biblical injunction it was the duty of the saved to save others. The emphasis on the worthiness of man, implicit in the Romantic philosophy, reinforced the old Arminian doctrine of God's infinite love and mercy for all sinful men. If grace were extended by God to everyone, Kaffirs to Polynesians, then all men must be given an opportunity to accept it. "Working among the heathen," then, became a Christian duty.

The missionary enterprise began first at home in the West, where emigrants were streaming westward by the thousands. As people left the East and South to go West, they broke contact with many of those institutions—including the church—which exerted social controls. The great danger of the West, as Eastern clergymen saw it, was that it might be lost to the forces of skepticism, immorality, and materialism. This could not be allowed to happen: "Let no man at the East quiet himself," said the Reverend Lyman Beecher, "and dream of liberty, whatever may come of the West. . . . Her destiny is our destiny." There was also the possibility, of course, that by emigration or conversion the Catholic Church might win over substantial portions of the new country.[17]

Churches recognized that missionary societies provided the best means by which the West could be made both Christian and American. Presbyterians and Congregationalists, in fact, joined in a plan of union in 1801 to make their efforts in the newly settled lands

16. See T. S. Miyakawa, *Protestants and Pioneers: Individualism and Conformity on the Frontier* (Chicago, 1964), chapter XIV; and also William McLoughlin's introduction to Finney's *Lectures on Revivals of Religion* (Cambridge, 1960).

17. Lyman Beecher, *A Plea for The West* (Cincinnati, 1835), 270; "A Reformation of Morals . . . ," *Works* (Boston, 1852), II:92.

more effective.[18] The American Home Missionary Society, formed in 1826 by the Presbyterian, Congregational, Dutch Reform, and Associated Reformed churches, sent out 169 missionaries its first year. By 1850 it employed over a thousand agents, who organized churches in small settlements and subsidized them, founded seminaries and colleges, and established regional or state church organizations. The American Home Missionary Society was unusual in that it was a cooperative enterprise, since most denominations preferred to do their own work. Although the Presbyterians were involved in organizing it, they also created their own missionary system in 1802, expanded it into a Board of Missions in 1816, and in 1837 divided it into a Board of Domestic Missions and a Board of Foreign Missions.

Baptists, who had several state missionary societies, in 1814 founded a national group, the American Baptist Mission Union, which put fifty missionaries into the West during its first year. Methodists established their Board of Foreign Missions in 1819, but some of their state societies were more active. The Episcopal Church entered the missionary field late, forming its Domestic and Foreign Missionary Society in 1821. The Catholic Church, which had maintained missionaries in North America for two hundred years, was in no position to compete equally in the West. Bishop John Carroll of Baltimore, the only American bishop, suddenly in 1805 found the whole Louisiana Territory added to his jurisdiction, and not until the 1820s, after convincing the Vatican that he needed assistance, was he able to establish even minimal control over the Catholic population of the new country. The Society for the Propagation of the Faith, founded in France in 1822, began sending materials and missionaries to the West in small quantities soon after.[19]

The missionary was not the only Christianizing force on the frontier. The printed word was considered an equally potent tool, available where the missionary was not. Since the Bible itself was the most powerful agency of conversion, churches organized Bible

18. The Missionary Society of Connecticut, for example, was founded in 1798 to bring the Congregational Church to western Connecticut and the Ohio Reserve lands. All the New England churches had similar societies by 1812 and had penetrated as far as New Orleans.

19. Olmsted, *op. cit.*, 276–81. An excellent general study is Colin B. Goodykoontz, *Home Missionaries on the American Frontier* (Caldwell, Idaho, 1939).

societies to distribute it in the new territories. The American Bible Society, a national interdenominational organization whose aim was simply to distribute Bibles "without note or comment," appeared in 1816 under the sponsorship of notables like John Jay, Daniel Webster, and John Quincy Adams. A highly successful venture, the Society had 1,200 auxiliary groups in operation within thirty years and had penetrated even into Central and South America. The American Tract Society, organized in 1825, spent thousands of dollars yearly to distribute religious materials, including its *Evangelical Family Library* (fifteen volumes) and its *Religious Library* (twenty-five volumes). It also published a newspaper, *The Christian Messenger*, and hundreds of biographies, histories, classics like *Pilgrim's Progress*, and pamphlets on dueling, gambling, and kindred vices.

These and other societies shipped materials to churches and missionary societies for distribution, but they also developed a system of agents, or "colporteurs," who penetrated into places where neither mails nor churches usually went. The importing of such materials was crucial to the work of missionaries like Baptist John Mason Peck, who wrote back to the Massachusetts Missionary Society,

> The experiment I have made has fully answered my most sanguine expectations of the important advantages the cause would derive in Bible societies, and the distribution of mission pamphlets, magazines, and tracts. . . . As the people in all the settlements seldom hear preaching but once in a month, these silent monitors serve to keep alive impressions and feelings till the return of the preacher.

The denominations also set up their own publishing houses. The Methodist Book Concern, founded in 1789, was the oldest church press, and *The Methodist Magazine* (1818, renamed *The Methodist Review*) was the oldest official church journal. By 1850 there were 850 such magazines, 250 of them published in the West. Often the only reading material available in remote settlements and read to tatters by people of all ages, these publications had much to do with shaping religious culture on the frontier.[20]

20. Gaustad, *op. cit.*, 165–66; Henry Rowe, *History of Religion* (New York, 1924), 89, 102–5; Olmsted, *op. cit.*, 292–4. Among other journals were the *Connecticut Evangelical Magazines*, the *Massachusetts Missionary Herald*, the Unitarian *Panoplist*, and the *Presbyterian Missionary Magazine or Evangelical Intelligencer*.

As a result of these missionary efforts, the West was swiftly brought under church control. Churches appeared in the new settlements almost as soon as settlers did, bringing those "silent forces" of "order, morality, civic virtue, and national prosperity" which Eastern churches hoped for. Western society was thus immediately founded on a firmly Christian base and swiftly absorbed into the national cultural pattern.

Missionaries had tried to Christianize the Indians since the earliest days of settlement. As the tribes were either conquered or pushed westward, it became clear to the churches that if the Indian had any future, it would have to be a Christian one; conversion of the savage might be the only way to save him, not only for God but from extinction. At the turn of the century and after, various state and local missionary groups in New England and New York worked among the few Indians still left in the East, while others went West, where the bulk of the red population lived. Pietist sects like Moravians and Quakers had long sent missionaries among the tribes; Methodists and Baptists began to send preachers to Indians in the Ohio-Mississippi area in the twenties. Methodist Jason Lee followed the Lewis and Clark route to Oregon in 1834; Presbyterian Marcus Whitman established missions in the Oregon country only to be killed by his charges in 1847. Meanwhile, during the thirties, other missionaries went into Sioux country and a few others into the Southwest. The Jesuits established a string of missions in Missouri and Kansas, while Father Pierre-Jean DeSmet, a Belgian, set out in 1840 to the Columbia River country to found missions among the Flatheads and Kalispels. It was DeSmet, trusted by the Indians above any other Christian, who at the request of the Interior Department negotiated an extremely important treaty between the Sioux and the United States in 1868.[21]

Colonial churches established missionary societies among Negroes during the eighteenth century in both North and South. After 1800 Baptists and Methodists proselyted among the slaves with great energy; of the half-million blacks who were church members by the fifties, over 200,000 were Methodists and 175,000 were Baptist.

---

21. Gaustad, *op. cit.*, 158–60; Olmsted, *op. cit.*, 275–77. The theory advanced by Elias Boudinot in *A Star of the West* (1816) that the Indians were descended from the lost tribes of Israel helped to stir interest in missionary work among them.

Methodists in 1851 had ninety-nine full-time missionary workers in the slave states, the great majority of them Negroes themselves. These belonged to predominantly black congregations; some black churches, like the Bethel African Methodist Episcopal Church, the African Methodist Church, and the African Methodist Church Zion had their own missionaries and missionary societies.

Since the great mass of heathens lived overseas, Americans were duty-bound to carry the Word to them. The Congregational Association of Massachusetts in 1810 instituted a foreign missionary program; that same year Congregationalists formed the Board of Commissioners for Foreign Missions, which two years later sent five young men and their families to India. Baptists founded their Foreign Missions Convention in 1814; while in 1817 Presbyterians, Dutch Reformed, and Associated Reformed churches established their joint United Foreign Missions Society to "spread the Gospel . . . in the heathen and anti-Christian world." The Methodists soon were sending missionaries to Liberia and South America, and the Episcopal Church to Africa, China, and Greece; Lutherans began to send missionaries abroad in 1837. Wherever ships went and wherever there were souls to save—Alaska, the South Seas, India, the Far East, Africa, the Middle East—these intrepid servants of God journeyed with Bibles and hymnbooks. Their purpose was eloquently stated by young Hiram Bingham, just out of Middlebury College, who left New England in 1819 for the Sandwich Islands:[22]

The object for which the missionaries felt themselves impelled to visit the Hawaiian race was to honor God, by making known His will, and to benefit those heathen tribes by making them acquainted with the Christian way of life; to turn them from their follies and crimes, idolatries and oppressions, to the service and enjoyment of the living God and adorable Redeemer; to give them the Bible in their own tongue, with ability to read it for themselves; to introduce and extend among them the more useful arts and usages of civilized and Christianized society.

These men and women carried not only the Christian, but the American way of life with them, for their purpose was to "civilize" as well as to "Christianize" all such pagan and backward lands. Natives learned to pray, read the Bible, and observe the Sabbath—

22. Quoted by Gaustad, *op. cit.*, 173.

and also to dress, think, and act in Protestant American patterns. And after the missionaries came traders and investors and visitors.

American society between 1820 and 1870 was a disputatious, competitive, and individualistic society, changing and expanding, subject to a number of inner tensions. Religion, a very important part of that society, responded by calling all its own values into question. Part of this was the natural result of a Romantic era which demanded in its theology much the same kind of freedom it demanded in its politics. The evangelistic "Second Awakening" that swept the country after 1800 shook the older sects to their roots, added millions to church rolls, and made American society so deeply theological that Alexis de Tocqueville concluded in 1831 that "Religion is the foremost of the institutions of the country."[23]

Another reason for religious change was the growing concern of the churches with political and moral issues—slavery, communitarianism, unionism—which brought theology and reform together and sometimes split them apart as well. Since there was no way by law for any church to impose uniformity on its members, American churches had to try to find principles or positions that drew wide support from them. When this was unsuccessful, dissenters broke off to form new sects or split the old ones; in other cases, where by compromise or reorganization division was avoided, there was still change.[24]

The intense debates over doctrine which shook American Calvinist churches in the eighteenth century—over sin, free will,

23. Between 1800 and 1830 Methodist membership increased sevenfold, Presbyterian quadrupled, Baptist tripled, and Congregational doubled. During the first fifty years of the nineteenth century the number of Protestant church members grew from 365,000 to 3½ million; in 1800 one of every fifteen Americans was a Protestant church member, in 1835 one of eight, in 1850 one of seven. Cited in Charles C. Cole, *The Social Ideas of the American Evangelists 1826–1860* (New York, 1954), 13–16.

24. For general discussions of religion during this period, see W. W. Sweet, *Religion and the Development of American Culture* (New York, 1952); Olmsted, *op. cit.*, chapter 15; Sydney Ahlstrom, "Theology in America," in James W. Smith and A. Leland Jamison, eds., *The Shaping of American Religion* (Princeton, 1961); and the histories of American religion cited in the bibliography. During the first half of the nineteenth century there seemed to be no crucial conflict between religion and science, which was generally considered a useful adjunct to theology. For a typical essay, see "The Harmony of Natural Science and Theology," *The New Englander*, X (February, 1852), 1–21.

Christ's divinity, the granting of grace, the application of doctrine to living—were not resolved by the nineteenth. The First Great Awakening of the 1740s and 1750s and the rise of unitarianism after the 1790s had already divided the Congregational church into conservatives and liberals; finally, with the creation of the American Unitarian Association in 1825, the division was complete. The Unitarians thus became a separate sect of 125 churches (120 of them in New England) including the 25 oldest Calvinist churches in America.

Unitarians and Calvinists both accepted the Bible as revelation but disagreed as to the kind of revelation it represented and the degree of its importance. Unitarians tended to regard the Bible as record of revelation and history, not wholly infallible, subject to human error. To the Unitarians, the Bible did not always say what the orthodox Calvinist said it did. As their name implied, the Unitarians believed that the Bible indicated the unity, not the trinity, of God; it made Jesus not divine but rather the ideal human being and philosopher; it drew a much more encouraging picture of human nature than the Calvinist saw and indicated that, instead of being inherently and totally sinful, man possessed great potential for good. The essentials of salvation were, the Unitarians believed, already within man's nature, placed there by God; by following their consciences, respecting their reason, educating their intelligences, and living a life on Jesus' model, all men could attain salvation. Essentially, Unitarianism was New Testament Christianity with a humanistic and ethical emphasis. It believed, said one of its explicators, in "the fatherhood of God, the brotherhood of man, salvation by character, the leadership of Jesus, and the progress of mankind."

The controversy between Unitarians and Calvinists centered chiefly on their concept of man. As Emerson remarked, Calvinism stood for man's liability to sin, whereas Unitarianism stood on man's capacity for virtue—neither ruled out the other's possibility, but the difference in emphasis divided them. Behind all the arguments within nineteenth-century Calvinism lay this disagreement over the nature of mankind and his ability to take care of his own ethic and his own soul. The error of orthodox Calvinism, William

Ellery Channing said, was "the attempt to exalt God by denying man freedom of will and moral power."[25]

Universalism, like Unitarianism, emphasized the optimistic possibilities of human nature and denied the orthodox principle of eternal damnation; there might be punishment after death for sins committed in life, the Universalists believed, but for disciplinary purposes only, with eternal salvation granted eventually by God to all. Brought to New England from England in 1770 by John Murray, who was minister to Boston's First Universalist Society, "universalism" became an organized church in 1790 when its believers met in Philadelphia to adopt a plan of church government and articles of faith. After Murray's death Hosea Ballou, a New England Baptist, became the leader of the movement. In 1805 Ballou and the Universalists decided to accept the central doctrines of unitarianism, and although Universalists and Unitarians maintained separate identity as sects, they continued to cooperate over the years.[26]

A different tactic of adjustment was that represented by the "New Haven Theology," developed at Andover and Yale by the Reverend Nathaniel Taylor and his followers. Influenced by the Scottish philosophy, the "New Haven" school was centered on the issue of free will and responsibility. Sin was a voluntary transgression of known moral law; man was free to choose between good and evil, and his salvation depended upon his own choice. In addition, Taylor and his group seemed willing to accept what was essentially the Unitarian position concerning revelation, declaring that Calvinism was after all "a rational faith of rational human beings" and that the Bible "ought to be tried at the bar of reason." Since this went too far along the Unitarian road, it failed to satisfy Congregationalist conservatives, while it did not go far enough to satisfy the liberals. In 1833 the conservatives called for a union of orthodox ministers to combat Taylorism and founded Hartford Seminary to

25. For a general account of the controversy see Frank H. Foster, *A Genetic History of New England Theology* (Boston, 1907). An analysis of the Calvinist-Unitarian controversy is J. Harotunian, *Piety Versus Moralism* (New York, 1932). A useful study of Channing is Robert L. Patterson, *The Philosophy of William Ellery Channing* (New York, 1952).

26. The best explanation of Universalist doctrine is in Ballou's own *Nine Sermons on Important Doctrinal and Practical Subjects* (Philadelphia, 1835).

defend Congregationalism against it. Yet Taylor's compromise had its adherents; preached by the powerful Presbyterian evangelist Lyman Beecher, it succeeded in creating still another division in Calvinism's ranks.[27]

The transcendentalist movement of the thirties and forties stirred up New England's already troubled theological waters. Since it presented new ideas about human nature, knowledge, and the nature of internal and external truths, transcendentalism had to be considered within a religious context as well as a philosophical one. Either directly or by implication it raised questions about such doctrines as revelation, redemption, miracles, and even about the nature of Deity itself. Whatever its debt to Kant and Plato, transcendentalism was—in a broad sense—a religion. Its origins lay in what Emerson called "the religious sentiment," which the philosophers provided an apparatus to express. The movement was, as Frederic Carpenter has characterized it, an extension of the "piety of Puritanism," a reassertion of the mystical basis of religion.[28] Yet not all transcendentalists—or near-transcendentalists—were ministers, nor were there more than a small minority of New England ministers who were transcendentalists at all. There was no transcendental creed, church, seminary, or congregation; it had none of the characteristics normally associated with a sect. Yet it influenced—in some cases decisively—the course of contemporary theological doctrine and contributed substantially (though less visibly) to the country's liberalizing, questioning religious mood. Transcendentalism's greatest effect was felt in the Unitarian churches, where

27. Ahlstrom, op. cit., 254–60. The complete study is Sidney Mead, Nathaniel William Taylor (Chicago, 1942). See also Ahlstrom's article, "The Scottish Philosophy and American Theology," Church History, XXIV (September, 1955), 257–72, and Earl A. Pope, "The Rise of the New Haven Theology," Journal of Presbyterian History, XLIV (March–June, 1966), 2–45, 106–22.

28. Frederic I. Carpenter, Emerson Handbook (New York, 1953), 18. On the relationships of transcendentalism to Unitarianism and Calvinism see Carpenter, 128–32; William R. Hutchinson, The Transcendentalist Ministers (New Haven, 1959); and Alexander Kern, "The Rise of Transcendentalism," in H. H. Clark, ed., Transitions in Literary History (Chapel Hill, 1953), 309–13. Kern points out that of the thirty most influential transcendentalist writers, all except one (Ellery Channing) were ministers or teachers, all attended Harvard, and all were New England-born.

men like Theodore Parker, George Ripley, and James Freeman Clarke held pulpits and offices.[29]

Specifically, transcendentalism shared and reinforced a number of ideas which Unitarianism had emphasized in its critique of Calvinism. Like the Unitarians, transcendentalist ministers did not accept the Calvinist doctrines of depravity, predestination, or salvation by grace alone; they, like the Unitarians, did not fully trust Biblical revelation, and they rejected ritual, formal creeds, and other marks of institutionalized religion. All these the transcendentalists discarded in favor of belief in an immanent Oversoul, free will, an optimistic view of human nature, and revelation by intuition through Nature as symbol. But rejection of God as a "person" (in the traditional anthropomorphic concept of deity) in favor of God as abstract law or principle of harmony went too far for many Unitarians. To reject all form, all organization, all association in favor of self-reliance seemed too much. Intuitionalism alone was not sufficient to reveal God's truth; the symbols of Nature were not enough to contain the full message Christians needed. The Boston Unitarian Association nearly expelled Theodore Parker in 1843 for his address on "The Transient and Permanent in Christianity," and as late as 1857 Harvard Divinity School refused to allow him to address the senior class.[30]

Horace Bushnell, who entered Yale at the time the New Haven theology was at its height, at first accepted Nathaniel Taylor's theology and then found it wanting. In his first book, *Christian Nurture* (1846, revised 1861), he set forth what he called the principle of Christian education, "that the child is to grow up a Christian, and never know himself of being otherwise." Christianity, then, was not a matter of proof or of conversion; a person should assume that he was saved and that he could make correct choices. To Bushnell the starting point of the Christian experience began with a feeling of the Spirit of God; theology simply interpreted this

29. Cf. Kern, *op. cit.*, 309–11. The standard study of transcendentalism is Octavius B. Frothingham, *Transcendentalism in New England* (New York, 1876). A useful study of its theology is contained in Ronald V. Wells, *Three Christian Transcendentalists* (New York, 1943).

30. A full account is C. H. Faust, "The Backgrounds of the Unitarian Opposition to Transcendentalism," *Modern Philology*, XXXV (February, 1938), 297–34. See also Hutchinson, *op. cit.*, chapters 2–5.

experience and formulated it. Thus all theological arguments disappeared, for it was no longer important whether God was one or three, but merely that men felt either to be so. Bushnell later developed his conviction that the most important principle of Christianity was love, evidenced by Christ's sacrifice; and that salvation came from a spiritual union through love with God. His God-is-love theme, at first rejected even by many of his liberal contemporaries, gained gradual acceptance later in the century and reappeared in different form in the Social Gospel movement.[31]

Presbyterianism, too, was racked by internal dissent. Many old-line ministers, disturbed by liberalizing trends, considered themselves "Old School" Presbyterians in contrast to younger "New School" men. The Old School counseled strict adherence to the Westminster Confession; New School liberals were willing to accept modifications of the creed. The differences were less doctrinal, however, than temperamental; Old School men feared the attractions of Taylor and the New Haven theology as well as Unitarianism and Universalism.[32]

There were other disagreements among Presbyterians, over missions and publications, over questions of church polity, over reform activities. New School ministers tended to participate in reform societies, whereas Old School men, fearing further division, hoped to keep their churches out of such things as abolitionism.

The conflict reached its climax at the General Assembly of 1837, when Old School leaders abrogated the Plan of Union, withdrew from most of the interdenominational societies to which the church belonged, and read out of the church the restive synods of Western Reserve, Utica, Geneva, and Genesee. The New School synods applied for readmission in 1838, were refused, and formed another

---

31. Olmsted, *op. cit.*, 300–1. The standard biography is T. T. Munger, *Horace Bushnell* (New York, 1899); more recent is Barbara Cross, *Horace Bushnell: Minister to a Changing America* (Chicago, 1968); H. Shelton Smith, ed., *Horace Bushnell* (New York, 1968) is a useful source. The leading exponent of Bushnell's doctrine of divine love reflected in human love was Henry Ward Beecher, who during his pastorate at Brooklyn's Plymouth Church was probably the nation's best-known preacher.

32. The Reverend Albert Barnes of Philadelphia was brought before the Presbyterian Assembly on charges of error and although acquitted in 1836, his case left bitter feelings behind. The Reverend Lyman Beecher, charged with heretical preaching, was twice acquitted but forced to explain his views in public to the satisfaction of his superiors.

General Assembly. The division was complete, with about half of the original denominations under the New School Presbyterian Church. In actuality the New School group was never so liberalized as the Old School believed it to be, but the breach was not healed until reunion in 1869.[33]

Lutheran churches in America, since they were strongly unified by linguistic and ethnic bonds, were less subject to stress than the older native sects. Yet the impact of evangelism and the era's demand for theological flexibility influenced Lutheranism too. Although a national General Synod was organized in 1820, Lutheran churches tended to remain in independent synods, often determined by the dominant language of the congregation. Samuel Schmucker, an American-born German Lutheran, represented a liberalized, Americanized force in Lutheranism. As professor of theology at Gettysburg Seminary he introduced a number of modifications in Lutheran attitudes and doctrines. Increased German immigration in the forties and fifties, however, created a division among American Lutherans. The "confessional" group believed that the churches should hold strictly to the Augsburg Confession and should use the German language in services. An "American" group believed that in a new country the old rules might be loosened to conform more closely with the American social environment.

Headed by Schmucker and the Gettysburg faculty, the "Americanists" favored freer worship, modifications of the confessional theology, and even the introduction of certain evangelistic techniques. Further immigration brought conservative reinforcements. Carl F. W. Walther, who came to Concordia Seminary in 1839, was unhappy with what he considered the looseness of the Gettysburg group and the General Synod and helped to organize the Missouri Synod in 1847; later other conservative elements withdrew to form the General Lutheran Council. Lutheranism tended to divide along linguistic as well as theological lines, and Schmucker's last attempt

33. A good brief account is Olmsted, *op. cit.*, 311–14. Andrew C. Zeno, *Presbyterianism in America* (New York, 1937), chapters IV and V, is a useful summary. The United Presbyterian Church, founded in 1858, represented the end of a different division among Scots Presbyterians which dated from the eighteenth century. The Cumberland Presbyterians of Kentucky and Tennessee broke away to form their own Presbytery in 1810–1813 after an argument with the General Assembly over evangelism and predestinarianism, and rejoined it in 1906.

to unite all American Lutherans on a common platform in 1855 failed. The church itself, nevertheless, prospered despite division and remained a strongly conservative force in German and Scandinavian-populated areas.[34]

The most serious division within the American Episcopal Church derived not from American but English sources. American Episcopalianism was traditionally low-church.[35] After 1815, however, the high-church wing of Episcopalianism (chiefly in New York) began to gain greater prominence. The emergence of the Oxford Movement in England, led by John Henry Newman, Edward Posey, and Richard Froude at Oxford in the eighteen-thirties, sharpened the division in America. The Oxford group revived Episcopal interest in liturgy and ritual, believing that Anglicanism needed a return to the energy and sincerity of an earlier Catholic Christianity. American high-church leaders were attracted to this new Anglo-Catholicism, enough so that Bishop Moore of Virginia warned against an American "revival of the worst evils of the Romish system." While it was clear that low-churchmen dominated the General Convention, nonetheless a number of American clergymen showed increased interest in ceremonialism.

What could have been a serious rift never developed, partly because the high-low division was never so broad as it seemed; partly because the Oxford Movement never found substantial American support; and partly because William Muhlenberg, rector of the Church of the Holy Communion in New York, developed a satisfactory compromise, which he called "Evangelical" Catholicism. His memorial, presented to the House of Bishops in 1853, proposed

34. Abdel Wentz, et al., *A Basic History of Lutheranism* (3 vols., Philadelphia, 1955); Vergilius Ferm, *The Crisis in American Lutheran Orthodoxy* (New York, 1927). The General Synod, formed in 1821, suffered various defections; in 1861 the conservative elements formed the General Council; in 1886 Southern Lutherans formed their own United Synods. Danish and Finnish Lutherans had independent synods. The Buffalo Synod was formed in 1845 and the Iowa Synod in 1854. The Synod of the Norwegian Evangelical Church was organized in 1853, while more revivalistic Lutherans had formed the Evangelical Lutheran Church of America in 1846. The Swedish Scandinavian Evangelical Augustine Synod came in 1860.

35. High Church and Low Church, distinctions made in the Church of England in Queen Anne's time, were terms which distinguished between those of Anglo-Catholic and those of Anglo-Protestant emphasis in regard to church documents and sacraments.

"a broader and more comprehensive" system which would provide for "as much freedom in opinion, discipline, and worship as is compatible with the essential faith and order of the Gospel." Although his petition was not adopted, it suggested the spirit in which the two factions could operate without schism.[36]

Even the Society of Friends, which allowed the individual Quaker nearly unlimited freedom to follow his "inner light," suffered from internal dispute. The attractions of evangelism led some Friends toward positions which seemed close to Methodism, while Unitarianism attracted others. One of the opponents of the new liberalism was Elias Hicks, a Long Island Quaker who believed in returning to the simple revelation of the Inner Light without the aid of clergy or scripture. In 1827–28 the Hicksite Quakers withdrew from the Philadelphia Yearly Meeting and founded their own. Other Hicksites in Ohio, Indiana, and Illinois followed. Later, evangelicalism slowly gained support within other Meetings, until singing, paid ministers, and planned meetings became fairly common. The original Philadelphia Meeting did not correspond with other Meetings and did not join the evangelically oriented Five Years Meeting in 1887.[37]

Divisions, disputes, and secessions within secessions continued to complicate the contemporary religious picture. Typical was the case of the Church of God, a product of the revivalist movement within the German Reformed Church which also drew support from Baptists and Methodists. The Reverend John Winebrenner, forced to sever connections with his own German Reformed Church in Pennsylvania because of his revivalist beliefs, organized a number of small congregations known as Churches of God, which emphasized baptism by immersion, observance of the Lord's Supper, the washing of feet of the saints, and other strict Biblical observances. In 1830 several of these congregations joined in a group called the General Eldership of the Church of God, which in 1845 added the

36. Olmsted, *op. cit.*, 318–20.
37. For histories of the Friends, see Rufus M. Jones, *The Later Periods of Quakerism* (London, 1921, two volumes); Charles F. Holden, *The Quakers in Great Britain and America* (New York, 1913); and Elton Trueblood's general summary of Quaker principles and influence, *The People Called Quakers* (New York, 1966).

phrase "of North America" to its name. It prospered, and encouraged other sects with similar names.[38]

Conflict over slavery led to the organization of the Southern Baptist Convention in 1845; other divisions led to eighteen or more minor groups of Hardshell, Softshell, two Seed-in-the-Spirit, Dutch Run, and other quasi-Baptist sects. The Freewill Baptist Church, founded during the evangelistic fervor of the late eighteenth century, had over 60,000 members by 1845. The Christian Church was the result of a union in 1820 of three evangelical groups, one Methodist, one Baptist, and one Presbyterian, the last led by evangelist Barton Stone. Some left (as Stone did) to join the Disciples of Christ in 1832, but the rest maintained a separate existence until the Christian Church merged with the Congregationalists in 1930.

The Campbellites, or Disciples of Christ, were by far the largest of the new churches to appear during the period. Thomas Campbell, a Scots-Irish Presbyterian, hoped to return to that primitive Christianity which had "neither creed nor name but only loyalty to Christ." "All that love our Lord Jesus Christ, in sincerity" were welcomed into his church, whose aim was "to restore the original gospel and order of things." Campbell severed relations with the Synod and in 1809 organized the Christian Association of Washington (Pennsylvania) as an independent religious society. His son, Alexander Campbell, organized the society into a church and in 1813 it gained admission into the Baptist Association. Alexander Campbell slowly evolved a theology, assisted by a Scottish immigrant, Walter Scott, based on a simple formula of baptism and conversion. Groups in Virginia, Kentucky, Pennsylvania, and Tennessee began to join the Campbellites, calling themselves Churches of Christ or Disciples of Christ. Since Barton Stone's Christian Church had much in common with the Campbellites, the two joined in 1832. The Church used both names—Christians and

38. Elmer T. Clark, *The Small Sects in America* (New York and Nashville, 1937), 81–82. The Church of God (Anderson, Indiana) seceded from the original church in 1880; the Church of God as Organized by Christ seceded from the Mennonites; the Church of God of West Virginia seceded from the Millerite Adventists; the Church of God Apostolic had connections with none of these.

Disciples of Christ—and by the time of its first national meeting in 1849 had more than 100,000 members.[39]

The American Jewish community at the opening of the nineteenth century was small (perhaps 3,000) and well established.[40] Jews served the Revolutionary cause well and after the peace held full citizenship rights everywhere but in Maryland. Most American Jews were Sephardic, of Spanish and Portuguese origin; almost all were of the merchant class, concentrated in the Eastern and Southern seaboard cities. During the early years of the century, however, immigration of Ashkenazic Jews (whose rituals differed) increased, from Germany, Poland, and Middle Europe. From the 1830s to the Civil War the Jewish population steadily grew—15,000 in 1840, 50,000 in 1850, 150,000 in 1860. These later arrivals were predominantly German-speaking, less well educated than their predecessors, and generally poor. They tended at first to become peddlers, small shopkeepers, low-wage laborers; later better-educated and more prosperous Jews followed, and with them a new set of rabbinical and lay leaders.

Later Jewish arrivals also brought with them the current European conflict in European Jewry between "reform" and orthodox Judaism which involved changes in synagogue worship, church government, and religious education.[41] The demands of these newcomers for liberalization were reinforced by a native reform movement, begun in the twenties in the city temples—Har Sinai in Baltimore, Emanu-El in New York, Sinai in Chicago—while other synagogues introduced such innovations as mixed choirs, organs, sermons, and services in English.

Reform moved more slowly in Europe than in the United States,

39. Olmsted, *op. cit.*, 309–11. For historical studies of the church, see Winifred Garrison and Alfred DeGroot, *The Disciples of Christ* (rev. ed., St. Louis, 1958) and David E. Harrell, Jr., *Quest for a Christian America: The Disciples of Christ and American Society to 1866* (Nashville, 1966). S. Morris Eames, *The Philosophy of Alexander Campbell* (Bethany, W. Va., 1966) is the best study.

40. Good histories are Nathan Glazer, *American Judaism* (Chicago, 1957) and Oscar Handlin, "Judaism in the United States," in Smith and Jamison, *op. cit.*, 122–61. Handlin's *Adventure in Freedom* (New York, 1954) is a useful general history; Hyman Grinstein, *The Rise of the Jewish Community of New York 1654–1860* (Philadelphia, 1947) is a specialized study.

41. David Philipson, *The Reform Movement in Judaism* (New York, 1931).

where rabbinical leaders like Leo Merzbacher, David Einhorn, and Samuel Adler, in the forties and fifties, were strong influences for change. The most influential was no doubt Rabbi Isaac Meyer Wise, who came to the United States from Bohemia in 1846. Passionately Americanized and possessed of an excellent command of English, Rabbi Wise published a modernized prayerbook, *Minhag America* (1857), and later founded the Union of American Hebrew Congregations to serve the cause of an Americanized, modernized Jewish religion and culture. Opposition to Reform Jewry came from a number of conservative leaders, but by the eighties, out of two hundred of the larger American synagogues, only ten or so were still Orthodox. The Order of B'nai B'rith (Sons of the Covenant), organized in 1843 to promote culture and philanthropy among Jews, was an important factor in social and educational work among the soaring Jewish urban population.

Of the flood of immigrants (about 25 million) who arrived on American shores during the first half of the nineteenth century, a large number were Catholic. Their sudden entry into a predominantly Protestant society created certain strains. In 1840 there were 660,000 American Catholics, in 1850 1,600,000, in 1860 3,100,000, making it the largest single denomination in the nation.[42] Fortunately for the American Catholic Church, it had settled several internal problems before the surge of Irish and German immigrants arrived, so that it was able to handle the sudden influx. The most difficult problem had been the recent rivalry between French and Irish factions; establishment of new dioceses and increased Irish influence helped to settle part of the problem. More difficult to solve was the need for priests and nuns. There were never enough, and since there were no American orders, all had to come from abroad. However, the Society of Jesus, once suppressed, revived swiftly; Marianists, Christian Brothers, Brothers of the Sacred Heart, Franciscans, Benedictines, and others established American

42. Theodore Roemer, *The Catholic Church in the United States* (St. Louis, 1950); chapters XII, XIII, XIV document this growth. In 1840 there were also fifteen Catholic colleges, twenty-seven seminars, and thirty-eight academies. A good brief history is John Tracy Ellis, *American Catholicism* (Chicago, 1969); see also Henry Browne, "Catholicism in the United States," in Smith and Jamison, *op. cit.*, 72–122; and Thomas McAvoy, C.S.C., *A History of the Catholic Church in the United States* (Notre Dame, 1969).

seminaries in the forties and fifties and took in American applicants. Ursulines, Carmelites, and other orders worked in the
schools.[43]

The primary Catholic problem, however, was to transform a
church, whose members and leaders were predominantly foreign,
into an American religious institution. One powerful instrument in
this process was the school. Since Catholic schools were not allowed
in the colonies, parochial schools appeared soon after independence.
Though the parochial system grew, before 1840 only a relatively
small percentage of Catholic students were in Catholic schools. By
1840 there were only about two hundred parish-supported Catholic
schools in the country, most of them in the West.

A second device for naturalizing and unifying Catholicism was
welfare and charity work. The Catholic immigrant needed help
from the day of his arrival, and the Church provided him with most
of it. Charitable orders and organizations brought the Church and
the individual together at every age and level, through orphanages,
hospitals, poor societies, homes for the aged, and the like. A third
factor was the Catholic press. Bishop England established the first
American Catholic weekly newspaper in 1822, *The United States
Catholic Miscellany*, which went into thousands of homes; in 1850
there were over twenty such weeklies published over the country.
The Boston *Pilot*, perhaps the best known, achieved a respectable
national circulation.[44]

The swift growth of the Catholic population alarmed some
Protestants when it was reported that Catholic missionaries were
gaining converts in the West and when Catholic immigration
poured into the Eastern cities at an unprecedented rate. Tensions
began to rise in the thirties. Language and cultural differences between new Catholic and older Protestant groups, combined with the
American workman's fear of "cheap foreign labor," led to increased
friction. A group of New York ministers, in 1830, launched an anti-
Catholic newspaper, *The Protestant*. Samuel F. B. Morse (inventor
of the telegraph) wrote a series of articles in 1834 under the title

43. The Sisters of Charity, the first religious community for women in the
United States, was organized in 1808. The Paulists, founded in 1849 by five
American-born priests, was the first native American order of its kind.

44. Cf. the discussion in Ellis, *op. cit.*, chapter II. See also John O'Grady,
Catholic Charities in the United States (Washington, 1930).

Foreign Conspiracy Against the Liberties of the United States, which charged the Catholic hierarchy with a plot to subvert the American government—the first step of which was the shipment to America of Europe's most useless and ignorant poor.

Nativist editors soon saw such "Romish plots" everywhere, and after 1836, when *The Awful Disclosures* of one Maria Monk claimed to expose the vices of convent life, scurrilous anti-Catholic publications appeared in profusion. Well-known ministers like Lyman Beecher sermonized against the Catholic menace; the American Tract Society published anti-Catholic pamphlets; and in 1843 the American Protestant Association of ministers was formed to "awaken the attention of the community to the dangers which threaten the liberties . . . of these United States from the assaults of Romanism." Encouraged by the fanatic wing of the nativist movement, mobs made sporadic attacks on Catholic buildings and meetings in several large cities during the forties and fifties. Anti-Catholicism entered politics via the Native American Party and the Know Nothings, who put candidates in the field in 1854, 1855, and nominated a presidential candidate, Millard Fillmore, in 1856. By this time, however, the movement had lost much of its force.

The fifties was a crucial decade for American Catholicism, for its leaders had to pick their way carefully through a thicket of sensitive issues, particularly during the controversy over slavery. Official doctrine did not hold slavery to be necessarily evil, or a violation of natural or divine law; the Church officially opposed the slave trade while reiterating the moral obligations of slaveholders to slaves. The Ninth Provincial Council in 1858 took no stand on slavery—by then an issue of crisis proportions—saying only that Catholics "should be free as to all questions of policy and social order, within the limits of the law and Christ." As a result, Southern pro-slavery and Northern antislavery Catholics could hold opposing views without dividing their Church. Catholicism thus survived the slavery controversy, the argument over disunion, and the war itself, without appreciable difficulty.[45]

Neither Jews nor Catholics, in the opinion of orthodox and evangelical ministers, constituted so great a threat to American religion

45. For a complete study, see Madeleine H. Rice, *American Catholic Opinion in the Slavery Controversy* (New York, 1941) .

as "infidelity," a term loosely applied to current deviations from established Protestant Christian doctrines or values. There was still a strong, though minor, strain of "infidel" thought, inherited from eighteenth-century deist thinkers like Elihu Palmer, Thomas Paine, and Ethan Allen. Although the deist brand of "infidelity" almost disappeared during the evangelical decades, Palmer, Paine, and Allen were still in print and had active descendants in such "free-thinkers" as George Evans, Abner Kneeland, Gilbert Vale, George Houston, and others. Evans, Vale, and Houston founded the National Tract Society, in fact, to counteract what they called "the heaps of trash annually scattered through the country by the American Tract Society."[46]

After 1830 there seemed to be renewed interest in "freethinking." Admirers of Paine in 1827 formed the Free Press Association to promote his writings, Voltaire's, and others'. Other societies—usually little more than loosely organized discussion groups—sprang up in cities and frontier communities; the "village atheist," as Mark Twain drew him in Judge Driscoll of *Pudd'nhead Wilson,* was a familiar type in the forties and fifties. Boston had the First Society of Free Enquirers and the impudently titled Infidel Relief Society; New York had its Moral Philanthropist Society and the Philosophical Library Association. There were similar societies in Pennsylvania, Ohio, Indiana, Illinois, and points South; St. Louis had a Society of Free Enquiry and even a settlement so small as Mineral Point, Wisconsin, had an "Eclectic School" in 1845. Typical discussions were of the kind sponsored by the Boston Free Discussion Society in October, 1845—"Whether the Christian Religion Has an Immoral Tendency?" and "Is There Evidence to Prove the Super-human Character of Jesus Christ?" Some of these societies combined in the thirties to form a national group, the United States Moral and Philosophical Society, which although it met annually until 1842 was not particularly successful. In 1845 a Convention of Infidels of the United States met in New York, counting 196 delegates from eleven states, and founded the Infidel Society for the Promotion of Mental Liberty, which held annual meetings until 1854.

46. Histories of freethought and religious dissent are Albert Post, *Popular Freethought in America 1825–50* (New York, 1943) and Martin Marty, *The Infidel: Freethought and American Religion* (Cleveland, 1961).

"Infidels," however, were never organization-minded, and their conventions were usually not well attended.

The "infidel press" was especially active in these years, particularly feared by the orthodox. There were about thirty "freethinking" publications between 1825 and 1860, some reasoned and sophisticated, others jejune and denunciatory. Most were ephemeral, although Gilbert Vale's *Beacon,* Abner Kneeland's *Boston Investigator,* John Harmon's *Ohio Watchman,* and Robert Jennings's *New York Free Enquirer* were rather widely distributed.[47] These newspapers offered "infidel" books by mail, reprinted extracts from Volney, Allen, Paine, and Voltaire, and reported "the misdeeds and hypocrisies" of churches and ministers. Preachers inveighed against them from rural and city pulpits; missionary societies warned against them; the church press attacked their editors bitterly. Freethinking editors offered to debate their opponents anywhere; Robert Owen, who founded New Harmony in Indiana and "rejected all absurd and unnatural systems of religion," met the Reverend Alexander Campbell in a famous encounter in Cincinnati in 1828. The debates drew hundreds and lasted for six days, during which each man spoke for as long as twelve hours.[48]

It was never precisely clear what "infidelity" was. It might be a kind of anticlerical skepticism derived from Paine and Allen; it might mean the denial of creation as given in Genesis; it might simply mean that one had doubts about Christ's divinity.[49] Almost any deviation from the orthodox could be so labeled, and there was a tendency to include the charge in political discussion. Nor was there an accurate estimate of "infidelity's" support. Ministers and missionaries, fearful of skeptical or merely lethargical congregations, no doubt magnified the threat, not only out of sincere regard for Christianity but because infidelity gave them a visible opponent

47. Albert Post, *op. cit.,* 235–6, has a complete list of these publications.

48. These were published as *A Debate on the Evidences of Christianity* (two volumes, Cincinnati, 1829). Campbell, a doughty debater, took on infidels from New York to Illinois for years. Peter Cartwright, the Methodist evangelist, was the nemesis of village atheists and *in extremis* was not averse to punching his adversary.

49. See, for example, Samuel Gridley Howe, "Atheism in New England," *The New England Magazine,* VII (December, 1834), 500–09; and VII (January, 1835), 53–62. *The Spirit of the Pilgrims* devoted its entire volume III (1830) to the question "What Constitutes Infidelity?"

and provided a useful foil for the evangelistic crusades of the thirties and forties. The attack on it was savage and relentless, waged through sermons, pamphlets, journals, courts of law, and camp meetings. Books appeared by the dozens; Noah Worcester and Lyman Beecher each wrote several best-selling attacks, while over 100,000 copies of David Nelson's *Cause and Cure of Infidelity* (1836) were distributed by the American Tract Society alone.[50]

Since infidelity led directly to immorality, "freethinkers" were constantly attacked as depraved, vice-ridden men; delegates to one freethought convention were reported in the press as displaying "the bloated countenances of the victims of intemperance and crime." *The New England Magazine* advised merchants not to sell to known infidels and recommended that all decent homes be closed to them. Several states passed laws (later declared unconstitutional) redefining blasphemy and attaching new penalties to it. The *cause célèbre* of the period was the arrest and conviction in 1834, under an eighteenth-century blasphemy law, of Abner Kneeland of Boston. After four trials and appeals he was finally sentenced to sixty days, appealed it to the Supreme Court, which after two years of delay upheld the sentence. Kneeland served his time in 1838, moved to Iowa, founded a colony named Salubria, and ran for office on the Democratic ticket.[51]

After Kneeland's conviction, the crusade against freethinking and infidelity began to abate. Catholicism seemed for the moment more dangerous, the Pope a greater opponent than Paine. Most of all, despite the dire warnings, it seemed obvious to the public that Kneeland and the shade of Tom Paine had not really endangered America's faith.

The divisions, debates, and schisms in the major and minor denominations over the first half of the nineteenth century were

50. Post, *op. cit.*, chapter II. The press was prone to wild calculations; *The New England Magazine* in 1834 claimed there were over 50,000 "infidels" in New England alone, while another journal estimated at least five and a half million in the nation at large.

51. See H. S. Commager, "The Blasphemy of Abner Kneeland," *New England Quarterly*, VIII (March, 1935), 29–41; and Leonard Levy, "Satan's Last Apostle in Massachusetts," *American Quarterly*, V (Spring, 1953), 16–30, for accounts of this landmark case, which became entangled in Whig-Democratic politics. Two hundred and thirty Bostonians, among them Parker, Channing, Ripley, Alcott, and Emerson, signed a petition asking for suspension of Kneeland's sentence.

manifestations of a larger spirit of enthusiasm that derived from the Romantic era's sensitivity to emotionalism and its trust of feeling. American religious history was always turbulent from its beginnings, but the thrust of the times encouraged a willingness to believe in faiths beyond the usual bounds of credibility. Leaders and cults offered attractive alternatives to traditional, Christian, Bible-based methods of getting at the truth, finding salvation, and discovering God.

Millennialism and adventism (belief in Christ's return after a thousand years and the establishment of a new Kingdom of God) had been a consistent thread in Christianity for centuries. In combination with the excitements of nineteenth-century revivalism, both burst forth in sudden popularity. The primitive Christianity of some evangelist sects encouraged literal readings of the Bible (particularly Daniel and Revelations) which predicted a coming day of judgment, Christ's appearance, and the sanctification of the holy. There were a number of predictions about the Second Coming, but the chief prophet of millennialism was William Miller, an upstate New York farmer and Baptist convert who, after studying the Bible for fourteen years, announced in 1839 that Christ would perhaps come again in 1843 or 1844.

Miller's lectures, published in 1838, received wide attention and gained him many followers. In 1842 and 1843 the Millerites held a series of nationwide revival meetings to prepare believers for the event. On March 14, 1844, Miller set the date for Christ's arrival at some time between then and May. When nothing happened in May, Miller recalculated the date as October 22, when "the Lord will appear visibly in the clouds." *The Advent Herald*, Miller's paper, issued its final number on October 21 and hundreds of Millerites waited in churches or in the fields, but the 22nd passed without incident. Some of his followers returned to their original churches in disillusionment; many, however, simply assumed that the calculation had been in error. Miller, a sincere, baffled man, said that he would choose another date, but "not until God gives me more light." In 1845 a number of the remaining adventist groups formed a loose organization, and though Miller died in 1849, the movement continued under other leaders. Many of his followers later joined the Seventh Day Adventists who developed a denominational organization in 1860, formulated on an essentially Baptist theology.[52]

The Millerite excitement had scarcely abated when interest in spiritualism replaced it. The possibility of piercing the veil that separated dead and living had always appealed to the mystically minded, and the American popularity of Swedenborgianism reinforced it. Emanuel Swedenborg, a Swedish mystic who died in 1772, explained in a series of books that there was a spirit world beyond life in which men could attain final perfection, and that the living could, under the right conditions, communicate with them. Linked with the contemporary interest in mesmerism (hypnotism), Swedenborgianism came to be recognized by theologians and philosophers (including Emerson) as a quasi-religious system of some importance and its concept of a "New Church" attracted substantial numbers of intellectuals.[53]

Spiritualism's earliest explicator was Andrew Jackson Davis, the "Poughkeepsie Seer," who established clairvoyant communication with Swedenborg himself, among others, and who became a well-known lecturer on the subject. As a boy, Davis had been hypnotized by a traveling mesmerist and later claimed to have direct access in a self-hypnotic state to all fundamental religious truths. His ramblings while in a trance, translated and published as *The Great Harmonia* (1850–52), went through thirty-eight editions over the next thirty years and became the basis for an emergent spiritualist cult.[54]

More influential than Davis in confirming belief in spiritualism were the Fox sisters, Margaret and Katie, adolescent daughters of a New York State farmer, who in 1848 heard, on the floor and walls of their home, rappings which spelled out messages. After a series of

---

52. For accounts, see W. P. Garrison, "American Isms," *Harper's Magazine,* XXXIII (April 1, 1882), 1–5; and Elmer Clark, *op. cit.,* chapter 2.

53. "New Church" theology rejected the Trinity and Christ's atonement, making man's free will the instrument of salvation. After death one went either to a heavenly sphere, where one literally became an angel, or to hell, where he was a fallen angel. The heavenly world was much like the human world, extended to ultimate perfection.

54. The best sources of information on Davis are his autobiography, *The Magic Staff* (New York, 1857), and his *Philosophy of Spiritual Intercourse* (New York, 1851). See also Robert Delp, "Andrew Jackson Davis, Prophet of American Spiritualism." *Journal of American History,* XX (June, 1967), 43–57.

local appearances the sisters gave public and private exhibitions in New York and other cities, at which all the apparatus of the "séance"—moving tables, rappings, ghostly hands, spirit "controls" from "the other side"—were quickly developed. Tests and investigations proved little; publicity attracted thousands of converts and dozens of imitators, while some ministers gave the movement religious meaning by suggesting that spiritualist techniques might truly bridge the gulf between the here and the hereafter. (Some years later Katie Fox said that they had made the rapping sounds by cracking their toe knuckles, but her confession was discounted by most believers.) Séance circles and spiritualist groups quickly spread, and out of them a methodology and theology gradually developed. Eventually with the founding of the National Spiritualist Association in 1893, a loosely organized Spiritualist Church took shape.[55]

Mormonism provided the best illustration of the millennialist, utopian, prophetic trends in nineteenth-century American religion, and by all odds the most successful. Its founder, Joseph Smith of upper New York State, reported in 1823 that he had been visited by the Angel Moroni, who revealed to him the existence of a book written on golden plates recounting the history of a lost race in North America. In 1827 Smith reported that he had discovered these plates near his home at Palmyra and in 1830 he published a translation of them as *The Book of Mormon*. The book was a narrative history of pre-Columbian America, inhabited by fugitives from the destruction of Babel, followed by the Lamanites (Indians) and the Nephites, or chosen of God, who created a rich and complex culture (as evidenced by the mound builders' remains) only to be exterminated by the Lamanites. The Book of Mormon thus coincided with several popular historical themes—Indian history,

55. Earl Wesley Fornell, *The Unhappy Medium: Spiritualism and the Life of Margaret Fox* (Austin, Texas, 1964) is the best source. Essentially, the Spiritualists believed that each individual continued to live after death in a glorious hereafter; that these spirits maintained an interest in the world and the persons they had left; and that because of their release from worldly concerns they could provide ethical and spiritual guidance. Contemporary journals are filled with discussions. See, for example, "Spirit Manifestations," *The New England Magazine of Literature, Science, and the Arts*, II (1853), 22-6, 86–90, 152–60; "Modern Spiritualism," *The Christian Examiner*, LXI (November, 1856), 353–89; "Spiritualism Tested by Science," *The New Englander*, XVI (1858), 225–71; "Modern Necromancy," *North American Review*, LXXX (April, 1855), 512–28.

the riddle of the mound builders, the lost tribes of Israel, and Scriptural history—and attracted a number of believers. With six converts, Smith organized the Church of the Latter-Day Saints in 1830; he also received two more revelations, one of which, the Book of Enoch, prophesied the construction of a New Jerusalem at which all the lost tribes would unite and the Kingdom of God would prevail on earth.

In 1831 Smith's colony moved to Ohio, where he spent the next few years constructing a theology (drawn from successive revelations), which tended to resemble the evangelical Christianity of the time. The Saints developed, however, their own distinctive church polity, with a rigid hierarchy of apostles, priests, bishops, elders, preachers, teachers, and deacons. They also accepted the inspiration of the Book of Mormon, special revelations of various kinds, and the creation of a special and complicated priesthood of believers.

After their colony's bank failed in the 1837 panic, the Mormons moved to Missouri, but the antagonism of their "gentile" neighbors soon drove them to settle at Nauvoo, Illinois, where they prospered. Nauvoo, in fact, by 1845 was the largest city in the state, and by legislative permission a relatively independent city-state in itself. Attacks from nearby communities only strengthened the Mormons' cohesiveness, while Smith organized his own militia for protection. In 1843, however, he announced that he had received a divine revelation authorizing polygamous marriages, a pronouncement that worried some Mormons and shocked the non-Mormon public. What was practically a civil war developed between Nauvoo and neighboring towns. Smith and his brother Hyrum were jailed in 1844 and killed by a mob in June. When the state legislature repealed the city's charter in 1845, Mormons were forced to move.[56]

Brigham Young led the Nauvoo Mormons westward, one of the most brilliantly executed mass movements in history, and in 1848 they reached the Great Salt Lake, where they established themselves as the State of Deseret. Carefully supervised groups arrived on timetable schedules until all were present at Salt Lake City. They built irrigation systems, set up sawmills and gristmills, established a tithing system to insure against lean years, and opened cooperative stores to do the community's business. Never quite fully integrated

56. Robert B. Flanders, *Nauvoo: Kingdom on the Mississippi* (Urbana, 1965) is an excellent account.

into the mainstream of American theology, the Mormon venture still remains unique among millenarian religions and communitarian experiments. As no other sizable deviationist Christian group was able to do, it combined the theological and secular elements of religious life into a unified ethos and a viable society.[57]

Until the second decade of the nineteenth century American churches were nearly unanimous in their opposition to slavery. The Baptist General Committee in 1789 adopted a resolution declaring slavery "a violent deprivation of the rights of man and inconsistent with a republican government"; the New York and Pennsylvania Presbyterian synods called for the abolition of slavery two years earlier. Among Congregationalists, who were almost wholly opposed to the institution, individual congregations frequently passed antislavery resolutions.[58]

That emancipation of all American slaves was necessary and desirable, most Protestant clergy agreed; how to accomplish it presented problems. The majority of ministers and congregations did not want to be drawn into the controversy as it developed after the turn of the century, but realizing that it seemed inevitable, adopted various kinds of antislavery positions. Colonization of the ex-slave in Africa appeared to be the most desirable solution, and the American Colonization Society, formed in 1817, was fully endorsed within five years by the Presbyterian General Assembly, the Baptist General Convention, the Methodist General Conference, and the General Convention of the Protestant Episcopal Church.

It was soon clear that colonization did not work. The emergence of the abolitionists, who demanded immediate emancipation—here and now—further exacerbated differences among the churches and

57. See A. Leland Jamison, "Religions on the Christian Perimeter," in Smith and Jamison, *op. cit.,* 212–16. For more extensive studies of the Mormons, see Thomas O'Day, *The Mormons* (New York, 1957) and Ray West, *Kingdom of the Saints* (New York, 1957). One group, the Reorganized Church of the Latter-Day Saints, settled in Missouri. Another under James Strang moved to Wisconsin and later to Beaver Island in Lake Michigan, where Strang was murdered. The best single study of the relationship between the Mormon experience and American culture is the volume of readings edited by Marvin S. Hill and James B. Allen, *Mormonism and American Culture* (New York, 1972).

58. Olmsted, *op. cit.,* chapter 19, "The Churches and the Slavery Controversy." See also John L. Bodo, *The Protestant Clergy and Public Issues 1812–1848* (Princeton, 1954).

clergy. Much of the support for abolitionism in its early phases came from evangelical leaders who saw in the movement both Christian "usefulness" and a way of promoting social perfection. One means of abolishing slavery, they argued, was to convert the slaveholder from "sin" so that he would voluntarily free his slaves and so destroy the system. *"The churches must take right ground on the subject of slavery,"* said Charles Grandison Finney in *Lectures on Revivals of Religion* (1835):

It is a great national sin. . . . Let Christians of all denominations meekly but firmly come forth, and pronounce their verdict, let them clear their communions, and wash their hands of this thing, let them give forth and write on the head and front of this great abomination, *SIN*.

Under Finney's inspiration, preachers like Theodore Weld and Marius Robinson dedicated themselves to the cause of the slave with the same fervor as they preached perfectionism; it was no accident that the Western center of perfectionist theology, Lane Seminary and Oberlin, produced thirty-two abolitionist agents. Meanwhile, within the churches the controversy centered on two related issues: whether slavery was Biblically justified; and whether it was or not, if it was *morally* justifiable in nineteenth-century America. Examining the institution in the light of scriptural teachings, Southern clergymen (and some Northern ones) argued that the Bible, especially the Old Testament, sanctioned slavery and that nothing in the teachings of Christ denied it. Northern clergymen (and a few Southern) claimed exactly the opposite.[59] Each could find dozens of passages to support his position. The specific point of conflict between pro- and antislavery churchmen and parishioners was, however, less theological than practical—what should the relationship be between the churches and the abolitionist movement? To what extent, and in what ways, should church bodies become involved in the struggle for or against the system? Every major religious body debated these questions after

59. Weld's *Bible Against Slavery* (1837) and Thomas Stringfellow's *Scriptural and Statistical Views in Favor of Slavery* (1856) represent typical examples. There were at least fifty books published on the issue between 1835 and 1860, and numerous debates between clergymen, published and unpublished. A good summary is provided by Arthur Y. Lloyd, *The Slavery Controversy* (Chapel Hill, 1939), chapter V.

1830, until the issue became, as the Methodists put it, "reformation or division."

The Baptists were the first to divide; in 1843 the Southern churches withdrew to organize the Southern Baptist Convention. The Methodists came next. Many Methodist congregations and ministers began organizing antislavery societies in the thirties, and at the annual General Conferences contests developed over whether or not the church should adopt an official position on slavery. As the moderate position gradually eroded, it became obvious that division was inevitable. At the 1844 General Conference, after eleven days of debate, Southern delegates withdrew and met in 1845 to form the Methodist Episcopal Church, South. The Presbyterians maintained a semblance of unity until 1857, when twenty-one Southern presbyteries left the General Assembly to form what eventually became the Presbyterian Church in the United States. Two statements published on the same day—November 21, 1835—illustrated vividly why the division of American Protestantism seemed inevitable, and why it took over a century to heal it.[60] A body of South Carolina Presbyterians resolved:

. . . that in the opinion of this presbytery, the holding of slaves, so far from being a sin in the sight of God, is nowhere condemned in his Holy Word—that it is in accordance with the example, or consistent with the precepts of patriarchs, prophets and apostles; and that it is compatible with the most fraternal regard to the best good of those servants whom God may have committed to our charge. . . .

In Michigan, another Presbyterian Church resolved:

. . . that this synod believe the buying, selling and owning of slaves in this country to be A Sin Before God and man: that the system of American slavery is a great moral, political, physical and social evil, and ought to be immediately and universally abandoned—and that it is our duty, . . . to endeavor to hasten the happy day of universal emancipation.

From neither position could there be retreat.

---

60. Quoted in Gaustad, *op. cit.*, 190. The division in the Methodist churches, typical of other Protestant sects, is well explained in David G. Matthews, *Slavery and Methodism: A Chapter in American Morality 1780–1845* (Princeton, 1965).

CHAPTER 9

The Study of Mind, Body, and Idea

THE two major influences in American philosophy during the first three quarters of the nineteenth century were Scottish realism and philosophical idealism. The "common sense" philosophy, developed in Scottish academic circles in the closing years of the eighteenth century, provided a theory of knowledge more acceptable to the times than Locke's empiricism, Berkeley's idealism, or Hume's skepticism.[1] During the Revolutionary era the major strain of American philosophy was Lockean empiricism, which fitted admirably with the political and scientific interests of the times. As Locke's popularity faded in America and Britain, Americans found a satisfactory replacement in the philosophy of "common sense," developed by such men as Francis Hutcheson, Thomas Reid, Dugald Stewart, James Beattie, and Adam Ferguson, all of them well known in American intellectual circles.

The first important emissary of the common-sense school to arrive in the colonies was John Witherspoon, who left Scotland to become president of the College of New Jersey in 1768. Witherspoon soon

1. The best treatments of the Scottish system are still James McCosh, *Intuitions of the Mind* (1860) and *The Scottish Philosophy* (1875). A recent study is Daniel S. Robinson, *The Story of Scottish Philosophy* (New York, 1961). Useful studies of philosophical trends in the United States are I. W. Riley, *American Thought: From Puritanism to Pragmatism and Beyond* (New York, 1923); P. R. Anderson and M. H. Fisch, *Philosophy in America* (New York, 1939); and especially Herbert W. Schneider, *The History of American Philosophy* (New York, 1946).

made Presbyterian New Jersey (Princeton) a Scottish stronghold, aided by another emigrant, Archibald Alexander, who lectured in Princeton's theological school. At Harvard, Scottish texts were introduced in 1792 by Professor David Tappan, and by 1810 the common-sense philosophy was taught at least equally with Locke in a majority of American colleges and universities. Samuel Stanhope Smith, one of Witherspoon's students who later succeeded him as Princeton's president, explained the American variety of the Scottish school in his *Lectures . . . on Moral and Political Philosophy* (1812). Men possess, said Smith, two sets of senses, external and internal. External senses provide knowledge of the outside world, which passes through the nerves and becomes ideas in the mind. These ideas group by association and are made into new ideas by rational organization and synthesis. Internal sensations are of three kinds: first, those of the mind itself, which originates first principles such as the idea of God, the existence of the soul, or the certainty of will; second, those of beauty and taste; third, those of morality, or ideas of good and bad. These senses are common to all men.

It followed, then, according to the Scottish school, that men possessed an innate, reliable "moral sense," which could be trusted to provide answers to moral questions. The exact nature of this sense was never precisely defined, nor was its existence ever doubted. Some, following the older school of Shaftesbury and Hutcheson, saw the moral sense as more or less intuitional, a perception of "obligation" that one felt without extended reflection. The majority of Scots thinkers, however, tended to define it as a more rational, reflective power, its decisions supported by education and experience.

In opposition to Berkeleian idealists, the Scots claimed that "real objects" had an existence of their own, independent of the mind, and that they could be perceived as "real." This was an assured, "self-evident" truth, intuitively deduced. If the reality of things could be thus intuitively established, so could moral, political, and ethical truths and other "first and fundamental" assumptions about justice, right, God's existence, the laws of nature, the soul's immortality, and so on. By extending this method of establishing truths, Scottish philosophy furnished a way of organizing clusters of orthodox ideas and values and of rationalizing their existence. The Scots philosophers' insistence on the reality of innate ideas, and their acceptance of the validity of intuitional knowledge, prepared the ground for the seeds of German philosophy, Platonism, Neoplatonism, and Oriental thought that later bloomed into the New England transcendental movement.[2]

Scottish philosophy provided, then, a means by which men could establish workable standards of religious, aesthetic, and moral truth, for it gave to the human mind, as Thomas Reid explained, the power to make those "original and natural judgments" which "serve to direct us in the common affairs of life, when our reasoning faculty would leave us in the dark." These judgments, he continued, "make up what is called the *common sense of mankind,*" providing men with "first principles" on which they may act. This was an extremely useful weapon against the skepticism of Hume and the rationalism of the deists, as well as an affirmation of the older belief in a "moral sense." Most convenient of all, it was a unified, compact system which destroyed nothing and gave more or less satisfactory answers to bothersome theological questions.[3]

The basic optimism of the Scottish philosophy fitted American needs admirably, especially its assumption that all men, whatever their condition, possessed an inherent moral sense which could be strengthened and improved by proper education and application. The principles of "common sense" gave reason to believe that the average individual could fulfill those obligations which the American political system placed upon him. It furnished a way of establishing the philosophical validity of those "self-evident" truths on which the American system rested; it was also a straightforward and sensible method of looking at life and considering its problems, one which could be easily codified and illustrated. Scottish philosophy, wrote the Reverend John Gros of Columbia College, gave "rules for the direction of the will of man in his moral state, such rules to serve for the guidance of the individual, community, and nation."

The Scottish system also had particular value in that it suited current theories of human nature and knowledge. The philosophers of the early eighteenth century concluded that the mind, distinct from the body, had a pattern and function of its own. It possessed

2. See E. W. Todd, "Philosophical Ideas at Harvard, 1817–1837," *New England Quarterly,* XVI (1943), 63–90.

3. Sidney E. Ahlstrom, "The Scottish Philosophy and American Theology," *Church History,* XXIV (1955), 257–72.

three sets of powers: the understanding, reason, or "perception," by which men reasoned, reflected, remembered, and created ideas out of experience; the "passions," "sensibilities," or "affections," by which they comprehended the emotions; and the will or "volition" which enabled them to act on motivations provided by the reason and the emotions. Scottish philosophy, with its acceptance of innate judgments, was thus easily adapted to contemporary psychology.

The Scottish approach became the quasi-official philosophy of nineteenth-century America, generally accepted as the proper way to understand, direct, and control man's thoughts and actions. By 1810 the majority of courses in Moral Science or Natural Philosophy, taught in nearly every institution of higher learning, were founded on common-sense principles. Samuel Stanhope Smith (Witherspoon's successor), Francis Wayland at Brown, Mark Hopkins of Williams, and others published influential texts which spread Scottish doctrines through the country's colleges. Few educated Americans, in the generations between 1790 and 1870, were not familiar with the concepts of the Scottish school. Its concepts, taught year by year to successive generations of college students, were a major influence in the development of American thought throughout the nineteenth century.

The expansion of education in post-Revolutionary America, particularly at the collegiate level, meant that philosophy became a "taught" subject with an important place in the curriculum. It was customarily divided into two—or sometimes three—parts as Natural, Mental, and Moral philosophy, taken usually during the third and fourth years of study. The Scottish variety, which was easily systematized into rules that could be taught, written on examinations, and tested by experience and observation, fitted academic requirements very well. The preponderance of Yale and Princeton theologians on most college faculties meant that a course in Moral Philosophy was likely to be Scottish. Such courses placed history, theology, science, law, government, economics, and social relations within a single ethical framework, instructing the student how to choose the morally correct course of action in his own life.[4]

Course titles might vary, but in general Natural Philosophy came

4. Wilson Smith, *Professors and Public Ethics* (Ithaca, 1956), chapter II, provides an excellent discussion of these courses. See also George Schmidt, *The Old Time College President* (New York, 1930), chapter V.

to mean the study of science; Moral Philosophy the study of ethics and theology; and Mental Philosophy the study of the mind and its powers, or psychology. Thus Jacob Abbott's edition of Abercrombie's *Philosophy of the Moral Feelings* (1833), a popular text, assisted the student to "investigate the Moral Feelings of the Human Mind and the principles which ought to regulate our volitions and our conduct." Philosophy thus became, in its academic version, received rather than speculative; its aim was to organize and codify rather than to explore or test ideas. Francis Wayland, in his *Elements of Moral Science* (1835), suggested that a philosophy text ought "to exhibit what was true" rather than discuss what was doubtful. In this way, as Joseph Blau has observed, philosophy became subject matter rather than wisdom, conclusions rather than speculations.[5]

The introduction of philosophy courses into the schools meant, of course, a demand for texts, of which literally hundreds appeared over the century. Bishop William Paley's *Principles of Moral and Political Philosophy* (1785) dominated the field for a number of years, while his *Natural Theology* (1812) was also a standard text in which the student found proofs from nature of the existence of God and of His attributes and powers. (Paley's famous analogy of Nature as a Watch, which if studied and understood revealed its Maker, was familiar to all educated people in the early nineteenth century.) His utilitarianism, however, disturbed some teachers, who felt that his idea of right as "the utility of the moral rule alone, which constituted the proper obligation to it," was less Christian than it should be.[6] Paley's books by 1830 were challenged by adaptations of Scottish texts, among them Wayland's *Elements of Moral Science* (1835), Jasper Adams's *Elements of Moral Philosophy* (1837), and Asa Mahan's *Science of Moral Philosophy*

5. Joseph Blau, *Men and Movements in American Philosophy* (New York, 1952), chapters I and II, provides an excellent discussion of the academic philosophy of the period.

6. Wilson Smith, *op. cit.*, chapters III and IV. Smith, p. 215, points out that Paley's *Principles* was used for fifty-three years at Yale, forty-seven years at Harvard, forty-nine years at Columbia, thirty-nine years at Brown, and twenty-five years at Amherst. See also Wendell Glick, "Bishop Paley in America," *New England Quarterly*, XXVII (1954), 347-355; and Wilson Smith, "William Paley's Theological Utilitarianism in America," *William and Mary Quarterly*, XI (July, 1954), 402-25.

(1848) .[7] Wayland's was both typical and influential, passing through numerous editions and selling 200,000 copies over sixty years. Rejecting Paley's utilitarian ethic of measuring an act against its consequence, Wayland taught that the *intent* of the act provided the proper moral standard by which to test it, a position much more suitable to the American Calvinist temperament. Divided into Theoretical Ethics (dealing with the Moral Sense and the Christian basis of virtue) and Practical Ethics (man's duties to God, society, and his fellowman), the book furnished the student with a minimum of disputation and a maximum of usefulness.

Courses in Moral Philosophy began to disappear, however, after 1850, as the clergyman gradually lost his place as chief adviser to American society, to be replaced by the lawyer, doctor, and scientist. The new secular and state colleges and universities tended less often to choose clergymen as presidents, while the increasing secularization of academic life meant that it was no longer feasible to teach a course that pretended to include everything from economics to epistemology. The great issues of the times—slavery, war, expansionism, industrialism—simply did not lend themselves to classroom solutions, nor could the rules in the texts provide answers. By the seventies, the old-fashioned Moral Philosophy course had virtually disappeared from the curriculum.[8]

Wayland's belief that intent, rather than result, furnished a standard for moral action, in effect substituted a more intuitive and personalized basis for moral judgment in place of the older, rationalistic moral sense. This was itself a reflection of the much wider shift in American philosophy which characterized the middle four decades of the nineteenth century—that is, its increased intuitionalism, its acceptance of the "feelings" or "inner promptings" as guides for determining truth and morality. This tendency was

7. Others were Archibald Alexander, *Outlines of Moral Science* (1852); Wayland's *Elements of Intellectual Philosophy* (1854); Mark Hopkins, *Lectures in Moral Science* (1862); Joseph Alden, *Christian Ethics* (1866); and James Fairchild, *Moral Philosophy, or the Sense of Obligation* (1869).

8. Wilson Smith, *op. cit.*, 202–4. Of forty-eight teachers of moral philosophy between 1830 and 1860, Smith lists thirty-nine who were clergymen. O. W. Holmes's *Elsie Venner* (1861), in which the family doctor replaced the minister as counselor and moralist, represented the new trend.

already present, of course, as a powerful component of both the Romantic movement and of church evangelicalism.

A new force for change in American philosophy came from Germany—via English and French sources—to appear in New England as "transcendentalism," a Kantian term which expressed rather vaguely its chief doctrines. Transcendentalism was a diverse, individualistic trend in philosophy, hardly to be called a school. Yet those who included themselves within the term displayed a sufficiently common temper and cast of thought to warrant consideration of it as a movement. Transcendentalism had strong religious elements, so much so that its own chronicler, Octavius B. Frothingham, thought it should be "more justly regarded as a gospel" than a philosophy, yet since it dealt with problems of knowing, believing, and acting, it had pertinent philosophical implications.[9]

Knowledge of Kant and German Romantic philosophy came to America in the twenties and thirties from England through Coleridge and Carlyle, and from France through Cousin and Jouffroy. The appointment of Karl Follen as Harvard's first professor of German (1828), and study abroad by such young scholars as George Ticknor, George Bancroft, Edward Everett, and Joseph Cogswell, quickly brought Germany to American attention. James Marsh's edition (1829) of Coleridge's *Aids to Reflection* became a standard text for American scholars; so too was Carlyle's *Sartor Resartus* (1838), a persuasive restatement of Kant's ideas. What appealed to American philosophers was Kant's concept (broadened beyond his original intentions) of the "practical reason" as an ethical guide and of the "categorical imperative" as a principle of morality. Equally interesting was the theory of knowledge suggested by his "pure reason," which seemed to be an intuitive source of truth. Nor were the Germans the only source of inspiration; the transcenden-

9. See Blau, *op. cit.*, chapter IV; O. B. Frothingham, *Transcendentalism in New England* (New York, 1876) ; H. W. Schneider, *op. cit.*, chapter V. Generally accepted as leaders of the movement were Ralph Waldo Emerson, William Ellery Channing, Theodore Parker, Bronson Alcott, George Ripley, James Freeman Clarke, James Marsh, F. W. Hedge, Caleb S. Henry, Margaret Fuller, and briefly, Orestes Brownson. William R. Hutchinson, *The Transcendentalist Ministers* (New Haven, 1959) is an excellent survey of its religious aspects.

talists read Plato and the Neoplatonists again, Oriental philosophy, and the older Berkeleian idealists.

Transcendentalism was an eclectic habit of mind rather than a system. James Freeman Clarke was once quoted as saying that transcendentalists were "a club of the likeminded, I suppose because no two of us thought alike." Ralph Waldo Emerson, the young minister who resigned his pulpit in 1832, soon became its most eloquent spokesman, beginning with *Nature* (1836) and continuing through *Self-Reliance, The Over-Soul,* and other essays. Emerson was certainly as much a poet as philosopher; James McCosh of Princeton never considered him a philosopher at all, but as a writer whose thoughts were like "strung pearls, without system or correction." James Marsh, president of the University of Vermont, was a sound scholar whose transcendentalism was conservative; Theodore Parker, a militant minister, translated transcendental perfectibility into active social reform; Frederick Hedge, an émigré Harvard professor, was perhaps the most philosophically knowledgeable of the group; Orestes Brownson, who had been Presbyterian, Universalist, and Unitarian, moved away from transcendentalism toward Catholicism.

The heart of transcendentalism lay in its theory of knowledge. Neither Locke nor the Scots gave convincing answers to the question, How do we know? Transcendentalists therefore went beyond reason; affirming the validity of intuitive truth, they assumed that knowledge was available to every man within himself. Like the idealists, they postulated two realms: a palpable, perceptible world of sensations; and an unseen world beyond, of pure ideas, beauty, truth, and goodness. Here neither the Lockean reason nor the Scottish common sense could penetrate. But each man had within him two primary powers, Reason and Understanding (terms adapted from Kant and Locke) which operated in these separate realms. The Understanding, a rational power, dealt with the facts and laws of the physical world and provided logical proofs for rational knowledge. The Reason, an intuitive sense despite its name, could pierce beyond the material world into the suprarational, "transcendental" realm of "ultimate reality" that lay behind phenomenal appearances. This transcendental Reason thus perceived truth directly by "transcending" the barriers of sense and temporality. It was, George Bancroft wrote in 1835, not that faculty which deduces inferences from the experience of the senses, but that higher faculty, which from the infinite treasures of its own consciousness, originates truth, and assents to it by the force of intuitive evidence; that faculty which raises us beyond the control of time and space, and gives us faith in things eternal and invisible.

Man's mind was thus a sensitive instrument which discovered truth in two ways—by rational analysis through the Understanding; and intuitively through the Reason, that "highest power of the Soul," wrote Emerson, which "never *reasons*, never proves, it simply perceives, it is vision."[10]

Transcendentalism, however, was more than epistemological speculation; it was a way of finding an answer to what Emerson called "the practical question of the conduct of life, How do I live?" It had religious, ethical, and social implications for the times. Unlike the older orthodox view that the ability to know God directly was granted only to the elect, transcendentalism held that Reason was every man's birthright. Because of this, all men were inherently worthy and spiritually equal, an idea quite compatible with current democratic thought. "Practically," wrote Octavius Frothingham, "it was an assertion of the inalienable worth of man; theoretically, it was an assertion of supernatural attributes to the natural constitution of mankind."[11]

Transcendentalism was also powerfully individualistic. Each in-

10. See Emerson's letter to Edward Emerson, in Ralph L. Rusk, *The Letters of Ralph Waldo Emerson* (New York, 1939), I:412–3; and Bancroft's "The Office of the People . . . ," in *Literary and Historical Miscellanies* (New York, 1855), 409. An exceptionally clear statement of "the Truths of Pure Reason" is "A Chapter on Intuitive Truths," *The New Englander*, XXII (July, 1844), 359–71, which lists twelve truths, verifiable by the Reason, as "the foundations of all our knowledge." The Kantian influence is strong but difficult to assess. Few Americans read German well, and Kantian German was particularly difficult; no doubt many of those who absorbed Kantian ideas did so via intermediaries, explanations, and reviews. Kant distinguishes two categories of mind, Understanding and Reason. The function of the first was to impose "categories" on experience, from which inductive reasoning derived. The Reason, on the other hand, asked categorical questions as they are, not necessarily based on experience. In Kantian terms, the Reason did not actually yield knowledge, but rather asked questions which might lead to knowledge. Followers of Kant, however, gave greater importance to the Reason than Kant originally ascribed to it; it became, as they interpreted it, a power superior to the Understanding and capable of providing a superior kind of knowledge. They kept the term Understanding, however, to indicate inductive knowledge.

11. *Op. cit.*, 136.

dividual's claim to equality and justice rested on his ability to consult his intuition; ethically, the belief in the validity of one's own intuitive truth led toward each man's responsibility for himself. "Trust thyself," wrote Emerson. "Every heart vibrates to that iron string." Transcendentalism thus had much in common with the optimistic, individualistic, egalitarian spirit of Jacksonian democracy, although Emerson could never bring himself to unqualified approval of Old Hickory. Transcendentalism really meant, as one of its followers phrased it, "that men are free, and claim the right to think for themselves in religious as well as in political matters." It emphasized the worth of the individual and the principle of self-reliance; it admired the man of action and original thought; it believed in the value of instinctive, individual judgment, rather than in those of authority and convention. It said, in Emersonian terms, "God is in every man," which in the final test was not so far removed from what the Jacksonians meant.[12]

On the other hand, although it was an interesting, provocative set of ideas, the influence of transcendentalism on the mainstream of American philosophical thought was not large, nor did it cause a major stir in academic circles. Transcendentalism was chiefly influential as a literary-religious phenomenon, neither formalized nor taught, never pursued very far beyond its own generation. A collection of ideologies loosely grouped around a Kantian-Coleridgean core, it was parochially New England and far too abstract and subtle to mix with the main currents of American philosophy. Transcendentalism was never able to deal effectively with the powerful economic and social forces even then reshaping contemporary American life, nor was it able to adjust to all the new ideas that shook the biological and physical sciences after the fifties. Transcendentalism could not transcend science, or industrialism, or technology, or Darwinism. By the latter decades of the century, new winds of philosophical doctrine—pragmatism, naturalism, instrumentalism—had blown much of it away.

Formal philosophy in the United States took notice of the Germans—Kant, Schlegel, and Hegel—in still another way. Scottish

12. A good summary of Emerson's ideas and of transcendentalism in New England is that of Frederic Carpenter, *Emerson Handbook* (New York, 1953), 124–137. An excellent collection of documents is George Hochfield, *Selected Writings of the American Transcendentalists* (New York, 1966).

realists like James McCosh never accepted the neo-Kantian Reason or any of the "ingenious theories" of the transcendentalists, preferring to wait, he said, "until they can be shown to be founded on the inherent principles of the mind." Other orthodox philosophers accepted German idealism in part or fitted it into the Scottish system one way or another. Laurens P. Hickok, at Union College, one of the few who fully understood Kant, made probably the best adaptation of his work in *Moral Science* (1853, revised 1880). Others worked out their own versions of German thought through the rest of the century.[13] A group in St. Louis, known as the St. Louis Hegelians, was especially influential in the formal development of German philosophy. William T. Harris and Henry Brokmeyer organized a Kant Club in 1858, which despite its name specialized in the study of Hegel. Harris translated Hegel; helped to found *The Journal of Speculative Philosophy* (1867), devoted to German thought; and later (with Bronson Alcott) organized the Concord School of Philosophy. Harris and others continued to argue for the intuitive, speculative method, opposing the new trends in philosophy with a dogged faith in the Reason's ability to find "ultimate reality."

"Mental philosophy" (the term "psychology" did not come into use until the 1840s) began to separate from "moral philosophy" and formal academic philosophy shortly after 1820. The "moral science" course in colleges, for example, came gradually to mean the study of ethics, or political philosophy, or economics; whereas "natural philosophy" tended to divide into the various sciences. The distinction was made clear by George Payne's *Elements of Mental and Moral Science* (1829), which defined mental science as "the study of the *capabilities* of the mind" and moral science as "the study of the *rectitude* of the mind." Mental philosophy, or psychology, soon became a separate subject with its own specialized textbooks and vocabulary. The rise of psychology as a separate study derived, in part, from the Enlightenment's—and Romanticism's—interest in man, and in part from empirical philosophy's curiosity about the nature of knowledge. Since all of man's actions

13. See Schneider, *op. cit.*, chapter 36, "Schools of Idealism."

depended on *what* he knew, *how* he knew it had consequences for the study of every aspect of human activity.[14]

There were two ways in which this question of knowledge might be answered: the one speculative, deriving from the formal philosophical tradition; the other experimental, deriving from natural science. In the first instance, psychology could draw upon the Lockean-Scottish tradition, which taught that the operations of the mind could be explained in terms of a collection of inborn, inherent, native powers or "faculties," located in the brain and common to all men.[15] These included such powers as willing, understanding, memory, and so on, as well as the moral faculty of judgment. They developed in different stages and to different degrees in different people, thus accounting for personality differences, mental disorders, "genius," and the like.

Locke and his followers postulated a number of powers within the mind, among them understanding, the affections, power, will, motive; others, like Benjamin Rush, identified more, including "the principles of faith, conscience, and the sense of Deity." Later philosophers usually reduced the number of categories of faculties to three, which under various names were recognized as the reason, the emotions or sensibilities, and the will. Whatever the names, "three faculty" psychology became standard in Europe and America by the earlier nineteenth century.[16] Faculty psychology was well suited to the Kantian-Coleridgean picture of the mind, for all one needed to do to make it fit was to identify the faculties with instincts. Thus Theodore Parker made faculty psychology transcen-

14. The history of early American psychology is treated by A. A. Roback, *A History of American Psychology* (rev. ed., New York, 1964), chapters 1–7; Jay W. Wharton, *American Psychology Before William James* (New Brunswick, 1939) ; and R. C. Davis, "American Psychology, 1800–1885," *The Psychological Review*, XXXIII (November, 1936) , 47–92.

15. Joseph Haven's *Mental Philosophy* (1857) chapter II defined a faculty as "the mind's power of acting, of doing something, of putting forth some energy, and performing some operation. The mind has as many distinct faculties, as it has distinct powers of action, distinct functions, distinct modes, and spheres of activities."

16. Reason or perception was the faculty by which men reasoned, reflected, and created ideas from experience; through the sensibilities or propensities or affections or passions men comprehended emotions such as hate, greed, love, anger, etc.; men acted by the will or volition on the motivations provided by the other two faculties. See Schneider, *op. cit.*, chapters XIX–XX; and Frank M. Albrecht, *The New Psychology in America*, unpublished dissertation, Johns Hopkins, 1960.

dental by labeling the powers of the mind as "the instinctive intuition of the divine, the instinctive intuition of the just and right, and instinctive intuition of the immortal." Joseph Haven's *Mental Philosophy* postulated six "intuited truths" in the mind; and Noah Porter's *Human Intellect* (1868) found eight.[17]

Faculty psychology, in one form or another, and occasionally mixed with German intuitionalism, dominated psychological theory until the 1880s. One of the first and most influential texts was Thomas C. Upham's *Elements of Intellectual Philosophy* (1827), later revised as *Elements of Mental Philosophy* (1831) and after numerous other revisions still in print in 1886. Upham, who based his system on the Scottish pattern but borrowed freely from others, defined the faculties as Intellect, Sensibilities, and Will, with several subdivisions under each. Frederick Rauch's *Psychology* (1840), one of the first American books to use the term (although it was already in use in England), was, as the author explained, "the first attempt to unite German and American mental philosophy"; also German-oriented was Asa Mahan's *Lectures on Mental and Moral Philosophy* (1841) and his *System of Intellectual Philosophy* (1845). For twenty years after Upham's first book, the publication of psychology texts averaged one per year.[18] Academic philosophers organized and codified the faculty theory, made it available to student and layman, and familiarized the public with its vocabulary, its concepts of personality, and its theories of knowledge and action. Not until the appearance of the new physiological and associationist psychology of the eighties and the work of such men as William James and G. Stanley Hall was the dominance of faculty psychology brought into question.

Faculty psychology, however, rested wholly on speculation. The first serious attempts to find out by experimentation how the mind worked, and how psychology could be practically applied, came with two imported systems, mesmerism and phrenology. Speculative philosophy had already established the possibilities of connections

17. Quoted in John Weiss, *The Life and Correspondence of Theodore Parker* (Boston, 1864), II:454–5.

18. Other important texts were Samuel Schmucker, *Psychology* (1842); Leicester Sawyer, *Elements of Mental Philosophy* (1846); Laurens Hickok's *Rational Psychology* (1848); Hubbard Winslow, *Intellectual Philosophy* (1852); Noah Porter, *The Human Intellect* (1868); John Bascom, *The Principles of Psychology* (1869); and James McCosh, *Psychology* (1888).

between mind and body; Benjamin Rush, for example, suggested in his *Influence of Physical Causes on the Moral Faculty* (1786) that there might be chemical-physiological reasons for certain kinds of actions. Since faculty psychology postulated that the mental powers had their seat within the brain, it was only logical to focus attention on the construction and operation of that organ so that the faculties could be located, measured, classified, and analyzed.

"Mesmerism" or "animal magnetism," developed by the German physician F. A. Mesmer in the eighteenth century, seemed to offer an excellent physiological basis for psychological research. Mesmerism (the term "hypnotism" was not used until the forties) was a mixture of the old seventeenth-century "humours" theory of human behavior, the popular "electrical fluid" theory of the eighteenth, and more recent theories of intuitional psychology. Essentially, Mesmer tried to explain thought and behavior in "scientific" terms. He assumed the existence of an electriclike "irradiating power" which emanated from all things (but with especial strength from stars, the human body, and metals) which under the direction of an "indwelling spirit" exerted force on other things. The workings of the mind, then, could be explained in physical terms, and the connections of mind and body by laws of electrical theory. Mesmerism, however, moved away from psychology toward faith healing, "magnetic" therapy, and other applied uses.[19]

Phrenology, however, was a different matter. Developed by Gall, Spurzheim, and others in Germany and by George Combe in England, phrenology was based on the belief that the shape of the head indicated the shape of the brain, which in turn indicated the development of the faculties of the mind within the brain. Phrenology, after 1820, swiftly became a full-fledged science.[20] It assumed that if the faculties of the mind are each located in specific areas of the brain, the configuration of each person's skull reflects the devel-

19. Cf. I. W. Riley, *op. cit.*, chapter IV. Charles Poyen, *The Progress of Animal Magnetism in America* (1837) is a useful contemporary source. See also Eric Carlson and M. M. Simpson, "Perkinsism vs. Mesmerism," *Journal of the History of the Behavioral Sciences*, VI (January, 1970), 16–25.

20. For information, see John D. Davies, *Phrenology: Fad and Science* (New Haven, 1955); Robert Riegel, "Early Phrenology in the United States," *Medical Life*, XXXVI (July, 1930), 361–76; and Riegel, "The Introduction of Phrenology into the United States," *American Historical Review*, XXXIX (October, 1933), 73–78. The works of Orson Fowler, especially his *Practical Phrenology* (1849) and *Human Science or Phrenology* (1873), are especially useful contemporary sources.

opment of those faculties, so that a trained scientist can, by observing the skull, interpret the mental pattern of the individual. The individual, in turn, can alter his personality by exercising or suppressing those faculties which, by reason of their under- or over-development, cause him to think and act as he does,[21]

for the mental faculties are susceptible of great alteration by training. They can be strengthened or weakened, according as the condition of the mind requires for its amendment the one or the other.

Instead of three faculties of the mind, however, phrenologists found it much more complicated, since the human skull displayed anywhere from thirty to fifty protuberances and hollows that indicated mental traits.[22]

Spurzheim visited the United States in 1832 for what amounted to a triumphal tour; George Combe, who followed, was welcomed with equal enthusiasm. Lorenzo and Orson Fowler, brothers who moved from the country to New York City in 1835, soon became the leaders of the movement. Almost everyone believed in phrenology, and almost everyone knew and used its terminology—Poe, Whitman, Emerson, Hawthorne, and Horace Mann, among others. In the space of years between 1825 and 1855 there were seventy-two books published on phrenology; in addition, phrenologists founded a number of societies, schools, and journals like *The American Phrenological Journal,* established in 1848 to "PHRENOLOGIZE OUR NATION, for thereby it will REFORM THE WORLD." Not all believed all of it, of course, and the argument often waged hot, but the system withstood attack for another generation.[23]

21. R. H. Collyer, *A Manual of Phrenology* (Dayton, 1842) , from which much of this explanation is taken.
22. Dr. Charles Caldwell, "Phrenology Vindicated . . . ," *American Phrenological Review and Miscellany,* II (December, 1839) , 97–111. S. R. Wells, *The New Illustrated Self-Instructor in Phrenology and Physiology* (New York, 1875) listed forty-two faculties: Amativeness, Conjugality, Parental Love, Friendship, Inhabitativeness, Continuity, Vitativeness, Combativeness, Destructiveness, Alimentativeness, Acquisitiveness, Secretiveness, Cautiousness, Approbativeness, Self-Esteem, Firmness, Conscientiousness, Hope, Spirituality, Veneration, Benevolence, Constructiveness, Ideality, Sublimity, Imitation, Mirthfulness, Individuality, Form, Size, Weight, Color, Order, Calculation, Locality, Eventuality, Time, Tune, Language, Causality, Comparison, Human Nature, Agreeableness.
23. There were dozens of attacks and replies, but typical are "Craniology," *The United States Review and Literary Gazette,* II (May, 1827) , 124–38; "Phrenol-

Phrenology had much to offer. It was more than a psychological system, for what one learned about human nature from it could be applied directly to actual situations; the concept of the individual that it projected reinforced the individualistic, democratic spirit of the age. Phrenology told a man what he was and told him how to improve himself. It was easily understood, easily explained, and so "clear, simple, and natural," wrote Samuel Gridley Howe, "that he who runs may read, and every reader may comprehend." It provided a practical educational psychology, since the development of one's mental faculties could be prescribed and measured. It explained criminality and insanity—Dr. Amanah Brigham, a phrenologist, founded the first periodical of its kind in English, *The American Journal of Insanity* (1844); and Dr. Charles Caldwell, another phrenologist, published a pioneer study in criminology, *New Views of Penitentiary Discipline,* in 1827. Medically, phrenology attracted attention to neurology and psychiatry, but more significantly it suggested to doctors that the mind could be scientifically explored, that mental phenomena could be studied objectively and explained by natural causes. Phrenology was the first psychological theory that could be tested experimentally—which destroyed it—but it did help to introduce the experimental method to psychology.

Some of the more orthodox theologians accused phrenologists of denying free will and God's direction, since phrenology claimed that character and action were determined by physical causes. They replied that it instead showed God's infinite wisdom in making man perfectible, capable of self-correction. Far from encouraging infidelity, said Orson Fowler, phrenology proved God's existence— what was the organ of veneration for? Most of all, phrenology provided a kind of popular psychology of hope, despite its oversimplifications, for it said in its fashion what more sophisticated thinkers such as Emerson and Channing were saying too—that each individual was unique in himself, that he had within him the power to make himself wiser and better. Orson Fowler's motto— "Self Made or Never Made"—differed little from Emerson's doc-

---

ogy Vindicated," *New England Magazine,* VII (December, 1834), 433–44; "On the Humbug of Phrenology," *Gentleman's Magazine,* VII (July, 1840), 62–69; "Phrenology," *North American Review,* XXXVII (July, 1853), 59–84.

trine of Self-Reliance. The Reverend James Freeman Clarke put it well by writing that phrenology:[24]

inspired courage and hope in those who were depressed by the conscious-ness of some inability. . . . Phrenology showed us how, as Goethe says, our virtues and our vices grow out of the same roots; how every tendency has its danger, and every dangerous power may be so restrained and guided as to be a source of good. . . .

The study of mental illness had progressed rapidly in the United States before phrenology encouraged more intensive research. Al-though treatment of the insane was much more enlightened and humane by the 1830s, the theory of insanity was still largely unexplored. A few doctors, following Benjamin Rush, suggested that mental illness might have physical origins, while others experi-mented with mesmerism and hypnotism. No distinction was made between the mentally retarded and the mentally disturbed; some physicians still treated both with drugs, confinement, and massive bleedings. The rise of psychology as a separate branch of research, however, changed the basis of theorizing about the aberrations of the mind. Upham's *Elements* in its 1839 edition included an entire section on "Imperfect and Disordered Intellectual Action"; and when he wrote the volume on insanity for *Harper's Family Library* in 1840, Upham made the brilliant suggestion that "the causes of mental irregularity" might be in the mind itself, in elements "intimately connected with the mind's interior nature and secret impulses." This took the study of insanity and mental deficiency away from medicine and placed it within psychology. New develop-ments came swiftly. Dr. William Sweetser's *Mental Hygiene* (1843) was the first book to recognize psychosomatic illness, while the title itself suggested analogies between emotional balance and physical health. The Association of Medical Superintendents of American Institutions for the Insane, which became the American Psychiatric Association, was founded in 1844, the same year that Brigham's *Journal of Insanity* appeared. For the first time, during the forties, psychologists separated the insane from the idiot and the feeble-minded, differentiating their treatment. Whether mental illness and deficiency were the results of disorder in or injury to the brain

24. Davies, *op. cit.*, 169. On Walt Whitman's use of phrenology, see Harold Aspiz, "Educating the Kosmos," *American Quarterly*, XVIII (Winter, 1966), 655-67.

(as English and German authorities held) or whether their causes were emotional rather than physical (as the French contended) was a matter for long debate, nor was it settled for another generation. Still, the point was that insanity and idiocy were being defined in psychological terms and considered as psychological problems.[25]

By 1820, American medical science was apparently better than ever before. Although standards varied widely, the profession had established most of the necessary basic medical institutions—societies, schools, certification procedures, hospitals, journals—which had not existed fifty years earlier. Communication with British and European research was quickly reestablished after the War of 1812, so that American doctors were well aware of the latest foreign developments. However, basic medical research in the United States was scanty, hampered by lack of record-keeping and of funds. Medicine was still a battlefield of conflicting theories. There were Cullenians and Brunonians, "bleeders," "sweaters," "purgers," "vomiters," and "blisterers," although most of the better-trained physicians now avoided the savage therapy of some of their predecessors.[26]

Lacking a theory to explain the causes of disease, physicians did not know how to diagnose, classify, or attack them. In 1836 *The Boston Medical and Surgical Journal* listed sixteen different kinds

25. See Richard H. Shyrock, "The Beginnings"; Henry Bunker, "American Psychological Literature"; and Albert Deutsch, "The History of Mental Hygiene," in Gregory Zilboorg, *One Hundred Years of American Psychiatry* (New York, 1944).

26. See Russel B. Nye, *The Cultural Life of the New Nation 1776–1830* (New York, 1960), 75–81, for a sketch of medical theory 1776–1830. Cullenians, followers of Scottish physician John Cullen, believed disease originated in debilitation of a "nervous force" emanating from the brain. Brunonians, following Dr. John Brown, considered disease an imbalance of "excitability" in the body. Most diseases were to be cured, therefore, by exciting or suppressing tensions. Depressants including bleeding, sweating, purgation, blistering, and diuretics; there were four methods of bleeding, eighteen purgatives, eleven emetics, and six blistering agents in common practice. Excitants included mercury, iron, copper, lime, iodine, wine, fruits, alcohols, and fifteen other stimulants. Prescriptions became extremely complicated, with one for "rickets and muscle strains" containing a combination of twenty-eight different excitants and depressants in a solution of lard, suet, and wine. See Henry B. Shafer, *The American Medical Profession 1733–1850* (New York, 1936), 96–115.

of "doctors" then in practice, among them root, herb, magnetic, botanic, hydropathic, and floral.[27]

Despite improvements in medical theory and practice, it was obvious that American mortality rates were rapidly rising. Deaths from degenerative and malignant diseases remained constant; deaths from infectious and epidemic diseases (especially among children) rose enormously. Scarlet fever, measles, croup, whooping cough, and diphtheria killed children by the thousands; pulmonary tuberculosis (or "consumption") killed young and old alike; enteritis, malaria, typhus, typhoid, asthma, Asiatic cholera, rheumatism, yellow fever, gonorrhea, and various fevers were endemic, although vaccination seemed to be reducing smallpox. Neither country nor city life was particularly healthy. An Illinois country doctor in the fifties could predict, as one did, more or less what his seasonal practice would be—winter, pneumonia (called "winter fever"), colds, coughs, diphtheria; spring and summer, dysentery, "summer complaint" (a diarrhea that struck infants), various cuts, bruises, and accidents; autumn, "chills and fevers," the "ager" or the "shakes." Diphtheria was not supposed to be communicable, and tuberculosis neither communicable nor curable.[28] Malnutrition and hookworm, neither one yet recognized by doctors, were widespread in the West and South. The most dreaded epidemic diseases were cholera, typhoid, and yellow fever. In Boston, between 1840 and 1845, 40 percent of all deaths were children under five; the average age of death for the city's total population 21.43 years. In Massachusetts during the fifties, the life expectancy for males was 38.7 years; for females 40.9 years. In the nation at large the rate for males was about 35.[29]

The nation's greatest medical problems lay in the growing cities, which provided concentrations of poverty and disease such as Americans had never before known. Disease in the city was visible

27. John A. Krout and Dixon Ryan Fox, *The Completion of Independence* (New York, 1944) , 293.

28. Edgar Martin, *The Standard of Living in 1860* (New York, 1942) , 240–1.

29. Richard Shyrock, *Medicine in America* (Baltimore, 1966) , chapter I; Dirk J. Struik, *Yankee Science in the Making* (Boston, 1948) , 236. A yearly attack of malaria was considered normal on the frontier. Remedies included sassafras tea, bourbon and boneset, soot in boiling water, slippery elm, and so on. The standard sailor's cure for gonorrhea was application of gin and black pepper.

and violent; urban conditions for illness were well-nigh perfect, with substandard housing, inadequate sanitation, infectious food supplies, and few effective health regulations. New York City still had hogs scavenging its streets in 1849, and only seventy miles of sewer in the city. House privies and water closets drained into underground vaults where the sewage soaked into the ground or was hauled away. In poorer sections, sewage often ran into drain ditches which emptied into the nearest stream. An 1852 housing report in Cincinnati revealed one tenement with 102 people and one privy. Garbage collection was sporadic, street-cleaning casual. Urban mortality rates rose as city population increased. New York, a typical case, had a death rate of about 21 per 1,000 in 1810 and 37 per 1,000 in 1857, or an increase of 80 percent. Savannah, in a natural malarial pocket, had a death rate during the twenties and thirties of 70 per 1,000.[30]

Constant waves of epidemics ravaged the cities yearly. Cholera swept most of the country's major cities in 1832, 1849, 1850, 1854, and 1866. (The microorganism responsible was not identified until 1883.) Yellow fever struck in 1841, 1850, 1853, and 1855; for reasons never understood, it lessened in Northern cities after 1825 but increased in virulence in the South. In New Orleans in 1847 yellow fever left 2,000 dead, while in 1852 it killed 1,300 in one week and 8,000 over the three summer months. At what point and to what degree did government—local, state, and national—assume responsibility for the health of its urban citizens? Even the most rudimentary statistical studies showed a clear correlation between living conditions and the death rate. The fact that Boston's mortality rate began to decline after the city began regular street-cleaning seemed to indicate some relationship between filth and disease, while physicians noticed that typhoid epidemics hit hardest at those areas of New York City where "waste water drained into yards and alleys . . . , and broke into cellars and foundations."

Since diseases like cholera and yellow fever penetrated the better sections of cities and killed the wealthy as well as the poor, city community leaders joined eagerly with physicians and social reformers in demands for protection. Control of epidemic diseases required quarantine, isolation, and sanitation, all of which could

30. Charles N. Glaab and A. Theodore Brown, *A History of Urban America* (New York, 1967) , 84–88.

be accomplished only through government action. After 1820, cities and states began to establish Boards of Health which passed laws, fixed health standards, gathered vital statistics, and encouraged medical research. The Boards usually had limited authority, but they did succeed in introducing health legislation at local levels and consolidated public support. After 1858 many Boards met at National Sanitary Conventions and during the Civil War worked closely with the United States Sanitary Commission. The fact that five-sixths of all war deaths were attributable to disease called tragic attention to the problem and led to the creation of a national body, the American Public Health Association, in 1872.[31]

Medical education, meanwhile, was improved and extended. In 1810 there were six medical schools in the United States (Columbia, Pennsylvania, Dartmouth, Harvard, Yale, and Transylvania), but during the next decade twenty more appeared, between 1830 and 1840 thirty more, and between 1840 and 1850 at least another thirty.[32] Some of these were second- and third-rate institutions, of course, inadequately staffed and funded; others were little more than diploma mills. Almost any physician or group of physicians could start a medical school, get it attached to a college, and obtain a state charter. State and local medical societies could do little; Jacksonian legislatures, fearful of "monopolies," hesitated to pass laws controlling such enterprises and in some states actually opposed them. Attempts at licensing by medical societies bogged down in battles between rival schools of medical theory, political partisanship, and claims of preferential treatment.[33] Anyone with a

31. Richard Shyrock, "The Early Public Health Movement," in *Medicine in America*, 126–38; and chapter XII of *The Development of Modern Medicine* (New York, 1947). For epidemics, see John Duffy, *Epidemics in Colonial America* (Baton Rouge, 1953); Charles E. Rosenberg. *The Cholera Years* (Chicago, 1962); and John Duffy, *Sword of Pestilence: The New Orleans Yellow Fever Epidemic of 1853* (Baton Rouge, 1966).

32. Francis R. Packard, "Some Medical Schools Founded During the First Half of the Nineteenth Century," *A History of Medicine in the United States* (New York, 1963), II:735–823. Cincinnati had a medical school as early as 1819, New Orleans in 1834, St. Louis in 1840. Rush Medical College in Chicago opened in 1837, when the city had only 3,000 population. For a complete account, see William F. Norwood, *Medical Education in the United States Before the Civil War* (Philadelphia, 1944).

33. By 1845 ten states had repealed their licensing laws, eight had never had any, and only three made serious efforts to enforce what they had. See Richard Shyrock, *Medicine and Society in America 1660–1860* (New York, 1960), 149–61;

theory about the cause and cure of disease could open a school for training practitioners. Such schools, which flourished especially in the South and West, ground out hundreds of "doctors" who opposed any attempts at regulation. Although figures are difficult to obtain, one authority has calculated that there were 11,000 medical school graduates in the decade 1841–51 who called themselves "doctor," a ratio of doctors to population five times as high as that of France, the most medically advanced nation in Europe. As one editor of a medical journal wrote sadly in 1857, the profession seemed to be "a body of jealous, quarrelsome men, whose chief delight is the annoyance and ridicule of each other."[34]

Almost all doctors were in general practice, and despite popular belief, a doctor's income was not high. Practically all treatment took place in the doctor's office or at the patient's home; there were only 149 hospitals in the entire country in 1873. Most physicians charged according to a "fee table" fitted to the economic realities of his practice. A country doctor might make $3,000 a year; an aggressive city physician in the fifties could make $80,000.[35]

The better medical schools built their curriculum about courses in anatomy, physiology, and chemistry, followed by instruction in materia medica, pharmacy, obstetrics, and elementary surgery. Requirements for licensing, although they varied widely, usually required at least some study with a physician and two courses at a medical college. Dissection still faced public opposition, but it was usually part of the medical course, rigorously controlled by law. However, the American Medical Association, founded in 1847, gradually began to require longer terms of study, interning, higher faculty qualifications, and more rigorous examinations. In 1849 the

Packard, *op. cit.*, chapter XII; and Joseph B. Kett, *The Formation of the American Medical Profession* (New Haven, 1968), chapter I.

34. Shyrock, *Medicine and Society*, 147, 250 ff.; Kett, *op. cit.*, chapter II.

35. Shafer, *op. cit.*, 160–62. A Washington, D.C., fee table in the forties, for example, showed that an office visit and a prescription cost $1, a night visit $5–10, and one beyond the city limits $8 and up. Cures for gonorrhea cost $10, syphilis $15, delivery of a child cost $21 by day and $15 by night, operations $40–100, minor amputations $5, vaccination $3, stitching up cuts $3. However, a later study showed that 75 percent of medical school graduates left the profession, presumably for financial reasons, within five years.

Association established examining boards which approved qualified schools, the first major step in certification.

The period 1830–60 also saw the emergence of such ancillary medical professions as pharmacy and dentistry. Horace Hayden, a soundly trained physician, lectured on dentistry at the University of Maryland as early as 1825 and helped to found the Baltimore College of Dental Surgery in 1840, the first institution to grant the D.D.S. degree. That same year dentists in New York formed the American Society of Dental Surgeons, and only four years later the first dental supply house, the S. S. White Company, appeared in Philadelphia. Technically, American dentistry was well advanced; dentists made good false teeth for $8 to $20 during the twenties and used gold fillings by 1825. Although dentists were not considered to be part of the medical profession, they were not discriminated against by physicians, as they were in Europe. Dental schools developed rapidly after 1840 and soon American dentistry was probably the best in the world.[36]

Nursing was not yet a profession, and almost all nurses were males; there were about eight or nine thousand of them in the country at the outbreak of the Civil War, casually trained if at all. The idea that a woman might nurse a man or another woman, and might be trained to do so, had not yet occurred to the medical profession. A few hospitals trained women as nurses in the fifties and sixties, but nursing as a career for women was not established until after the Civil War.[37] Although many doctors continued to compound their own medicines, pharmacy emerged in the thirties as a supplementary medical profession. The Philadelphia College of Pharmacy (1821) was a pioneer; Massachusetts College in Boston followed in 1823, New York City College in 1829, the University of Louisiana in 1838, and the University of Maryland in 1843. Pharmacists had stiff competition from manufacturers and purveyors of "patent" medicines, but they attained professional status fairly

36. James E. Dexter, *A History of Dental and Oral Science in America* (Philadelphia, 1876), 10–20. Other prominent dental schools of the period were Ohio College (1845), Pennsylvania College (1856), Philadelphia College (1863), the New York College of Dentistry (1867), and Harvard Dental School (1867). The American Dental Association was founded in 1859.

37. Edgar Martin, *op. cit.*, 223–7.

soon. The American Pharmaceutical Association, founded in 1852, was but five years younger than the American Medical Association.[38]

Despite considerable progress in education and organization, the medical profession in the pre-Civil War years faced a number of very real problems. Division and disarray within its ranks, lack of regulatory laws, and wide variations in standards tended to undermine public confidence. There were still epidemics, a great deal of sickness and suffering, and high mortality rates. Despite optimistic talk of the future, the public could contrast the great strides made by the physical and biological sciences with the floundering uncertainties of medical science, much to the latter's disadvantage. It seemed to the public that all old theories of disease were wrong and all new ones uncertain; the best medical authorities admitted that they did not know what caused diseases, or what cured them, nor did they even know how to identify and classify them. Until medical science could evolve a workable body of general theory, it had to compete with such rival systems as phrenology, dietary reform, mesmerism, and faith healing.

One of the most difficult problems for the medical profession was that presented by the "patent" medicine. If all illness came from a single cause, or if all diseases were variations of a single basic disease, as older medical theory postulated, then a medicine that removed the cause or cured the master disease was logically possible. Many claimed—sincerely and insincerely—to have found it. It also seemed equally logical (as early medical theory proposed) that if God put diseases on earth he also put their cures on earth too; thus patent medicines advertised themselves as "Natural remedies" or as curing by "Nature's Way." The idea of healing oneself appealed to the average American's self-reliance, to say nothing of his pocketbook; for that matter, most patent medicines were often more palatable (and sometimes safer) than those prescribed by some physicians. There were so many common nagging ills the doctors could not cure—worms, fevers, rheumatic pains, headaches, colds, "irregular bowels," "general weakness," "female complaints"—that the ordinary man could hardly be blamed for trying something which promised relief. Patent laws lent themselves easily to proprietary remedies; legislation concerning such medicines was lax; the

---

38. Shyrock, *Medicine and Society*, 117–53; Packard, *op. cit.*, 525–26.

rise of newspapers and magazines gave manufacturers a magnificent opportunity to advertise them.[39]

The sudden popularity of patent medicines in the early nineteenth century reflected the current lack of public confidence in medical science; a drug catalogue of 1771, for example, listed not one such medicine, while one for 1804 listed ninety.[40] Samuel Lee of Connecticut, who patented his "Bilious Pills" in 1796, made a fortune from them over the next forty years. Richard Lee of New York City, in the twenties, sold Grand Restoratives, Elixir, and Worm-Destroying Lozenges; Michael Lee of Baltimore made and sold almost exactly the same array of cures in the thirties. Thomas Dyott of Philadelphia, who sold at least a dozen medicines, founded a school to train apprentices and salesmen, and price-cut a good many of his competitors out of the market. William Swaim's "Swaim's Panacea" was a household word, while Dr. Benjamin Brandeth, who spent $100,000 a year on advertising, by 1862 was taking in $600,000 a year.[41] There were perhaps two hundred patent medicines on the market in 1865. Many did little good or little harm; on the other hand, some contained sufficient opium or alcohol to create addicts and alcoholics. They wasted the money of rich and poor, raised false hopes in the ill and aged, and kept the sick from seeking medical help. Nor was there much the medical profession could do.

Much more serious threats to orthodox medicine, however, were posed by three rival systems which appeared almost simultaneously in the thirties and forties—hydropathy; "Thomsonism," or botanic medicine; and homeopathy—all supported by well-organized

39. A useful summary is D. L. Dykstra, "The Medical Profession and Patent and Proprietary Medicines During the Nineteenth Century," *Bulletin of Medical History*, XXIX (1955), 401–19.

40. See James Young, *Toadstool Millionaires* (Princeton, 1961), 31–93, for the most comprehensive study of patent medicines in this period.

41. Young, *op. cit.*, 75–89 *passim*. Swaim's mixture contained sarsaparilla, oil of wintergreen, and corrosive sublimate, a dangerous mercury compound that undoubtedly killed some who took it. Brandeth's Pills were merely a powerful purgative. Other medicines popular in the period were Hunter's Red Drop, Madam Gardion's Specific, and Mothe's Capsules (all for venereal disease); Wishart's Cordial, Morse's Indian Root, Dr. Ticknor's Antiseptic Refrigerant, Merchant's Gargling Oil, Swift's Botanic Blood Balm, and the famous Hostetter's Bitters.

groups and all offering easily understood and believable theories of disease and cure to a receptive public. The hydropathic school of medicine was built on the theory that the internal and external use of water was a natural and effective curative for the majority of ills, excepting broken bones and obvious surgical cases.[42] The idea was of course not new; the curative powers of bathing were known to the Greeks and Romans, while the eighteenth century's interest in mineral springs and spas carried over into the nineteenth. The water cure could be self-administered, except in its more complicated forms; was simple, logical, and gave the individual responsibility for his own health.[43]

American interest in hydropathy in the early nineteenth century came from the work of Vincenz Priessnitz, who in 1829, in Silesia in Germany, opened a hydropathic hospital with forty-five patients. He devised eighteen different kinds of baths (not including sponges, showers, and various internal dosages), combining his water cure with a strict regimen of grain, vegetables, and exercise. By 1843 he had 1,500 patients and his methods were known all over the world. German hydropathy was introduced to the United States by R. T. Trall, who opened a water-cure hospital in New York in 1844, and by Joel Shew, who opened his at Lebanon Springs, New York, in 1845. Trall and Shew were skillful publicists. Shew's *Water-Cure Manual* (1847) and Trall's *Hydropathic Encyclopaedia* (1857) both sold in the thousands; Shew's periodical, *The Water-Cure Journal,* had a subscription list of 10,000 per month in 1850 and 50,000 a month in 1855. Trall, Shew, and others (among them Orson Fowler, the phrenologist) made extravagant claims for hydropathy, listing over fifty diseases it could cure. Other hydropathic doctors elaborated the system by introducing steam baths,

---

42. The most complete study is Harry B. Weiss and Howard Kemble, *The Great Water Cure Craze: A History of Hydropathy in the United States* (Trenton, N.J., 1967). An excellent contemporary estimate is "The Cold Water Cure," *The New Englander,* V (April, 1847), 150–61.

43. Hydropathy rested on two assumptions. First, that water, since it was nature's most plentiful chemical compound, must have many uses as yet undiscovered; and second, that the body could cure itself by the use of "natural" agents of which water was obviously the most natural. Artificial drugs, chemicals, "sanatives and elixirs" were dangerous substitutes for nature's remedies; actually, they tended to paralyze the body's ability to eliminate diseased matter and thus hindered cures. See "The Cold Water Cure," *op. cit.,* 160–1, for a summary of these arguments.

Turkish baths, sitz baths, wet-sheet treatments, and other refinements.[44]

Shew, Trall, and others formed the American Hydropathic Society in 1849, reorganized later as the American Hygienic and Hydropathic Association of Physicians. A number of hydropathic training schools opened in the fifties, but the majority of hydropaths (an ominous sign for the older medical schools) were traditionally trained physicians; of those listed in *The Water-Cure Journal*, in fact, about 70 percent were M.D.s. By the mid-fifties there were at least thirty major water-cure institutions, stretching from Maine to Mississippi, not including dozens of mineral-springs hotels and resorts which advertised hydropathic treatments.[45]

It became clear by the sixties, however, that hydropathy was moving away from medical theory toward reform. Since many of the ills that water could cure were caused by "bad air, improper light, over-exertion, unregulated passions . . . and unphysicological voluntary habits," as Trall wrote, it was best to begin with the causes. Many hydropathic institutions therefore adopted an anti-tobacco, anti-alcohol, anti-coffee-and-tea regimen and gave instruction in dress reforms, religion, and sex as well as the usual baths and dosages. (A few even had matrimonial bureaus.) By the seventies, the hydropathic element in these institutions had almost disappeared, the emphasis placed instead on exercise, diet, mental calm, and personal and spiritual development. The institutions themselves generally became "sanitariums" or "health resorts."[46]

Samuel Thomson, the originator of "botanic medicine," was a New Hampshire farmer who based his cures on herb remedies, which, he said, combined with steam baths, restored the body to proper temperature and cured the disease.[47] Herb medicines were

44. H. F. Phinney's *The Water Cure in America* (1848) reported two hundred cures of difficult diseases, claiming endorsements by Longfellow, Lyman Beecher, Horace Greeley, Calvin Stowe, and other prominent people.

45. See George E. Walton, *Mineral Springs of the United States and Canada* (New York, 1883) for this aspect of the hydropathic movement.

46. Dr. John Harvey Kellogg in 1875 began a systematic study of the physiological effects of water and diet at his Battle Creek, Michigan, sanitarium, and in 1901 published *Rational Hydropathy*, marking the final transition from water cure to health reform.

47. All life, said Thomson, was composed of four elements—earth, air, fire, and water—maintained at the correct degree of heat. A drop in body heat caused ill-

the most important element; his prescriptions derived from sixty basic herb mixtures (patented in 1813) listed in a textbook which, with a license to practice, cost $20. In 1813 he joined forces with an itinerant evangelist named Elias Smith (whom he cured of "bilious cholic") who helped him promote his system nationwide. Thomsonism was especially popular in the rural areas and small towns of the South, West, and New England, where herb doctors had been known for generations.

There were sufficient botanical doctors in 1832 to hold a national convention; they published journals, founded schools, and established their own societies. Thomson, however, soon had a rival, Worcester Beach, who published a competing manual, *The American Practice of Medicine*, in 1833, based on an "Eclectic Medicine" composed not only of herbs but minerals, which Thomsonians would not prescribe. Both systems (and there was little difference) spread swiftly. By 1840 it was estimated that three to four million people were treated annually by "botanic" physicians.

Botanical medicine, whether Thomsonian or Eclectic, presented a serious threat to orthodox medical practice, for Thomson carried his attack on the profession into politics. Actually, he claimed, under his system men could cure themselves, despite claims to the contrary by the medical monopoly; botanic medicine was thus a blow against privilege, a popular movement to make health available to all at little cost. Since it was a "natural" system of healing, with its materia medica placed on earth by God's own hand, it therefore possessed a kind of divine sanction. Thomson, an ardent Jacksonian, managed to convey the impression that Old Hickory himself approved of the system, and it was not unusual for anti-

---

ness by affecting glandular and organic processes; the cure therefore lay in restoring the proper temperature by steam baths and "natural" botanic medicines. For more complete explanations, see Kett, *op. cit.*, chapter IV; J. C. Furnas, *The Americans* (New York, 1969), 442–5; and F. L. Packard, *op. cit.*, II:1227–30. Thomson's theory obviously reflected a mixture of the old "humours" school, Cullenian and Brunonian theory, and hydropathy. Botanic medicine was also buttressed by an old folk theory that for every disease within a geographical area, there must be a plant that treats it, placed there by a kindly deity. This theory received support from the work of botanists, especially from Constantine Rafinesque's *Medical Flora; or Manual of Natural Botany of North America*, published in Philadelphia 1828–32. John D. Rockefeller's father was a botanical doctor in Ohio, where in the 1830s about one-third of all doctors were Thomsonians or Eclectics.

monopoly and workingmen's political groups to endorse it. Divisions within the ranks, however, and Thomson's death in 1843, robbed the movement of much of its force, and many of its adherents moved into hydropathy, dietary reform, and temperance.

The basic principle of botanic medicine suggested another approach to the problem of health—through diet. Since food and water were the mainstays of life, supplied in profusion by Nature and a kindly deity, the key to health might well be through diet and bodily discipline, or "nature's way." Dietary reform, since it placed the responsibility for his own well-being on each individual, and since it seemed to fit into the pattern of other self-generated quasi-medical systems like hydropathy and mesmerism, appealed to the public quickly. "Physical reform," editorialized the *Boston Health Journal* in 1840, "is second to no other in importance—we believe it lies at the foundation of others, and that wherever it is effected, there will the efforts of other reformers be effectuated."[48]

In truth, many nineteenth-century ills probably were the result of American dietary habits. Food was often poorly prepared under unsanitary conditions, and overindulgence in eating was particularly common; people ate stupefyingly huge meals of fried foods, fat meats, and few and overdone vegetables, all in prodigious amounts. Cookbooks recommended a standard "three meat, three dessert" menu for the average home meal, whereas a ceremonial banquet might offer thirty different meats and fishes at a single sitting, to be consumed over a five- to seven-hour span. Pork, salt or fresh, or in the form of bacon and ham, was the staple of American diet. Gout, dysentery, and dyspepsia were pervasive alimentary ailments. The *Encyclopaedia Americana* in 1830 said of dyspepsia that "all classes and ages suffer from its attacks. Few are so happy as to pass through a life of ordinary duration, without undergoing protracted struggles with this malady."[49] Physicians, who had no effective remedies whatever for dietary ills and no information of value on nutrition,

48. Quoted by Richard Shyrock, *The Development of Modern Medicine* (New York, 1947), 118, see also 253–7.

49. An excellent popular history of dietary reform is Gerald Carson, *Cornflakes Crusade* (New York, 1957). A dinner served for William Appleton of Boston in the fifties, for example, included oysters and fish, five meats, five birds, five kinds of pie, and three puddings. Records left by a typical farm family in Illinois in the forties showed three meals a day of coffee, hominy soaked in lard, and pork in one form or another for weeks at a time.

could offer only emetics, laxatives, drugs, and bloodlettings. In addition, the nineteenth-century American bathed seldom, took little regular exercise, rarely opened windows, and avoided sunlight.[50]

William Metcalfe, an English clergyman, brought a shipload of converts to Philadelphia in 1817 to establish a vegetarian church and colony. Vegetarianism flourished in the United States, one of its chief exponents being Dr. William Alcott, Bronson Alcott's cousin, who declared that "a vegetable diet lies at the basis of all reforms." The American Vegetarian Society, founded in 1850, published *The American Vegetarian*, later renamed *Food, Home and Garden*. A number of medical men seriously experimented with diets. Dr. Isaac Jennings of Ohio advocated a diet of spring water and wheat bread; Dr. Russell Trall, also a hydrotherapist, proposed one based on milk and sugar; Dr. James Caleb Jackson combined dietary reform, hydrotherapy, and physical exercise as the basic regimen of a "health sanitarium" at Dansville, New York, in 1858, the prototype of dozens of similar institutions established later in the century, when the diet-health movement reached its peak.[51]

The most influential figure in the movement, however, was undoubtedly Sylvester Graham, who after beginning his career as a temperance lecturer in 1830 evolved the most comprehensive and convincing body of theory of any of the health proponents of the era. Since a healthy body resisted illness, Graham reasoned, and the right food made a healthy body, diet therefore must be the most important weapon in fighting disease. He began with bread, man's most common food, advocating the use of "natural" or unbolted wheat flour (exemplified in "Graham bread" and "Graham crackers") and moving on to the development of an entire "natural diet" of grains, vegetables, fruit, and water. Tobacco, coffee, tea, pickles, spices, liquors, fried foods, and many meats were gradually added to the taboo list. Margaret Fuller, for example, when she visited Horace Greeley in New York, found that his diet consisted of beans, potatoes, boiled rice, milk, and Graham bread. Graham's

50. Richard H. Shyrock, "Sylvester Graham and the Popular Health Movement," *Mississippi Valley Historical Review*, XVIII (December, 1931), 172–84, is an excellent summary of health trends in the earlier nineteenth century.

51. See Carson, *op. cit.*, for accounts of this movement. Dr. Jackson invented Granula, the progenitor of cereal breakfast foods.

program was soon extended to include sensible dress, personal hygiene, exercise, sex habits, and culture of the mind. "Grahamite" boarding houses and hotels appeared in the cities, ladies formed health clubs, health and diet magazines appeared everywhere, and dozens of camps and sanitariums were established on Graham's principles. Later, in the nineteenth and early twentieth centuries, a whole health industry grew from his teachings.[52]

Graham and the dietary reformers, unlike the patent medicine manufacturers, had an overall beneficial effect on American public health and posed much less of a threat to the medical profession. Convincing a generation that it ate too much meat, starch, and fat, and making the public conscious of its need for physical exercise and self-discipline, was in itself a major contribution to the nation's health. While it may have smacked occasionally of cultism, the dietary movement's emphasis on sun, air, personal cleanliness, and sensible food habits did far more good than most other such paramedical systems. On the other hand, the popularity of Grahamite and other diets did encourage the acceptance of simplistic cure-alls and did little to augment public confidence in the medical profession, since they were based on so-called natural cures.

The most serious threat of all to traditional medicine was homeopathy, which had impeccable medical credentials and a sophisticated theory behind it. The last of the "single-cause" theories of disease, homeopathy's central postulate was that most illnesses were forms of an internal irritation which upset the body's "vital principle"; illness could be cured by the prescription of drugs which produced an effect like the disease—that is, "like cures like."[53] Samuel Christian Hahnemann's *Organon of the Rational Art,*

---

52. See Mildred V. Naylor, "Sylvester Graham, 1794–1851," *Annals of Medical History,* IV (May, 1942) , 236–40; Shyrock, *op. cit., Mississippi Valley Historical Review;* J. C. Furnas, *The Americans* (New York, 1969) , 440–42; Carson, *op. cit.,* chapter IV. Graham's *Lectures in the Science of Human Health* (1837) provided a cornerstone for the movement. The American Physiological Society, also 1837, was founded to propagate his ideas, while the American Health Convention in 1838 advocated courses in hygiene, diet, and physiology in the public schools. There were about eighty health magazines published in the United States between 1830 and 1890, the most prominent being Graham's own *Journal of Health and Longevity.* His popularity on lecture tours prompted some newspapermen to label him "The Peristaltic Persuader."

53. See Kett, *op. cit.,* chapter V; and William King, ed., *The History of Homeopathy and Its Institutes in America* (New York, 1905) , 4 volumes.

published in Germany in 1810, a convincing exposition of the theory, became the handbook of the movement.[54] Hans Gram, an American-born Dane, opened a homeopathic office in New York in 1825 and converted others; William Wesselhoeft practiced in Massachusetts; and Constantine Hering went to Pennsylvania, where he founded Allentown Academy (later the Homeopathic College of Pennsylvania), the most influential of the early homeopathic training institutions.[55]

Homeopaths had nothing to do with politics, fads, or diets, and had fairly rigorous professional training in chemistry, pharmacology, surgery, physiology, and botany. They did not directly attack other theories; they simply claimed that their methods strengthened the body's natural tendency to cure itself, while "allopathic" (from "allos," Greek "aller," or traditional) medicine tended, as one homeopath said, "to ignore nature and her powers." The system immediately attracted public support. By the mid-thirties graduates of homeopathic schools were in practice in most of the states; there were homeopathic medical societies; and homeopathic journals, books, and manuals circulated widely. The meeting held in Cincinnati in 1849 to form a national professional organization attracted a thousand delegates. Homeopathy was simple to explain and logically consistent; it shared terminology and training with orthodox medicine and made use of all the advances of chemistry, physiology, and instrumentation that were available to other physicians. In most communities homeopaths and allopaths were accorded equal status.

However, as basic medical research improved, homeopathy gradually waned. Certain absurdities in homeopathic practice—for

54. Disease, said Hahnemann, was a general derangement of an "immaterial vital principle" that kept the entire body in balance. There were three chronic "miasmas" which caused imbalance—syphilis, sycosis (inflammation of the hair follicles), and psora (a skin itch). The disordered "vital principle" could right itself under normal conditions but needed assistance when disarranged by abnormal miasmic imbalance. The process of re-establishing inner harmony was best initiated by small doses of drugs which produced symptoms similar to the disease, producing a physical state which would stimulate the vital principle to greater effort, thus helping the body to heal itself. Homeopathy (similarity of feeling) owed obvious debts to the inoculation principle and to the Brunonian theory of "excitability."

55. The Hahnemann Medical College of Philadelphia opened in 1848, New York Homeopathic College in 1860, and the Hahnemann Medical College of Chicago the same year.

example, the extreme dilution of drugs and their multiplication—
had adverse effects on public opinion. Later in the century, in a
head-on collision, allopathic medicine won and homeopathy disappeared. Yet, as Dr. Oliver Wendell Holmes, one of its most effective critics, wrote, it made a not inconsiderable contribution to
medical progress by helping to eliminate "the system of over-
drugging, and overdosing" as well as the massive bleedings and
purgations that so long characterized medical practice.[56]

Despite the appeal of such alternate medical systems, the problem
of establishing professional controls, and the difficulty of regaining
public confidence, the medical profession during the decades 1830
to 1860 did make significant advances. First, the introduction of
statistical methods into medical record-keeping quickly proved of
inestimable benefit to theoretical research. Vital records, of course,
had been kept since the eighteenth century, often in hit-or-miss
fashion, but the medical profession's lack of statistical tools made
them of limited use.[57] Without statistics, it was impossible to establish relationships between the treatment of an illness and its result
or to check the accuracy of old and new theories. The usefulness of
statistical mathematics, which developed swiftly in England and
France, was immediately apparent to medical researchers; for the
first time it was possible to gain accurate information about the
incidence and treatment of disease, about death rates and public
health, about such socially significant matters as accidents, suicides,
venereal disease, insanity, alcoholism, and so on.

Statistics were equally important in establishing regulations for
public health. The statistical work of such men as Lemuel Shattuck,
Edward Jarvis, and George S. Shattuck of Massachusetts proved to
be of especial importance. They were among the founders of the
American Statistical Association, formed in 1838, while Lemuel
Shattuck's report on public health to the Massachusetts legislature
in 1850, although it lay unnoticed in the files for another thirty
years, was one of the most important medical documents of the

56. Holmes's devastating essay, "Homeopathy and Kindred Delusions," appears
in *Writings* (Boston, 1901), IX:1–102.

57. Records of the Philadelphia yellow fever epidemic of 1793, for example,
seemed to indicate that patients who received treatment died faster than those
who did not, but no one could analyze the information the records contained. For
the importance of statistics to the public health movement, see Struik, *op. cit.*,
234–36.

century. Also, by the sixties the physician had at hand a whole new series of drugs (or older drugs about which he now knew much more), among them morphine (discovered 1804), quinine, strychnine, emetine, iodine, ergot, epsom salts, and a dozen more. He also had a number of new, sophisticated instruments which made diagnosis more rapid and accurate—the clinical thermometer was in general use by the thirties; the stethoscope, ophthalmoscope, otoscope, and graduated hypodermic needle by the sixties. The improved microscope, for example, provided new information about the role of microorganisms in disease and pointed the way toward parasitology, bacteriology, and eventually antisepsis.

The strongest influence on American medicine was France, the most medically advanced of any nation. By 1830 Paris had thirty hospitals and 5,000 medical students, while Pierre Louis and others were making it a science, based on systematic observation. Under French influence, the old "single-system" theories of disease—that it was caused by imbalances of fluids, or nerves, or humours, or electricity, and so on—were quickly destroyed. In the thirties, American medical students began to leave English and Scottish medical schools, which had trained most American physicians up to that time, for France and Germany. Oliver Wendell Holmes studied in Paris under the great Louis before returning to take his M.D. at Harvard in 1836; other well-known Americans like James Jackson, Henry Bowditch, William Gerhard, and Alfred Stillé were also Paris-trained.[58] The French concept of tracing disease or illness to a specific organ or bodily part—that is, pathological medicine—was the greatest single factor in redirecting medical research in the United States. Illness could now be studied not as a person dying of "inflammation of the lungs," but as an example of a general pulmonary condition which could be identified as tuberculosis, pneumonia, bronchitis, or pleurisy. Pathological medicine naturally led to surgery; once illness could be traced to a particular part of the body, it was logical to open the body to find and remove the cause.

Nineteenth-century American surgery was crude, as it was everywhere, usually learned by trial and error and limited to the body surfaces or extremities—amputating limbs, lancing boils, removing

58. Richard Shyrock, "The Influence of French Medicine in Europe and America," *The Development of Modern Medicine,* 170–92.

tumors, and the like. To quiet patients, surgeons used bloodletting, drugs like opium and henbane, soporifics such as brandy and "water of nightshade," or they simply numbed the limb by cutting off the blood supply with a tightened strap. American surgeons were as skilled and daring as any. Amos Twichell did a ligation of the carotid artery in 1808, Ephraim McDowell a laparotomy in 1809, and Horatio Jameson removed a jawbone in 1821, all before anaesthesia. America's greatest contribution to medicine, of course, was anaesthesia. The work of Crawford Long, W. T. G. Morton, Charles Jackson, and Horace Wells culminated in the successful use of ether in surgery at Massachusetts General Hospital on October 16, 1846, a landmark in medical history. Subsequently Drs. Morrill Wyman and Henry Bowditch (1850) were among the first to tap the pleural cavity, Erastus Wolcott did the first nephrectomy (1861), John Bobbs the first cholecystectomy (1867). American surgeons contributed to, as well as learned from, the great surgical techniques being developed in contemporary Europe and England.[59]

Although American medicine suffered from external competition and internal confusion, it made substantial progress during the pre-Civil War years. There were still physicians who sweated and purged, patent medicine manufacturers who made fortunes, and "steam doctors" or Eclectic physicians who dosed patients with herbs, but there were more and better doctors being trained and more research in medical theory than ever before. Much was being discovered about drugs, hygiene, and sanitation. The growth of medical societies—thirty-four state and local societies by 1865— established professional standards, raised morale, and provided means of professional cooperation. Americans were in constant communication with British and European practices, and well abreast of the work in epidemiology, antisepsis, microbiology, and surgery that soon would irrevocably change the nature of medical theory and practice. Physicians also had a larger number of publications to serve as means of internal communication. There were, in fact, 213 different medical journals published in the country before 1850; although many lasted no more than a few issues, at least twenty major publications remained.[60] Developments in support-

59. Allen O. Whipple, *The Evolution of Surgery in the United States* (Springfield, Illinois, 1963); Francis Packard, *op. cit.*, II:1053–1119.

60. George Daniels, *American Science in the Age of Jackson* (New York, 1968), chapter I.

ing sciences, such as chemistry, biology, and physiology, stimulated medical research and were quickly absorbed into it. Dr. Samuel Gross of Cincinnati, looking into the future from 1861, could see nothing ahead but progress. The next half century, he wrote, would see one of the "most widespread revolutions in medicine that the world has ever witnessed . . . destined to convulse the profession, and exert a most powerful influence upon the practice of the healing art."[61]

61. Shafer, *op. cit.*, 249.

CHAPTER 10

Educating a Nation

LINKED with the great social movements of the eighteenth and early nineteenth centuries, both in Europe and America, was the belief that truth would set men free. Knowledge was considered to be one of the most powerful instruments of social change; every cultural institution, therefore, was called upon to distribute learning, so that each individual could fulfill his own and his society's potential. Schools—from kindergarten to university—were of course considered the primary means of supplying the populace with what it needed to know, but beyond them were other agencies of education, new and old, which could be brought into the service of the people.[1]

One of these agencies was the Sunday school. In the seventeenth century children received instruction on Sundays in some New England churches, a practice that continued sporadically into the eighteenth century. In 1780, however, a philanthropist, Robert Raikes, established a charity school in England for poor children which met on Sundays, their only time for instruction. The Sunday School Society which derived from Raikes's classes enrolled a quarter-million English children within the decade.

A few Americans founded schools on the English pattern, but it

1. For expressions of this feeling, see "Popular Education," *North American Review*, XXIX (July, 1829), 241–58; and "Diffusion of Knowledge," *Ibid.*, XXX (April, 1830), 293–313.

was not until after 1800 that the idea took hold.[2] The organization of the Union Society of Philadelphia (1804) marked a new start; cities like Pittsburgh, New York, Boston, and Baltimore soon followed. These schools, aimed at children six to fourteen, emphasized (as the English schools had) the skills of literacy, adding Bible study and Christian principles to instruction in reading and writing. Staffed by voluntary lay teachers, supported by lay contributors, and sponsored by lay societies, these Sunday schools—although they often met in churches—were not solely religious schools.

Promoted by groups like the American Bible Society and the American Tract Society, the movement spread quickly; in 1824 the various societies combined in the American Sunday School Union, which served them as a coordinating and publishing agency. Controlled wholly by laymen (clergymen could not serve as officers), the Union's function was to bring schools to communities where no group or church maintained one of its own. Meanwhile, age boundaries were widened to include preschool infants, young adults, and, later, older people.[3]

The Union also embarked on a huge publishing program, issuing in its first six years over six million books and sponsoring three periodicals; through its services one could buy an entire twenty-four-volume library for $10. It helped to establish six thousand Sunday schools with enrollments of four million, and it founded a thousand libraries. The Union could proudly say that for a whole generation of Americans it encouraged "a prevailing habit of reading and thinking . . ., produced habits of sobriety, temperance, and reverence for the Sabbath . . ., and has done specific, visible, and tangible service to the State."

2. "The Sunday School Movement in the United States," *Encyclopaedia of Religion* (New York, 1945), 745-47; E. Wilbur Rice, *The Sunday School Movement* (Philadelphia, 1917); and Marianna C. Brown, *The Sunday School Movement in America* (New York, 1961) provide good general information. Sunday schools were established in Virginia in 1785 and South Carolina in 1790. The Sabbath, or First-Day School Society of Philadelphia (1790), was one of the earliest successful urban ventures.

3. Sunday schools usually had four grades: an infant section, emphasizing reading and writing skills; an elementary section, concentrating on spelling and advanced reading; the Scripture grade, devoted to Bible study; and a senior section, with advanced Bible study and discussion groups. See Frederick C. Packard, *A Popular Sketch of the Rise and Progress of Sunday Schools in the United States* (Philadelphia, 1845).

The interdenominational nature of the Sunday school, however, did not satisfy some churches, who while supporting the Union saw advantages in having their own schools for their own purposes. The Methodist Episcopal Church in 1827 organized its own, the Unitarians theirs in 1830, and the Lutherans in the same year. By the forties most Protestant denominations had their own Sunday schools, stressing catechical training, confirmation classes, and denominational theology. By 1860 the Union, recognizing the trend, suspended operations except to sponsor yearly conventions. Nonetheless, the interdenominational, lay-controlled Sunday school, over the thirty-odd years of its existence, was an educational agency of real importance and a valuable adjunct to the early public schools.[4]

Beyond the schools there existed a multitude of societies, associations, and institutes to educate the general public. Following the British example, hundreds of mechanics' and workingmen's "institutes" appeared in the thirties; "young men's associations," debating societies, "literary" societies, and other organizations provided instruction to people at low cost and with minimum requirements for enrollment.[5]

The Franklin Institute, founded in Philadelphia in 1824, was typical; its purpose was

the advancement of science and the mechanic arts, the increase of useful knowledge, the encouragement of invention and discovery, and the education of the public in the achievements of science and industry.

Such institutes flourished in every major city and most smaller ones; wealthy philanthropists like Lowell (Boston), Peabody (Baltimore), and Cooper (New York) endowed their own, which were, in effect, people's colleges. In addition, some cities opened the public schools to evening classes for those who, "by nature of their occupation, are prevented from attending day schools." Between 1830 and 1850, twelve cities held regular night schools, a practice expanded considerably in the fifties and sixties.[6]

4. A brief account is William Bean Kennedy, *The Shaping of Protestant Education* (New York, 1966), chapters I and II.
5. See "Popular Lectures," *The New Englander*, VIII (May, 1850), 201, and "Young Men's Associations," *Christian Examiner*, XV (September, 1833), 120-33.
6. Malcolm S. Knowles, *The Adult Education Movement in the United States* (New York, 1962), 27-30. Cleveland, for example, in 1850 enrolled 135 students in its first night class. In Buffalo evening classes were so crowded in 1851, the first year, that it increased the number to twelve; Cincinnati opened a night high school in 1856.

In rural areas the agricultural societies, after a slow start, organized institutes and sponsored discussion groups. In 1839, beginning in Massachusetts, state boards of agriculture held farmers' institutes, which, although they distributed information chiefly about farming, were also in effect educational agencies. The United States Agricultural Society, formed in 1852, reported in 1860 that there were 941 agricultural societies in the country which held institutes; and with the establishment of the Department of Agriculture in 1862, the federal government itself assumed responsibility for rural education.

The most effective means of popular education during the nineteenth century, however, was the lyceum, a self-supporting, locally controlled, voluntary association that played a vital role in the development of American culture. Although the "Thursday lecture" and similar community meetings were part of a long American tradition, the formal organization of the lecture system as a public service did not come until the 1820s, beginning with a pamphlet published in 1826 by Josiah Holbrook, suggesting an "American Lyceum of Science and the Arts." Lyceums, he believed, would diffuse useful knowledge, produce good citizens, and "raise the moral and intellectual taste of our countrymen."[7]

Millbury, Massachusetts, established the first lyceum on Holbrook's plan in 1826; within two years there were a hundred and by 1834 three thousand in fifteen states. In 1831 lyceum delegates met in New York to form the American Lyceum Association, which organized a nationwide chain of local, county, and state lyceums. By the forties every state had lyceums which not only sponsored lectures but maintained libraries and museums, organized classes, and published teaching materials. They were formed, said a contemporary participant, "for the mutual improvement of their members and the common benefit of society. . . . All declare, by joining a lyceum, that they wish to extend their knowledge, and from the

7. Carl Bode, *The American Lyceum: Town Meeting of the Mind* (New York, 1956) is the best study. See also Cecil B. Hayes, *The American Lyceum* (Washington, 1932) and David Mead's study of the lyceum in Ohio, *Yankee Eloquence in the Middle West* (East Lansing, 1951). Holbrook was influenced by similar agencies in England and was preceded by Augustus Woodward, who founded the Detroit Lyceum in 1818; see Richard Weaver, "Prelude to an Institution," *Michigan History*, LIV (Spring, 1970), 29–45.

manner in which they associate each may become, by turns, a learner and a teacher."

The real strength of the lyceum system lay at the local level, and despite the symmetry of its table of organization, the state and national societies soon began to break up. The American Lyceum Association itself ended in 1839 and many of the state societies were gone by the mid-forties, but the lower-level organizations thrived into the seventies, when most of them were absorbed into commercial, professionally run lecture agencies which emphasized entertainment rather than culture. For thirty years or more, however, the lyceum's impact on American culture was enormous.[8] It was of great assistance to the leaders of the public school movement and operated as a lobby for it. But more important, it served cities, towns, and the newer communities of the West as a focus for the kinds of cultural activities that neither church nor school provided. "Here is a pulpit," wrote Emerson, who knew from experience what impact the lyceum could have, "that makes all other pulpits ineffectual."

A well-run lyceum might present, over a season, lectures on literature, science, philosophy, history, music, and current events, as well as scientific demonstrations, humorous talks, and travelogues. Almost every intellectual figure of the times appeared on the lyceum platform—Agassiz, Melville, Beecher, Webster, Everett, Sumner, Phillips, Mrs. Stowe. There were national favorites like Henry Giles, who spoke on Cervantes, Burns, Shakespeare, Hawthorne, and other literary figures; Parke Benjamin and John G. Saxe, witty popular poets; John B. Gough, a reformed alcoholic; world traveler Bayard Taylor, who spoke on Egypt, Japan, Palestine, and Russia, sometimes dressed in appropriate costume; "Dr. Boynton," who lectured on electricity, geology, and physics. What they gave their audiences was culture in easily assimilated form, reaching an enthusiastic, literate public that no other agency touched so effectively.[9]

8. Bode, *op. cit.*, believes that the lyceum as originally conceived—that is, as an informal, mutual and self-improvement educational agency—began to change into a "lecture system" in the late forties, turning gradually into a commercialized system after the Civil War when professional booking agencies like Redpath (1868) and Pond (1878) dominated the field.

9. For the lecturer, the lyceum was a valuable source of income. Three-quarters of Emerson's essays began as lectures, while nearly all of Taylor's travel books

Still, advocates of culture agreed, the best educational tool was a book. Access to books—as Franklin and his generation proved—was the key to learning. Franklin's first public venture, his Philadelphia Library Company (1731), was the progenitor of dozens of such libraries over the next century, aimed, as Franklin's original prospectus said, at the improvement of "citizens in the middle and lower walks of life." By Jackson's time, the demands of special-interest groups for their own libraries changed the situation considerably.

"Subscription" libraries on Franklin's plan were not, in a sense, "public" libraries, since they charged a fee and restricted circulation to members. "Association" libraries, another form of subscription library, were controlled by voluntary associations of individuals who contributed money to buy books for their common use. These might be debating clubs, literary societies, "Young Men's" or "Young Ladies' " associations, or "athenaeums" which (on the British model) maintained book collections and reading rooms like the Boston Athenaeum Society's.[10]

Although association libraries were open to any who could pay the fee, their cost, a Boston newspaper pointed out in 1824, was "incompatible with the means and wants of a great part of society." This had already occurred to William Wood, a wealthy New England merchant, who in 1819 began gathering books for "mechanics' and merchants' " libraries and who established a library for seamen at Brooklyn Navy Yard. Wood, by tireless effort, encouraged clerks and apprentices in the Eastern cities to form (as Franklin had) associations of their own which, with outside support, could collect books fitted to their needs. Soon, by the thirties, nearly every city had one or more such libraries, supported partially by fees and

---

were adaptations of his lecture series. Emerson lectured fifty-six times in Ohio alone over a seventeen-year span; Taylor was there eighty-five times over sixteen years. For one Cincinnati lecture Emerson received $471, which covered the expenses of his entire lyceum tour. See Bode, *op. cit.*, 224–35. In Marshall, Michigan, one could hear Emerson for $1, which included an oyster supper.

10. Useful sources of library history are Charles S. Thompson, *The Evolution of the American Public Library* (Washington, 1952) and Thelma Eaton, ed., *Contributions to American Library History* (Champaign, Ill., 1961). These associations also sponsored lectures and discussions and kept "cabinets" of scientific and historical materials for study. For a specialized study, see C. K. Bolton, "Proprietary and Subscription Libraries," in Eaton, 91–99.

by contributions from philanthropists, employers, and in a few instances from civic funds.

The larger mechanics' and apprentices' associations did far more than simply circulate books. The Boston Apprentice Library, for example, subscribed to dozens of magazines, twenty newspapers, held classes in literature and elocution, sponsored lectures, and published an eight-page newspaper of its own. The "mercantile" libraries, though similar, were directed at the needs of young men in business—clerks, officeboys, messengers, and others who were preparing for careers in banks, stores, clearinghouses, and the like. The spread of public colleges and technical schools after midcentury, and the founding of public libraries, reduced the need for such associations, although some of them continued through the nineteenth century.[11]

In addition, there were "circulating" or rental libraries which charged a fee for borrowing books, usually in conjunction with a bookstore, stationery shop, or newsstand. Endowed libraries, established by wealthy philanthropists, lent books to members of the community under certain restrictions; churches organized their own libraries, supervised by the minister or a church officer. School libraries were sometimes opened to parents and citizens; several states had a rather extensive system of school district libraries, patterned on New York State's. Adding together all such library facilities, there were obviously many "public" libraries in nineteenth-century America, in the sense that there were collections of books open to the public everywhere, either free or for a nominal charge.

The concept of a free, public library was thus not unfamiliar to educationally minded citizens; Salisbury, Connecticut, in fact, opened a free library for children in 1803, supported by local

11. Thompson, *op. cit.*, 76–96. See also Sidney Ditzion, "Mechanics' and Mercantile Libraries," *Library Quarterly*, X (April, 1940), 70–91. The New York General Society, a mechanics' library, served over a thousand young men in 1829 from a ten-thousand-volume collection. The range of the New York Mercantile Society's shelf-list in the thirties revealed the members' interests—it bought subscriptions to *The Edinburgh Review, Blackwood's,* and *The North American Review;* sets of Burns, Irving, and Shakespeare; and books on French and Italian history. It had its own publication, *The Mercantile Library Reporter,* and its own professional librarian. In 1835 it bought a full eighty-five-volume set of *The Transactions of the Philosophical Society of London.*

appropriations.[12] Peterborough, New Hampshire, is usually credited with establishing the first library which was open to all residents of the town without charge, financed by public tax funds. Over the next twenty years similar libraries appeared in a few New York and New England small towns. The turning point came with the founding of the Boston Public Library in 1848, under the leadership of Joshua Bates, Edward Everett and George Ticknor.

The establishment of a free public library in a major metropolitan community, based on a carefully articulated plan of service to the public at large, provided the impetus the movement needed. The Astor Library in New York, the Peabody Library in Baltimore, and others followed suit. By 1860 the public library was firmly established as an integral part of the nation's cultural pattern. There were, that year, approximately 10,000 public libraries in the United States, with holdings of about eight million volumes. In comparison to the total number of libraries (there were 48,000 Sunday school libraries alone) this did not seem to constitute a large percentage, but since most of them were in urban areas, they served a disproportionately large segment of the public and provided a sound base for postwar expansion.[13]

The concept of the museum as an instrument of popular education developed simultaneously as part of the same trend toward the democratization of knowledge. Museum collections of various kinds, of course, had existed since the eighteenth century, but for somewhat different purposes. The earliest public museums derived from the historical societies which proliferated after the Revolution; as the new republic searched diligently for its historical identity, these collections gave the present tangible links with its past.[14]

12. See Thompson, op. cit., 114–28, on free public libraries; also Robert E. Lee, Continuing Education for Adults Through the American Public Library 1833–1964 (Chicago, 1966) , and J. L. Harrison, "The Public Library Movement in the United States," Eaton, op. cit., 30–42. Indiana's 1816 Constitution required each county to set aside 10 percent of its land sales for "the use of a public library," but few actually did.

13. The Boston Public Library was established in 1848, began to lend books in 1849, and was formally opened in 1852.

14. The Massachusetts Historical Society's and the New-York Society's collections were among the earliest and largest. See Thomas R. Adam, The Museum and Popular Culture (New York, 1939) , 5–8. For general treatments of museum history, consult Alvin Schwartz, Museum (New York, 1967) ; Herbert and Marie Katz, Museums, U.S.A. (Garden City, 1965) ; and particularly Laurence V. Cole-

Most common among early museums were those devoted to "natural history" or science—the earliest of all in America, in fact, was probably the collection of materials "relating to the Natural history of South Carolina" assembled by the Library Society of Charleston in 1773. As the teaching of science spread through the schools, colleges like Harvard, Yale, and Dartmouth brought together collections for instruction and for the edification of the visiting public. The new academies of science, like those in Philadelphia, New York, and Baltimore, gathered materials for study and display in their libraries and laboratories.[15] Private collectors also arranged "cabinets" for public display and entrepreneurs opened museums to the public for an entry fee. Charles Willson Peale's Philadelphia Museum (1785) was the hit of the era, so successful that his sons Rembrandt and Rubens opened similar museums in Baltimore and New York. Phineas T. Barnum, of course, led the field after he opened his own in 1842.[16] The growth of lyceums and libraries, too, contributed to the interest in museums; both often arranged educational displays, some of which (as Worcester's did) became the base for large and important collections.

The American museum, then, by midcentury, was considered—like the lyceum—as a useful instrument for popular education. Some, of course, like Barnum's, emphasized entertainment, but those controlled by academic societies, libraries, and schools did not. As the educational aspects of the museum received greater notice, changes in museum policy followed. A number of the more alert institutions arranged study collections for specialists and in-

man, *The Museum in America* (three volumes, Washington, 1939). A useful summary is that by Solan Weeks, "The Development of the Museum Movement in America," *Michigan History*, XVVI (March, 1962), 33–50.

15. Dartmouth and Harvard had museums in 1784; Yale's Peabody Museum was founded in 1802. The Maryland Academy of Science's museum dated from 1797, the Philadelphia Academy's from 1812, the New York Academy's (an ancestor of the American Museum of Natural History) from approximately 1818. Many state geological surveys, after completing their work, gave their collections to college museums.

16. See H. and M. Katz, *op. cit.*, chapter I. Edmund Savage's "Columbian Gallery" in New York (1801) was purchased by John Scudder, whose American Museum (1812) was purchased by Barnum, who also bought Rubens Peale's. Rembrandt Peale's Baltimore Museum building (1814) was the first structure to be built in the United States specifically for the purpose.

troduced a system of changing exhibits for the month-to-month visiting public, a policy still followed by most museums. In the fifties, another development altered the entire museum concept; that is, the preservation of the "historic house" or "historic site" by restoring it to its original condition, which gave the visitor an increased sense of realism and participation. The first such reconstruction was Hasbrouck House, which had once served as Washington's headquarters, in 1850. The most rapid development of this kind of museum activity, however, came after the Civil War, inspired by the centennial celebrations of 1876.[17]

Visitors to the United States rarely failed to express amazement at Americans' almost compulsive reading habits. The nineteenth-century reading public, in contrast to Britain's and Europe's, was not only well educated (about 90 percent literacy in the white population) but already addicted to print. Boston had fifty bookstores by the 1770s, Philadelphia and New York thirty or more, and peddlers hawked books up to the edge of Indian country in the backwoods. By 1825 the libraries of the five largest cities in America had twenty times more books to *lend* than the entire country *owned* in Washington's youth. Americans of all classes simply took literacy as a matter of course. "Every mechanic worth anything at all," wrote a Boston publisher in the fifties, "must have a small library which he calls his own."

The newspaper, by the opening of the nineteenth century, had developed into a uniquely American institution. After the Revolution the rate of increase was proportionately far in excess of the growth in population—in 1801 there were about two hundred newspapers in the United States but in 1833 about 1,200. Active, energetic, sometimes scurrilous and not always honest, the American press was a vital component of American cultural life.[18]

All the elements for a journalistic explosion were present in 1830.

17. See Weeks, *op. cit.*, 38–40. By 1895 there were twenty such houses open to the public. The federal government began to take an active part in the preservation and restoration of historic sites and buildings in 1889, beginning with Indian cliff dwellings and Civil War battlefields, a policy which culminated in the Historic Sites Act of 1935.

18. For general histories of American journalism, see Frank Luther Mott, *American Journalism: A History of Newspapers* (New York, 3rd. ed., 1962); Robert W. Jones, *Journalism in the United States* (New York, 1947); and Sidney Kobre, *The Development of American Journalism* (Dubuque, 1969).

New steam-powered, double-column presses could print 4,000 copies an hour; the rotary press, introduced in 1847, produced 8,000. The increase in the population—which doubled between 1790 and 1830, and doubled again before 1870—created a tremendous market. As a result, the United States was a nation of newspaper readers. Almost every town of moderate size had a daily paper, sometimes several, and even remote frontier settlements could boast a weekly. Very little happened in the nation, anywhere at any level, that did not appear in the press, which was a matter of great importance in a democratically based culture.

Journalism was a highly competitive business, chances for profit or loss great, casualties high. The appearance of the "penny press," or cheap mass-circulation paper, was preordained by market conditions. Benjamin Day's New York *Sun* (1833) showed the possibilities for a new kind of paper, priced at a cent, which printed a wide range of news that included scandal, sports, a bit of sex, and anything else of interest.[19] Day's formula was so successful that his daily circulation reached 19,000 in a few years (passing the London *Times*) but the *Sun* was quickly overtaken by James Gordon Bennett's New York *Herald* (1835), which not only printed everything the *Sun* did but added a financial page, a society page, illustrations, and telegraphic news. Bennett's aim was frankly to sell papers; he made the newness of news important, inventing the "scoop" or "beat" to give the reader a sense of immediate involvement.

Bennett's formula was followed and expanded by some editors, played down by others. Horace Greeley's New York *Tribune* (1841) exerted a powerful influence because of Greeley's domination of New York journalism. The New York *Daily Times* (1851), under Henry J. Raymond, emphasized political independence and extensive foreign coverage. All major cities had at least one eminent paper—such as Boston's *Atlas*, the Philadelphia *Ledger*, the Pittsburgh *Gazette*, Cleveland's *Plain Dealer*, the Chicago *Weekly Democrat*, and smaller cities too had papers like the Hartford *Courant*, the Toledo *Blade*, and the Springfield *Republican*. It was also an age of powerful editors who had personal followings and

19. Day's paper may have been the first to use advertising as a major source of revenue, thus helping to reduce the sale price. On the "penny press," see Kobre, *op. cit.*, chapter 8, "Penny Press Leaders."

great influence—Parke Godwin and William Cullen Bryant of the New York *Post,* James King of the San Francisco *Bulletin,* George Kendall of the New Orleans *Picayune,* George Prentice of the Louisville *Journal,* John M. Daniel of the Richmond *Examiner,* Joseph Medill of the Chicago *Tribune,* Murat Halstead of the Cincinnati *Commercial.* No nation at any time was perhaps so thoroughly covered by the press, nor at any other time in American history were newspapers so politically and culturally influential. The South was less well served than the West and North. The total circulation of all daily papers in the South before 1860 was less than the combined sales of the New York *Herald* and the New York *Tribune;* furthermore, fewer Southern than Northern or Western papers were politically independent.[20]

The American newspaper, as it developed during its era of expansion, was an educational and cultural medium of major importance. It existed in greater numbers and variety than anywhere else in the world. It was unusually mobile, quickly following population wherever it went—Minnesota, for example, had forty printing offices before it became a state. It was localized, regionally centered, tied closely to the community, reflecting local society, issues, and interests; there could never have been a *national* American newspaper under such conditions. In addition, it was relatively free, in comparison to the press of England and Europe, of government controls and censorship.

Magazines, like newspapers, proliferated in response to the market—some 3,000 of them were being published in 1860—and like newspapers they differed widely in quality, permanence, and circulation.[21] The wave of magazine publishing that flooded the years after 1790 began to recede by 1830, with a few survivors, like the *North American Review* (1815) and the *American Quarterly Review* (1827), entrenched in a relatively small, well-educated market. The *Knickerbocker* (1833) published in New York and the

20. Allan Nevins, *Ordeal of the Union* (New York, 1947), III:80–91 is an excellent brief treatment of the newspaper in the period.

21. The 1860 census listed 3,383 magazines, of which the majority were labeled "political publications" and "religious publications." See Edgar Martin, *The Standard of Living in America in 1860* (New York, 1942), 313–30, for useful statistics. The standard reference is Frank Luther Mott, *A History of American Magazines* (five volumes, Cambridge, 1938–68), but a good summary of magazine publishing during the period is Kobre, *op. cit.,* chapters 6 and 16.

Southern Literary Messenger (1834) published in Richmond were excellent literary journals but, like the *North American,* were restricted to upper-class readership. Political magazines, such as *The Democratic Review* (1837) and *The American Whig Review* (1845), appealed to special interests and never reached mass circulation. The most important political publication was probably the Washington *Globe,* founded in 1830 by Francis Blair and ably edited by John Rives, whose purpose was to furnish accurate reports of Congressional debates, helping to make the American public the best-informed politically of any in the world.

The first magazine to tap the huge popular market was *Graham's* of Philadelphia (1826), which under the aggressive editorship of George Graham set the pattern for the market-oriented, mass-circulation magazine to come. Since Graham paid exceptionally well, he attracted contributors of the stature of Lowell, Poe, Cooper, Willis, and Longfellow, as well as romancers like Ann S. Stephens and Mrs. Emma Edbury. *Graham's* was challenged by several competitors—*The Saturday Evening Post,* under Henry Peterson; N. P. Willis's New York *Mirror;* and *Harper's New Monthly Magazine* (1850), which soon dominated the field. Fairly expensive and consciously literate, *Harper's* printed novels, poetry, essays, articles, and specialized in illustrations. It sold 200,000 an issue by 1860 and had no real rival except the *Atlantic* (1857).

Louis A. Godey, in 1830, recognizing the potential market represented by millions of educated, feminist-conscious women, founded *Godey's Lady's Book,* specializing in female-slanted fiction, poetry, articles, and, most important, illustrated fashion news. Edited by Sara Josepha Hale for forty-one years, *Godey's* became a household standard. The success story of the era, however, was that of Robert Bonner, a young newspaperman who bought the New York *Ledger* on a shoestring in 1851 and made it into a periodical that fitted halfway between a newspaper and *Harper's.* Bonner paid high prices for popular writers like Mrs. E. D. E. N. Southworth and Sylvanus T. Cobb, and equally good fees for prestigious intellectuals. His payment of $10,000 to Edward Everett for a series in 1858 set a new standard. By 1860 the *Ledger's* circulation exceeded 400,000 a week.

Even Bonner, however, was eventually eclipsed by Henry Carter, a young Englishman who took the name of "Frank Leslie" and entered the field with *Frank Leslie's Illustrated Newspaper* (1855), followed by *Frank Leslie's Lady's Magazine, Frank Leslie's New Family Magazine,* and *Frank Leslie's Budget of Fun,* thus covering the market spectrum. *Harper's* entered the lucrative illustrated newspaper business in 1857 with its own, *Harper's Illustrated Weekly.*

Widely circulated as these journals were, their impact on popular thinking probably did not equal that of the religious magazines and the farm journals, whose individual circulations may have been less but whose numbers were far greater. Sectarian religious journals appeared by scores. There were nationally known church magazines like *The Methodist Quarterly* and *The Christian Examiner* and many smaller journals, often with regional interests, like *The Southern Presbyterian Review* and *The Baptist Magazine.* Rigidly sectarian, acrimonious in debate, and zealous in opposition to things like gambling, dueling, drinking, and other habits, they were powerful forces in molding public opinion. The farm journals, which printed a great deal of nonagricultural material, reached a segment of the public no other magazines did. There were many of them—*The Southern Cultivator, The American Agriculturalist, The Southern Field and Fireside, The Horticulturalist, The New England Farmer, The Country Gentleman,* and so on—often skillfully edited, covering a wide range of cultural interests. They carried general news, historical essays, travel articles, book reviews, and scientific information, as well as articles on health, sports, fashion, and education—but seldom partisan politics.[22]

The market for popular books offered similar possibilities.[23] Booksellers and publishers, during the 1820s, developed a different kind of relationship than before, more to their mutual advantage. Whereas previously they worked together to produce and sell a book, the publisher now printed it and sold it to the bookseller,

22. Albert Demaree, *The American Agricultural Press, 1819–1860* (New York, 1941) is the best source. Edmund Ruffin's *Farmer's Register* (1833) was particularly influential in the South, John S. Wright's *Prairie Farmer* (1840) in the Midwest. Wright for years maintained a reading room in Chicago for farmers visiting the city.

23. On the history of book publishing, see Hellmut Lehmann-Haupt, L. C. Wroth, and Rollo Silver, *The Book in America* (New York, 1952); Roger Smith, ed., *The American Reading Public* (New York, 1963); and William Miller, *The Book Industry* (New York, 1949).

who resold it to the customer at a profit. Book publishing thus became a professionalized business venture; by the thirties several of the great publishing houses—Harper, Matthew Carey, Thomas, Cummins and Hilliard—were established in the major cities. Meanwhile the invention of improved oil lamps (later gas) meant more reading hours per day for everyone, while the expanding network of roads and railroads meant cheaper and wider distribution for reading matter of any kind.

Publishers could never have produced the acres of print demanded by this huge audience, however, without a succession of technological innovations in the mechanics of printing. New processes for making paper improved the product substantially; meanwhile the number of paper mills in the country went from 150 in 1830 to 400 in 1840, 550 in 1860, 742 in 1880, and so on. Stereotyping came in 1811, electrotyping in 1841. David Prince in 1813 invented the cast plate, replacing the old plate of handset type that had to be broken up and reset.

New machines and methods seemed to appear every few years. Cheap cloth bindings, which drastically reduced costs, came after 1812; an improved bookbinding machine came in 1823; folding and sewing machines in the fifties, a backing machine in 1870, a gathering machine in 1900. During the 1830s the Napier and Hoe cylinder presses made the flatbed press obsolete; with steam power they could spin out thousands of impressions per hour from plates set by the new typesetters. The publishing industry by the 1830s could turn out books as rapidly as nails or matches.

The first revolution in cheap publishing came in the 1840s. The depression of 1837 nearly wiped out the book market, forcing publishers to try new methods of getting it back. One way to lower publishing costs, and thus price, was to use newspaper presses; a news sheet folded once, to make four pages, made a cheap booklike format. Furthermore, newspapers paid no special tax, were granted special mailing rates, and—in the person of the postman—had free delivery service. Even subscription payments could be franked free in the mails.

Taking advantage of this, Rufus Griswold and Park Benjamin founded a weekly periodical in New York called *Brother Jonathan;* although they called it a newspaper, it was really a collection of fiction. Their success brought on the flood—*The New Yorker, The*

New World, The Corsair (which openly pirated books), and a dozen others. Book publishers and regular newspapers retaliated with "supplements" on newsprint, selling them first at fifty cents, then at twenty-five cents, later at six-and-a-quarter cents.

After a time it all became somewhat ridiculous. Prices came down to five and six cents; issues increased in size and unwieldiness until a paper like *The Boston Notion* offered 104 square feet of reading for a nickel. In 1843 the Post Office Department changed the situation by charging book rates for papers and supplements, but cheap books remained. The major publishing houses, among them Harper, Lea and Blanchard, Post, and others, kept their paper-covered books on the market for twenty-five to seventy-five cents, bringing out new ones from time to time. Never again was the American reading public without a low-priced, mass-produced book.

American educational theory in the nineteenth century was drawn chiefly from European sources. Reports of the "new schools" of England and Europe, especially Germany's, were eagerly quoted in the American press and brought home by American visitors. Much of the current excitement derived from Jean-Jacques Rousseau's *Émile* (1762), which had challenged traditional educational psychology by asserting that the child had inborn natural instincts—curiosity, a love of activity, a capacity for sensation—which prepared him for education. A child should be educated, then, "in harmony with the nature of children," through "the natural development of mind," by contact with Nature and experience and not solely through books and externally imposed disciplines.

The most influential of the educational theorists who followed Rousseau was Johann Pestalozzi, a German Swiss, who also believed that the purpose of education was individual and social betterment. He experimented with new materials and methods, and with working out new relationships between teacher and pupil; like Rousseau, he stressed learning by the "object method," that is, by relating experience to knowledge. (A child, for example, learned numbers by counting stairsteps or windowpanes.) He also emphasized educating children for practical life, advocating vocational training as well as cultural and intellectual learning, an idea especially attractive to American educators.[24] His writings and the experimental school at Yverdon in Switzerland, of which he became director in 1805, drastically altered the course of American educational thinking. Pestalozzi's system required a much greater understanding of child psychology, which meant professionally skilled teachers. His emphasis on "natural" teaching and "object learning" made science an essential part of the curriculum. To focus attention on the development of the individual child meant a child-centered —not a teacher- or book-centered—school; as Emerson said, "Respect the child, wait and see the product of Nature." Then too, Pestalozzi's concept of learning as individual progress, and his belief in education as an agent of change, placed the school directly in the stream of contemporary reform movements and put it in a quite different social perspective.

Contemporary educational psychology was based on the "faculty" psychology of the times, derived from Locke's "powers of the mind." The mind, it was believed, was separate from the body, composed of "faculties" which could be identified, stimulated, and developed by exercise, training, and the provision of proper materials for their growth. The number and functions of these faculties tended to be vague, but in general they were all included in three general sets of powers: the understanding (reason, intellect, "head"); the sensibilities (affections, emotions, "passions"); and the will (volition, choice). This psychology, easily explained and understood, furnished a serviceable basis for the learning process. It was also equalitarian, minimizing the effects of heredity, environment, and cultural background, for it was assumed that all persons possessed these faculties, regardless of color, sex, economic or social condition. Faculty psychology fitted admirably into the Pestalozzian methodology, furnished a useful pattern for teacher training, and obviously reinforced the argument for free public schools.[25]

Americans who traveled in Europe, and Europeans who came to the United States, brought the new ideas across the Atlantic very

24. Frank D. Greaves, *Great Educators of Three Centuries* (New York, 1912) contains useful summaries of the ideas of the major educational philosophers. See also Joseph J. Chambliss, *Origins of the American Philosophy of Education* (The Hague, 1968), 6–25.

25. Vivian Thayer, *Formative Ideas in American Education* (New York, 1965), contains more complete discussion.

quickly. Joseph Neef, one of Pestalozzi's assistants, came to Philadelphia to found a school in 1809 which became the model for a number of similar experiments. In 1818 Professor John Griscom toured Britain and the Continent, and his report, *A Year in Europe* (1819, reprinted 1824), in the opinion of Henry Barnard became "the single most influential educational work of the nineteenth century." After Griscom, other Americans visited the Yverdon school, among them Alexander Bache, Horace Mann, Henry Dwight, Henry Barnard, George Bancroft, Joseph Cogswell, William Woodbridge, and Calvin Stowe, all of whom later lectured or wrote on German and Swiss educational theory.[26] A report on German education, published by French educational philosopher Victor Cousin and translated in 1834, was also widely read by American educators; educational journals discussed Pestalozzianism with enthusiasm, while major general journals, such as *The North American Review* and *The New England Magazine,* published essays and articles on the new education.[27]

Meanwhile experimental schools, modeled on various European schools, flourished and fell—among them schools founded by such men as George Bancroft, Bronson Alcott, and Robert Owen. American "normal" or teacher-training schools quickly adopted the new ideas, disseminated through such books on pedagogy as Samuel Hall's *Lectures on Schoolkeeping* (1829), Jacob Abbott's *The Teacher* (1833), and David Page's *Theory and Practice of Teaching* (1842). Warren Colburn's *First Lectures on Arithmetic* (1821), based on Pestalozzian principles, a standard text for a half century, was as much a landmark in the history of education as

26. Calvin Stowe's *Elementary Education in Europe* (1837), commissioned by the Ohio legislature, was distributed free to Ohio schools and reprinted for use in Massachusetts, Pennsylvania, Virginia, and North Carolina. Horace Mann's report to the Massachusetts legislature in 1843 was circulated throughout the country. Alexander Bache (Franklin's grandson) published a similar widely distributed report on his European tour in 1843.

27. Among these journals were Albert and John Pike's *Academician* (1818–20); William Russell's *American Journal of Education* (1826–30), which became *The American Annals of Education* (1831–39); *The Common School Journal* (1838–42); Henry Barnard's *American Journal of Education* (1855–66); Horace Mann's *Common School Journal* (1839–42); and *The Ohio School Journal* (1846–50). See B. A. Hinsdale, "Notes on the History of Foreign Influences Upon Education in the United States," *Report of the Commissioner of Education,* I (1897–1898), 618–21; S. C. Parker, *Modern Elementary Education* (New York, 1912), 297–98.

Webster's blue-backed speller.[28] Endorsed by the National Teaching Association in 1865 as its official pedagogical theory, Pestalozzianism remained the dominant American educational philosophy until the eighties, when it was gradually modified by the influence of another European, Johann Friedrich Herbart.[29]

Pestalozzi's insistence on the training of skilled teachers particularly impressed his American disciples. Professional teacher training was already accepted in Europe, but the American concept of "keeping school" rather than "teaching school" was far more general. Samuel Hall opened a private training institute, the first of its kind in America, in Vermont in 1823, and James Carter another in Massachusetts in 1827. In 1839 Massachusetts opened the first state-supported teacher-training school at Lexington. The New York legislature in 1832 designated certain academies as training schools (called "normal schools" from the French *norm,* meaning *standard* or *model*) , but by 1860 there were only eleven in the country, scattered from Massachusetts to Illinois.[30] Some cities, however, among them Boston, New York, Trenton, Baltimore, and St. Louis, had their own training schools, while some academies and colleges added training courses to their curricula.

Another result of Pestalozzi's emphasis on "useful" education and

28. Neef's *Sketch of a Plan and Method of Education* . . . (Philadelphia, 1808) became a standard text in teacher-training courses. He would teach students nothing, said Neef, but would provide them with opportunities to develop their own mental powers as nature intended. George Jardine's *Outlines of Philosophical Education* (1818) , published in Scotland, was also widely used in the United States. Jardine emphasized Neef's concept of teaching as allowing the student to learn, and advocated greater research into the learning process, believing that there was a "science of the mind" that could be applied to teacher training. James G. Carter, a New Englander, extended Jardine's ideas in his *Letter to the Hon. William Prescott* . . . (1824) and numerous articles in the *American Journal of Education* about "scientific" teacher training. See Chambliss, *op. cit.,* 15–22.

29. See W. S. Monroe, *A History of the Pestalozzian Movement in the United States* (Syracuse, 1907) .

30. W. L. Magnum, *The American Normal School* (Baltimore, 1928) is a good treatment; an additional useful source is Merle Bowman, ed., *Teacher Education in America* (New York, 1965) . Other state schools appeared at Albany (1844) , Ypsilanti, Michigan (1849) , and Illinois (1857) . Wages, however, failed to reflect increased training. In 1847 Massachusetts paid a male elementary teacher the nation's highest wages, $24.50 a month, and the highest-paid woman teacher $10.00 a month. Vermont paid the nation's lowest for men, $12.00 a month, for women $4.75 a month.

vocational training was the experimental "manual labor" school, or "labor institute." If experience were the best teacher, as Pestalozzians believed, work itself was clearly a valuable learning experience. A number of European schools were established on this basis and widely copied in the United States. Combining "learning and labor" (the motto of Oberlin College, founded 1833) appealed to American practicality and also helped a poor student pay his expenses. Encouraged by the Society for Promoting Manual Labor in Literary Institutions, formed in 1831, dozens of such schools appeared in the thirties and forties, while some already established colleges introduced "manual labor departments." The movement gradually faded, but the concept of "working your way through college" did not.

When the nineteenth century opened, no state had a system of public elementary, secondary, or higher education. In 1860 every state had at least the first two, while several had public colleges and universities. Traditionally, it was assumed that the responsibility for education of the child rested with his parents and that education was either a private or a religious enterprise. The private academy, the charity school, the church school—these were the usual educational agencies. Yet within the space of a generation the demand for schools that were not only free and open to the public, but of a different kind with different aims, forced the development of a uniquely American system.

The great push for public schools came from a number of different sources, and for a number of sometimes contradictory reasons. It came from humanitarian reformers and societies, who thought of mass education as a way of eventually eliminating crime, poverty, and degradation from American life; significantly, many of the leaders in the public-school movement were prominent reformers— Calvin Stowe, Lyman Beecher, Frances Wright, Thomas Gallaudet, Robert Owen, among others. Societies specifically concerned with promoting public education, like the Society for the Public Schools and the American Institute of Instruction, were often partners with other reform groups. Workingmen's organizations made demands for public schools part of their political platforms year in and year out. Conservatives, for their part, often regarded mass education as a protection against revolution and anarchy. Extension of the voting franchise to the laboring classes gave them unprecedented political power, which, to be wisely used, had to be used by educated voters. Daniel Webster favored public schools as "a wise system of police, by which property and life, and the peace of society, are secured."

Similarly, businessmen believed that better-educated workers supplied a larger skilled labor market and a greater number of consumers. Education could turn poor and paupers into wage earners for the benefit of all concerned. "The very taxes of a town," *The American Journal of Education* pointed out, "in twenty years will be lessened by the existence of a school which will continually have sent forth those who were so educated as to become not burdens but benefactors." Anti-Catholic elements were certain that more public schools would offset parochial ones; nativists thought public schools would quickly make Americans out of immigrants. And also, of course, the public school was regarded as a powerful democratizing force, one which cut across class and economic and cultural lines to create a naturally "American" society. The school was "the great equalizer of all conditions of men . . . the balance wheel of the social machinery."[31]

The demand was not only for a different kind of school, supported by and open to the public, but for a different kind of education, one more relevant to the needs of contemporary society. To Americans of the twenties and thirties "education" had a number of meanings. Learning for its own sake, or for the individual's sake—to develop his personal potential, improve his spiritual life, expand his intellect—was desirable and legitimate. At the same time, culture was not enough; education ought to be useful, functional, practical, productive of social good. Schools should train young men "for the ordinary business of merchant, farmer, and

31. Clarence J. Karrier, *Man, Society, and Education: A History of American Educational Ideas* (Glencoe, Ill., 1967), chapter III; Stuart Noble, *A History of American Education* (rev. ed., New York, 1961), chapter IX. Full studies of the public school movement are Paul Monroe, *The Founding of the American Public School System* (New York, 1940); Sidney Jackson, *America's Struggle for Free Schools* (Washington, 1941); Rush Welter, *Popular Education and Democratic Thought* (New York, 1962). See also Lawrence Cremin, *The American Common School* (New York, 1951); Merle Curti, *The Social Ideals of American Educators* (New York, 1935), chapter II; R. Freeman Butts and Lawrence A. Cremin, *A History of Education in American Culture* (New York, 1953), and Rena Vassar, *A Social History of American Education* (Chicago, 1965).

mechanic"; surely, said a group of Pennsylvania civic leaders in the thirties, "to write a common business letter, promissory note, bill or account, and in proper form, is the least that should be required of our common schools."

In addition, education ought to produce better and more patriotic citizens; schools should not only teach Americans how to vote properly, but should reinforce, wrote Horace Mann, "those articles in the creed of republicanism which are accepted by all, believed in by all, and which form the common basis of our political faith." The school also served with the church as a base for training a moral society of moral individuals. Though the public school was not a theological seminary, Mann agreed, it should "inculcate Christian morals . . . and welcome the religion of the Bible." In summary, the argument for the public school represented the thinking of relatively conservative, middle-class Americans; it was to teach useful skills, absorb the immigrant, secularize education, protect republican institutions, train responsible citizens, and instill in society the prevailing middle-class cultures, as represented by the content of Webster's *Speller* and McGuffey's *Reader*.[32]

On the other side of the issue were those who could see no reason why parents who could afford to educate their own children should pay to educate others'; if education was a personal, family, or church responsibility, the state had no business in assuming it. Others thought public education a plot to discredit religion by abolishing the denominational school; still others that it encouraged a dangerous leveling tendency. "I hope you do not conceive it necessary," wrote a correspondent to the Raleigh, N.C., *Observer,* "that *everybody* should be able to read, write and cipher." Many slaveholders quite naturally opposed the whole scheme. W. H. Trescott wrote in *DeBow's Review* that education in the South must be based on two principles: first, "that the state is not required to provide education for the great bulk of the laboring classes"; but required only "to afford that degree of education to

32. R. Freeman Butts, *The College Charts Its Course* (Philadelphia, 1939), 213–33; Karrier, *op. cit.,* 72–4. For representative contemporary discussions, see "National Education," *The York Review,* III (July, 1838), 149–95, with essays by Thomas Wyse, E. C. Wines, and Calvin Stowe; and Orville Dewey, "Popular Education," *North American Review,* XXXVI (January, 1833), 73–99.

every one of its white citizens which will enable him intelligently and actively to control and direct the slave labor of the state."[33]

The bitterest struggle over public education centered on its cost. Private and state endowments, land grants, licensing fees, and the like were never satisfactory methods of financing schools, and state support in its early phases was often inefficient and inconsistent. Tax support was obviously the only workable method, but this raised the basic issue of the debate—is education, paid for by the state, the inalienable right of every child? There were no easy answers. Nonetheless, between 1830 and 1860 the majority of Americans came to two conclusions about free, tax-supported education. They agreed that, first, each child possessed a natural right to education, guaranteed by the state, sufficient to provide him with economic security and the ability to exercise responsible citizenship; second, that the public schools should be nonsectarian, open to all qualified youth regardless of religious belief or financial status (but not regardless of color), and to be supported by funds raised by taxation of all citizens. The "will of God," wrote Horace Mann,

places the *right* of every child that is born into the world to such a degree of education as will enable him, and as far as possible will predispose him, to perform all domestic, social, civic, and moral duties. . . .

Massachusetts led the way in organizing public schools. James Carter, whose *Essays Upon Popular Education* (1826) was one of the first important publications in the movement, helped to write the Massachusetts Education Act, which shaped the state system and centralized its supervision and planning. The Act, passed in 1837, established a State Board of Education to which Horace Mann, a prosperous, reform-minded lawyer, was appointed secretary. A shrewd and practical man as well as a dedicated reformer, Mann dominated American public education in its early years. During his twelve years as secretary to the Board, Mann saw state appropriations doubled, two million dollars spent on buildings, teachers'

33. Butts, *op. cit.*, 200–02; *Southern Literary Messenger*, XIII (November, 1847) , 686; *DeBow's Review*, XX (January, 1856) , 148. An excellent collection of documents is Carl Gross and Charles Chandler, *A History of American Education Through Readings* (Boston, 1964) .

salaries raised by half, the school year lengthened by a month, and three teacher-training schools founded.[34]

Henry Barnard, who was made secretary of the Connecticut Board when it was appointed in 1838, was equally influential. Barnard founded the *American Journal of Education* (1855), the first nationally recognized professional educational journal, went West to become president of the University of Wisconsin, and later became United States Commissioner of Education. Mann's and Barnard's accomplishments were repeated in state after state, old and new; the new states in the Northwest Territory organized public systems of education as soon as they were admitted to the Union. Things moved more slowly in the South, where private academies and tutors had long educated the children of the planting class, but the Southern states were not so laggard as they seemed—in 1860 one Southern white child in seven was in school, as compared to one in six in the North. There was strong agitation among middle-class Southerners for public schools, and although the Civil War interrupted the trend, every Southern state by 1868 had established the pattern of a public school system.[35]

The tremendous increase in the number of schools caused great changes in the organization of the schools and their curricula. During the twenties, a child went to preparatory school at ages six to ten, and to an academy until fourteen or fifteen. In the forties he was sent to primary school from six to nine, to intermediate school from nine to twelve, and to grammar school from ten to fifteen. During the fifties most school systems were divided into elementary schools (ages six to fourteen) and academies and high schools (fourteen to seventeen or eighteen). Different systems might vary, but generally the principle was established that a pupil moved upward through graded stages, passing levels of competence, rather than by age alone.

34. See Lawrence Cremin, ed., *The Republic and the School: Horace Mann and the Education of Free Men* (New York, 1966); Louise Hall Tharp, *Until Victory: Horace Mann and Mary Peabody* (Boston, 1953); and E. J. F. Williams, *Horace Mann* (New York, 1937).

35. See Noble, *op. cit.*, chapter X, for a convenient summary. See also sketches of educators of the period in Merle Curti, *op. cit.*, chapters III, IV, and V, including the work of Calvin Stowe in Ohio, Caleb Mills in Indiana, Calvin Wiley in North Carolina, and others. Stowe's *Report on Elementary Public Instruction* (1839) was reprinted and distributed by the thousands in Massachusetts, Michigan, Pennsylvania, Virginia, and North Carolina.

The academy, developed in the later eighteenth century to replace the old "Latin school," was admirably adapted to the needs of the changing times. Financed by tuition fees, or subsidies from church or state or both, it taught what was needed, experimented with curricula, and prided itself on being the "poor man's school." To the classical curriculum, if students wanted it, academies added composition, mathematics, modern languages, sciences, or practical business courses. Some academies admitted girls; there were also academies for girls only, usually called "seminaries." Flexible, responsive to students' needs, and close to home, the academies merged easily into the public system and became high schools, some of which were first called "free academies."[36]

The public high school, like the academy, at first tended to maintain a two-track curriculum, the "classical" course and the "English" course (so-called because it was not Latin-based). The classical course emphasized such studies as rhetoric, literary study, and classical learning; while the other, as Boston Latin School said, "fitted the student more directly for active life, and . . . a foundation for eminence in his profession, whether mercantile or mechanical." However, the distinction gradually disappeared as both curricula introduced new subjects and changed the teaching of old ones—mathematics soon ranked next to the classics as a cultural study, and English literature, formal grammar, the sciences, civil government, and economics, along with bookkeeping, accounting, and business law, entered the high schools in the sixties. High schools (some admitting girls) to prepare students both for collegiate and noncollegiate careers were well established in the public school system after the Civil War.

As schools changed, so did schoolbooks. Post-Revolutionary American schools found British-originated books unacceptable, and as soon as the war was over American-written and American-published texts—particularly grammars, readers, and geographies—were on the market. Books in mathematics, the sciences, and philosophy, where nationalistic materials were less relevant, did not appear until later.[37] Since teachers were not always well trained, the textbook was usually the focus of the schoolroom. In an over-

36. See Leonard V. Koos, *The American Secondary School* (New York, 1922) for a complete study.

37. Charles Carpenter, *A History of American Schoolbooks* (Philadelphia, 1963), and John A. Nietz, *The Evolution of American Secondary Textbooks*

crowded school, or one with an unskilled teacher, reciting from the text was the most efficient method of learning and the one most easily tested. Teaching aids such as blackboards, globes, maps, and demonstration equipment did not enter the classroom until the later thirties, after lyceum lecturers had proved their effectiveness. A student in a poor school was lucky to have a slate and a book; he memorized the book, which gave him not only facts but concepts and attitudes which an untrained teacher might not be able to provide.

If, as contemporary educational theory presumed, schools were to teach morality and national pride, textbooks furnished excellent tools with which to do it. Webster's *Speller* was intended, he wrote, to instill children with "just ideas of religion, morals, and domestic economy" on the one hand, and "ideas of national character" and "American principles" on the other. Spellers introduced children very early to the meanings of words such as "republic," "tyranny," "liberty," "popery," and "monarch." Children learned from readers like *McGuffey's* that "God gives a great deal of money to some persons, in order that they may assist those who are poor," and to "Try, try again," and that "Governments derive their just powers from the governed."[38]

The speller provided the basic nonclassical text after 1750, and although Webster's dominated the market it had powerful competitors. Spellers contained a great deal of reading material (Hume, Addison, Goldsmith, Johnson, Blair, among others) and served as general cultural texts until "readers" began to displace them in the early nineteenth century. Lindley Murray's combined reader and speller was outselling Webster's by that time, but William Holmes McGuffey's *First Eclectic Reader* (1836) introduced a new kind of reading text. His books were graded in difficulty, profusely and aptly illustrated, and dealt with close-to-home experiences like ball-playing, farm chores, going to the store, and family life. He also

---

(Rutland, Vt., 1966), are excellent sources. Noah Webster's speller, grammar, and reader were published between 1783 and 1790; books like Caleb Bingham's *Columbian Orator* (1797) and Lindley Murray's *English Reader* (1799–1805 eds.) continued to sell well into the nineteenth century.

38. Ruth Miller Elson, *Guardians of Tradition: American Schoolbooks of the Nineteenth Century* (Lincoln, Nebraska, 1964), 1–5. See also Henry Steele Commager, "McGuffey and His Readers," *Saturday Review of Literature,* June 16, 1962, 50–53.

instilled more effectively than most others the virtues of thrift, work, morality, and patriotism. McGuffey was blessed with a shrewd sense of the interests of the times, and of a child's own interests as well; he also had a publisher with an aggressive sales organization. Literally millions of American boys and girls knew "Twinkle, Twinkle, Little Star," and "The Boy Stood on the Burning Deck," "The Boy Who Cried Wolf!," as well as the words of Washington, Patrick Henry, Webster, and Clay from McGuffey's pages. His *Sixth Reader* appeared in 1857, but by that time he had already edited a series of *Speakers* which were popular into the eighties. Truthfully it was said of him that he "taught millions to read and not one to sin."[39]

Among other standard texts were grammars—Webster's, published in 1784 but revised; Lindley Murray's (revised in 1808), Bullion's, Weld's *Parsing Book*—and rhetorics like Ebenezer Porter's *Analysis,* James Boyd's *Elements,* and Henry Day's *Elements of the Art of Rhetoric,* published in 1850 with twelve editions over the next ten years. Rhetorics not only taught composition and discourse, but served as texts for literary history and creative writing. Elocution texts, or "speakers," were much like readers, the selections of course chosen for reading aloud and dramatic expression. Handwriting was taught from copybooks, usually British in origin. Most schools taught the "Buckham Script," based on George Buckham's *Universal Penman* (London, 1733–34), until the publication of Joseph Perkins's *Practical Penmanship* (1830, 1836), which taught three different scripts for different purposes. Several new styles were introduced in the forties, until Platt R. Spencer, in 1848, devised a script which utilized the advantages of the newly invented steel penpoint. Spencer treated handwriting as an expressive art, and the flowing, ornamented Spencerian style gradually displaced the others for two generations.

The wave of expansion in higher education that began immediately after the Revolutionary War did not begin to recede until

39. Carpenter, *op. cit.,* chapters V, VI. Other popular readers were Samuel Woods's *New York Readers,* William Darby's *United States Readers,* John Pierpont's *National Readers,* Charles Merriam's *Springfield* series, "Peter Parley's" series, and Hilliard's readers. Changes in the teaching of reading also helped to displace the speller. The Jacotot method, imported from France, abandoned the old letter-by-letter alphabet method for teaching by word recognition.

1870. The earliest colleges were predominantly religious in aim; of the "colonial nine" in existence in the 1780s, seven were founded by Protestant church groups.[40] The sectarian, denominational nature of the eighteenth-century college established the pattern for the subsequent development of collegiate education through the first half of the nineteenth century. The college's purpose, for the most part, was to furnish young men with a broad cultural background and to prepare them for the professions, particularly law and the ministry.

During the early years of the republic, however, colleges' functions were extended and diversified, as the public asked them to produce not only cultured gentlemen but useful and patriotic citizens. Those states which did not have universities set about at once to charter them—North Carolina (1789), Georgia (1785), Maryland (1784), Tennessee (1794), Vermont (1791), South Carolina (1801). Colleges proliferated wildly in the closing decades of the century and the early years of the nineteenth. Whereas nine colleges were founded between 1636 and 1776, at least fifty were established (though not many survived) between 1776 and 1800.[41]

The expansion of collegiate education in the postwar period brought into focus the long struggle for control, implicit in eighteenth-century American education, between the church-related college and the publicly supported university. In five of the thirteen original states, a particular church denomination dominated society (Virginia, New York, Massachusetts, Connecticut, and New Hampshire), and in them the established universities (William and Mary, Harvard, Yale, Columbia, and Dartmouth) held exclusive rights over higher education. With the exception of Columbia all

40. Harvard (1636, Congregational) ; William and Mary (1693, Anglican) ; Yale (1701, Congregational) ; Princeton (1746, Presbyterian) ; Brown (College of Rhode Island, 1764, Baptist) ; Dartmouth (1769, Congregational) ; Rutgers (Queens, 1770, Reformed). Columbia (King's, 1754) and Pennsylvania (College of Philadelphia, 1755) were nondenominational. Catholic Georgetown was founded in 1789.

41. See Donald G. Tewksbury, *The Founding of American Colleges and Universities Before the Civil War* (New York, 1932). Among these were: Washington, Maryland (1782) ; Hampden-Sydney (1776) ; Washington and Jefferson (1800 ff.) ; Transylvania (1784) ; Charleston (1785) ; Franklin (1787) ; Vermont (1791) ; Williams (1793) ; Bowdoin (1794) ; Greenville, Tenn. (1794) ; Blount, Tenn. (1794) ; Union (1795) ; Middlebury (1800).

these universities had deep religious roots and powerful church connections.

State politicians made several attempts to secure control of the private, denominational colleges, but the settlement of the Dartmouth College case of 1819, ably argued in a five-hour speech by Daniel Webster before the United States Supreme Court, finally gave a legal victory to the forces of private sectarian education. The Dartmouth case established two principles: that state institutions were subject to state, not denominational, control; and that denominational colleges established by minority sectarian groups, once having obtained a charter, were to be free from state interference. The way, therefore, was opened for public and private institutions of higher education to develop separately, with the victory to the most powerful. State educational systems, during the first half of the nineteenth century, never managed to gain sufficient financial support to establish themselves as serious rivals to the church-related colleges. The churches fought them everywhere and usually won.[42]

The most important factor in the victory of religion in higher education after 1800, however, was the wave of evangelistic fervor that swept over American churches during the first forty years of the nineteenth century. Dozens of church colleges, particularly in the West, sprang up overnight. Of the seventy-eight permanent colleges and universities existing in the United States in 1840, thirty-five were founded after 1830, almost all under church sponsorship.[43]

42. George P. Schmidt, *The Old Time College President* (New York, 1930), 96. State legislatures were pinchpenny in their appropriations to state universities. The University of Missouri waited twenty-eight years for its first state appropriation and the University of Michigan twenty-three. State universities, or those partially state-supported, chartered or founded after 1800 included Ohio (1804), Miami (1809), Virginia (1819), Missouri (1839), Alabama (1821), College of Louisiana (1825), Nashville (1826), Indiana (1828), Mississippi (1830), Delaware (1833), and Michigan (1837). See Tewksbury, *Founding of Colleges*, chapter III, for an extended discussion.

43. See George P. Schmidt, *The Liberal Arts College* (New Brunswick, 1957), chapter II, for a survey of the religious impulse in higher education; and Butts, *The College Charts Its Course*, chapter VII. Many of the colleges founded between 1820 and 1860 quickly disappeared. Gaustad, *op. cit.*, 168–70, lists as joint Congregational-Presbyterian colleges Western Reserve (1826), Knox (1836), Grinnell (1846), and Ripon (1850). Methodists founded McKendree (1828), De Pauw (1832), Ohio Wesleyan (1841), Northwestern (1851), and Willamette (1842).

State institutions in the Western states fared poorly in the race for educational supremacy. The cost of public education was high, and the major share of the West's resources available for education was usually channeled into the denominational colleges which, an observer remarked, were "known to be places for the diligent inculcation of spiritual Christianity, as well as the truths of science and the grace of literature."

The Catholic church, during the same period, founded St. Mary's (Baltimore, 1805), St. Joseph's (Bardstown, Kentucky, 1824), and St. Louis (1833). Southern states had no tradition of state-supported education, though one was in the making. Wealthier families sent their sons North (Harvard in 1820 had fifty Southern students, Princeton forty-two, and Yale forty-two), while poorer families sent theirs to the church colleges which dominated the South and Southwest.[44] Of the total number of colleges in existence in 1860, Presbyterians controlled forty-nine, Methodists thirty-four, Baptists twenty-five, Congregationalists twenty-one, Catholics fourteen, Anglicans eleven, and Lutherans six.

The tremendous expansion of collegiate education and the rivalry between state and sectarian institutions caused serious deterioration in the quality of American higher education. The proliferation of colleges scattered energies and strained limited financial resources. Colleges sprang up everywhere, wrote President Philip Lindsley of Nashville in 1829, "like mushrooms on our luxuriant soil."[45] The evangelistic reaction against the Enlightenment's rationalism and tolerance encouraged many of the new

Baptists founded, among others, Denison (1831), Shurtleff (1835), and Baylor (1845). Baptists, Methodists, Presbyterians, and Congregationalists founded about half of all such colleges begun before 1860. Lutherans established Wittenberg (1842), and The Disciples of Christ Butler (1850); Evangelical-Reformed churches founded Heidelberg (1850) and Quakers Earlham (1847). Kenyon (1824) was Episcopalian, Oberlin (1833) Congregational.

44. Presbyterians supported Hampden-Sydney (Virginia), Davidson (North Carolina), Erskine (South Carolina), Oglethorpe (Georgia), and Centre (Kentucky). Baptists founded Richmond (Virginia), Wake Forest (North Carolina), Furman (South Carolina), Howard (Alabama), and Union (Tennessee). The Methodists had Randolph-Macon and Emory-Henry in Virginia, Trinity in North Carolina, Emory in Georgia, and La Grange in Alabama. In the East, where older church colleges already existed, the impetus of renewed religious enthusiasm helped to found Waterville, Colby, Amherst, Washington, Asbury, and Wesleyan.

45. See Richard Hofstadter and W. F. Metzger, *The Development of Academic Freedom in the United States* (New York, 1955), 212 ff.

colleges to be defenders of the faith against theological subversion, rather than true educational institutions. They were too often expected to produce orthodox church members, missionaries, and ministers—rather than young men interested in science, humanities, government, and the free pursuit of truth.

Demands for changes in American higher education soon arose from three sources. Jacksonian society wanted access to higher education for students from a broader range of society than before. This meant new standards of preparation and admission, and a new curriculum more clearly geared to vocationalism. The growth of a diversified urban society, coupled with the development of an increasingly powerful agrarian and mechanical class, required reconsideration of the objectives of higher education as well as its curriculum. The great expansion of scientific and technical knowledge hit the colleges and universities like a blow. There was so much more to know, and so much more to use; what there was to know changed the way men looked at themselves, their society, and even their universe.

The traditional curriculum, by the thirties, plainly failed to satisfy contemporary needs. Education, wrote a New England editor, ought to "have a relation with the state of society, and the wants and conditions of the community for which it is intended as a preparation." Was education keeping up with knowledge? Were the colleges aware of the changing nature of American society? Many of the young men who studied in Europe in the twenties and thirties found much to criticize in the American system. Twenty-five Americans studied at German universities alone before 1830—among them George Bancroft, Edward Everett, Joseph Cogswell, F. H. Hedge, and Theodore Woolsey—who brought back glowing reports of what they saw. At the same time, critics at home found some of American higher education irrelevant, out of touch with the American character. "A few only," said Albert Gallatin, "are destined for the learned professions . . . , but all want such degree of useful and practical knowledge, which can be acquired during the earliest years of life. It is that want which is generally felt, for which there is a loud and well-founded clamor, and which ought to be satisfied."[46]

Some colleges moved with the times, others resisted. Union Col-

46. Richard Starr, *The Beginnings of Graduate Education in the United States* (Chicago, 1953) , 62.

lege's President Nott in 1828 dropped the Latin and Greek requirement and established a "scientific" curriculum parallel to the
classical course. Amherst allowed its students some flexibility in
choosing required languages and, like Union, offered a parallel
scientific course, which did not succeed. Vermont and Nashville
allowed students some elective choices, while Nashville (under
liberal President Lindsley) introduced vocational training. Hampden-Sydney, Wesleyan, and Hobart, like Union, for a time offered a
parallel alternative to the classical curriculum. North Carolina, as
early as 1795, planned a curriculum which allowed a student to
"apply himself to those branches of learning in science alone which
are absolutely necessary to fit him for his desired profession in life,"
though it never went into full effect.[47]

The conflict within the ranks of higher education between 1820
and 1860 was most clearly illustrated by the University of Virginia's
introduction in 1826 of an experimental, innovative curriculum;
and on the other hand, by Yale's quelling of its "rebellion" of 1828.
Jefferson intended Virginia as a state university in more than name.
It was to offer broader and more advanced studies than other
American universities, and it was to be open to that "aristocracy of
talent" of which Jefferson spoke, whether poor or rich—the Virginia
legislature, in fact, provided scholarships for one student from each
senatorial district. Reflecting Jefferson's own example, the curriculum struck a balance between pure and practical learning. The
educated man, said Jefferson, valued knowledge for its own sake,
but he also recognized the need for a university in which "all the
branches of science useful *to us,* and *at this day,* should be taught to
the highest degree." Virginia did not realize all of Jefferson's aims,
but it exerted considerable influence on educational thinking over
the next thirty years and provided a model for some of the new state
universities soon to be founded in the South and West.[48]

Yale, Harvard, and Princeton, however, stood fast. Harvard resisted the young men who brought back ideas of reform from
Germany; Princeton maintained its old curriculum without much

47. Butts, *op. cit.,* chapter VII, discusses these and other experiments with curriculum.
48. Daniel J. Boorstin, *The Lost World of Thomas Jefferson* (Boston, 1960),
217-25; R. J. Honeywell, *The Educational Work of Thomas Jefferson* (Cambridge,
1931).

change despite student unrest. Yale, under the presidency of the
Reverend Jeremiah Day, established a wall against innovation that
defied attack for another generation to come. In response to a near-
revolt among students and younger faculty in 1827, the Yale Report
of 1828, a product of a faculty-administration committee, refused to
budge. Noting that some European and American colleges were
introducing new subjects, "chemistry, mineralogy, geology, political
economy, etc.," Yale would continue to emphasize the old studies
and let other schools take care of utilitarian needs. It would have
on its campus "no experimental farm or retail shop, no cotton or
iron manufactory." Yale's prestige and power carried the day and
made the Report of 1828 the greatest rearguard action in the history
of American higher education. Almost all of the major changes in
college and university curricula came after 1850, concurrent with
the rise of the state university and the redirection of higher education for the needs of another age.[49]

The majority of denominational colleges were as conservative as
Yale and the Eastern universities they looked to as models. After
1830 the Methodists and Baptists began to rival the Presbyterians
and Congregationalists in college-founding activities. Religious
groups moved into the new communities with the first settlers, ready
to found a college, provide the area with ministers and civic leaders,
and to save it from "atheism, infidelity, the slaveholder, and the
Pope." In Illinois it was said that "a settler could hardly encamp on
the prairie but a college would spring up beside his wagon." Some
of these "log-cabin colleges" were hardly worthy of the name; on
the other hand, some were adequately financed and well staffed.
But not many survived. Of five hundred colleges founded in sixteen
states between 1820 and 1860, four out of five disappeared by reason
of competition, internal dissension, lack of financing, shifts of
population, and natural disasters.[50] Those which survived, how-

49. For an account of the Yale rebellion and the Report, see Butts, *op. cit.*,
118–25, and Schmidt, *Liberal Arts College*, 53–56. To those who believed that
the study of a modern foreign language might substitute for the study of a
classic language, the Report advised, "Let a page of Voltaire be compared with a
page of Tacitus."

50. Schmidt, *Liberal Arts College*, 76–84. For statistics on survival rates and
types, see Tewksbury, *op. cit.*, 28, 90, *passim*. The westward wave of migration
after 1830 produced colleges like Beloit, Carleton, Whitman, Wabash, Grinnell,
Alma, Adrian, Olivet, Hillsdale, Ripon, Albion, Knox, DePauw (Indiana Asbury),
Northwestern, Denison, Mercer, Willamette in Oregon and the College of Cali-

ever, left an indelible mark on American education. Localized, slow to experiment or change, fiercely independent, they tended to preserve older values and life-styles.

Most colleges, public and private, were inadequately financed. The history of American higher education through much of the nineteenth century is one of constant struggle against debt. Gifts and bequests occasionally provided aid, but they were infrequent and remarkably small. Some colleges resorted to lotteries; Yale, Harvard, Rutgers, and Princeton all used this device, and the legislature of New York in 1841 approved lotteries for Hamilton and Union. In the log-cabin frontier colleges a yearly "begging tour" by the college president was an established custom. During the 1830s, Eastern colleges discovered the value of alumni as a source of finance, with results not always quite as anticipated.[51] Most colleges depended primarily on tuition fees for solvency, though many students found it hard to pay even the most modest charge. The struggle of the public-supported nonsectarian college to survive was long and desperate.

Early attempts to create state universities were not wholly successful. Georgia, North Carolina, South Carolina, Vermont, Tennessee, Maryland, Ohio, and Kentucky (Transylvania) were all founded during the closing decades of the eighteenth century and the early nineteenth, but their educational level was not high and state support for them capricious. Control of state schools was usually centered in boards of citizen-trustees who were often appointed by the boards themselves or by private, not public, agencies which had vested religious or economic interests of their own. The denominational colleges were powerfully entrenched; attacks on "godless" state universities were convenient to make; and the presidents of most state universities were often themselves ministers. The idea of a tax-supported university, controlled by state legislatures or nonsectarian boards, financed by regular appropriations from public

---

fornia. Catholic colleges, too, followed the westward movement; by 1860 there were fourteen permanent Catholic colleges, most of them controlled by teaching orders, among them Notre Dame (1842), St. Louis (1818), Dubuque (1852), St. Johns (Minnesota, 1857) and San Francisco (1855).

51. Princeton's Alumni Association, the first, was founded in 1826, Pennsylvania's in 1835. Schmidt, *Liberal Arts College*, 13.

funds, was simply not yet acceptable to a substantial majority of American society.[52]

The new states in the West were educationally a *tabula rasa*. The heavy influx of denominational schools and New Englanders tended to perpetuate the Eastern, religious-college pattern. However, these new states and territories had strong relationships to the federal government, and it was natural for them to assume that government, among its other responsibilities, would furnish schools for their population. The Ordinance of 1787 provided grants of land "given perpetually for the purposes of a university"; beginning in 1804, every state from Ohio to the Mississippi admitted to the Union received federal land for a university. Federal law, in fact, required the states to guarantee that these lands actually would be used for the purpose.

In most of the new Western states, therefore, provision for a university was co-existent with the state itself. Indiana's constitution of 1816, for example, established a system "from township schools to a State University, whose tuition shall be gratis and equally open to all." Although such federal land grants were by no means enough to support the universities, they did suggest the pattern for future development. Out of this policy, completely foreign to the Eastern Yale-Harvard-Princeton model, came Ohio (1804), Indiana (1821), Michigan (1837), Iowa (1847), Wisconsin (1848), Minnesota (1851), and Alabama (1831), Missouri (1839), Mississippi (1844), Louisiana State (1860), and Kentucky (1865).[53]

Whatever their hopes, these state universities found the going hard. Always underfinanced, they faced the hostility of the denomi-

52. John S. Brubacher and William Rudy, *Higher Education in Transition* (New York, 1968), 145–48. For additional discussions, see Richard Hofstadter and C. DeWitt Hardy, *The Development and Scope of Higher Education in the United States* (New York, 1952); George W. Pierson, "American Universities in the Nineteenth Century," in Margaret Clapp, ed., *The Modern University* (Ithaca, 1950) and Theodore Crane, ed., *The Colleges and the American Public 1787–1862* (New York, 1963).

53. Typical of the state universities' philosophy was the statement in Michigan's early catalogues that its intent was "to make it possible for every student to study what he pleases and to any extent that he pleases. Nor can it be consistent with the spirit of a free country to deny to its citizens the possibilities of the highest knowledge."

national colleges and their legislative allies.[54] But they also had strong supporters among the laboring, agricultural, and mercantile population, who wanted not colleges training ministers and lawyers, but "colleges for the people" which would teach a young man how to make a better living. "Where are the universities, the apparatus, the professors, and the literature, adapted to any one of the industrial classes?" asked one critic. "Echo answers, Where?" Jonathan Turner, a Yale graduate who taught at Illinois College, made an eloquent and typical "Plea for a State University for the Industrial Classes" to the state legislature in 1850. What Illinois needed, he wrote, was a university of "a high order, in which should be taught all those things which *every* class of citizens must desire to learn," and one "which teaches all that is needed for all the varied professions of human life."[55]

Specialized technical education developed slowly. West Point, the railroad and canal companies, and industrial technologists supplied most of the nation's engineers; Rensselaer Polytechnic Institute, established in Troy, New York, in 1824 by a wealthy manufacturer, was the nation's only first-class technical school. Union College added a department of civil engineering in 1845; two years later Harvard founded Lawrence Scientific School and Yale added what became the Sheffield School. Brown, Pennsylvania, and Dartmouth entered technical education in the fifties, and Brooklyn's Polytechnic Institute opened in 1854.

But these were not what Turner and others like him had in mind. President Wayland of Brown put his finger on the problem when he commented that in a nation of farms and machines there were forty-two theological schools and forty-seven law schools, but no schools at all to provide "the agriculturalist, the manufacturer, the mechanic, and the merchant with any kind of professional preparation."[56] Michigan and Pennsylvania, in 1855, established

54. Indiana University was controlled by church interests for some years; denominational groups delayed the founding of the University of Illinois until after the Civil War; the battle was so close for a time in Michigan that the legislature at one point nearly withdrew all state support from the university, leaving it only federal land-grant funds.

55. Gross and Chandler, *op. cit.*, 172–4. Turner called also for vocational institutes and applied research, urging college faculties to "apply existing knowledge directly and efficiently to all practical pursuits . . . and to extend the boundaries of our present knowledge in all possible practical directions."

56. Brubacher and Rudy, *op. cit.*, 63–5.

the kind of college of which Wayland spoke,[57] but the majority of them came after Congress passed the Morrill Land Grant Act in 1862, which gave each state 30,000 acres of public land for each of its congressional representatives, the proceeds to be used for education in agriculture, engineering, and military science. These land-grant universities opened a new era in American higher education.[58]

A major principle of the women's rights movement was a demand for equal education, commensurate with woman's social role and domestic responsibilities. Schools were opened to girls in the late eighteenth century, though boys and girls were kept apart and the female curriculum was much less demanding—music, drawing, painting, light reading, English, perhaps French. In the early decades of the nineteenth century, academies for girls (or "seminaries") multiplied, although tuition fees restricted attendance to daughters of the more prosperous. Private girls' schools, some established in the eighteenth century, spread swiftly after 1800 (at least twenty were founded before 1825), many of them teaching at least some solid subjects like geometry and mathematics along with the politer accomplishments. The spread of public schools, and the drain of young men into business, factories, and to the West created a demand for teachers that could be met only by young women; it was no accident that the first female institutes also trained teachers. The lyceum, a powerful educational force, was also open to women; newspapers and magazines and books made information and culture available to girls at home.

Despite the agitation for women's rights, there were many men and women who opposed female education as defeminizing and useless. Educating girls to the age of fifteen or so seemed to be acceptable; higher education was a different matter. It was not clear what usefulness a woman might find in Latin or higher mathematics, when, as one newspaper said in 1828, the "most acceptable degree" for a young lady was "the degree of M.R.S." On the other hand, proponents of female education argued that educated women made better wives and mothers—"Mothers," said Horace Mann,

57. Now Michigan State University and Pennsylvania State University.
58. For a full account, see Earle D. Ross, *Democracy's College: The Land Grant Movement in the Formative Stage* (Ames, Iowa, 1942). For developments in higher education after 1865, see Lawrence R. Veysey, *The Emergence of the American University* (Chicago, 1965).

"determine to a great extent, the very capacity of our rulers' minds." Women could contribute to social progress, the reformers explained, equally with men.[59]

The founding of first-rate seminaries such as Emma Willard's at Troy (1824) and Mary Lyon's at Mount Holyoke (1836) furnished precedents for the next logical step, a college for women. The earliest was Georgia Female College (Wesleyan College) at Macon, Georgia, which received its charter in 1836 and granted degrees in 1840. Rockford College for Women opened in 1847; Female Normal Institute and High School (Milwaukee-Downer) was given the right to grant degrees in 1851; Elmira College received its charter in 1853. Oberlin College in Ohio enrolled four freshman girls in 1837, thus becoming the first co-educational college, but no more than a half-dozen others followed its example.[60] The quality of education in some women's colleges was not especially high, and in the few co-educational schools girls were often discriminated against in the curriculum. The American Women's Education Association, formed in 1852 to set standards and encourage improvement, was of great assistance in raising the caliber of women's colleges, but the older colleges and universities were not receptive to women, nor did female colleges attract significant popular support.

The new state universities in the West, however, quickly opened their doors to girls. These were public institutions, and girls' parents paid taxes; women had always found more equal treatment on the frontier, and in the new Western communities women had important responsibilities. Among the state universities which enrolled girls from their founding were Utah (1850), Iowa (1856), Kansas (1860), and Nebraska (1871). Wisconsin, Indiana, Mis-

59. See the discussion of educational theory in Curti, *op. cit.,* chapter V; and Noble, *op. cit.,* chapter 13. William Goodsell, *The Education of Women* (New York, 1923) and Thomas Woody, *A History of Women's Education in the United States* (two volumes, New York, 1929) are standard sources. An excellent brief summary of trends in the thirties and forties is that of Schmidt, *Liberal Arts College,* chapter IV.

60. The young women, who deserve to be remembered, were Mary Hosford of Oberlin; Mary Kellogg of Jamestown, New York; Elizabeth Pratt of New York City; and Caroline Mary Rudd of Huntington, Connecticut. Miss Kellogg did not complete the course; she married James Fairchild, who became the college's third president. Fairchild's sister Emily was probably the first woman in the United States to receive a graduate degree, obtaining an M.A. at Oberlin in 1847. A good brief account is "The Barrier Seemed Impassable," *Oberlin Today,* XXI (1963), 1–11.

souri, Michigan, Ohio State, Illinois, and California all admitted women in the sixties and after. The barriers against women at Eastern universities held until 1872, when women were granted admission and certain educational rights at Cornell. The tradition of separate and presumably equal colleges for men and women was firmly established in the East, however, and none of the major private universities followed Cornell's example.[61]

The curriculum of the American college remained virtually unchanged for the first hundred and fifty years until, during the first half of the nineteenth century, its assumptions were challenged, its organization attacked, and its content questioned. The issue at stake was, fundamentally, what shall be taught, and to what purpose? A society in transition, a public that expected new and different things from education, students whose aims were diverse and contemporary—these were powerful forces of change, despite the influence of the Yale Report.

The central issue lay in the inadequacy of the curriculum to contain the great explosion of knowledge that occurred in the eighteenth and early nineteenth centuries. There was simply so much more to know than ever before that the traditional curriculum could not possibly contain it. The older generalized science course was rapidly being divided into chemistry, botany, mineralogy, geology, paleontology, and physics. No course in "moral philosophy" could teach the new psychology, economics, or politics—so "political economy" courses appeared, ethics, natural law, and so on. Furthermore, fewer students came to college with the intention of entering law, the ministry, or public service, and the traditional curriculum failed to satisfy them.

Critics raised other questions. Was education primarily religious and moral, its purpose to educate the student for a cultured, Christian life; or was it secular, aimed at finding and applying knowledge to personal and social ends? Should college produce moral men, trained citizens, or wage earners, or were these mutually exclusive aims? What should be the balance of "new" studies (psychology, the sciences, political economy) and classical ones

61. Mabel Newcomer, *A Century of Higher Education for Women* (New York, 1959); and Mary A. Bowker, *Catholic Colleges for Women* (Washington, D.C., 1933).

(rhetoric, Latin, moral philosophy) ? Should colleges train an elite, professional class of "leaders," or open their doors to everyone; should there be as many kinds of colleges and universities as there were needs?

One attempt to answer some of the criticisms of the college curriculum was the parallel course of study, set up for students whose needs were not met by the traditional "classical" curriculum. Miami, for example, in 1825, organized an "English-Scientific" course which allowed the student to take a modern language instead of a classical one and included mathematics and political economy. A number of colleges experimented with similar parallel curricula, using English literature, modern history, and applied science as alternatives. Other colleges introduced an elective system, allowing students limited substitutions, as Jefferson had done with his Virginia plan. Neither of these innovations was particularly successful; conservative faculties, safe behind the walls of the Yale Report, easily held off changes of this sort through the forties.

The most viable alternatives to the traditional curriculum were those introduced into college life by the students, who erected—much to the puzzlement and concern of faculty and administration—an informal educational system of their own which incorporated most of the changes the formal curriculum rejected. The college literary societies and clubs, which appeared in the eighteenth century and proliferated in the nineteenth, provided active and exciting extracurricular centers of education on every campus. With names like Athenian and Parnassian and Aeolian, these societies organized programs of lectures, readings, and discussions which accomplished much that the curriculum did not. Men like Webster, Emerson, Choate, Everett, and Bancroft were pleased to lecture to them; their book collections often outnumbered the college library's or the president's.[62] They founded magazines, published speeches, launched debates, awarded prizes for academic attainment, and gathered collections of paintings and statuary. Through them the student found a world of music, art, politics, and ideas that he did not find within the classroom.

Most of these societies were displaced or absorbed by the Greek-letter fraternities which began to appear in New England and New

62. Frederick Rudolph, *The American College and University* (New York, 1962), 113–30, 221–36.

York colleges in the fifties. By midcentury there were fraternities in all major universities and most small colleges, introducing to the campuses a kind of sophisticated social life that administrations did not quite know how to handle. In addition, students introduced athletics and games into the college environment. Gymnastics and physical education courses appeared in some colleges in the twenties, brought back from Germany by travelers, but in the forties students were organizing boat races, foot races, wrestling, swimming, and boxing matches, and were playing early versions of baseball and football. The next step, attaching these activities to the college itself, was not far away.

In 1850 a committee of the Massachusetts General Court requested Harvard—no less—to make such modifications in its curriculum as to produce "better farmers, mechanics, and merchants," while a Georgia editor, echoing the common complaint, warned that universities, to supply the needs of the state, must produce "practical men, civil engineers, to take charge of public roads, railroads, mines, scientific agriculture, etc."[63] By this time some faculties and administrations were listening and cracks in the defensive wall appeared here and there. Yale in 1852 admitted civil engineering. Harvard began granting a Bachelor of Science degree in 1852 and Yale a Bachelor of Philosophy (essentially a "parallel course" degree) in 1852; before the close of the decade these degrees appeared at Michigan, New York University, North Carolina, and Iowa, among others. Yet to most university administrations the function of education still seemed to be the production of a cultivated professional elite—as President Lord of Dartmouth said, a college education was *not* for those who intended to "engage in mercantile, mechanical, or agricultural operations." President Francis Wayland of Brown thought the time was ripe for change, but when he attempted to revise Brown's curriculum, he was deposed by his faculty and his successor promised that the university would return to "educating a sterling class of citizens" rather than "conferring degrees upon the unfortunate."[64] Reform and redirec-

63. Brubacher and Rudy, *op. cit.*, 98–116.
64. Rudolph, *op. cit.*, 135, 238–40. Wayland's *Thoughts on the Present Collegiate System in the United States* (1842) and his *Report to the Corporation of Brown University* (1850) form the most incisive critique of early higher education. Wayland wanted to introduce courses in applied science, agriculture, and

tion of American higher education would have to come later, primarily from the new state universities, technical schools, and agricultural and mechanical colleges created after the Civil War.

Despite constant criticism and occasional student revolts, methods of classroom instruction changed little over the first half of the nineteenth century. Within the system there were, of course, both inspired and pedestrian teachers, but the system gave the innovator small chance. The recitation method, based on a textbook, was the most common for smaller classes. The classroom was not intended to be a place for discussion (debating and literary societies provided that) but rather where the teacher tested knowledge of an assigned book by asking questions about it. With a good book and a skilled teacher the experience could be educationally exciting; with poor ones, it could be deadly. As enrollments soared, lecturing to large classes became simply economic necessity; lecturing became, in fact, the most widely used instructional method of the century. Brilliant lecturers had reputations far beyond the colleges they taught in; there were also equal numbers of dull ones. The single most important innovation in teaching came with the use of the laboratory method in the sciences (derived chiefly from the lecture-demonstrations of the lyceum) in which the student watched the professor perform an experiment, and later might duplicate it himself under the teacher's supervision. Amos Eaton, famous as a lyceum lecturer, introduced it at Rensselaer in 1824 (he also took students on field trips), but laboratory instruction was common in only a few colleges before the fifties. It was developed chiefly at the new agricultural and mechanical colleges after 1855.

Examination in the colonial colleges was chiefly by disputation—that is, the defense of a thesis—and although this method had almost disappeared by 1820 (numbers alone prevented the practice), it continued in smaller schools. Written examinations became standard in the thirties and after, graded by marking systems of great diversity and questionable accuracy. Some colleges used the Yale system of *optimi, second optimi, inferiores,* and *peiores;* some used a four-grade system (like William and Mary's) with detailed explanations; Columbia used *proficient* and *deficient.* Such systems

---

teacher training at Brown; he suggested alternative courses for nondegree students and a liberalized disciplinary system, a revised fee structure, and he hoped to abolish the aristocratic residential colleges.

were quickly replaced by numerical grades—Yale used 4 as a base, Harvard at different times a base from 8 to 20. Some colleges gave grades a moral component, or judged students' attitudes; a student might get one mark for his command of information and another for his assiduity (or lack of it), or have demerits subtracted from his grades for disciplinary reasons. Occasionally colleges gave cash prizes for high grades or recognized attainment by choosing the better students for class orations, arranging them in order of importance in the program and noting whether they were given in Latin or English.[65]

When education was made a responsibility of society, incumbent on all its members, it was expected to undertake a variety of responsibilities—for individual self-development, for civic duty, for economic security, for moral and ethical training, for social progress and betterment. The American educational system, then, emerged from its formative period with its future course virtually charted. It would be pluralistic, diverse, flexible, responsive; there was no national ministry, federal agency, or state church to impose a permanent pattern of control over it, nor was it likely that any could. It would be, to varying degrees but nonetheless consistently, closely tied to the public, whether it was in state or private hands. Sectarian schools were run by boards of trustees who represented the church members who financed them; public schools were run by boards elected or appointed by the state. In any case, the public element of education was always assumed, and education was always considered to be directly related to society. If the public paid for education, it expected education to meet its requirements; it had to be both practical and abstract, train both thinker and doer, mean all things to all men. Its function was simple and clear—"to diffuse," one commentator said, "the greatest amount of learning to the greatest number of people." No other educational system in the world was ever asked to accept such varied obligations or to respond to such a diversity of needs.

65. Mary L. Smallwood, *An Historical Study of Examinations and Grading Systems in Early America* (Cambridge, 1935), 12–13, 28–35, *passim*.

Bibliography

The Frame of American Belief

Useful studies of American nationalism are Hans Kohn, *American Nationalism* (New York, 1957); Paul C. Nagel, *This Sacred Trust: American Nationality 1798–1898* (New York, 1971); and Yehoshua Arieli, *Individualism and Nationalism in American Ideology* (Cambridge, 1964). An earlier broader study is Merle Curti, *The Roots of American Loyalty* (New York, 1946). Paul C. Nagel's *One Nation Indivisible: The Union in American Thought 1776–1861* (New York, 1964) is a valuable treatment of the idea of unionism in nationalistic thought. Edward McNall Burns' *The American Idea of Mission* (New Brunswick, N.J., 1957) is an earlier study of the idea, later applied to "manifest destiny" by Frederick Merk, *Manifest Destiny and Mission in American History* (New York, 1963). Albert Weinberg's *Manifest Destiny* (Gloucester, Mass., 1958) is another study of the principle, while Ernest C. Tuveson, *Redeemer Nation: The Idea of America's Millennial Role* (Chicago, 1968) is an excellent background book. One of the best brief summaries of American Romanticism is G. H. Orians, "The Rise of Romanticism," in Harry H. Clark, ed., *Transitions in American Literary History* (Durham, N.C., 1954); two general studies of Romanticism in its American and European contexts are W. T. Jones, *The Romantic Syndrome* (The Hague, 1961); and Robert Gleckner and Gerald Ensue, eds., *Romanticism* (Englewood Cliffs, N.J., 1970). Arthur Ekirch, *The Idea of Progress in America 1815–1860* (New York, 1944) is easily the best and most available source; excellent summary treatments are those in Stow Persons, *American Minds* (New York, 1958) and Ralph H. Gabriel, *The Course of American Democratic Thought* (New York, 1940). For surveys of the period and bibliographies, see Edward Pessen, *Jacksonian*

America: Society, Personality, and Politics (Homewood, Ill., 1969) ; Douglas T. Miller, *The Birth of Modern America, 1820–1850* (New York, 1970) ; Glydon Van Duesen, *The Jacksonian Era 1828–1848* (New York, 1959) ; and Clement Eaton, *The Growth of Southern Civilization 1790–1860* (New York, 1961) . Clinton Rossiter's *The American Quest 1790–1860* (New York, 1971) is an excellent study of the search for identity and unity that characterized the early National period.

The Thrust of Reform

Two useful brief collections, with excellent introductions, to the period of reform are Henry Steele Commager, *The Era of Reform 1830–1860* (Princeton, 1960) ; and David B. Davis, *Antebellum Reform* (New York, 1967) . The relevant chapters of Allan Nevins, *Ordeal of the Union,* volume I (New York, 1947) provide equally useful surveys, while Alice Felt Tyler's *Freedom's Ferment: Phases of American Social History to 1860* (Minneapolis, 1944) is still a standard source. The relationships between contemporary ideas of moral responsibility and reform are treated in Clifford S. Griffin, *Their Brother's Keepers: Moral Stewardship in the United States 1800–1865* (New Brunswick, N.J., 1960) , while those between religion and reform in the period are studied in Timothy M. Smith, *Revivalism and Social Reform in Mid-Nineteenth Century America* (Nashville, 1957) ; Charles C. Cole, Jr., *The Social Ideas of the Northern Evangelists 1826–60* (New York, 1954) ; and C. Joseph Nuesse, *The Social Thought of American Catholics* (Washington, 1945) . For books on the peace movement, see Merle Curti, *The American Peace Crusade 1815–1860* (Durham, N.C., 1929) ; W. Freeman Galpin, *Pioneering for Peace: A Study of American Peace Efforts to 1846* (Syracuse, 1933) ; and Peter Brock, *Pacifism in the United States* (Princeton, 1968) . Merle Curti's study of Elihu Burritt, *The Learned Blacksmith* (New York, 1937) contains additional information. John A. Krout, *The Origins of Prohibition* (New York, 1925) was the first comprehensive treatment of the temperance-prohibition crusade; J. C. Furnas' *Life and Times of the Late Demon Rum* (New York, 1965) is a sprightly, informal history; Joseph R. Gusfield, *Symbolic Crusade: State Politics and the American Temperance Movement* (Urbana, 1963) is a good specialized study. For the history of women's rights, one might well begin with Elizabeth Cady Stanton, *et al., History of Woman Suffrage* (Rochester, 1889) , the original; later studies include Eleanor Flexner, *Century of Struggle: The Woman's Rights Movement in the United States* (Cambridge, 1959) ; William L. O'Neill, *Everyone Was Brave: The Rise and Fall of Feminism in America* (Chicago, 1969) ; Robert E. Riegel, *American Woman: A Story of Social Change* (Rutherford, N.J., 1970) ;

and O'Neill's collection of documents, *The Woman Movement* (New York, 1969). Two valuable studies of American social movements are Robert Bremner's *American Philanthropy* (Chicago, 1960) and *From the Depths: The Discovery of Poverty in the United States* (New York, 1964); older but useful is Frank D. Watson, *The Charity Organization Movement in the United States* (New York, 1922); whereas John O'Grady, *Catholic Charities in the United States* (Washington, D.C., 1930) is a good specialized study. On prisons, see Blake McKelvey, *American Prisons* (Chicago, 1936), and W. David Lewis, *From Newgate to Dannemora: The Rise of the Penitentiary in New York, 1790–1845* (New York, 1965), while it treats only New York State, offers additional information on prisons in general. Robert S. Pickett, *House of Refuge: Origins of Juvenile Reform in New York State 1815–1847* (Syracuse, 1969) likewise provides information on juvenile reform beyond the state. Albert Deutsch, *The Mentally Ill in America* (New York, 1937) and David J. Rothman, *The Discovery of the Asylum: Social Order and Disorder in the New Republic* (Boston, 1971) are excellent sources for contemporary attitudes toward mental illness; see also Samuel W. Hamilton, "The History of American Mental Hospitals," in Gregory Zilboorg, ed., *One Hundred Years of American Psychiatry* (New York, 1944). Helen Marshall's *Dorothea Dix: Forgotten Samaritan* (Chapel Hill, 1937) and Harold Schwartz, *Samuel Gridley Howe, Social Reformer 1801–1876* (Cambridge, 1956) are informative biographies. There are several histories of American communal experiments; three of the most useful are Mark Holloway, *Heavens on Earth* (New York, 1951); Arthur E. Bestor, *Backwoods Utopias* (Philadelphia, 1949); and Vernon F. Calverton's early but interesting *Where Angels Dared to Tread* (New York, 1941). Margaret Fellows, *The Shaker Adventure* (Boston, 1941) and Edward Andrews, *The People Called Shakers* (New York, 1953) deal with the followers of Mother Ann Lee: Oneida is treated in Robert A. Parker's biography of Noyes, *A Yankee Saint* (Boston, 1935) and Karen L. Carden, *Oneida: Utopian Community to Modern Corporation* (Baltimore, 1969). Studies of abolition and proslavery abound. The best overall treatment is Louis Filler, *The Crusade Against Slavery 1830–1860* (New York, 1960); a useful collection of documents is William H. and Jane Pease, eds., *The Anti-Slavery Argument* (Indianapolis, 1965). Gilbert H. Barnes, *The Antislavery Impulse* (New York, 1933) is the pioneer study of the relationship of evangelicalism and abolition; Donald G. Mathews' *Slavery and Methodism 1780–1845* (Princeton, 1965) is a study of one church and the problem. William S. Jenkins, *Pro-slavery Thought in the Old South* (Chapel Hill, 1935) and Arthur Y. Lloyd, *The Slavery Controversy* (Durham, 1939) are expositions of the traditional Southern argument. A recent study of the argument in the South is Robert F. Durden, *The Gray and the Black: The*

Confederate Debate on Emancipation (Baton Rouge, 1972). Martin Duberman, *The Antislavery Vanguard* (Princeton, 1968) and Hazel Wolf, *On Freedom's Altar: the Martyr Complex in the Abolition Movement* (Madison, 1952) re-evaluate the abolitionists. Richard Curry has edited a collection of essays, *The Abolitionists* (Hinsdale, 1973) with an excellent, annotated bibliography: Lewis Perry, *Radical Abolitionism* (Ithaca, 1973) studies the role of anarchism in the movement. Lorman Ratner, *Powder Keg: Northern Opposition to the Antislavery Movement 1831–1840* (New York, 1968) surveys Northern opinion; while Eugene Berwanger, *The Frontier Against Slavery* (Urbana, 1967) considers the reaction of the frontier to abolitionist controversy and racial feeling. Aileen S. Kraditor, *Means and Ends in American Abolitionism* (New York, 1969) is a good discussion of the Garrisonian division within the antislavery movement. Russel B. Nye, *Fettered Freedom* (East Lansing, 1963) is a study of the controversy as it affected civil liberties. For relations between American and British reformers see Christine Bolt, *The Antislavery Movement and Reconstruction: A Study in Anglo-American Cooperation 1833–1870* (London, 1969); and Betty Fladeland, *Men and Brothers: Anglo-American Antislavery Cooperation* (Urbana, 1972).

History and Literature in a Romantic Age

An excellent general history of American literature is Robert E. Spiller, *et al.*, *Literary History of the United States* (three volumes, New York, 1948); on nationalism in American literature see Benjamin Spencer, *The Quest for Nationality* (Syracuse, 1957). A useful collection is George Boas, ed., *Romanticism in America* (New York, 1961). For publishing history consult H. Lehmann-Haupt, C. C. Wroth, and Rollo Silver, *The Book in America* (New York, 1952); Frank Luther Mott, *A History of American Magazines 1741–1850* (New York, 1930); and William Charvat, *Literary Publishing in America 1790–1850* (New York, 1939). John Pritchard's *Return to the Fountains: Some Classical Sources of American Criticism* (Durham, 1942) and his *Literary Wise Men of Gotham: Criticism in New York 1815–1860* (Baton Rouge, 1963) are important special studies; for general treatments of the history of criticism see Pritchard's *Criticism in America* (Norman, Okla., 1956); Clarence A. Brown, *The Achievement of American Criticism* (New York, 1954); Floyd Stovall, ed., *The Development of American Literary Criticism* (Chapel Hill, 1955); William Charvat, *The Origins of American Critical Thought 1810–1835* (Philadelphia, 1936); and John Stafford, *The Literary Criticism of "Young America"* (Berkeley, 1952). Scholarship concerning American authors can be followed in *American Literary Scholarship*, published yearly by the Duke University Press,

Durham, N.C. The following are selected biographical and critical works about major American authors: Eleanor Tilton, *Amiable Autocrat* (New York, 1947), a life of O. W. Holmes; Martin Duberman, *James Russell Lowell* (Boston, 1966) and Leon Howard, *Victorian Knight-Errant: James Russell Lowell* (Los Angeles, 1952); Sherman Paul's study, *The Shores of America: Thoreau's Inward Exploration* (Urbana, 1961), Walter Harding's biography, *Thoreau, Man of Concord* (New York, 1960), and his useful *Thoreau Handbook* (New York, 1959). General histories of the American novel include Edward Wagenknecht, *Cavalcade of the American Novel* (New York, 1952); Alexander Cowie, *The Rise of the American Novel* (New York, 1951); and Arthur H. Quinn, *American Fiction* (New York, 1930). Walter Blair, *Native American Humor* (New York, 1937) is a standard reference, and a good collection is James R. Aswell, ed., *Native American Humor* (New York, 1947). The best introductions to Cooper are Donald Ringe, *James Fenimore Cooper* (New York, 1962), and James Grossman, *James Fenimore Cooper* (New York, 1949). There are a number of biographies of Poe, of which one of the more recent and trustworthy is Edward Wagenknecht's *Edgar Allan Poe: The Man Behind the Legend* (New York, 1963), although Arthur H. Quinn, *Edgar Allan Poe* (New York, 1941) is still useful. Critical studies are Edward H. Davidson, *Poe* (Cambridge, 1959) and Vincent Buranelli, *Edgar Allan Poe* (New York, 1961). There are more than fifty books on Hawthorne and over a hundred on Melville. A good biography of Hawthorne is Edward Wagenknecht's *Nathaniel Hawthorne: Man and Writer* (New York, 1961) and a fine short study is Terence Martin, *Nathaniel Hawthorne* (New York, 1965). Newton Arvin's *Herman Melville* (New York, 1950); Leon Howard's *Melville* (Berkeley, 1951); and Jay Leyda's *Melville Log: A Documentary Life of Herman Melville* (two volumes, New York, 1951) are excellent sources for the general reader. Popular literature and "best-sellers" are treated in James D. Hart, *The Popular Book* (Berkeley, 1951) and Frank L. Mott, *Golden Multitudes* (New York, 1947). Harriet Beecher Stowe and *Uncle Tom's Cabin* are the subjects of Charles H. Foster's study, *The Rungless Ladder: Harriet Beecher Stowe and New England Puritanism* (Durham, 1936). Older studies of American historians and the writing of American history include John S. Bassett, *The Middle Group of American Historians* (New York, 1917); Michael Kraus, *A History of American History* (New York, 1937) and William F. Hutchinson, ed., *The Marcus W. Jernegan Essays in American Historiography* (Norman, Okla., 1937). Good selections appear in Harvey Wish, ed., *The American Historians* (New York, 1962), while Donald Sheehan and Harold Syrett edited a collection of essays on historians, *American Historians* (Columbus, Ohio, 1960). Excellent general studies are H. Hale Belott, *American History and American Historians*

(Norman, Okla., 1952); George H. Calcott, *History in the United States 1800–1860* (Baltimore, 1970); Bert J. Loewenberg, *American History in American Thought* (New York, 1972); David Van Tassel, *Recording America's Past* (Chicago, 1960); and David Levin's brilliant study, *History as Romantic Art* (Stanford, 1959).

Poetry and the Public Arts

Surveys of American poetry covering the early national period are Hyatt H. Waggoner, *American Poets from the Puritans to the Present* (Boston, 1968) and Roy H. Pearce, *The Continuity of American Poetry* (Princeton, 1961). A fine study of the New England poets is George Arms, *The Fields Were Green* (Stanford, 1953). A good anthology, with bibliographies and reading notes, is Gay Allen, Walter Rideout, and James Robinson, *American Poetry* (New York, 1965). The standard biography of Bryant is Howard H. Peckham, *Gotham Yankee* (New York, 1950); a useful brief critical study is A. F. MacLean, Jr., *William Cullen Bryant* (New York, 1964). For Poe, see the books cited in chapter III, and also Robert Regan, ed., *Poe: A Collection of Critical Essays* (New York, 1967). Killis Campbell, *The Mind of Poe and Other Studies* (Cambridge, 1932) contains essays on Poe's ideas and art. For Longfellow, the best recent biography is Newton Arvin, *Longfellow: His Life and Work* (New York, 1963); for Whittier, John B. Pickard, *John Greenleaf Whittier* (New York, 1961); and Whitman Bennett, *John Greenleaf Whittier: Bard of Freedom* (Chapel Hill, 1941). Among the dozens of studies of Emerson, particularly valuable are Sherman Paul, *Emerson's Angle of Vision* (Cambridge, 1952) and Stephen Whicher, *Freedom and Fate: An Inner Life of Ralph Waldo Emerson* (Philadelphia, 1953); the standard biography is Ralph L. Rusk, *Life of Ralph Waldo Emerson* (New York, 1949). A good Holmes biography is Eleanor Tilton's, cited in chapter III; for critical studies, see the introduction to S. I. Hayakawa and H. M. Jones, *Oliver Wendell Holmes* (New York, 1939) and M. R. Small, *Oliver Wendell Holmes* (New York, 1962). The best recent biography of Whitman is Gay Allen, *The Solitary Singer* (New York, rev. ed., 1967). Additional studies of Whitman include James E. Miller, *Walt Whitman* (New York, 1962) and Roy H. Pearce, ed., *Whitman: A Collection of Critical Essays* (Englewood Cliffs, N.J., 1962).

General histories of music in the United States are H. Wiley Hitchcock, *Music in the United States* (Englewood Cliffs, N.J., 1969); Gilbert Chase, *America's Music* (New York, 1966); John Tasker Howard and George K. Bellows, *A Short History of Music in America* (New York, 1957); and Paul Henry Lang, *One Hundred Years of Music in America* (New York, 1961); a good specialized study is Irving Lowens, *Music and Musicians in Early*

America (New York, 1964). Alan Lomax, *The Folk Song in North America* (London, 1969), is a standard source. Sigmund Spaeth, *A History of Popular Music* (New York, 1948), and David Ewen, *Panorama of American Popular Music* (Englewood Cliffs, N.J., 1957), chart the course of American popular songs; see also the relevant portions of Russel B. Nye, *The Unembarrassed Muse* (New York, 1971). John H. Mueller, *The American Symphony Orchestra* (Bloomington, Ind., 1957) is a useful history. For studies of rhetoric and oratory, consult William P. Sanford, *English Theories of Public Address* (Columbus, Ohio, 1931); Robert T. Oliver, *The History of Public Speaking in America* (Boston, 1965), and William N. Brigance, ed., *History and Criticism of American Public Address* (two volumes, New York, 1943). There are many collections of American speeches, but one of the most available is Warren Choate Shaw, *The History of American Oratory* (Indianapolis, 1928).

Standard histories of the American stage are Glen Hughes, *A History of the American Theater* (New York, 1951); Arthur H. Quinn, *The History of the American Drama from the Beginnings to the Civil War* (rev. ed., New York, 1943); and Oral Coad and Edwin Mims, Jr., *The American Stage* (New Haven, 1929). David Grimstead's *Melodrama Unveiled: American Theater and Culture 1800–1850* (Chicago, 1968) is an invaluable study; so too is Richard Moody's *America Takes the Stage* (Bloomington, Ind., 1955); while Moody's collection of plays, *Dramas from the American Theater 1726–1909* (Cleveland, 1966) is one of the most useful of its kind. Garff B. Wilson, *A History of American Acting* (Bloomington, Ind., 1966) is an essential source.

Painters, Builders, and Stonecutters

There are several good histories of American painting, among them Edgar Richardson, *Painting in America* (New York, 1965); Virgil Barker, *American Painting* (New York, 1950); and Alan Burroughs, *Limners and Likenesses: Three Centuries of American Painting* (New York, 1965). Painting, sculpture, and other arts are treated in Oliver Larkin's distinguished *Art and Life in America* (New York, 1949); and the essays in Wendell Garrett, Paul Norton, Allan Gowans, and Joseph T. Butler, *The Arts in America: the Nineteenth Century* (New York, 1969). The social contexts of art are studied in Neil Harris, *The Artist in American Society, 1790–1860* (New York, 1956) and Lillian Miller, *Patrons and Patriotism: The Encouragement of the Fine Arts in America 1790–1860* (Chicago, 1966). Special studies of nineteenth century painting are: James T. Soby and Dorothy C. Miller, *Romantic Painting in America* (New York, 1943); Edgar Richardson, *American Romantic Painting* (New York, 1944); John

I. H. Baur, *American Painting in the Nineteenth Century* (New York, 1953) ; and Barbara Novak, *American Painting of the Nineteenth Century* (New York, 1969). Supplemental studies are James T. Flexner, *That Wilder Image: The Painting of America's Native School from Thomas Cole to Winslow Homer* (Boston, 1962) ; and Yvon Bizardel, *American Painters in Paris* (New York, 1960). Harry T. Peters, *Currier and Ives* (New York, 1929) is still a key book. Lorado Taft's *History of American Sculpture* (New York, 1930) is interesting because of its eminent author's viewpoint; Albert T. E. Gardner, *Yankee Stonecutters* (New York, 1945) was a pioneer study, still useful; Wayne Craven, *Sculpture in America* (New York, 1968) is the best modern history. Margaret Farrand Thorp, *The Literary Sculptors* (Durham, 1965) ; and Nathalia Wright, *Horatio Greenough, The First American Sculptor* (Philadelphia, 1963) are studies of individual sculptors.

Marcus Whiffen, *American Architecture Since 1780: A Guide to the Styles* (Cambridge, 1969) is an invaluable brief handbook; Wayne Andrews' *Architecture in America: A Photographic History* (New York, 1960) is an equally invaluable pictorial history. Fiske Kimball, *American Architecture* (Indianapolis, 1928), though among the first architectural histories, still has much to offer; the first volume of James M. Fitch, *American Building* (rev. ed., Boston, 1966) covers the nineteenth century; Wayne Andrews, *Architecture in America* (New York, 1960) and John Burchard and Albert Bush-Brown, *The Architecture of America* (Boston, 1961) are good one-volume general histories. Important studies of architecture within its cultural contexts are Wayne Andrews, *Architecture, Ambition, and Americans* (New York, 1955) and Allan Gowans, *Images of American Living: Four Centuries of Architecture and Furniture as Cultural Expression* (Philadelphia, 1964). Henry Forman, *The Architecture of the Old South* (Cambridge, 1948) ; and Talbert Hamlin, *Greek Revival Architecture in America* (Oxford, 1944) are useful specialized books. Carl Condit, *American Building Art: The Nineteenth Century* (Chicago, 1960) is far the best study of the building technology of the period.

The Other Americans

General studies of racial theory in American history are Oscar Handlin, *Race and Nationality in American Life* (Boston, 1957) ; and William Gossett, *Race: The History of an Idea in America* (Dallas, 1963). Vincent Freemarck and Bernard Rosenthal, eds., *Race and the American Romantics* (New York, 1972) is a collection of nineteenth century writings, while George Frederickson, *The Black Image in the White Mind* (New York, 1971), Claude Nolen, *The Negro's Image in the South* (Lexington, 1967) are especially valuable for an understanding of racial attitudes in the period. Histories of immigration include: Marcus Hansen, *The Atlantic Migration: 1607–1860* (Cambridge, 1940) and his *Immigrant in American History* (Cambridge, 1940). Carl Wittke, *We Who Built America* (rev. ed., 1967) is a standard source. The adaptation and assimilation of English and Scottish immigrants, whose history is often neglected in favor of that of minorities, is well treated in Charlotte Erickson, *Invisible Immigrants* (Coral Gables, 1972). A useful collection of essays is that edited by Bruce A. Glasrud and Alan M. Smith, *Promises to Keep: A Portrayal of Non-Whites in the United States* (Chicago, 1972). A recent general study is Philip Taylor, *The Distant Magnet: European Emigration to the United States* (New York, 1971).

Recent interest in Indian history has produced a number of general and specialized studies. For collections of documents, see Wilcomb Washburn, ed., *The Indian and the White Man* (Garden City, 1964) and Jack D. Forbes, *The Indian in America's Past* (Englewood Cliffs, 1964). Clark Wissler, *Indians of the United States* (rev. ed., Garden City, 1966); William Γ. Hagan, *American Indians* (Chicago, 1961); Harold Driver, *Indians of North America* (rev. ed., Chicago, 1969); Alvin Josephy, *The Indian Heritage of America* (New York, 1968); and D'Arcy McNickle (himself an Indian), *Indian Tribes of the United States* (London, 1962) are all good sources. Peter Farb, *Man's Rise to Civilization* . . . (New York, 1968) is anthropologically-oriented; Roy Harvey Pearce, *The Savages of America* (Baltimore, 1953) is a study of the Indian and the concept of savagery. Studies of reformers and the Indian problem are Bernard Sheehan, *Seeds of Extinction: Jeffersonian Philanthropy and the American Indian* (Chapel Hill, 1973); Robert W. Mardock, *The Reformers and the American Indian* (Columbia, Mo., 1971); and Robert F. Berkhofer, Jr., *Salvation and the Savage: The Analysis of Missions and the American Indian Response 1787–1862* (New York, 1972). The collection of essays edited by Nancy Lurie, *North American Indians in Historical Perspective* (New York, 1971) is important.

The best single-volume history of the Negro in America is John Hope Franklin, *From Slavery to Freedom* (rev. ed., New York, 1967); an excellent collection of essays is Melvin Drimmer, ed., *Black History* (Garden City, 1967). For bibliographical aids, see Erwin Welsch, *The Negro in the United States: A Research Guide* (Bloomington, Ind., 1965); and Elizabeth W. Miller, *The Negro in America, A Bibliography* (Cambridge, 1966). A good collection is August Meier and Elliot Rudwick, eds., *The Making of Black America* (New York, 1969); see also their *From Plantation to Ghetto* (New York, 1966). Benjamin Brawley, *A Social History of the American Negro* (New York, 1921, repr. 1968) still has relevance. The best general study of

slavery is Kenneth Stampp, *The Peculiar Institution* (New York, 1956);
recent and good is John W. Blassingame, *The Slave Community: Plantation
Life in the Antebellum South* (New York, 1972). Studies of Northern
attitudes are Leon Litwack, *North of Slavery: The Negro in the Free States
1790–1860* (Chicago, 1961) and V. Jacque Voegeli, *North of Slavery: The
Negro in the Free States 1790–1860* (Chicago, 1967). Carter G. Woodson,
The Mind of the Negro as Reflected in Letters (Washington, 1926) and
Earl E. Thorpe, *The Mind of the Negro: An Intellectual History of Afro-
Americans* (Baton Rouge, 1961) are sources for the study of black thought
in the period, while Robin Winks, *The Blacks in Canada* (New Haven,
1971) is a fine study of fugitives and others in Canada. Margaret Butcher,
The Negro in American Culture (New York, 1956) is a good general source.
Sterling Brown, *Negro Poetry and Drama* (New York, 1937); Vernon
Loggins, *The Negro Author* (New York, 1931); Herman Dreer, *American
Literature by Negro Authors* (New York, 1950); and Benjamin Brawley,
Early American Negro Writers (Chapel Hill, 1935) provide treatments of
black literary history in the nineteenth century. Collections are Vernon F.
Calverton, *An Anthology of American Negro Literature* (New York, 1929)
and Sterling Brown, Ulysses Lee, and Arthur Davis, *The Negro Caravan*
(New York, 1941). Alain Locke's *Negro and His Music* (New York, 1936),
Locke's *Negro in Art* (Washington, 1948); John Rublowsky, *Black Music
in America* (New York, 1971); and Lindsay Patterson, *The Negro in Music
and Art* (New York, 1968) are useful sources. See also Miles Fisher, *Negro
Slave Songs in the United States* (Ithaca, 1953) and Newman I. White,
American Negro Folk Songs (Hatboro, Pa., 1965). Carter G. Woodson, ed.,
Negro Orators and Their Orations (rev. ed., New York, 1969); Frederick
G. Detweiler, *The Negro Press in the United States* (Chicago, 1922);
Carter G. Woodson, *The Education of the Negro Prior to 1861* (Washing-
ton, 1919); Horace M. Bond, *The Education of the Negro in the American
Social Order* (New York, 1934); Dwight O. W. Holmes, *The Evolution of
the Negro College* (New York, 1934); and E. Franklin Frazier, *The Negro
Family in the United States* (rev. ed., New York, 1966) are other sources of
information on nineteenth century black life. Histories of the Negro church
are: Carter G. Woodson, *The History of the Negro Church* (Washington,
1921); Ruby F. Johnston, *The Development of Negro Religion* (New
York, 1954); and E. Franklin Frazier, *The Negro Church in America* (New
York, 1964).

Nature as Law and Machine

Collections of documents concerning the history of American science are
Nathan Reingold, ed., *Science in Nineteenth Century America* (New York,

1946) ; and John C. Burnham, ed. *Science in America* (New York, 1971). The essays collected in David Van Tassel and Michael Hall, *Science and Society in the United States* (Homewood, Ill., 1966) are important; the best study of the period is George Daniels, *American Science in the Age of Jackson* (New York, 1968). Edward Dana, ed., *A Century of Science in the United States* (New Haven, 1918) though outmoded in approach contains useful information. Dirk Struik, *Yankee Science in the Making* (Boston, 1948) is excellent on science in New England, and A. Hunter Dupree, *Science in the Federal Government* (Cambridge, 1957) is essential. Bernard Jaffe, *Men of Science in America* (New York, 1944) is biographical; Walter and Mabel Smallwood, *Natural Science and the American Mind* (New York, 1941) place science in an intellectual and social context. Ralph S. Bates, *Scientific Societies in the United States* (New York, 1945) deals with the organization of science; Book III of Perry Miller's *Life of the Mind in America* (New York, 1965) is informative and suggestive. The issue of *The Journal of World History* (VIII, 1965) titled "Science in the American Context" carries essays by Edward Lurie on "Science in American Thought"; William Stanton on early anthropology, "The Scientific Approach to the Study of Man in America"; and Frederick Kilgour, "Technological Innovation in the United States." Studies of particular sciences include: George P. Merrill, *The First Hundred Years of American Geology* (New Haven, 1924) ; Aaron Ihde, *The Development of Modern Chemistry* (New York, 1964) ; R. T. Young, *Biology in America* (Boston, 1922) ; William A. Lacy, *Biology and Its Makers* (New York, 1928) ; Joseph Ewan, ed., *A Short History of Botany in the United States* (New York, 1969) ; Harry B. Humphrey, *Makers of American Botany* (New York, 1961) ; David E. Smith and Jekuthiel Ginsberg, *A History of Mathematics in the United States Before 1900* (Chicago, 1934) ; and Dirk J. Struik, *A Concise History of Mathematics* (rev. ed., New York, 1967). A good introduction to the history of American astronomy is Bessie Z. Jones, *Lighthouse of the Skies: The Smithsonian Astrophysical Institute* (Washington, 1965). Among biographies of scientists the following are outstanding: Edward Lurie, *Agassiz: A Life of Science in America* (Chicago, 1960) ; Frances Williams, *Matthew Fontaine Maury* (New Brunswick, 1963) ; A. Hunter Dupree, *Asa Gray* (Cambridge, 1959) ; John F. Fulton and Elizabeth Thomson, *Benjamin Silliman* (New York, 1947). William J. Youmans, *Pioneers of Science in America* (New York, 1896) contains information on many minor figures.

For the history of technological development in nineteenth-century America, see John W. Oliver, *The History of American Technology* (New York, 1956) ; and the earlier chapters of Courtney R. Hall, *A History of American Industrial Science* (New York, 1954). Carroll W. Pursell, Jr., *Readings in Technology and American Life* is the best collection of documents: the most comprehensive history of technology is that edited by Melvin Kranzberg and Carroll Pursell, *Technology in Western Civilization* (two vols., New York, 1967). The journal, *Technology and Culture,* is an indispensable source; Brooke Hindle, *Technology in Early America* (Chapel Hill, 1966) while concerned with an earlier period, is valuable for backgrounds. Roger Burlingame, *March of the Iron Men* (New York, 1938) and *Engines of Democracy* (New York, 1940) comprise a two-volume survey of nineteenth-century science, technology, and invention in an economic and social setting. Burlingame's *Backgrounds of Power* (New York, 1949) covers the history of mass production in the United States. H. J. Habakkuk, *American and British Technology in the Nineteenth Century* (Cambridge, England, 1962) is an excellent comparative study, and Mitchell A. Wilson, *American Science and Invention* (New York, 1954) is a good pictorial history. The development of scientific agriculture and of agricultural education is treated in Alfred True, *A History of Agricultural Experimentation and Research in the United States 1607–1925* (Washington, 1937, repr. 1968), USDA miscellaneous publication #251. Specialized studies include: for agricultural technology, Stewart Holbrook, *Machines of Plenty* (New York, 1955) and Reynold Wik, *Steam Power on the American Farm* (Philadelphia, 1953); technology and domestic life, Walter Buehr, *Home Sweet Home in the Nineteenth Century* (New York, 1965) and Siegfried Giedion, *Mechanization Takes Command* (New York, 1948); the railroad, George Rogers Taylor, *Transportation Revolution 1815–1860* (New York, 1951) and Albert Fishlow, *American Railroads and the Transformation of the Antebellum Economy* (Cambridge, 1965). Henry B. Comstock, *The Iron Horse* (New York, 1971), is a history of the locomotive. Carl Condit, *American Building Art: The Nineteenth Century* (New York, 1960) is the definitive source on construction engineering. On engineering, see R. S. Kirby and P. G. Laurson, *The Early Years of Modern Civil Engineering* (New Haven, 1922) and R. S. Kirby, S. Withington, A. B. Dabney, and F. G. Kilgour, *Engineering in History* (New York, 1956). For consideration of the impact of technology on American intellectual life, see Leo Marx, *The Machine in the Garden: Technology and the American Ideal* (New York, 1964); Marvin Fisher, *Workshops in the Wilderness* (New York, 1967); and the early chapters of Charles Sanford, *Quest for Paradise* (Urbana, 1961).

The Life of the Soul

Especially useful studies of religion in the United States are Edwin Scott Gaustad, *A Religious History of America* (New York, 1966); and Sidney Ahlstrom, *A Religious History of the American People* (New Haven, 1972).

Briefer histories are: Clifford Olmsted, *Religion in America, Past and Present* (Englewood Cliffs, N.J., 1961); Winthrop Hudson, *American Protestantism* (Chicago, 1961), John Tracy Ellis, *American Catholicism* (Chicago, 1969); and the essays collected in James W. Smith and A. Leland Jamison, eds., *The Shaping of American Religion* (Princeton, 1961). W. W. Sweet, *Religion in the Development of American Culture 1765–1840* (New York, 1952) and Sidney Mead, *The Lively Experiment: The Shaping of Christianity in America* (New York, 1963) are excellent sources of statistical information. For evangelism in the nineteenth-century churches, see Charles C. Cole, *The Social Ideas of the American Evangelists 1826–1860* (New York, 1954); Timothy Smith, *Revivalism and Social Reform* (New York, 1957); William McLoughlin, ed., *The American Evangelicals 1800–1900* (New York, 1968); Bernard A. Weisenberger, *They Gathered at the River: The Story of the Great Revivalists* (Boston, 1958); W. W. Sweet, *Revivalism in America* (New York, 1944); William McLoughlin, *Modern Revivalism* (New York, 1959); and chapter III of Perry Miller, *The Life of the Mind in America* (New York, 1965). Winthrop Hudson, *The Great Tradition of the American Churches* (New York, 1953) treats voluntaryism as a characteristic of American religion; John L. Bodo, *The Protestant Clergy and Public Issues 1812–1848* (Princeton, 1954) considers the social thought of the clergy; Robert T. Handy, *We Witness Together* (New York, 1956) is a study of the missionary movement. The argument over slavery in the Southern churches is considered in H. Shelton Smith, *In His Image, But . . . : Racism in Southern Religion 1780–1910* (Durham, 1972). Smaller sects and cults are treated in Charles W. Ferguson, *The Confusion of Tongues* (Grand Rapids, Mich., 1936) and Elmer T. Clark, *The Small Sects in America* (rev. ed., 1949). For histories of the various sects, see Andrew Zenos, *Presbyterianism in America* (New York, 1937); Emory S. Bucke, *The History of American Methodism* (three vols., New York and Nashville, 1964); Elton Trueblood, *The People Called Quakers* (New York, 1966) and Rufus M. Jones, *The Later Periods of Quakerism* (two vols., London, 1921); Abdel Wentz, et al., *A Basic History of Lutheranism* (three vols., Philadelphia, 1955); Winifred Garrison and Alfred DeGroot, *The Disciples of Christ* (rev. ed., St. Louis, 1958). Octavius B. Frothingham, *Transcendentalism in New England,* first published in 1876, is still the classic source in a new edition (New York, 1959); William K. Hutcheson, *The Transcendentalist Ministers* (New Haven, 1959) is a valuable additional study. For Catholicism, see Theodore Roemer, *The Catholic Church in the United States* (St. Louis, 1950); Theodore Maynard, *The Story of American Catholicism* (rev. ed., New York, 1960); and Thomas McAvoy, *A History of the Catholic Church in the United States* (Notre Dame, 1969). John Tracy Ellis, ed., *Documents of American Catholic His-*

tory (Milwaukee, 1956) is an excellent collection; Robert Trisco, *The Holy See and the Nascent Church in the Middle Western United States 1826–1850* (Rome, Italy, 1962) is a useful book on the Catholic Church on the frontier. Nathan Glazer, *American Judaism* (Chicago, 1957) is the best brief history; Oscar Handlin, *Adventure in Freedom* (New York, 1954) is excellent and informative; David Philipson, *The Reform Movement in Judaism* (New York, 1931) is a key study. Two shorter histories of Mormonism are Thomas F. O'Dea, *The Mormons* (Chicago, 1964) and Ray B. West, *The Kingdom of the Saints* (New York, 1957). See also the volume of essays edited by Marvin S. Hill and James B. Allen, *Mormonism and American Culture* (New York, 1972). For American freethinkers and agnostics, see Martin Marty, *The Infidel: Freethought in American Religion* (Cleveland, 1961) and Albert R. Post, *Popular Freethought in the United States* (New York, 1943).

The Study of Mind, Body, and Idea

Standard histories of American philosophy include Herbert Schneider, *History of American Philosophy* (New York, 1946); P. R. Anderson and M. H. Fisch, *Philosophy in America* (New York, 1939); and Joseph K. Blau, *Men and Movements in American Philosophy* (New York, 1952). A useful collection is Paul Kurtz, *American Thought Before 1900* (New York, 1966). Two chapters of the original classic, I. W. Riley, *American Thought from Puritanism to Pragmatism* (repr., New York, 1923) are still valuable for study of the philosophy of this period—chapter V, "Realism," and chapter VI, "Transcendentalism." Daniel Robinson, *The Story of Scottish Philosophy* (New York, 1961), and O. B. Frothingham's classic *Transcendentalism in New England* (repr., New York, 1959) are valuable specialized studies; an excellent anthology is Perry Miller, ed., *The Transcendentalists* (Garden City, 1957). For the history of psychology in the United States, see Jay W. Wharton, *American Psychology Before William James* (New Brunswick, N.J., 1939); A. A. Roback, *A History of American Psychology* (rev. ed., New York, 1964); and J. K. Hall, Gregory Zilboorg, and H. A. Bunker, eds., *One Hundred Years of American Psychiatry* (New York, 1944). Madeleine B. Stern's *Heads and Headlines. The Phrenological Fowlers* (Norman, Okla., 1971) is an excellent study not only of the leaders of the phrenological movement in the United States but of the theory itself. The most eminent work in the history of American medicine has been that of Richard H. Shyrock, which includes *The Development of Modern Medicine* (New York, 1947), *Medicine and Society in America 1660–1860* (New York, 1960); and his collection of essays, *Medicine in America* (Baltimore, 1966). Francis R. Packard, *The History of Medicine in the United*

States (two vols., New York, 1931) contains additional information. A comprehensive modern study of homeopathic medicine is Martin Kaufman, *Homeopathy in America: The Rise and Fall of a Medical Heresy* (Baltimore, 1971). *The Bulletin of the History of Medicine* is a current source, as is Genevieve Miller, ed., *A Bibliography of the History of Medicine in the United States and Canada* (Baltimore, 1964).

Educating a Nation

A pleasant and useful introduction to popular education and culture of the period is Carl Bode, *The Anatomy of American Popular Culture 1840–1861* (Garden City, 1959). On the Sunday school, consult Marianna C. Brown, *The Sunday School Movement in America* (New York, 1961); E. Wilbur Rice, *The Sunday School Movement 1780–1917* (Philadelphia, 1917); and Frank Lanbard, *A History of the American Sunday School Curriculum* (New York, 1927). Malcolm S. Knowles, *The Adult Education Movement in the United States* (New York, 1962) is informative, as is Robert E. Lee, *Continuing Education for Adults Through the American Public Library 1833–1864* (Chicago, 1966). For the lyceum movement see Carl Bode, *The American Lyceum* (New York, 1956) and C. David Mead, *Yankee Eloquence* (East Lansing, Mich., 1951); older but useful are Cecil B. Hayes, *The American Lyceum* (Washington, 1932); and John S. Noffsinger, *Common Schools, Lyceums, Chautauquas* (New York, 1925). Charles S. Thompson, *The Evolution of the American Public Library* (Washington, 1952) is standard; one may also consult John D. Marshall, *An American Library History Reader* (Hamden, Conn., 1961); and Thelma Eaton, ed., *Contributions to American Library History* (Champaign, Ill., 1960). Lawrence V. Coleman's *The Museum in America* (three vols., Washington, 1939) is standard, but also useful are Thomas R. Adam, *The Museum and Popular Culture* (New York, 1939); and Alvin Schwartz, *Museum: The Story of America's Treasure Houses* (New York, 1967). Sources for the history of newspapers and magazines are Frank Luther Mott, *American Journalism* (rev. ed., New York, 1962); Sidney Kobre, *The Development of American Journalism* (Dubuque, Ia., 1969); Robert W. Jones, *Journalism in the United States* (New York, 1947) and Frank Luther Mott's monumental *History of American Magazines* (five vols., Cambridge, 1938–68). Book publishing and marketing are treated in Hellmut Lehmann-Haupt, C. C. Wroth, and Rollo Silver, *The Book in America* (New York, 1952); William Miller, *The Book Industry* (New York, 1949); and Roger Smith, ed., *The American Reading Public* (New York, 1963).

Among the numerous histories of American education, the following are useful: Adolph E. Meyer, *An Educational History of the American People*

(New York, 1957) ; Harry A. Good, *A History of American Education* (New York, 1963) ; Rena Vassar, *A Social History of American Education* (Chicago, 1965) ; S. Alexander Rippy, *Education in a Free Society* (New York, 1967) ; Stuart G. Noble, *A History of American Education* (New York, 1954) ; and R. Freeman Butts and Lawrence A. Cremin, *A History of Education in American Culture* (New York, 1953). Among treatments of the development of educational philosophies, see Merle Curti, *The Social Ideas of American Educators* (New York, 1935) ; Clarence J. Karrier, *Man, Society, and Education: A History of American Educational Ideas* (Glenview, Ill., 1967) ; Vivian T. Thayer, *Formative Ideas in American Education* (New York, 1965) ; and Joseph J. Chambliss, *The Origins of the American Philosophy of Education* (The Hague, 1968). On the creation of free schools, the following are good sources: Lawrence A. Cremin, *The American Common School* (New York, 1951) ; Sidney Jackson, *America's Struggle for Free Schools* (Washington, 1941) ; Rush Welter, *Popular Education and Democratic Thought* (New York, 1962) ; Paul Monroe, *The Founding of the American Public School System* (New York, 1940) ; and Lawrence Cremin, ed., *The Republic and The School: Horace Mann on the Education of Free Men* (New York, 1966). The best biography of Mann is Louise Hall Tharp, *Until Victory: Horace Mann and Mary Peabody* (Boston, 1953). Frederick Rudolph, *The American College and University* (New York, 1962) is an excellent history of higher education; see also Margaret Clapp, ed., *The Modern University* (Ithaca, 1950) ; Elbert V. Wills, *The Growth of American Higher Education* (Philadelphia, 1936) ; R. Freeman Butts, *The College Charts Its Course* (Philadelphia, 1939) ; George P. Schmidt, *The Liberal Arts College* (New York, 1957) ; and Donald G. Tewksbury, *The Founding of Colleges and Universities Before the Civil War* (New York, 1932). Useful collections of documents in the history of education are: Carl Gross and Charles Chandler, eds., *A History of American Education Through Readings* (Boston, 1964) ; Richard Hofstadter and Wilson Smith, eds., *American Higher Education: A Documentary History* (Chicago, 1961) ; and Theodore R. Crane, ed., *The Colleges and the Public 1787–1862* (New York, 1963). Specialized studies are Richard Hofstadter, *Academic Freedom in the Age of the College* (New York, 1961) ; George P. Schmidt, *The Old Time College President* (New York, 1930) ; Albia Godbold, *The Church College of the Old South* (Durham, 1944) ; Richard J. Storr, *The Beginnings of Graduate Education in America* (Chicago, 1953) ; Merle Borrowman, ed., *Teacher Education in America* (New York, 1965) ; Charles Carpenter, *A History of American Schoolbooks* (Philadelphia, 1963) ; John A. Nietz, *The Evolution of American Secondary School Textbooks* (Rutland, Vt., 1966) ; and Ruth M. Elson, *Guardians of Tradition: American Schoolbooks of the Nineteenth Century* (Lincoln, Nebr., 1964).

Index

Abbott, Jacob, 107, 325
abolitionism, *see* slavery; names
actors and actresses, 146–57; *see also* theater; names
Adams, Jasper, 325
Adams, John, 1–2, 11, 26, 104
Adams, John Q., 13, 15, 79, 138, 248, 294
Adams, Sarah, 236–7
Adrian, Robert, 249
African Methodist churches, 223–4, 296
African Union Society, 222
Agassiz, Louis, 200, 241–2, 246, 253–4, 256, 258, 361
agriculture: education, 360, 392–3, 397; immigrants, 202–6; journals, 370; research, 249–50; slavery and, 62; societies, professional, 240; technology, 259, 261, 270–1
Aiken, George, 155
Alcott, Bronson, 24, 33, 57, 374
Alcott, William, 350
Aldridge, Ira, 233
Allen, Ethan, 4, 311, 312
Allen, George, 78
Allen, Richard, 223
Allen, William, 14
Allen, Zachariah, 243, 272
Allston, Washington, 164, 174, 177, 180, 185
Amana Colony, 56, 204
American Academy of Arts and Sciences, 240

American and Foreign Anti-Slavery Society, 63
American Anti-Slavery Society, 63
American Art-Union, 186, 188
American Association for the Advancement of Science, 242, 247
American Bible Society, 35, 294, 358
American Chemical Society, 240
American Colonization Society, 66, 221, 318
American Female Reform Society, 42
American Geological Society, 240
American Home Missionary Society, 293
American Hydropathic Society, 347
American Journal of Education, 377, 380
American Journal of Insanity, 336
American Journal of Science, 240
American Lyceum, 246
American Lyceum Association, 360–1
American Medical Association, 342–3
American Party, 207
American Peace Society, 40–1
American Pharmaceutical Association, 344
American Philosophical Society, 240
American Phrenological Journal, 335
American Protestant Association, 310
American Psychiatric Association, 337
American Public Health Association, 341
American Quarterly Review, 85, 368
American Review, 243

417

74 75 76 77 10 9 8 7 6 5 4 3 2 1